FIRST LADY FLORENCE HARDING

MODERN FIRST LADIES

Lewis L. Gould, Founding Editor

TITLES IN THE SERIES

Edith Kermit Roosevelt: Creating the Modern First Lady, Lewis L. Gould

Helen Taft: Our Musical First Lady, Lewis L. Gould

Ellen and Edith: Woodrow Wilson's First Ladies, Kristie Miller

First Lady Florence Harding: Behind the Tragedy and Controversy, Katherine A. S. Sibley

Grace Coolidge: The People's Lady in Silent Cal's White House, Robert H. Ferrell

Lou Henry Hoover: Activist First Lady, Nancy Beck Young

Eleanor Roosevelt: Transformative First Lady, Maurine Beasley

Bess Wallace Truman: Traditional First Lady, Sara L. Sale

Mamie Doud Eisenhower: The General's First Lady, Marilyn Irvin Holt

Jacqueline Kennedy: First Lady of the New Frontier, Barbara A. Perry

Lady Bird Johnson: Our Environmental First Lady, Lewis L. Gould

Pat Nixon: Embattled First Lady, Mary C. Brennan

Betty Ford: Candor and Courage in the White House, John Robert Greene

Rosalynn Carter: Equal Partner in the White House, Scott Kaufman

Nancy Reagan: On the White House Stage, James G. Benze, Jr.

Barbara Bush: Presidential Matriarch, Myra G. Gutin

Hillary Rodham Clinton: Polarizing First Lady, Gil Troy

Laura Bush: Texas Roots, Global Impact, Jill Abraham Hummer

FIRST LADY FLORENCE HARDING

BEHIND THE TRAGEDY

AND CONTROVERSY

KATHERINE A. S. SIBLEY

UNIVERSITY PRESS OF KANSAS

© 2009 by the University Press of Kansas
All rights reserved
Published by the University Press of Kansas (Lawrence, Kansas 66045),
which was organized by the Kansas Board of Regents and is operated
and funded by Emporia State University, Fort Hays State University,
Kansas State University, Pittsburg State University, the University of Kansas,
and Wichita State University

Library of Congress Cataloging-in-Publication Data
Sibley, Katherine A. S. (Katherine Amelia Siobhan), 1961–
First lady Florence harding : behind the tragedy and controversy /
Katherine A. S. Sibley.
p. cm. — (Modern first ladies)
Includes bibliographical references and index.
ISBN 978-0-7006-1649-7 (hardback)
ISBN 978-0-7006-4184-0 (paperback)
ISBN 978-0-7006-3576-4 (ebook)
1. Harding, Florence Kling, 1860–1924.
2. Presidents' spouses—United States—Biography.
3. Harding, Warren G. (Warren Gamaliel), 1865–1923. I. Title.
E786.2.H37S53 2009
973.91′4092—dc22
[B]2008052807

British Library Cataloguing-in-Publication Data is available.

EU Authorised Representative Details: Easy Access System Europe
Mustamäe tee 50, 10621 Tallinn, Estonia | gpsr.requests@easproject.com

For Joe, with love

CONTENTS

Editor's Foreword

ix

Acknowledgments

xi

Introduction

1

Chapter 1. Early Life, Marriages, and Ohio Politics, 1860–1915

8

Chapter 2. Washington Life and the Presidential Campaign, 1915–1921

32

Chapter 3. Inaugural Year, 1921

70

Chapter 4. Defining the Job, January–August 1922

98

Chapter 5. Crisis and Convalescence, September 1922–June 1923

143

Chapter 6. Crossing the Country, June–August 1923

179

Chapter 7. Harding's Death and
Its Aftermath, August 1923

203

Chapter 8. Widowhood, August 1923–November 1924

236

Notes

267

Bibliographic Essay

335

Index

343

EDITOR'S FOREWORD

Few women in American history have been the subject of more sustained scorn and criticism than Florence Kling Harding. Married to a president who is perceived as a failure in office, Mrs. Harding has been depicted as an amalgam of shrew, harpy, and, in some of the wilder scenarios, even a murderer of her husband. If there was any first lady who seemed beyond rehabilitation, Florence Harding appeared to qualify for that unhappy status. Professor Katherine A. S. Sibley has now written a study of Mrs. Harding as first lady from 1921 to 1923 that restores the humanity to her subject and demonstrates the innovative contributions that Florence Harding made in her brief tenure in the White House.

Sibley is able to achieve this impressive feat of scholarship because she has done what other writers about Mrs. Harding have not done—examine the primary sources in detail. Working with manuscripts held in Washington, D.C., Ohio, and other parts of the country, Sibley constructs a narrative of Florence Harding's life that dispels old myths and undermines the textbook clichés about her time in the national spotlight. The portrait of the Harding marriage is nuanced and fair. The legend of Nan Britton receives the skeptical treatment it merits, while she explains well Warren Harding's dalliance with Carrie Phillips.

Sibley is at her best in examining the impact that Florence Harding had on the institution of the first lady. After the reclusive approach of Edith Wilson from 1919 to 1921, Mrs. Harding threw open the White House to the public. She used the emerging techniques of celebrity such as movie cameras and expanded newspaper coverage to humanize her role. Sibley brings out the identification that the American citizenry felt with Mrs. Harding during the time of the first lady's near-fatal illness in 1922.

The sudden death of Warren G. Harding in August 1923 is the climax of the story that Sibley tells. She brushes away the silly myths surrounding the president's fatal illness and looks in detail at how Mrs. Harding responded to the tragedy. The result is a narrative that illuminates why Harding's passing struck Americans with such force at the time, and yet why this national empathy proved so fleeting. Florence Harding's own death soon followed. In the succeeding years, her reputation plummeted. With the expert work of Katherine Sibley, Mrs. Harding has at last found a biographer who can give this neglected and derided first lady a full measure of justice and insight.

Lewis L. Gould

ACKNOWLEDGMENTS

Just as Florence stood shoulder to shoulder with her husband in their mutual life's work, so too have so many librarians, colleagues, friends, and family done the same for me, offering their support and assistance in the conception, gestation, birth, and development of this book. For their help, I would like to thank the archivists, librarians, and staff at the Library of Congress, the Ohio Historical Society, the Marion County Historical Society, the First Ladies Library, the Ohio State University, Saint Joseph's University, the Marion Library, the American Heritage Center, the White House, the White House Historical Association, the Palace Hotel, and the Harding Home, especially John Earl Haynes, Jeffrey Flannery, Liz Plummer, Bill Markley, Lisa Long, Teresa Carstensen, Lisa Wood, Gale Martin, Martha Regula, Chris Dixon, Mary Martinson, Sam Norris, Shannon Bowen, William Bushong, Bill Allman, and Melinda Gilpin.

Scholars including Craig Schermer, Kristie Miller, Catherine Forslund, Carol Singley, Phillip Payne, Nancy Beck Young, Carl Sferazza Anthony, John Dean, Scott Gilbert, Jo Alyson Parker, Mark Aultmann, and Julius Fraser offered their inspiration and suggestions as this study developed. I am grateful as well to the organizers, commentators, and audiences at recent meetings of the National Council of Public History, the Western Association of Women Historians, and the International Society for the Study of Time, as well as the Pennsylvania Humanities Council, the Swarthmore Public Library, and Congregation Beth Israel, who all provided opportunities for me to discuss Florence Harding and her legacy. Marion Harding experts Mike Perry, Carol Davidson, Shelby Needham, and Jim Carpenter assisted me with photographs and correspondence not otherwise available. Research assistants, including Elliott Drago, Steve Weinberg, and Chris Klosko, wound patiently through many microfilm reels. Sue McFadden was also tireless in pushing this project along in so many ways.

{ *Acknowledgments* }

A researcher could not find a kinder and more gracious historian and host than Trella Hemmerly Romine. I first met her at the Marion County Historical Society when she was a youthful eighty-eight years old; she insisted I cancel my hotel reservation and stay with her, and she took me on a tour of the local Harding haunts, including the president's birthplace. She has provided me with research materials, contacts, and many stimulating talks about Florence, most memorably as we walked through her beautiful garden, Terradise, and its adjoining prairie, which she did so much to save. How fitting that the Ohio Historical Society recently granted her the Edward J. Tiffin Award, its highest honor. I would not have met Trella without Robert Ferrell's introduction; Bob has been a tremendous inspiration and a source of encouragement, humor, and helpful criticism from the very beginning of this project. Lewis Gould, too, was an awesome and patient editor, who took a sharp pencil to the manuscript to its great benefit (but all errors and oversights remaining are mine). He also unearthed many treasures for me to further investigate, including those in the online archive of eBay. At the University Press of Kansas, Fred Woodward, Larisa Martin, Susan Schott, and Sara Henderson White have been gracious and helpful.

Family and friends, including Liz Fletcher, Annie Horsley, George Sibley, Mern Sibley, Gay Walley, Jamie and Steven Horwitz Fram, Amy Fantalis, Nina Bakisian, Sara Starr, Ruth Wuenschel, Selene Platt, Sharon Boyd, Fiona Harris Stoertz, Linda Hauck, Karen Locke, Mary Anne Moore, and Lauri Mansky offered treasured support and assistance during the writing of this book. Jonah and Marin have provided their own kinds of joy to this project; they have no memory of life without Florence and have put up with her clinging long in our lives. Even more so has my sweetheart, Joe, who has shared me with this other woman for most of our marriage, with humor and patience. This book is lovingly dedicated to him.

FIRST LADY FLORENCE HARDING

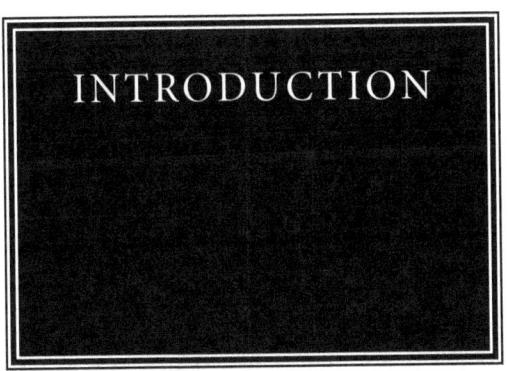

INTRODUCTION

Although Eleanor Roosevelt has been credited as having "shattered the ceremonial mold in which the role of the First Lady had traditionally been fashioned," the first cracks in that mold were indelibly made by an earlier occupant of that office, Florence Kling Harding.[1] Eleanor's role is relatively well known; Florence's, however, is not, though the journalists of her time recognized that her influence would assist them in reaching the president.[2] As the *Philadelphia Ledger* pointed out, "She shares his life in a fuller, deeper, and wider measure than do the wives of most public men."[3] Florence wrote and corrected the president's speeches and weighed in on his choices for important cabinet posts. One reporter noted in 1922, "perhaps no wife of a president, at least within recent years, has entered into the White House duties with more energy and zest than Mrs. Harding."[4] She took a pioneering role in Harding's campaign and in his presidency; as a "politician," some thought, she outdid her husband![5]

Her role in enhancing his career was important to her, as it had been for years; Florence's influence in Warren's professional life started well before they reached Washington. She assisted him in turning his struggling newspaper in Marion, Ohio, into a lucrative enterprise, and she consistently encouraged his aspirations for more ambitious elected offices. She was indeed his "drum major."[6] Throughout, Harding acknowledged his wife's importance to him, and this was surely among the reasons he never left her for Carrie Phillips, even if their affair lasted for nearly fifteen years. As first lady, Florence did not ignore the traditional ceremonial role of White House hostess, either. Instead, she reveled in it. She hosted many teas, dinners, and public gatherings, sometimes with exhausting numbers of guests; these events became the subject of adulatory newspaper articles.

Nevertheless, Florence Harding has been one of the most maligned and despised of American first ladies. In a recent historians' poll, she ranked thirty-seventh of thirty-eight occupants of the post, situated just behind Mary Todd Lincoln and ahead of Jane Pierce. She was dead last in her background and integrity![7] Consistently, Florence's influence in her husband's management of the country has been portrayed in a negative light. Despite the immense popularity of her husband and herself when in office, events after their deaths changed their administration's reputation dramatically and have affected Mrs. Harding's legacy to this day. Allegations—and later convictions—in the case of Secretary of the Interior Albert Fall's oil leases at Wyoming's Teapot Dome and shady dealings in Attorney General Harry Daugherty's Justice Department, with its toleration of bribery, kickbacks, and other corrupt practices in regulating the liquor trade, were damning.[8] Like the Teapot scandal, the Hardings soon transformed into cartoons. Although little evidence exists that they had any awareness of Fall's or Daugherty's misdeeds, this was a muckraking era, and their friends' malfeasance left lasting stains on them both.[9] Florence's efforts to burn her husband's papers (although only a fraction of them) and the closeting of the remainder by Harding family members and associates in the Harding Memorial Association for decades after the president's death have only contributed to suspicions about the couple. This book is the first to offer a full treatment of Florence as first lady, rather than as a supporting actress in a drama of scandalous dealings, womanizing, and illicit booze, the all-too-typical scenario in books on the Hardings. Such depictions have prevented a clear understanding of how much this husband and wife were loved in their time, as witnessed among the thousands who braved weather, hour, and inconvenience to attend their receptions and parades, as well as Warren's two public funerals.[10] This unfaltering negative perspective has also made it difficult to see how pathbreaking a first lady Florence Harding was. This biography seeks to provide a fuller view of her role in the White House, one that takes into account her deeply held passions and her many contributions, as well as the daunting challenges she faced. In this study, I have resorted to a much broader range of sources than previous biographies have consulted so that I can better situate Florence in her time—a convulsive postwar era highlighted by women's activism and Hollywood celebrity culture—as well as portray her as a fully evolved human being, not a caricature. Florence Harding was a transitional first lady as well as a woman of complexity and depth. Socially progressive and gracious with the public, Florence was also privately anxious and chronically ill. Yet her inner strength was immense.

This picture will no doubt come as a surprise to many readers. After all, compared with the popular dismissal of Harding as a crook, Florence's treatment has been even nastier. Her place in history has been colored by a particular kind of denigration related to her sex and also her age; she was sixty when she entered the White House. Gaston B. Means, the jail-serving government investigator whose notorious diaries were encapsulated in 1930's *The Strange Death of President Harding*, helped establish this image by dismissing her as "a little drab woman, strong-minded, self-willed, older than her husband by nine years [actually, it was about five and a half], . . . clinging with tenacious ferocity to the illusions of youth." Even worse, she was "ambitious, worldly, greedy for power."[11] Journalist Mark Sullivan suggested that she was relentlessly uptight: "aggressive and talkative," "sparrow-like," her face "too shinily rouged," her clothes "too trimly tailored." "A nervous, rather excitable woman . . . strident," added Alice Roosevelt Longworth.[12] More recent books, meant to be revisionist, still often paint a negative portrait.[13]

One of the most common ways historians have attacked Florence has been through aspersions about her femininity. In the late 1960s, Francis Russell impugned her "deficiency as a female" owing to her "domineering" nature: "the withered harridan [President Harding] ironically called the Duchess";[14] she was "sexless, with the brittle quality of an autumn leaf."[15] Russell went even further in a letter to a trusted Marion confidant: if she had been only "warm, sensuous, buxom," he attested, her husband "might have led a very successful life as a Marion editor" and never attempted the presidency. Instead,

Russell claimed she was "hermaphroditic."[16] Though Russell's study is now forty years old, *The Shadow of Blooming Grove* was the first to use the long-sealed Harding papers and remains a standard work in the field. But his approach, with its inexorably negative (and inaccurate) emphasis on Florence's personal and physical attributes, has not only obscured her achievements, but also made it difficult to recognize this extremely popular first lady.

As archival materials, newspaper articles, and other sources used in this book show, Florence in fact brought in a spirit of fun and wide access to 1600 Pennsylvania Avenue almost from the minute she moved in on March 4, 1921. Americans adored her and her folksy ways, from public receptions to Easter egg rolls. This approach also characterized her relationship with the press. She liked spontaneous discussions with journalists, especially women reporters—though she refused to be formally interviewed, claiming her reticence would better protect her husband. Her leadership in her husband's work and her unusually public role both confirm her status as a transitional figure.

Florence Harding came into the White House during a volatile moment in American history, as her husband's call for "normalcy" made clear. In the midst of a painful postwar depression, continued large-scale immigration, overseas revolutions, and the domestic and international legacies of World War I, from its hobbling veterans to its high-minded visions of world peace, the country's new administration faced unique challenges. At the same time, a new era of opportunity and prosperity was emerging with the enfranchisement of half of the population and the growth of a popular culture dominated by movies, radio, and the automobile. This unpredictable, free-wheeling atmosphere would have created more latitude for any first lady, but for the ambitious and outspoken Mrs. Harding, it was particularly appropriate. She became a celebrity herself, visible in newsreels, hobnobbing with Hollywood personalities, and exploiting media opportunities. So much was she "'snapped,' 'interviewed,' and 'movied,'" one paper wrote, that "Mrs. Harding is a 'star.'"[17] Befitting her starring role, a reporter added, "Nebraska and Iowa citizens are in love with Mrs. Harding."[18] The rise of mass marketing and advertising, along with women's increased visibility, also created a new interest in fashion, and the expansion of movies after

World War I fueled this trend, with film a vehicle for selling the clothes and furnishings of celebrities.[19] Florence was attuned to these developments, and as the first first lady to meet this appetite for style, she was besieged by New York designers who showered her with samples of chiffon and satin in shades of navy and lavender, known to be among her favorite hues.[20] "Harding blue" became her signature color, and a velvet, diamond-encrusted neck band was her standard accessory. Florence took much care with her dress, her look, and her public image, as befitted her position; journalists noted that "her clothes are decidedly smart"; they were "quiet, but rich."[21]

As movie stars became ever more prominent, Florence welcomed such well-known actors, singers, and directors as the Gish sisters, Al Jolson, and D. W. Griffith both to the front porch during the campaign and the White House after. Their visits provided superb photo opportunities, a term that Florence practically invented. What a first lady did was news and worthy of media attention, she fully recognized, and she welcomed the chance for snaps, although she always claimed she did not photograph well. She liked pictures with photogenic and interesting subjects, including visiting delegations of Filipino women, Native Americans, Girl Scouts, or (always) their Airedale, Laddie Boy. She invited in journalists, especially, "the girls," for close-ups of White House affairs, so that they might get a full view of table decorations and even arriving guests at her big dinners.[22] Because she made herself so visible and accessible, in 1922 the entire country also knew of her frightening illness, and movie men waited at the steps of the White House to welcome the famous Dr. Mayo. It is nearly impossible to imagine such a scenario at the convalescing Wilson White House less than two years before!

As John Morello writes, her visibility, "unshaded" by her husband, "did wonders for her image and that of women in general."[23] Of course, she also spent hours alongside her husband, shaking hands with White House visitors, from prominent diplomats to the poorest immigrants. Unlike Edith Roosevelt, a very private first lady who often held flowers to avoid having to proffer her palm, Florence put forth a welcoming hand with a firm grasp, and she always had a word with her visitors.[24] In line with such a public presence, she became the first in her position to insist on Secret Service protection.

Florence Kling Harding also used her office as a forum for her ideas. The early 1920s were an auspicious time for female activism, and she was an enthusiastic supporter of women's political agency. She was, of course, the first woman to vote for her husband (who had once *opposed* women's suffrage!), and her visible role in the campaign brought a majority of women to vote for him as well.[25] Mrs. Harding hosted numerous women's organizations at the White House and addressed national gatherings and representative groups of Republican women. She also did not shrink at offending prejudices. She stood up for black defendants in the South, and she fully supported her husband's relatively progressive views on racial equality. She was, moreover, strongly interested in social welfare matters. She lobbied for better treatment for veterans and female prison inmates. Mothers of young men on death row appealed to her, too, believing Florence to be "the only person who could help" stop a hanging.[26] In addition, as an assiduous horsewoman in her youth and a lifelong dog lover, Mrs. Harding maintained a strong interest in the prevention of cruelty to animals, and she was sometimes sharp in her criticism of rodeos and other sports that she saw as hurting helpless beasts.

Fifteen months into the administration, Florence had a near-fatal recurrence of her kidney affliction, and as the first first lady to divulge such a life-threatening illness, she showed her rapport with the press and the people. After her lengthy convalescence and recovery, she participated in the longest trip ever conducted by a first lady up to that point when she joined her husband's cross-country jaunt to Alaska, known as the "Voyage of Understanding." Along the way, she gave spontaneous speeches (the first woman in her position to do so), energetically greeted crowds, and showed that she was indeed "the first of all the wives of our presidents who takes an actual hand in politics and is just as intense and enthusiastic . . . as if she were herself a candidate."[27] Sadly, her husband died on this trip, on August 2, 1923.

Rumors that she caused his death by poisoning him (supposedly in anger at his extramarital dalliances) have never lost their currency.[28] In fact, she was in shock, and the grace and determination with which Florence handled this calamity, including three funerals in as many time zones, a public grieving that lasted thousands of rail miles, and ceremonies organized in three cities, all testify to her strength and endurance.²⁹ She returned to live in Washington during her widowhood, but she fell ill once more with kidney disease in the summer of 1924 and died that fall. Glowing obituaries reflect that she had made a real connection in the hearts of Americans, which unfortunately did not long outlive her.³⁰

As a transitional first lady, one who "bridg[ed] the traditional and modern duties" of the post, Florence carefully tried to balance her support of women's advancement, as exemplified in her own career and causes, and the cherished importance of her home in the White House.³¹ She succeeded, according to journalist Constance Drexel, "retaining her feminine attractions and homemaking instincts, yet enlarging her vision to encompass the rest of humanity within her horizon."³² This was no easy task. Modern first ladies, expected to preserve long-treasured definitions of what has traditionally been a ceremonial post, have often found themselves toeing a fine line between their wishes to turn a potentially powerful position into a vehicle to promote desired causes, and the country's sentimental expectation that they remain demurely in the background and on the pedestal.³³ Florence offered a compelling example of activism and entertaining that could be emulated by others in her position, but as Hillary Rodham Clinton complained sixty-eight years later ("I suppose I could have stayed home and baked cookies and had teas"), full acceptance of this broadened role was slow to come.³⁴

As this book will detail, by her progressive causes, her celebrity, and her role in her husband's work, Florence Harding bequeathed an activist legacy to the women who followed her in the White House. As a result of her example, aspiring presidential wives are routinely expected to campaign with their husbands, and to be visible and accessible—as well as to adopt a celebrity status. As first ladies, they consistently adopt worthwhile causes in office, which they publicize. Moreover, they have become increasingly important in their contributions to their husbands' careers and legacies, as we see in the recent examples of Mrs. Johnson, Mrs. Carter, and Mrs. Reagan—not to mention Mrs. Clinton, the first first lady to run for president. The following pages will show just how Mrs. Harding helped reshape the office of first lady to make these changes possible in the span of just twenty-nine months.

CHAPTER 1

EARLY LIFE, MARRIAGES, AND OHIO POLITICS, 1860–1915

Born on the eve of the Civil War, on August 15, 1860, Florence Mabel Kling grew up in an era of contradictory expectations for women. The Victorian age, as it was called even in the United States, ushered in an era of activism, suffrage, and careers for women, despite its emphasis on a culture of domesticity and purity for them. Florence faced contrasting expectations even in her own family. Her father, Amos Kling, had hoped for a boy, and although she would have two younger brothers, Clifford and Vitalis ("Tal"), he stayed closest to her, his boy-girl. Florence was his companion, an expert horseback rider, and a lover of all animals, especially dogs. She and Warren would always have one: Gyp, the rat terrier; Hub, the Boston bull; Jumbo, the mastiff; and of course, Laddie Boy, the Airedale.

Florence was a tomboy who loved the outdoors and physical activity, especially riding her horse, Billy. She was tall and slim, with arresting gray-blue eyes. She was fun-loving and brave, too, "the only person in town to guide a bobsled down Gospel hill without dumping [out] . . . in the snowdrifts along Cucaw Creek," as a contemporary pointed out.[1] It was good that she had her father to share the outdoors with; her mother was not a healthy woman. Still, Mrs. Kling was a warm and kindly presence in her children's lives, in contrast to her stricter husband.

Florence and Clifford as toddlers.
Courtesy of the Marion County Historical Society, Marion, Ohio.

Amos Kling. Courtesy of the Marion County Historical Society, Marion, Ohio.

Amos Kling was of German ancestry, born June 15, 1833, in Lancaster County, Pennsylvania.[2] After working as a successful young farmer in Mansfield, Ohio, at the age of twenty-two he came to Marion, perhaps to taste town life.[3] He got a job as a clerk at Bain's Hardware for $9 a week, and before too long, in bootstrap fashion, he bought the store. On a trip to visit friends in New Canaan, Connecticut, in the late 1850s, he met Louisa M. Bouton, "a young lady

Louisa Kling. Courtesy of the Marion County Historical Society, Marion, Ohio.

remarkable for refinement, education, and beauty," said to be "the most popular girl" in her town. They married on September 27, 1859, in that Connecticut city before returning to Marion. Her family eventually moved to Ohio too, where Louisa's father set up a shoe business. It was Florence's French grandmother, she later said, who pressed upon her proper posture, always insisting she use chairs with straight backs.[4]

The Boutons were of Huguenot ancestry, having originally fled from France in the 1600s; some had been among the first settlers in Boston in 1635 before founding the New Canaan settlement. Owing to these early ancestors, including her great-great grandfather, Captain Edmund Richards, who was captured by the British in the Revolutionary War, Florence was eligible to join the National Society of Daughters of Founders and Patriots of America, which she did once in the White House.

On her father's side were plainer Pennsylvania Germans, whose outlook influenced Amos Kling's "economy and thrift." Her cautious father taught her to "walk in the middle of the country roads ... and to keep a watchful eye about her."[5] From her mother's side, then, she derived her cultured outlook, her elegance and grace; from her father's, her driven, purposeful approach to life. Amos would become a rich man, from real estate, from importing and selling horses obtained in Paris, and from assorted other pursuits.[6] The Marion Telephone Company, the Marion National Bank, and the Columbus and Toledo Railroad recruited him for their boards, and he owned a share of the Hotel Marion as well.[7] By the time Florence was in grammar school, they had moved from modest quarters atop a store to a white limestone mansion Kling had built.

Her father encouraged Florence to learn accounting by keeping the books for his store. He also took her on trips, and "she learned the way of men in a business world," including "ambition, forcefulness and shrewd judgment," traits that would stand her in good stead in the White House. Even earlier than that, these skills helped her cope with difficulties in her young life.[8] Amos also saw that she got a good education in music and the classics. Yet after only a year of study at the Cincinnati Conservatory of Music after high school, where she was becoming an accomplished pianist—practicing five to seven hours a day—and an increasingly independent woman, he called her home. Though Florence would grow up rich, and die that way as well, back in Marion as a young woman, she would taste the desperation of poverty, and she never forgot it.

When her father ordered her to return home from music school, she complied, but she defied his control by staying out late with young men. Skating rinks were a popular hangout for her, and it was likely at a local rink, the Merry Roll Round, where she grew close to

Florence's first home. Courtesy of the Library of Congress.

her neighbor, Henry "Pete" DeWolfe, despite their fathers' mutual antagonism.[9] The older DeWolfe, like Kling, was a successful businessman, though his son was not. She and Henry eloped in 1880, although it is not clear whether there was ever an actual wedding, because no record of one exists. In any case, their son, Marshall Eugene, was born just six months later, on September 22; Florence was barely 20. She soon knew her marriage had been a mistake. Pete half-heartedly tried some ill-fated business ventures while Florence taught piano to help pay the bills (for 25 cents an hour). But her husband was a drunk, had no interest in supporting her or their young son, and soon abandoned them.[10]

Florence's girlhood home. Courtesy of the Marion County Historical Society, Marion, Ohio.

When she divorced Pete in May 1886 (apparently the court accepted her claim that they were married), she charged him with "gross neglect of duty," took back her maiden name, and offered him monthly visiting rights to Marshall. It is doubtful he ever saw the boy.[11] After they separated, her former spouse continued to be a ne'er-do-well. A sometime resident of Columbus, he was spotted on the train from Marion inebriated on at least one occasion; he also attempted a train robbery. His exasperated mother declared he had no authority to collect money on her behalf.[12] The entire DeWolfe affair infuriated Amos, of course, who offered his daughter one choice: give up Marshall to his maternal grandfather. With her own equal "strength of will and character," Florence vowed to raise her baby alone, until this proved impossible on her earnings as a piano teacher. Florence resented the need to rely on Amos: "Woman has had no redress since she must depend upon the man for support."[13]

Still, she did not carry a grudge against Pete DeWolfe. Later she wrote in her diary, "The truth about most divorces is . . . one party is never *all* good and the other never all *bad*. Both are to blame and that makes philosophizing difficult." In her typical game-faced style, she noted "that short unhappy period in my life is dead and buried."

Young Florence. Courtesy of Shelby Needham.

Yet she continued to be haunted by "the dead embers of [her] unfortunate past," as she put it.[14] The marriage and its ending had happened to her at a time when such things were thought scandalous for women, and despite the changing mores of the 1910s and 1920s, she always wanted the episode kept private from the wider world. Her sensibilities, sadly, prevented her from having a full relationship with her future grandchildren. Later, she lamented to her friend and adviser, Kathleen Lawler, "I never lived; I never had any real life or

Marshall DeWolfe. Courtesy of the Marion County Historical Society, Marion, Ohio.

pleasure until after I was thirty years old." She was thirty-one when she married Warren G. Harding.[15]

On her own once again, she continued to teach piano to make her living, and it may have been during one of her lessons to Warren's sister, Charity, in their father's parlor that she met her future husband. Or she may have met him, too, at the Merry Roll Round. The young newspaper publisher often went with his friend and workmate Jack Warwick to relax there after a hard day in the pressroom in the mid 1880s. Harding also played waltzes for skaters with his band.[16] Wherever she met Harding, Amos Kling was furious once again at his daughter's taste in men. Although Warren's father, George, was a well-loved country doctor, Harding and his newspaper were considered unlikely to succeed, and the marriage was thus "beneath" his daughter. As family friend George Christian Sr. recalled, "Marion town and country from the east bank of the Whetstone to the west bank of the Scioto rocked under the storm of social war."[17] Meanwhile, Florence and her beau ambled happily and amorously in Marion's Lover's Lane, under the willow trees. Unlike her father, Florence had high hopes for her future husband and the role she could play in building him up, and herself too. They became a "husky, lusty, ambitious pair."[18] Amos, meanwhile, meanly disparaged the *Star* and its owner to business colleagues, intimating too that the Hardings were of African descent.

Warren, five years younger than Florence, had come to Marion with his family from nearby Caledonia in 1882. He was born on his grandparents' farm, in Blooming Grove, Ohio, a town of New Englanders of a reformist tendency: "prohibitionists, abolitionists, and straight out members of the whig and republican parties" (whence the source of Kling's rumors).[19] He and his seven younger siblings were the children of George Tryon Harding, a homeopath, and his wife, Phoebe. They were not well-off. The Hardings moved off the farm when Harding was six months old, eventually settling in Caledonia, but young Warren continued to work hard on his grandparents' fields. At fourteen, he attended Ohio Central College, walking more than seven miles each way. A glorified high school, it gained him a better than average education for the time, especially in history, math, and Latin. Family circumstances soon forced him to leave to earn money. He worked on the railroad, and he later taught school, but what he really loved (beside playing the alto horn in the Caledonia Aelonian Band) was the printing trade, which he tried first at college and continued at a Caledonia paper, the *Mirror*, beginning in 1882.[20] His politics were too Republican to stay at that Democratic paper, so in 1884, with his father's help—Doc Harding was now doing better with his own business centered in Marion—he bought the *Marion Star* (then known as the *Pebble*) for $300 with Jack Warwick and another friend.

Though he loved his father dearly, Harding worshipped his mother—who early on had believed he would be president.[21] Her influence helps explain to some degree his patience with Florence, who must have been trying at times. Phoebe was a saintly woman, and her son, basking in her love, reflected it. It is rare to find him remembered in any way but as a lovable man, despite his flaws.

Florence and Warren were married on July 8, 1891, at the house she and Warren had built on Mt. Vernon Avenue in Marion. George B. Christian Jr., the son of their dear neighbor and later Harding's secretary in the White House, served as ring bearer. Ironically, Florence never wore that ring, feminist as she was.[22] She also continued to use "Kling" as her middle name. She seems not to have been bothered by the difference in their ages, and she later told a friend that statistics showed that marriages with an older wife were "the happiest."[23] The house had been built in part with Kling money, thanks to Florence's mother. Facing the resistance of Amos, who refused to attend the wedding, Louisa snuck in the back door and witnessed the ceremony.[24] The *Star* reported their nuptials and noted their plans to travel to "Chicago, St. Paul, and the Northwest," where they got at least as far as Vancouver.[25] After they returned, Marshall became a frequent visitor at their home, staying there in summers during breaks from school; he was part of the family, nurtured and loved by Warren. Amos Kling, however, remained the boy's chief support, and he lived mostly at the Klings.[26] Three years after her wedding, Florence was reminded of her earlier life when Pete DeWolfe died of tuberculosis complicated by alcoholism. Neither Marshall nor Florence attended Pete's funeral.[27] Tension between Warren and Marshall flared later, when the young man proved in some ways as unreliable as his biological father. But Florence was always attached to him, and she kept the dog he gave her, Hub, close at the foot of her bed. Hub became the office dog at the *Star* but was later mysteriously poisoned.[28]

In the early days, Florence found herself frequently called on to assist with the *Star* while Warren checked himself into Dr. J. H. Kellogg's sanitarium in Battle Creek, Michigan. He regularly drove himself to exhaustion, overindulged to compensate, and then eventually, collapsed with nervous breakdowns—a pattern that repeated itself some five times between 1889 and 1901. Some of his prescriptions from this era include stomach remedies, like pepsin and aspirin, as well as something called uritone, an herbal appetite suppressant.[29] But this was a temporary condition for Harding. As his old friend, Christian, claimed, "he reformed and became 'the most temperate man in all things.'"[30] In the meantime, the illnesses compelled his wife to play an ever greater role at the *Star*. The paper began to thrive, despite Amos's continued cranky plottings against its owner.

Florence became vital to the paper's good fortune as she built up its receipts through nurturing its circulation and advertising base. She never hesitated at taking on the less glamorous aspects of the work either, scrubbing the office floor when necessary, as Joseph De Barthe noted: "It was her toil and ceaseless, uncomplaining efforts that finally lifted the paper from mediocrity to a firm and successful business basis."[31] Or, as William Allen White wrote chauvinistically, "she did a man's hard work."[32] Florence, like her husband, was imbued with "newspaper atmosphere." She loved to hear the clattering presses, smell the ink, drink in the news.[33] She "made it a habit to spend hours every day at the printing shop, often publicly caressing Warren," William Chancellor alleged.[34] Perhaps she did; certainly, her husband's career provided an outlet for her energies and talents. Indeed, his career became hers.

It was an exciting time to be in journalism too. During the Spanish-American War, she helped obtain the first direct wire report ever received in Marion, and thus gave the *Star* an international perspective. But she is best known for creating a system by which young boys delivered the paper and collected money from their customers, instead of purchasers having to come by the *Star*'s office.[35] She always had a special empathy for newsboys, likely occasioned by her difficult history with Marshall. She took on a motherly role with them, following their development, "moral and physical," and forming them into a tight group, which she closely monitored.[36] Indeed, when they let her down, she was known to spank them! One of her former boys, socialist presidential candidate Norman Thomas, did not remember this experience fondly and called her "a woman of very narrow mind." But many of the newsboys stayed close to her. One of them, Ora "Reddy" Baldinger, later took a post as military aide at the White House and stayed with her until she died. Despite her influence on the paper and a long-standing interest in politics, she never felt moved to write for the *Star*, even with all the issues she might have addressed in that fast-changing era, from a women's proper place to the role of America overseas.

She seems to have been well fulfilled in her role at the paper, and proud of her work, too: as she noted tartly of her husband, "He does well when he listens to me and poorly when he does not."[37] Warren agreed, and to him she was always the Duchess. In a jokey Christmas letter written some sixteen years into their marriage, Warren chuckled to a friend, "The Duchess has been bossing Santa Claus, because he stands for it and she likes to boss."[38] Her brother, Cliff, whom she was close to, also called her Duchess, or sometimes Deutcharino; Florence herself signed the name in some of her letters.[39] According to Francis Russell, however, all was not so fun; Harding used the moniker "as an unspoken protest" in response to "this domineering female." Robert Ferrell disagrees, however, and sees the term as "playful."[40] The *Marion Star* went even further, arguing that it was "a tribute to [her] charm and poise."[41] Domineering or not, Florence devoted herself to her husband's career, whether at the paper or later in public office. She soon saw how the growth of the *Star* was positioning him for greater prominence outside Marion. She liked to downplay her influence with such statements as, "Warren does the talking, and I do the baking for the family," but this was not quite so—although she did love to make waffles and cream caramel cake, especially when visitors came.[42] (She hated cooking, however.) As a contemporary journalist rightly asserted, for her, "It was evidently never a question of husband or career, which shall it be? It was both. That must be a very satisfactory way for a woman to solve the problem of her career. Standing back of a man in every possible way and on every possible occasion to make his career come true is something of a career in itself."[43]

Actually, Florence wanted to be beside him—or maybe in front. She always joined his political campaigns, beginning with his successful race for state senator in 1898, the same year he met the man who would be his principal promoter, attorney Harry Daugherty. Warren served as state senator for an unprecedented two terms before being elected lieutenant governor on November 3, 1902. As a senator, he lived in Columbus at the Great Southern Hotel, known as "the little capitol," for the three months of the year he needed to be at the legislative sessions.[44] Florence, who was greatly interested in this work, spent more time in Columbus than most wives, assisting him with not only political advice but in sartorial decisions.

They had a happy marriage, on the whole, those first fifteen years. Florence's view of marriage, that "the man and the woman, properly mated . . . are complements of each other, mutually helping, supporting, and sustaining," resembled the concept of "companionate marriage" popular among the more enlightened of the dawning century.[45] Their relationship seems to have been relatively egalitarian: before her illness, Florence always worked, and Harding did not mind assisting her at home.[46] They attended separate churches; he was a member of Trinity Baptist, she, a longtime pewholder at her mother's church, Epworth Methodist Episcopal. Spiritual guidance was important to her, and she called often upon the Reverend Jesse Swank, her pastor, even long after she left Marion. They had lots of friends, and as in the White House later, there was much jolly sociability at their home. Florence often treated her guests to piano performances.

She was less welcoming to uninvited guests, especially neighborhood kids who trespassed on her property. Proud of her garden—her passion for flowers would be evident in the White House too—she did not suffer anyone eating apples and pears from her trees uninvited. One Marion resident remembered as a child seeing her nail her fence shut, and then, when he and other neighborhood children tried to cross over, she pounced on them with "her large mastiff." After taking the children "by the ear" and admonishing them for stealing the fruit, she offered them freshly baked cookies and the promise of future apples—if they only asked her. "From that time on she was our friend," the man remembered. But she could no doubt be redoubtable, unlike her more huggable husband.[47]

One neighbor who got some hugs from him early in their marriage, according to historians Carl Sferrazza Anthony and Francis Russell, was their unhappily married neighbor, Mrs. Susan P. M. Hodder, whose intimacies with the *Star* publisher allegedly resulted in his first child. But the evidence for this affair is flimsy, based largely on Marion gossip.[48] Warren's ability to father children, moreover, remains highly questionable. In fourteen years of marriage before Florence became ill, they had none. Florence was then in her prime childbearing years, she was of course capable, and the Hardings loved little ones, so if he had had a child out of wedlock (or two, if Nan Britton is to be believed), why didn't he have any with Florence?[49]

The Hardings could at least look forward to the possibility of grandchildren when Marshall married in late 1907. His wife, Esther Neely, was the daughter of Marion's mayor, George Neely. She was barely seventeen years old, he a decade older. Although Marshall had attended the University of Michigan for two years and had worked periodically at the *Star*, he struggled in life. He also drank. Two years after the marriage, he was diagnosed with tuberculosis, just like his father, and the young couple moved to Colorado for his health. After spending some time in a sanitarium, Marshall joined Esther in Kersey, seven miles from Denver, and they tried farming, without much success. Marshall then decided he wanted to set up a newspaper, and he asked for $5,000 from his stepfather—who helped, although by now, he complained to friends about "my good for nothing drunken stepson."[50] Florence also supported him, but Marshall failed at this venture too.

Florence had her own worries at this time. In 1905, as Warren finished his term as lieutenant governor, she had fallen ill with her first bout of kidney disease, hydronephritis, which would affect her with periodic and often violent intensity for the rest of her life. This first attack was so bad that on February 24 she had to have an operation at a hospital in Columbus run by Dr. James Fairchild Baldwin, a pathbreaking women's doctor whose facility, Grant Hospital, was among the largest and best in the country. He surgically anchored her "floating" kidney in place. The incision had to be dressed twice each day, and Florence later recalled that this experience had led to her activism in assisting the suffering veterans of the World War. It took her a year to convalesce, and she never went back to work at the *Star*.[51] It may have been at this time that she wrote in her diary: "By the infirmities of a life of sorrow and fatigue I have reason to think I am not a great way off from, if not very near to, the great ocean of eternity and the time may not be long ere I embark on the last voyage."[52] Or she may have written it later; she would have numerous near-death occurrences with this ailment for nearly twenty years.

While she recovered, her husband found solace by beginning a relationship with Carrie Phillips, an attractive former schoolteacher whose husband, Jim, was also conveniently ill and recovering at Kellogg's in Battle Creek. Florence was not so far away; she convalesced at Dr. Charles Sawyer's neuropsychiatric sanitarium in Marion, later located in roomier quarters at White Oaks Farm just outside of town.[53] She did not have psychiatric troubles, other than those caused by an unfaithful husband and the traumas of her early life, but the place provided "some security, some foundation" to her.[54] The Phillipses and Hardings had been friends, and continued to be; Phillips ran a dry goods store in town. They had a daughter, Isabelle, but had sadly just lost their young son, creating further strain in their marriage.

The Phillips affair has been documented in dozens of love letters and poems Harding wrote to Carrie.[55] A selection of these may be found in Russell's own papers at the American Heritage Center in Wyoming, materials kept out of his book, *The Shadow of Blooming Grove*, by agreement with the Harding Memorial Association, and replaced with long ellipses. The letters reveal a warm and romantic man, uninhibited and florid, who referred frequently to Carrie's lips, thighs, and other intimate parts. Warren was smitten with Carrie, drawn both to her blonde good looks ("pre-Raphaelite," according to Russell) and her cosmopolitan aspirations for a life outside Marion. Despite long breaks later while she was in Germany and while Harding was in Washington, the affair lasted for fifteen years.[56]

Florence felt keenly the injustice life had dealt her: both illness and infidelity. In a forgiving mood, she could write of her husband, "vice often comes in at the door of necessity[,] not at the door of inclination"; more bitterly, she reckoned, "Love, to a man[,] is a sensation only never a complete giving of himself to one forever . . . a

The Hardings and Phillipses with two unknown men, Carrie Phillips seated on left, Florence on right. Courtesy of Mike Perry.

man has one conscience, one code, before marriage; another after."⁵⁷ These sentiments come from Florence's diary, found in an Ohio attic in 1997. It is a miscellaneous compilation, with many lists and nostrums: casts of symphony orchestras and opera directors, criticism of "hyphenated Americans," cures for hiccoughs, clues for getting out tea stains, and characteristics of astrological signs, as Florence found the stars a compelling guide through life. Yet the diary also includes penetrating observations about love and men that reveal some of the pain she endured. The material is almost entirely undated; it is scrawled in a thirty-five-page Women's Calendar from 1891, undoubtedly in her hand, but it seems mostly to come from the first two decades of her marriage (the latest clear date is 1912). Despite the indeterminate nature of the diary's chronology, it is one of the few extant examples of her innermost thoughts—expressions of bitterness, yes, but also unflagging determination to transcend these difficulties. The Phillips affair hurt deeply, and at her blackest moments, Florence felt that Warren had exploited her, referring cynically to "the misunderstood husband—he who makes his wife's frailties his excuse for the full Decalogue of sins and every other woman he meets." She felt oppressed by the burdens of a double standard: "To sanction the iniquity of man, but demand purity of woman, has become an attitude of society." It was still a "man's world," which forced women to "mute acceptance of disloyalty, faithlessness, and humiliation," she lamented. As she wrestled with this cloud over her marriage, she soothed herself by rationalizing the affair and her reaction to it. She would never leave her husband, although she certainly could have afforded to financially: "It is strange how life changes our standards . . . the happy wife is not the woman who has married the best man on earth, but the one who is philosophical enough to make the best of what she has got."[58]

Overall, her married life *was* good. When Florence was healthy enough to do so, the Hardings enjoyed traveling. In 1906, they vacationed in Cuba, opportunely meeting Alice Roosevelt on her honeymoon with Nicholas Longworth. The women became friendly, sharing their developing "occult" interests. Florence, at least, thought they became "good friends," but Mrs. Longworth always wrote about her with "disdain," according to her biographer.[59] Indeed, Alice Roosevelt's picture of a bitter, drinks-serving Florence at a card party in her 1933 book, *Crowded Hours*, has become one of the most indelible portraits of the first lady to this day.

The Hardings stopped in Daytona on the way back, staying at Amos Kling's vacation house. He, meanwhile, had tied the knot again, with Caroline Denman, widowed like himself, and younger than his daughter![60] He had mellowed and had forgiven Florence and her husband; the Klings traveled to Europe with the Hardings the following summer.[61] Kling paid for the voyage, a delightful time of eating good food, taking pleasant walks on the promenade deck, and reading and snoozing in the ship's library. They visited such cities as Oxford and Stratford, Berlin and Nuremberg (known for its beer, Harding pointed out happily), as well as Paris.

The Hardings often vacationed with the Phillipses, too, despite the complications, and from February to April 1909, they were all in Europe, including Germany (introducing Carrie to her future home). The following year, both couples traveled to the Isles of Shoals not far from Portsmouth, New Hampshire. They stayed at President Taft's summer White House there. It is not clear exactly

Florence in Florida. Courtesy of the Marion County Historical Society, Marion, Ohio.

when Florence learned of her husband's affair, but many in Marion were aware of it by 1910, when local gossip convinced Carrie to make plans to go to Berlin with her daughter—that is, if Harding would not marry her first.[62] Of course, the worldly Mrs. Phillips seems to have been keen to leave the confines of small town life by then anyway. The affair may have explained why Florence decided to accompany her husband on the Chatauqua speaking circuit; as she wrote sarcastically in her diary, "there is no devotion like a husband's provided he is far enough out of his wife's sight to do as he pleases." Some of the other speakers objected to Florence intruding on their homosocial circle and alleged that she tagged along to keep an eye on him.[63] More likely, though, the trips afforded her the opportunity for travel and interesting talks. She liked both, and throughout their marriage, she always traveled with her husband whenever possible. Warren had become a Chatauqua speaker in 1906; he was soon recognized as a "spellbinding" one, and one of his most popular presentations addressed Alexander Hamilton. He served on the circuit every summer for years and was well paid for his appearances.[64]

Florence soon had something else to preoccupy her; in part because of her urging, her husband, who had been happy back in his printer's apron with the opportunity to make periodic Hamiltonian orations, decided to run for governor of Ohio in 1910. Florence had long been a champion of his political potential and was likely getting a little bored in Marion. Unfortunately, he lost to Democratic incumbent Judson Harmon by 100,000 votes; 1910 was a tough year for the GOP, with the party faithful split already between adherents of the former president, Teddy Roosevelt, and those of the current occupant of the White House, William Howard Taft, foreshadowing 1912's election debacle. For Harding, his four-year absence from politics, as well as his support for Prohibition, which this German beer lover had extolled in the *Star*, were likely also of no benefit. Marion was a small Midwestern town with 10,000 people, but it had fifty bars, and dryness was not appealing. The Hardings decided to use the free time profitably and visit Europe in the winter and spring of 1910–11 with the Phillipses. Florence, who still considered Carrie a friend, was willing to downplay her suspicions, but this grew increasingly difficult. The two couples took their last trip in 1911, to Bermuda. By the end of that summer, Carrie insisted, Harding had to divorce Florence, or she would move away. Meanwhile, Mrs. Phillips finalized her plans to leave for Berlin and enroll her daughter in school there.[65]

Harding would not leave his wife, of course; he knew how vital she was to his working and political life. That summer, several historians have alleged, Florence ripped open a letter from Carrie addressed to her husband and learned of the affair. *She* then forced Warren to consider a divorce.[66] Whether or not this actually happened, certainly by the summer of 1911, Florence would have known that Carrie was planning to leave, lessening the requirement for such an ultimatum. The Hardings themselves got away that summer, for another European trip, this time with Frank and Evaland Scobey, their old friends from the Ohio senate who had moved to San Antonio.

As they left, Harding wrote a fervent, desperate letter to Carrie, knowing she was slipping away: "I stand more than willing. . . . *I'm yours* now, any time—for all time." Despite page after page of panting prose, he still would not give her what she wanted: a divorce from Florence. Carrie resolved to live in Berlin for an indefinite period; she felt at home there. Russell's notes show she did come back, secretly, in 1912 and 1913, but as long as Florence was breathing, Warren would not leave her. Carrie seems to have found solace in other affairs.[67]

Despite Harding's loss in the governor's race, that election had given him a certain national prominence, and he now regularly gave speeches on behalf of President Taft; he and Florence were among the vast crowd invited to the Taft twenty-fifth wedding anniversary extravaganza at the White House in 1911. This new recognition within the GOP may have also cemented Warren to Florence. With his growing visibility, he needed her more than ever. In 1912, he put the president's name in for nomination for reelection at the Republican convention in Chicago, and he "strafed" Roosevelt with vigor.[68] That November, though, Taft was defeated by the Democratic candidate, Woodrow Wilson, in a four-way race with progressive Teddy Roosevelt and socialist Eugene Debs.

That did not stop Florence from seeing once again even bigger possibilities for her husband, as did his old friend Harry Daugherty, when an open Senate seat came up for 1914. In part to reunite Republicans and Progressives after that divisive 1912 race, Harding was cultivated as a bridge candidate. Meanwhile, Florence suffered through another serious attack in the winter of 1913. She was ill for much of the next year, convalescing at White Oaks.[69] Other family developments, including her father's death, her son's continued ill health, and her husband's chance to run for higher office, all spurred her to recover.

Amos's death in October 1913 left her $35,000 and her son, $25,000. Sadly, Marshall's own ailments worsened. His wife must have worried how she would care for their growing family, including a daughter, Eugenia, born in 1911, and a son, George Warren, born in 1914. Marshall may have been a challenging young man who never made much of himself, but his wife and children were especially dear to the older Hardings. Florence loved her grandchildren and would make sure they did not starve. Nevertheless, she was reluctant to spend much time with them. In part, that was because Warren's new life in the Senate soon took her to Washington, but she passed up opportunities to see them even when back in Marion, perhaps because of her desire to keep this part of her life very private—not because of something so petty as embarrassment about being old enough to be a grandmother, as some have alleged, but because of their connections with her past life.

Harding, meanwhile, defeated the venerable Joseph Foraker in the spring 1914 Ohio primary—Foraker had already served two terms in the Senate and been defeated in his last try in 1908—and won the Republican nomination. By that summer, Florence was well recovered from her illness and could once again assist her husband in Ohio's first popular general election of a U.S. senator. The election season started in a leisurely way in September 1914, after the Hardings visited Lake Placid and the Adirondacks; Florence went to work writing some of his speeches.[70]

Meanwhile, the start of World War I in Europe had brought the possibility of homefront battles. Carrie was back in Marion, and her relationship with Harding seems to have resumed, whether Florence was aware of it or not. Having lived in Germany made Mrs. Phillips ever more impatient with Marion's provincialism. Harding assuaged her with a new Buick. But he and Florence would soon be in Washington, and their affair was nearing its end. It seems the two women had a final blow-up in 1916, with Carrie threatening a lawsuit. Both marriages remained intact, however, and afterward, except for her continuing pro-German sentiments, which drew critical attention as the United States entered the war, and her 1920 blackmail attempt of the Republican presidential nominee, Carrie largely disappeared from their lives.[71]

A much younger woman was now angling for the senator's heart: Marion neighbor Nan Britton, who began a correspondence with Harding in 1914, which would turn into an affair that resulted in the birth in 1919 of the "President's Daughter." Nan, who first knew of Harding when she had his sister Daisy as her high school teacher, seems to have developed a crush on him in 1910, when she was fourteen, and he, forty-five. Francis Russell, among others, claimed that the feelings ran deeper and more mutually than that, with Harding writing Nan long missives on the same kind of paper on which he inked his lusty poems to Carrie.[72] While there is no record of any letters from Harding of this sort in Nan's collection, recently opened to researchers at UCLA, her fantasies about the handsome candidate would soon turn into reality when she conceived a child, Elizabeth Ann, with him in the Senate Office Building.[73] Whether these continued with passionate embraces in the Oval Office, as her 1927 confessional claims, cannot be verified, but in 2015 DNA tests of Nan Britton's grandson, a 65-year-old construction worker named James Blaesing, showed what many scholars, including this one, had once doubted; Harding had a daughter with Nan Britton. Blaesing's DNA was akin to Harding's grand-nephews'.[74]

In Carl Anthony's book, Harding is described as having had as many as seven extramarital liaisons. Samuel Hopkins Adams hints at even more; he suggests that "there is no way of determining" how many there were. Yet Harding, despite the rumors as well as the excesses of his earlier lifestyle, as attested to by his friend Christian Sr., was not a man gargantuan in his appetites by the time he approached fifty. He was, for instance, a moderate consumer of alcohol, as his Secret Service agent took pains to point out—at a time and in a position when he could have imbibed as excessively as he wished. The chief explanation for Harding's reputed affairs seems to be to run him down and to undermine Florence, as Adams does regularly, alleging that "she ceased to satisfy his emotional, or perhaps his physical demands." This is unfair. Certainly her illness led him to find physical release with women like Carrie, but emotionally, and in many other ways, he continued to depend greatly on his wife.[75]

And her support paid off this time. On November 3, 1914, Warren G. Harding was elected senator over Democratic attorney general Timothy Hogan by 102,000 votes. His warm manner, good looks, and effective forcefulness as a speaker had all assisted him—as had Hogan's Catholic faith—despite the enmity of some "wets."[76] Friends like Scobey thought Harding should now consider running for president![77] With his looks and speaking ability, he seemed a natural candidate. There was plenty of time to think about it. As a result of the contemporary setup of the congressional calendar, although his service began on March 4, 1915, Harding's first session would not start until the following December, more than a year after his election![78] But the new senator was not ready to seriously contemplate higher office just yet. Neither was Florence.

Less than two months after Election Day, on New Year's Day 1915, Marshall died in Colorado of tuberculosis brought on by alcoholism. Thus, as she got ready for a new life in Washington,

Florence had to tidy up the ends of her son's, visiting his home in Colorado and helping to take care of his debts, and making sure his inheritance was "safely invested" for the children.[79] The Hardings had hoped to go to Burma that winter to see Harding's sister, Carolyn, but she and her husband had already returned home. Instead, they went west, ostensibly as part of a fact-finding trip—or junket. Harding gave some speeches along the way, visiting the Scobeys in San Antonio and some other friends, the Timkens, in San Diego. They also went to Hawaii to learn about sugar production. In Honolulu, they met Charles Forbes, who would later prove an embarrassment (and much worse) in the Veterans Bureau. Meanwhile, Hawaii was a delightful playground, with golfing and other games that Harding loved; as the new senator told Scobey, "Duchess is tickled over her triumph at Poker, and is hanging on to her coins for some special purpose in the Hawaiian Island."[80]

They returned by mid-March and were "well and reasonably happy," Harding told Scobey. With no obligations yet in Washington, they would be in Marion except for regular Chatauqua trips.[81] Florence's good health continued that summer, their last before going to the capital.[82] They found renters for their Mt. Vernon Avenue house; White Oaks Farm, with the Sawyers, would be their home when they returned for visits, except of course during the Front Porch campaign.[83] A Columbus paper proclaimed Florence a most satisfying Senate spouse: "a loyal wife, a charming hostess, a sympathetic neighbor and an ardent Republican of the stalwart type."[84] Stalwart and excited, the Hardings got ready for the next adventure in their lives.

CHAPTER 2

WASHINGTON LIFE AND THE PRESIDENTIAL CAMPAIGN, 1915–1921

SENATE WIFE

Although she had been well through the summer in Ohio, by October 1915, with less than a month to go before leaving for Washington, Florence felt wretched once again.[1] She was determined to come east nonetheless. She would not miss her husband taking the Senate oath, and so a special car was arranged. The Hardings at last left for Washington, D.C., on November 24, 1915, the day after she buried her son's ashes in the Neely plot in Marion. This ritual was a poignant one, so much tied with her now-unmentionable past as she began her new life in the nation's capital.

Unfortunately, the trip only made her sicker, and once she got there, she stayed in bed for weeks.[2] Despite being an invalid, she did not lack for company, as the kind Senate ladies came to call on her. Such calls were a matter of etiquette in those days, and she must have greatly appreciated it. Ironically, as first lady, she would introduce a procedure that saved everyone much calling by simply bringing all the congressional and Cabinet wives together at a large White House function. However, no such mechanism existed in 1915, a moment when there was no first lady in the White House, as Ellen Wilson had died the year before, and Edith Bolling Galt was not yet the second Mrs. Wilson.

The Hardings lived at 1612 Twenty-first Street Northwest, the former home of Hilary Abner Herbert, the secretary of the navy in the second Cleveland administration. The house came complete with furniture and servants, but the Hardings had their eyes on a new home, a $50,000 terraced neo-Georgian brick duplex at 2314 Wyoming Avenue, which they spent much of their first year renovating and decorating. Harding also joined the Chevy Chase golf club to make some social connections and to play the game; it was so exclusive that it took over two years for him to be a full member. Florence, once she recovered, turned her energy to readying their new home, which turned into an extensive project. Harding was still taking in $20,000 a year from the *Star*, plus $7,500 as a senator, so they could afford to make some significant fixes.[3]

The new house, in fact, was a small mansion, with a library, wicker room, sun porch, drawing room, and two guest rooms. They wanted new bathrooms on the first and third floors, an additional servant's room in the basement, and an expansion in the garage, which was big enough for three cars and included a separate toilet.[4] The new rooms also needed draperies, which Florence ordered (she chose braided antique velvet and silk), and of course furniture. She selected mahogany for their bedroom, and antique ivory enamel and walnut for the guest bedroom. She did compromise in some of her expenditures: the chauffeur got an iron bed and a cotton (not horsehair) mattress. Thus, Florence's room cost $600 to furnish and the chauffeur's, $71.50.[5] In total, their order came to $3,200 for furniture, and well over $700 for draperies.[6] It was a fitting house for a rising senator and his wife. Their "colored servants, well trained and efficient," were also paid well.[7]

With the other Senate spouses calling on her, Florence soon succeeded in making a number of friends. She kept these friends in the White House, too; she would have no pretensions that their Senate associations made them unsuitable for company at the executive mansion.[8] After all, she brought her Marion friends to Pennsylvania Avenue, and the ladies from her Columbus bridge club too.[9] Though illness initially prevented her from participating in activities with her new Senate friends, she kept up with their doings by reading the society pages, where members of her circle were often featured. By early 1916, she was feeling much healthier and liking her new role very much.[10] She was happily busy with the house planning and her husband's work, enjoying herself greatly—indeed, she was "full of ambition," and, as Harding was happy to tell Scobey, "better than she has been at any time within the last three years."[11] Florence told a reporter that it was "a quiet life, a pleasant one, and the problems are not so huge. I like it."[12] Her husband, who may have missed the "hurly and bustle" of the newspaper shop, liked it too. As one journalist noted later, he "looked like a Senator, he had the pose and build and declamation of a Senator . . . he did not speak often, but he was listened to . . . he expressed himself clearly and forcibly."[13] Harding had already been named to the commerce, coast defenses, and claims committees. Later he joined the Philippines committee, which had only irregular meetings.[14] After just a few months in the Senate, he was asked to be the temporary chairman of the Republican National Convention in Chicago and to give the keynote address there, following up his role in 1912 where he had introduced Taft, leading some to think a more important office was in the wings. He wrote his old Ohio friend, Malcolm Jennings, self-deprecatingly, "you know that I am unsuited to the higher position if it were possible for me to attain it." Jennings promised to help divert the giddying prospect, but, if matters settled on Harding for president in 1916, "you will have no right to refuse."[15]

Harding traveled the country that fall for the actual Republican nominee, Supreme Court justice and former New York governor Charles Evans Hughes. He gave speeches for other Republican candidates too, as far away as Wyoming and Utah, and often faced Wilson partisans, happy that "he has kept us out of war, or so they think, anyway." In Boston in October, remembering Florence's interest in fashion—an interest that would only expand during her years in Washington with their heightened opportunities for display of sartorial splendor—he told her that women were wearing dresses three inches above their shoe tops! There were "more young women with short skirts . . . than you can imagine." He would pick her up some new styles in New York.[16] Florence was at that moment back in Marion, staying at White Oaks, while their house was being readied; she made it a practice to visit her father-in-law in the mornings, and after her sister-in-law, Daisy, who lived with him, was off teaching school, Florence would stay and straighten the house, making herself useful to the older man.[17]

As they planned their return to Washington after the long summer and fall recess, Harding voted for Hughes in the presidential election. Florence, of course, could not—and not even her husband was sure she should yet! Harding came to support a suffrage amendment—and a Prohibition one too—primarily because, as a democratic sort, he thought voters should have a chance to determine the issue, not because he necessarily liked the idea.[18] Florence's health, meanwhile, was now improved enough for her to contemplate a role that fell very much within her sphere: entertaining at the new house, which was finally ready at the beginning of December.

As they settled into Senate life, with the world war looming ever larger, Florence's days grew more hectic. As she wrote a friend, "My life these days . . . [is] one of great rush. People coming and going all the time." There were luncheon engagements and calls to make, frequent houseguests, and visits to the manicurist and stylist, often all on the same day. Part of this was Florence's personality: she liked to be busy. But she also well knew, as she had for years, how important a contribution she could make to her husband's success, whether at the paper or in politics. "She was ambitious for herself and for Warren," well noted a woman who would become an especially close friend in those years, Evalyn Walsh McLean, who saw Florence Harding's determination first in the way she carried herself.[19]

Evalyn, married to Edward "Ned" McLean, the publisher of the *Washington Post*, was also known as the Hope Diamond heiress. She and Florence met in 1916 at the home of Congressman Nick Longworth and his wife, Alice Roosevelt Longworth. Mrs. Longworth had the Hardings over regularly for poker evenings, despite her disdain for them. She recalled later, "It is odd to have seen so much of people whom I never liked as I saw of the Hardings." But Alice knew it was important to make connections; her husband, an Ohio Republican congressman, could benefit from links with the state's junior senator. While the rest of them played poker, Florence would tend bar. When the players wanted a drink, Alice observed, "Mrs. Harding, who was watching the play of the hands, would obediently get up and mix a whisky and soda for them." Alice noted that the

Hardings "never liked me, and I can hardly blame them." Alice only visited Florence after she was in the White House.[20]

But Florence and Evalyn soon become close. Their husbands, Ned and Warren, would also become good friends, drawn together by poker, and Ned's other paper, the *Cincinnati Inquirer,* which was favorable to Harding.[21] At their first meeting, Evalyn had initially been more impressed with Warren herself, "a stunning man with a powerfully masculine quality to charm a woman," even if his pants were baggy, he wore unflattering suspenders, and he chomped on a plug of tobacco. Evalyn, more perceptively than Alice, saw he was "not a slob." Alice, of course, thought he was a crook too.[22] Evalyn noticed right away signs of Florence's age and illness: her neck was "withered" and her ankles, "thickly swollen." However, she also saw that Florence was "rich in spirit; a determined and a jealous wife."[23] Hearing a few weeks later that Florence had fallen ill, Evalyn went to visit her and was greatly moved by Mrs. Harding's struggle against her debilitating malady. A close friendship developed, despite their age difference; Evalyn was twenty-nine and had two young children (with two more to come), and Florence was a fifty-five-year-old grandmother. Florence, in turn, became gushingly fond of Evalyn, writing her: "I look upon you as one of my very tried and true friends."[24] Evalyn would not only provide Florence with close friendship, but also give her life much color and excitement, even though the younger woman's health was also often fragile. In the following years, and well into the presidency, the Hardings spent many happy hours with the McLeans at their various homes, from Washington to Florida. Their capital estate, Friendship, a former priestly retreat for Georgetown Jesuits in Cleveland Park, featured a garden with a fountain, golf and tennis courts, an indoor pool, and a ballroom. Florence thought it was "the nearest place to Heaven of anything on this earth."[25]

Still, in the midst of the luxury and the excitement of Washington, she did not forget those less fortunate left behind in Marion. If anything, Esther and Florence grew closer after Marshall's death in 1915. One paper suggested that Florence "diverted all the glow of her love" to the children now that her son was gone.[26] Esther's situation as a widow and single parent no doubt drew much empathy from her mother-in-law. Although the young woman would soon remarry, for a time her fortunes were constrained; the inheritance her late husband had received seems to have been tied up in investments. In April 1917, for instance, she wrote a long, plaintive letter to Florence urging the sale of a bond, which would bring her a much-needed $5,000. She also wanted to assert her right as her children's guardian, which would bring her control of the needed funds and permit her to settle their affairs should something happen to Florence. "I prefer to be guardian of my own kiddies," she pleaded; "at least give me credit for trying to take care of them myself—if a woman deserves any credit for caring for her own infants," she added. Likely Esther knew that Florence had been unable to do so with her own son! To reassure her thrifty mother-in-law, she added, "we live very simply—kids eat more bread and butter than anything else." She fixed her daughter's hats herself, even if she still needed "three or four new ginghams" for Jean that year. Esther, too, wasn't about to buy "tapestry, velours, and mahogany," but would be happy with oak furniture filled with imitation fiber.[27] Florence, of course, was buying a good deal of luxurious fabrics; in May 1918, she received a $600 bill for her last six months' worth of clothes, including satin, crepe, plush, silk, and taffeta gowns.[28] Yet rather than turn over the invested funds to her daughter-in-law directly, Florence continued to make interest payments to Esther. For years, she sent monthly checks of $35 to $50 for the children (somewhere between $350 and $500 per month in today's money). These would have been helpful amounts, but they did not give her daughter-in-law all the freedom she wanted with her money, either.[29]

By April 1917, the United States was at war, and Florence was soon preoccupied with another set of young people to assist. She and Evalyn, along with other Washington friends, did their part in helping the soldiers, setting her on a path of activism that would galvanize her once in the White House, when she assisted numerous disabled veterans. She busied herself on the home front in making cotton garments for the Red Cross ("I do not think she ever handled a sewing machine in her life," Harding chuckled to Scobey).[30] Florence also made numerous donations to charities and war bonds. The Hardings didn't get their long hiatus that summer either, owing to the war; Congress stayed in session for an unprecedented 567 days. But the Ohio senator still got in a trip to New Hampshire in October, to his friend Senator John Weeks's summer place, to play golf and poker, overeat, and smoke a lot of cigars.[31] He was contemplating a stag party trip to Hawaii, too, although he ended up passing on it when his close friends did not join in.[32] Instead, Florence and he planned a "leisurely" vacation that fall, including stops in Philadelphia, Corning, New York, St. Louis, and San Antonio, arriving at the Scobeys for Harding's fifty-second birthday. "Surprise me with a highball," Warren told his hard-drinking friend.[33] Apparently they had a delightful visit—and why not? Scobey was the "best friend I have in the world," as Harding once said; moreover, they also enjoyed spending time with other Scobey cronies, like influential Texas Republican R. B. (Gus) Creager. Afterward, they returned to Marion for Harding to roll up his sleeves at the *Star* and give his associate, George Van Fleet, a ten-day holiday while Florence visited her dressmaker in Columbus.[34]

In Washington, life would be more difficult that winter. Florence wrote a friend at Christmas that the city was packed with war workers, and it was "worse than freezing because there is little coal, and no inside overcoats at any public dispensary." She joked with a contemporary ditty: "My Tuesday's are meatless, My Wednesday's are wheatless . . . My house, it is heatless, My bed, it is sheetless . . . How I hate the damned Kaiser."[35] Although George Creel of the government's Committee on Public Information would have liked that last sentiment, he would have been unhappy with Florence's conclusions: tough times would hurt the Democratic administration, she thought. But her husband instead worried more about the "Bolsheviki . . . getting stronger in America every day."[36] More immediately dangerous than the Red Menace was the Spanish flu, which broke out in early 1918 with great force.

Meanwhile, the Hardings lived comfortably. They purchased nearly $85 (worth ten times that, at least, in today's dollars) in wine and "distillates" in one month in 1917. They ate well too, with large orders arriving every day or every other. Instead of being sheetless, their linens were laundered.[37] In November, perhaps getting ready for the holidays—and apparently not anticipating Prohibition—they bought about $600 worth of monogrammed cocktail, cordial, claret, and highball glasses and goblets. But Florence refused to get a dog, much to her husband's disappointment; she thought the city was no place for one.

In May 1918 Harding got away again for some weeks, to the Adirondacks with Senator Joseph Frelinghuysen and other friends, and to New England on a Chautauqua tour, earning $600 per week for his daily talks.[38] He also was besieged by Carrie that summer and planned to see her at the end of the tour. She was still pressing him to marry her.[39] Feeling squeezed and likely guilty, he referred to her cattily in communications with her husband. In one letter to Jim written while he was in Washington, Harding noted that he "doubt[ed] if Carrie knows" the meaning of "reasonable economy"; moreover, he added, she "always boasted how she could get on."[40] Carrie was, in fact, becoming an embarrassment and a liability with her pro-German views, demanding the freshman senator vote against the war and threatening that otherwise, she would reveal their affair to her husband and the world. Her attitude, as expressed in some of her letters, had attracted the interest of local law enforcement officials, who wondered about her loyalties.[41] Harding remained a war supporter, and he urged Jim Phillips to rein her in.[42]

But back in Marion that fall, voting for the last time without his wife in November, the senator and Carrie reconciled. A hot poem suggests the rekindling of the affair: "I love your mouth, I love your fire, I love the way you stir desire . . . I love you garb'd but naked, MORE!"[43] Before long, however, Harding was back in Washington, and his most tempting thoughts in the wake of the armistice that month were plans to play poker and golf with his buddies in Florida and Georgia.

While Carrie was still on his mind, "like a juggler," Russell contends, Harding was pursuing Nan Britton too. Russell was not alone in his assertions. Nearly every book on the Hardings alleges a close relationship with Nan that continued into the White House, even when credible evidence had yet to emerge to support these charges.[44] Samuel Hopkins Adams went so far as to assert they became common-law intimates: "They lived together on and off from 1916 to 1922, if not longer," he writes, with the result that "on October 22, 1919, their first child was born." And even though Russell's own letters show that Harding absolutely refused to divorce Florence and marry Carrie, his longtime mistress, he blithely borrows from Britton such Harding quotes as, "I'd like to make you my bride, Nan darling."[45] Anthony, too, faithfully transcribes Nan's version of events, from

Harding's bestowal of "several hundred-dollar bills" upon her to "a tryst in a large closet . . . adjoining the Oval Office."[46] While Britton's archive only showed Harding finding her a job during the war with U.S. Steel's Safety, Sanitation and Welfare Bureau in Manhattan, the 2015 revelations of their grandson's existence have at last confirmed the decades-long rumors.[47]

That Britton's story got into print at all at the time seems to have resulted from a sudden stoppage of funds from Daisy Harding, Nan's former teacher and Harding's sister, whom the younger woman had successfully blackmailed with her allegations after Harding's death. Daisy had sent varying sums to Nan in the mid-1920s, including payments of $65, $110, $125, and $400. To protect her brother's name, Daisy was trying to shut Nan up—which worked for a time, though it cost this schoolteacher about half her annual salary and added to the credibility of Nan's assertions.[48] When brother George Harding and sister Carolyn Votaw learned about the sordid business, they cut Nan off in 1926; within a year, she published her book, with the assistance of the Bible Corporation of America.[49] She made $50,000 on it—a lot more than she ever got from Daisy—for the benefit of the Elizabeth Ann Foundation, a dubious charity named after her daughter.

Four years after it appeared, in 1931, Nan slapped a Marion man, Charles A. Klunk, with a $50,000 lawsuit after he published a book that claimed hers was slanderously inaccurate. Attacking Nan's conclusions, Joseph De Barthe's *The Answer* also provided further persuasive evidence for her story being false. Harding and Florence had been married thirty-two years, yet there was no child, and De Barthe believed that an earlier case of mumps was the reason for Harding's infertility. Nan lost the suit; until 2015, nothing beyond her privately published book had ever surfaced to document this affair. Secret Service agent Edmund Starling also never mentioned her visiting the White House. But Carl Anthony, citing medical evidence, has suggested that the infertility in the Hardings' marriage may have been actually Florence's, owing to the onset of her kidney ailment after Marshall's birth.[50]

Florence *was* sick in January 1919, and Harding could have gotten away to make a baby then. But it is hard to believe that Harding would have left his own child without support, which is Nan's allegation. He supported Florence's son for years. He was not only a kind man, but he was also not hesitant to make quiet payments when the need arose, as Carrie's election-year blackmail reveals. It would have been unlikely for a man like Harding, a man "whose chief fault and failing was his loyalty to his friends" to have abandoned the daughter of a good friend like Dr. Britton and leave her "suffer[ing] to bear, unprotected and unprovided for, the pains of motherhood and the penalties of an unhallowed love," as De Barthe put it. Instead it seems likely that Harding was not entirely convinced of his paternity of the baby.[51]

Instead, during Florence's illness that winter of 1918–19, Warren was watching closely over *her*. In a four-day attack, she had nearly lost her life yet again.[52] The senator described her hydronephrosis to Scobey as "due to the secretions of the [kidney] which do not find an outlet through urinary channels. As a result, her kidney is swollen to 8 or 10 times its normal size," with excruciating pain. Florence did have her doctors, including Carl Sawyer, Dr. Harding, and a nurse on hand to assist, and Carl's father, Charles, was in close touch from Marion. Florence also had a recently widowed friend, Mrs. Boyd, staying with her for support. Her condition was dire, but Florence rallied, and when she was better, as Warren cracked to Scobey, he was ready for a "regular knock-out fight with her concerning the dog question."[53] Meanwhile, Mrs. Boyd was helping to buoy Florence's spirits. She had given "the Duchess exercise thinking of things to do where I am not on the job. Where the Duchess can't issue twelve separate and distinct orders in [as many] minutes we are going to send for the good undertaker and hang wife on the door," Harding chuckled.[54]

On a more serious note, he predicted to Scobey that Wilson's trip to France, in which the president had excluded any members of the opposition except diplomat Henry White, who merely "went as a Republican," was "a mistake." Yet, he added hopefully, "if we will only allow him to go on in his egotistic way, I think he will cease to be a strong factor in American political life."[55] Such commentary was only further justification for Scobey to continue to pester his friend to make a run for president himself. With Theodore Roosevelt's recent death in January 1919, Harding's opportunity looked plain to the San Antonian. Harding turned down the idea: "I should really be ashamed to presume myself fitted to reach out for a place of such responsibility." Neither did he want to bother "my many good friends" with it. Of course, it was "mighty gratifying" to hear Scobey's blandishments. Still, he noted he had other reasons to shy away, more selfish ones. If elected, "I am sure I should never have any more fun or any real enjoyment in life."[56]

Meanwhile, he was looking forward to his next fun. Florence, who was "depressed" at her invalidism, was keen to get out of town as soon as possible. By mid-February, she was much better. Not only could she "move about comfortably," but she was also looking forward to a trip to the South they were planning, including a visit to two of their favorite haunts, Augusta and St. Augustine, after Congress adjourned in March. Unfortunately, Texas was out of the question, Harding told Scobey: Florence "couldn't wear a corset and dress" yet — her condition was still too bothersome.[57] His friend wrote back jokingly that they must come to San Antonio all the same; "I will not wear a corset if she don't, and if it will add any to her comfort I will wear nothing but BVDs." They never did make it to San Antonio that spring. Florence, in her still convalescent condition, had dreaded the "long and weary railroad journey."[58]

She decided to stay in Washington with Mrs. Boyd, who remained their houseguest, while Harding went on his own to St. Augustine, staying at the luxurious Ponce de Leon Hotel. He enjoyed "motoring heaps" on Daytona Beach with cheap gasoline (22 cents), along with his friends, Senators Joseph Frelinghuysen, Frank Kellogg, Frederick Hale, and Gilbert Hitchcock, a Democrat from Nebraska. He told Malcolm Jennings they'd driven 500 miles.[59] And, he reported, the news from Washington was good: "Duchess is very much improved." By March 22, she had put on fifteen pounds and was up to walking a mile at a time.[60] He wrote to her just about every day, about his card games (where he detested his friends' rules), his golfing, and his day jaunts. From St. Augustine, the senatorial entourage went to the Hotel Bon Air in Augusta; Warren was grateful for Florence's encouragement of him staying down South longer. In Augusta, Harding had played thirty-six holes of golf in one day: "The golf is mental rest and good physical training. I am certainly vastly better. The only thing we do wrong is to eat excessively of sweets," he noted. They also enjoyed poker, and altogether it was a good "loaf" for him.[61]

But he wanted her to be better too: "Sorry you are not feeling fit. It is a fright to be out of sorts and more or less invalided all the time.

If you can think of any thing that will help, we will go the limit to have it." He missed her, too. "I think you could have made the journey 'comfy' enough," he insisted. Others too had mentioned their "disappointment" at her absence; the other senators considered her "a good sport." Moreover, "You would enjoy the bridge but you would probably be broke." Harding himself was already out $40.[62] As these sentiments express, Warren was fond of his wife and received much emotional support from her. Their marriage, despite its problems, was built on a deep bond. These sentiments also beg the question of how, in the midst of his crowded days in Florida and Washington, he could have had time to live with Nan; yet this period, early 1919, was said to be the height of their affair! That Harding could have dealt with the stress that squeezing in such a rollicking romance would have caused in his life is a testament to his personal vigor for such activities. As his presidential ambitions then indicate, the senator was not a man who was especially fond of pressure.

The presidential primaries were only a year away, and before he left for his Southern jaunt, Harding had a few words to say about such higher ambitions. After giving some talks in several Ohio cities that winter, he wrote Scobey, "the strain and incessant alertness incident to meeting several hundred people about exhausted my nervous strength. If I had to go through this sort of thing to be a candidate for the big job, I am sure I should want to surrender before I had begun ... winning ... is not worth the work and anxiety involved."[63] Harding knew himself well. It would be he who more often flagged during their huge handshaking marathons later in the White House; Florence, despite her fragile health, persevered.

Their good friend, Mrs. McLean, recalled him saying at this time, "Evalyn, I don't want it. I am satisfied to go right on being senator." It was a comfortable life, out of the direct spotlight, and he figured he could do it for two terms; his "little poker games, his little trips" satisfied him.[64] Similarly, Harding told his fellow senator and friend Albert Fall (R-N.M.): "I am happy in the Senate ... I want to stay there." Florence agreed with him, telling her eager friends, "just let it drop." After all, she liked going to Senate debates herself, and when well, she could often be seen in the gallery. She hectored journalist Charles E. Hard: "I'm on the warpath. ... I want you to stop your activity." Because of Florence's initial resistance, Hard believed that it was Harry Daugherty, not Florence, who later pushed Harding into the presidency.[65] Certainly their old Ohio friend and politico's influence was critical, but Florence, once she was fully in gear, was the vital engine in the campaign train. Political maneuverings in Ohio may have been even more important as a precipitating factor for Harding's entry in the race, however. By November 1919, Harding felt backed into a corner in his home state, where some of his foes were pushing for General Leonard Wood for president; they also made it clear that they were intriguing to nominate a competitor to run for Senate in his place, too, in the next election. He could not let his political base erode. As late as October 11, 1919, he was wistful about going back home: "I could be lots more happy living on a farm out in Ohio and giving a half day's attention each day to the newspaper shop at Marion," he sighed. That changed a month later, as he realized that such choices were being made for him. Harding decided to run.[66] Another pivotal factor in the decision was Florence's health, which was also largely intact after her crisis earlier in the year. Her political savvy and effective organizing abilities would be crucial in the race, he knew. Daugherty took over the campaign "as a matter of necessity," he said modestly, although he was looking for someone else "to take supreme control."[67] But this old friend was not well liked by Harding's other intimates and would remain a controversial campaign leader.[68]

Still, as Jennings noted perceptively later, Harding "is more the mastiff than the bulldog type . . . he detests quarreling and pugnaciousness and the rough and tumble of politics." Daugherty would serve as a useful buffer, and even more a fighter, and Harding knew that. Jennings also was well aware that Harding didn't want to be president—"political conditions forced him" to do it. He thus even more needed a pugilist like Daugherty.[69] As Boone noted later, Daugherty probably was essential to getting Harding chosen as the nominee in 1920, despite lacking the necessary "caliber in the legal profession" to deserve his later appointment as attorney general.[70] Harding correctly saw the Ohio lawyer as "loyal, very alert," and argued further, "he is vastly much the smartest politician in the bunch and the only one with vision and acquaintance to carry on a nation-wide campaign."[71] These "acquaintances" would be significant in raising money.[72]

Despite Daugherty's connections and tenacity, the Hardings continued to be plagued by many second thoughts, as their old friend George Christian Sr. recalled. At one point, "Florence . . . proceeded to express her views in language that could not be misunderstood." Worried, Christian privately urged Harding to tone her down—as if he could! He fretted, "She is a woman of strong character, so influential among her countless friends that I fear that she herself might damage your campaign." But Harding pooh-poohed such concerns, noting blithely: "No woman ever lived who objected to becoming, if possible, First Lady of the land."[73] Still, "Mrs. Harding was greatly worried," Christian Sr. recalled, "unable to overcome her doubts and fears that he would lose both the Senate and the presidency." Ironically, despite Florence's misgivings, in the long run, she and his close friends would all help push Harding to pursue a job he didn't really want.[74]

In early February 1920, he diffidently wrote Jennings, "I need not tell you that I would not wish to have the nomination unless it was the deliberate judgment of party leaders that mine was the best for the party. Probably it isn't. You know I have never taken myself seriously."[75] But ten days later, he was feeling a bit more confident: "the whole situation looks infinitely more promising than I have any reason to expect. I am beginning to feel now as though I am afraid I will be nominated."[76]

It was not going to be easy; the primaries were often keenly disappointing for him. After a particularly bruising battle in Ohio, which he barely won, Harding told his wife quite plainly, in Christian's recounting of it, that "more than anything else in the world he wished to remain in the Senate."[77] Thus, Florence had to work hard to keep him going, "stoutly insist[ing] upon going on to the finish." Her husband's supporters relied on her, as Kathleen Lawler, his presidential campaign assistant, noted, and "she used her influence."[78] Harding wrote Jennings, "She thinks she knows the game better than anybody and will pull it off alone unless some of us fool men ball things up, of course. But she is a good gal and a loyal scout."[79]

Indeed, once committed, Florence almost breathlessly threw herself into the campaign, although her vanity prevented her from finding a picture of herself she deemed suitable until late January.[80] She continued to be vexed by her image on film; one sympathetic observer, noting she was better looking in person, asked her, "what makes you take such ugly pictures, anyway?"[81] Florence rued that photographers just "can't seem to get my mouth," which usually appeared more stern in their images than it did in real life.[82] Her pictures, she thought, were "frightful," but "I know you've got to do it," she sighed to photographers.[83] At least she never allowed one of *him* to substitute for her, and chided Edith Roosevelt for permitting Teddy to do this: "I would like to see . . . President Harding, or any other man takes such liberty with me!"[84] Photographs, newsreels, sound recordings, billboards—all would be a hallmark of this first modern campaign, where Harding and his wife were sold like cornflakes—or Van Camp's pork and beans. The brains behind the marketing operation was Albert D. Lasker, an advertising pioneer, whose firm had the Van Camp's account and who convinced millions of housewives to give up boiling beans and buy the cans instead.[85] Lasker played a key role in building the president and his wife into celebrities themselves. He and Will Hays, the Republican National Committee Chairman, coordinated a highly successful campaign, as theaters played newsreels of the Hardings that effectively got the candidate far from the Front Porch. Sound recordings, too, were in demand for home use and for clubs; one man asked for a speech to play for his soldier's reunion, and Florence sent him the Americanism talk, along with buttons and other items.[86] The expenditure on these marketing tools came close to $1.5 million, out of a total expenditure on the campaign of $3 million.[87]

Perhaps nervous of dreaming too wildly of the possibilities of moving to the Big House—or perhaps because she did want to get her house ready to sell for that very reason—Florence looked into redecorating their home yet again, to the tune of $2,000. That spring, with similar nervousness, she also visited Washington psychic Madame Marcia with three other Senate wives, Mrs. Harry C. Woodyard, Mrs. Miles Poindexter, and Mrs. George Sutherland. They went on a whim after a game of whist, to find out which of them was going to be the next first lady. But of course, to Florence, astrology was no lark, and her husband was actually in the race. From this meeting, she and Marcia would form a relationship—and Florence took on an occult name, "Jupiter." Madame Marcia, whose real name was Marcia Champrey, called her "Child of destiny," and

Florence regularly sent her new clients; as Florence readily admitted, "I believe in astrology and the indication of the planets as to a man's or woman's fate." Earlier, the psychic had predicted that Ellen Bolling Galt, the future second Mrs. Wilson, would marry a president, and Mrs. Galt had promised her a "tent in the White House Grounds" if this transpired. But Madame Marcia said she had never after heard from Mrs. Wilson.[88]

Closer to the convention, Florence returned to Madam Marcia with her husband's horoscope. This time, she covered herself in a veil and took a streetcar to Marcia's. The psychic predicted that Harding would be nominated on Saturday, June 12, just after noon, following a long and contentious fight—this, when many were urging him to drop out and yield to stronger competitors.[89] Marcia predicted his ultimate victory in the fall election too, but added, "tragedy was written upon his brow."[90] Such cryptic warnings did not deter the future first lady. Now, she even more strongly urged her husband to stay the course, for which Marcia took some credit.[91] Florence looked for signs, too—had George Washington surveyed Marion County? Had Lincoln touched the head of Dr. Harding? Not content to rely on the stars, Harding stumped in Kansas, Oklahoma, Colorado, and Nebraska—states that he would later win in the fall election.

Florence was a "close student of astrology all her life," and as Lawler notes, she was hardly singular in her allegiance to this psychic: Marcia's waiting room was filled with many prominent wives, and husbands, too, all "waiting for the privilege of paying $5 each to hear something they desired . . . past or future."[92] Joel Boone, who knew Florence well during her illness and convalescence in the White House, recalled her connection with the mysterious: "when the nurse and I were trying to help her out of bed into a chair, I picked up [her] slippers and placed them on her bed. She quickly assumed a sitting position—when we thought she had no such strength—and scolding me said: 'Do not ever place slippers on a bed! You ought to know that is very bad luck.'"[93]

In her era, there was just as much skepticism by rationalists about astrology and other planetary imponderables as there is now—perhaps more. Professor William F. Ogburn of Columbia University noted in 1925 that superstition was "The greatest enemy to the spread of science," and included horoscopes in that blight.[94] Still, if it was possible to be scientific in one's approach to astrology, Florence was. She studied it precisely as she did "the science of political economy, and of government," wrote Lawler, who was fast becoming an intimate friend and adviser in the Harding entourage, yet was a doubter about the signs of the sky.[95] Florence's approach was strikingly similar to Nancy Reagan's astrologically driven presidential schedule planning sixty years later.

Although eager to see what the future would foretell, Florence wanted the past, or at least some parts of it, well buried. Thus, during the campaign, she did her best to ensure that her previous marriage was not mentioned. Warren respected her views, but this only blew up "a great mystery out of the unfortunate affair," spurring unwanted gossip, in Lawler's view. Mention of the "'DeWolfe' grandchildren" in the press ran into Florence's insistence that it was her "private affair." As she had once written grimly in her diary, "At sometime or another the sins of our youth come back to plague us." Lawler believed that Florence's approach was a "really serious political error, a tactical mistake."[96] But this marriage had happened to her at a time when such things were thought scandalous, at least for women, and despite the changing mores of the 1910s and 1920s, she still wanted the past under wraps. Florence's approach echoes that of Mrs. Lidcote in Edith Wharton's brilliant portrait of an older woman in "Autre Temps" (1907). Florence, like Mrs. Lidcote, was the woman who had "done something which, at the time [she] did it, was condemned by society." As a result, her "case had been passed on and classified," and Florence contributed to this outlook with her silence.[97]

Florence did not want to revisit her past, and thus she missed an opportunity to reach out to other women in similar circumstances. And while journalists had joyfully anticipated the White House becoming more lively with "two kiddies"—her grandchildren—"fine, upstanding young Americans ... romping through," they did not.[98] Thus few knew of her close relationship to these children. Florence well recognized that divorce remained scandalous; in Cecil B. DeMille's *Old Wives for New* (1918), an adaptation of David Graham Phillips's novel, the film's sympathetic treatment of divorce was considered "shocking."[99] Once Harding's Democratic opponent, James Cox, had been nominated, a man with his own divorce (after three children) and a much younger second wife, this effectively removed the potency of the issue from the campaign, yet Florence still kept mum on the topic.

THE NOMINATION

On June 5, the Hardings arrived at Chicago's LaSalle Hotel with the Longworths and several other friends. Harding's Capitol Hill colleagues for the most part liked him, and they would be key players at Chicago. Florence was even more important; she had helped keep him in the race when he would have gladly turned it over to someone else, such as General Wood or Senator Hiram Johnson (R-Calif.), and she would continue to keep his spirits high. By the time of the convention, Wood and Illinois governor Frank O. Lowden topped the list of likely candidates, and in early balloting got about 300 delegates each, while Harding had come to Chicago ranked sixth in a Literary Digest poll. Given the odds still against him, the Hardings focused on his being a viable second choice. That was fine to the senator, who "cheerfully plunged in" to canvassing over the next few days. As Florence urged him on, he began to rise, soon surpassing third-place Johnson.[100]

But Harding also had some influence of his own. The senator had been visibly active at the last two nominating conventions; his opponents had some ethical issues; and he was a "good harmonizer": people liked him. After much smoking and horse trading, and a lot of sweating through a Midwestern heat spell, just as Madame Marcia had predicted, he was nominated at noon on June 12, on the tenth ballot, in Chicago's stifling Coliseum. The nomination is often described as the product of a smoke-filled suite, room 404 of the Blackstone Hotel, where seven senators and a couple of others—including Colonel George Harvey, later ambassador to Britain, and Will Hays—did their dealing. (Florence would have found the room number highly auspicious: Harding would get just that many electoral votes in November!) But this picture of an orchestrated plot is a distortion. Harding earned the nomination in his own right, as a popular senator from an important state—even if it took ten ballots. He was a most popular second choice, and with Wood and Lowden supporters fighting at the top, Harding's nomination became the inevitable compromise.[101] Jennings could only affirm: "H. is liked and admired," effective as "a compromise candidate—or rather, a man upon whom all could unite as safe, sane and sure."[102] After 1912 and 1916, the Republicans badly wanted a man behind whom all could unify. The Republicans did not want a "superman," as they had had with Teddy Roosevelt, Taft, and Hughes; they did not want an exemplary individual who could lose them the White House yet again. They wanted someone like Harding, a man who called for "healing . . . normalcy . . . restoration . . . adjustment . . . equipoise."[103] This was picked up by their admen as well; Lasker and Hays made sure that any "wild-eyed" and "high brow" arguments were kept to a minimum.[104] Calvin Coolidge, the Massachusetts governor who had crushed the 1919 Boston police strike, was named Harding's running mate.

As soon as she heard the results at ten minutes past noon, Florence rushed to find Warren at the LaSalle Hotel. As she left the Coliseum, she was nearly crushed by enthusiastic supporters; "I thought I should be dismembered," she recalled. She too was excited, as Kathleen Lawler recalled, "almost hysterical," and when Harding came down to greet her at the hotel, she collapsed in his arms.[105] She soon busied herself greeting the delegates and other callers who came to their suite to congratulate him, and to hear the Republican Glee Club of Columbus sing out its joy. Hosting the visitors and the Glee Club in the Gold Room, their reception area at the hotel, was Florence's idea, a prelude of the many welcoming handshaking sessions to come in her life as first lady. She was thrilled to see the delegates, including the 140 women (out of 984 total).

Among those also visiting was a group of black delegates from South Carolina. Earlier, African American Texan H. R. Green had attempted to organize a campaign to have black delegations from as many states as possible seated at the state and national conventions. To that, Scobey scowled, "We are not going to stand for any negro nomination."[106] To their credit, both Warren and Florence were much more open-minded. But this was before the "black blood" issue had appeared.

Even as he greeted them all, however, Harding was not sure if he wanted the final victory. As he told Jennings that evening, "the idea of being president . . . [is] an enormous responsibility . . . one must divorce himself from his friends. . . . Jennings, my friends are important to me."[107] But he loyally carried on, likely because of those same friends. He could not now disappoint them—or his wife. This hesitancy would be picked up by more critical observers later, of course. Colonel Edmund Starling, a White House Secret Service operative, believed that Harding "should never have been president.... He did not want to be president. He was happy as editor and publisher of the *Marion Star*."[108]

FRONT PORCH

After a golfing holiday at the end of June with the Frelinghuysens at their New Jersey estate, the Hardings were back in Marion on July 5, where they planned to conduct their quest for the White House from their modest manse, much as another Ohioan, former president William McKinley, had done two dozen years before. Being at the porch allowed the Hardings a certain level of control over the campaign and the news it generated; it also lent the proper level of "folksiness," so much in contrast to the aloof Wilsons.[109]

And the folks came. Eagerly, 3,000 people awaited them there that day under the elms, oaks, and maples. But the campaign only really got going after Harding gave his acceptance speech in his hometown on July 22. Florence "sat on the edge of her seat and her lips quietly formed the words that were pronounced by the senator, for she knew his address by heart," one paper reported. As was often the case, she had assisted him in writing and learning it.[110] As Harding had told Jennings during one of these coaching sessions, "The Duchess is sitting by and listening and censors all that I say."[111] As Lawler noted, "She was his keenest, but at the same time his most sympathetic and constructive critic."[112]

Lawler would become a vital support to both Hardings in the campaign that exciting but stressful summer and fall as the election campaign heated up against the Democratic nominee, Ohio governor James Cox. A native of Lansing, Michigan, and a Catholic—a negative consideration to some outside the campaign—Lawler was a smart and resourceful young woman.[113] Her job was not easy, for she had to deal with both Florence, who, with "her nervous, high-tensioned state, with her desire to see things go ... felt she must do everything herself," as well as her husband, with his own "killing independence," who was at the same time much too available: "always ready; always approachable, always responsive, and always accommodating."[114] Both Warren, and especially Florence, came to rely on Lawler closely.

Warren, of course, still mostly leaned on Florence, who made herself indispensable in often maternal ways. As Lawler added, "she appeared more than a wife for she watched him as a mother would follow with approval the deeds and the triumphs of a son. His work was hers, his ambitions, his joys, his sorrows, were hers."[115] This thorough enmeshment, not surprisingly, affected their relationship. For instance, when he was late to return home to get ready for a dinner, she'd call him, and even break into his line if it was engaged. When he got back, she would have his clothes ready, "with a mother's forebearing smile, and with maternal tenderness." Lawler recalled that her patient husband (qua errant son) would say, "Don't get in a sweat... you are worth waiting for, even if I am not." And "Her happy laughter would ring out."[116] That is, until next time!

For much of the campaign, at least, she didn't have far to go to find him. The Harding porch—complete with McKinley's flagpole—was the epicenter of Republican electioneering in 1920, at least until the fall, when public clamor and campaign pressures forced him to canvass more widely. Yet the initial stay-at-home approach, chiefly orchestrated by Florence, was wildly popular. She knew this homey, inclusive, festival atmosphere would be tremendously effective, especially in comparison to the Wilsons, who still kept people off the White House lawn, by now unattractive under its thick clumps of sheep dung. The preparations for the throngs at the porch, and the crowds themselves, were exhausting, of course. But she loved it, and the excitement seemed to be good for her often rocky health: that summer of 1920, those "gripping weeks," she noted, were "one of the greatest epochs of all my life." Perhaps the greatest. On the cusp of the election, she told her friend Harriet Taylor Upton of the Republican National Committee, "It has been wonderful. Nothing on earth can ever approach, and nothing ever take away this glorious experience, regardless of what the future holds for us.... Such crowds, and such attentions, and such enthusiasm!"[117] Party leaders whipped up the enthusiasm too by spending $200,000 to make photos of the Hardings on their porch.[118] She wrote journalist Mark Sullivan, who also visited Marion that summer, that it was "a wholly beautiful,

{ *Washington Life and the Presidential Campaign* } 53

The Hardings, Nick Longworth, and the Weekses on the Front Porch, 1920. Courtesy of the Marion County Historical Society, Marion, Ohio.

heart-gripping experience ... greeting the splendid men and women who came to us and ... honored us by sitting around my own board."[119] Even the normally crabby Alice Roosevelt and her husband twice visited Marion then, and they enjoyed marching behind the Harding's car in one of the Front Porch parades; "we had great sport, and much fun," she wrote.[120] Meanwhile, poor Cox gave almost 400 speeches in twenty-four states. He was exhausted, hot, and hoarse.[121]

Typically, those Marion days began with visiting delegations assembling in a grove of trees near the house, waiting until 2:30 P.M., the assigned time for the daily parade to the porch. There, Harding would give a speech, shake hands, and eventually send everyone off, except the press, for whom he always felt a special fondness.[122] Of course, this visiting choreography was often violated, and the Hardings were good-natured about it. Their easygoing response was made possible in part by the hard work of Lawler, as well as their dear old friends and neighbors, the Christians, who were intimately involved in assisting the campaign. Young George's house became offices for the effort, taken over by stenographers, assistants, secretaries, and a publicity director, Judson Welliver; the older Christians saw their house used as an entertainment center.[123]

Despite the carnival atmosphere, there were many serious issues in the election, and many complications, including the veterans' bonus bill, the League of Nations, the postwar recession, and the expanding role of women.[124] Indeed, Florence's politically savvy and media-connected women friends often served as close sources during the campaign. She bounced ideas off them, and received theirs as well. Journalists knew she was influential. Ira E. Bennett, editor of the *Washington Post,* informed Mrs. Harding about his suspicions concerning the U.S. role in the Mexican elections, urging her to impress upon Warren, when he was elected, to put a stop to it.[125] He had a couple of other issues to raise with the Hardings as well, but strikingly, he approached Florence first.

Harding, of course, claimed to be for "normalcy" and "America first." His planks included a "businesslike government," a protective tariff and strong merchant marine, and highway construction—Harding was a keen driver. He also wanted immigration "standards" as well as benefits for veterans. Harding's platform, in fact, had a strongly progressive social agenda that included money for housing, aid to farmers, and efforts to promote women's employment and suffrage, to end child labor, and to stop lynching while introducing political rights for African Americans. In fact, his would be the last candidacy—Republican or Democrat—for decades to call for an end to lynching.[126] Sadly, in office, Harding never did much about the terror that still characterized life for many below the Mason-Dixon line. Much to the *Raleigh News and Observer*'s relief, Washington promoted none of the "anti-lynch hysteria that threatened further trouble in the peaceable and prosperous south."[127] Social welfare was also neglected; plans to create an agency to promote education were stillborn, although the administration did establish a Veterans Bureau and supported the short-lived Sheppard-Towner legislation and its clinics for women and children.

Back in "normal" Marion, meanwhile, the Front Porch was a smashing success. The crowds came all summer, close to half a million all told. Gray-headed Union veterans were there, and women's groups, and Indian chiefs (one aptly called Florence "Snow Bird," which means "busy worker").[128] Celebrities, including Al Jolson, Mary Pickford, Lillian Russell, Ethyl Barrymore, and Lillian Gish joined the Harding-Coolidge Theatrical League and campaigned for

Celebrities, including Al Jolson and Blanche Ring, surround the Hardings during the campaign. Courtesy of Ohio Historical Society.

the president. They also came to the Front Porch, sometimes more than once, swelling the ranks of those who hoped for a glance.

On August 24, seventy members of the league arrived by train in Marion and walked to the porch accompanied by bands and gaping autograph seekers. Al Jolson sang "Mammy" and "Avalon." He also made up a special song for Harding, "Mr. Harding, You're the Man for Us," which he sang as well. With the resultant singing and dancing, as well as that generated by other visiting actors like Blanche Ring, even the eminence of Charles Evans Hughes, also there that day, lost some of its grise. Harding was a celebrity, these actors suggested by their presence, showing the way in which the Hardings capitalized on the movie industry and the popular culture it spawned. This kind of marketing, and the use of numerous photo opportunities to sell the candidate, rather than simply relying on getting out the troops, would assist her husband to a landslide victory.[129]

By September, it was hot enough for the Hardings finally to take their show on the road, accompanied by Dr. Sawyer and George Christian Jr., beginning a series of campaign trips to complement the Front Porch. They took their first one, off to the Minnesota Fair in St. Paul, on the seventh. They returned in time for General Colored Peoples Day at the porch. The visitors had camped out and "covered the roofs of the houses and other buildings, sang from the treetops, and filled every available inch," Lawler reported. Wilson had been no friend of African Americans; Harding, by contrast, offered them two warm speeches that day, and in return got to hear many bands and choruses perform, which, Lawler affirmed, "was a never-to-be-forgotten feature . . . it was melodious and beautiful."[130] One song the visitors brought, "Harding Will Shine Tonight," was sung regularly during the campaign thereafter.

Harding's campaign reached out not only to African Americans, but to women. In October a throng of suffragists crowded around the porch, full of smiles at Harding's now-committed support for their cause. Florence greatly appreciated these calls from women.[131] She did not, however, appreciate the visit of one woman: Carrie Phillips. This was the visit—perhaps legendary—where various projectiles were hurled into the street. In one version, that of history professor Arthur Hirsch of Ohio Wesleyan University, who claimed to have been there as an eyewitness, Mrs. Phillips came strolling up to the porch. After she had exchanged a few words with Warren, "Suddenly Mrs. Harding appeared. A feather duster came sailing out at Mrs. Phillips, then a wastebasket. . . . Next came a piano stool. Not until then was there a retreat."[132] Cinematic as this is, it is hard to credit. First of all, there were so many surrounding the porch each day, that the wastebasket and stool—even a feather duster, if thrown with sufficient force—could have been dangerous to bystanders. Florence would have been fond of her piano stool, in any case; it's hard to imagine her willfully wrecking it.

Which is not to say that the porch didn't adversely affect the health of some of its visitors. First Voters Day turned out to be an unseasonably hot October day, though not hot enough to stop the Bicyclists Association from coming along for the ride with the nascent balloters, as well as the Pittsburgh Women's Republican Marching Club. While Harding went off to write his speech for the young voters, Florence took care of the guests, who swelled by the half hour. The sun baked them all, while Florence was "pulled and mauled on every side."[133] She kept at it until 1 P.M., despite the pleas of Lawler and Christian that she quit, even as people were dropping like overripe fruit; as Lawler noted, they sprawled out "on couches, chairs, steps, tables, the floor . . . the house bore a striking resemblance for a short time to an emergency hospital at the front." Florence, however, held up well; her assistant attested, "She could endure more physical pain and hardship and . . . more punishment than any human being I ever met."[134]

Once again, the heat drove them out of Marion, as did the calendar. With just weeks remaining until Election Day, they could no longer stay home. Florence would travel 20,000 miles with Warren, much of it in the less than ninety days before the election. In addition to the Minnesota trip, they went to Baltimore, and to Midwestern cities including Des Moines, Chicago, Omaha, Kansas City, Oklahoma City, and St. Louis. There was a southern trip including Chattanooga, a jaunt to Buffalo and Rochester, and then trips back to Dayton, Cleveland, and Akron, right into the heart of Cox territory. The traveling was not always safe. As Kathleen reported, during one of their stops, in West Virginia, a "mysterious [and] very suspicious parting of the rails" occurred just after their Pullman passed the spot. Lawler marveled that Florence, like her husband, was "entirely unconscious of any peril," yet perhaps the campaign sobered them. Florence would get herself Secret Service coverage in the White House. In another display of their trustingness, the Hardings never thought to examine the cornucopia of different foods sent their way. Food and drugs including "melons from Texas, berries from Maine . . . hams from Virginia, maple sugar and syrup from Vermont, cakes from Missouri . . . pie from the Conn pie belt . . . Smith Brothers cough drops . . . French perfumes . . . Dr. Ayers Ague cure and horse liniment" all arrived, often in large quantities, and Florence was prepared to have her cook prepare some of the more "tempting" items. Lawler put her foot down and prevailed: the items would be "buried or burned" after being suitably acknowledged."[135]

Rather than worry about food, Florence was fully focused on the campaign, and her organizing skills were honed to a high degree. As Lawler writes, "her rapier mind was flitting like a scintillating flame." She would, moreover, have no high-hatting by the others working with her; she stopped people in the habit of getting up whenever she walked into a room. It was inefficient, she pointed out.[136] There were some things she could not control, though, despite her thorough organization, as well as that of Republican National Committee chairman and überorganizer Will Hays. Two scandals hung over the Hardings, threatening the campaign and further spurring their campaign trips: first, Carrie, who seems to have successfully blackmailed the presidential candidate by the end of the summer, and second, the issue of Harding's racial makeup, a rumor that flared up several times during the campaign.[137]

Carrie was pressing Harding once again to quit politics, get divorced, and come back to Marion—or pay up. He wrote her in desperation: "To avoid disgrace in the public eye, to escape ruin in the eyes of those who have trusted me in public life . . . I will if you demand it as THE PRICE, return to Marion to reside . . . retire completely to obscurity." But there was no promise of marriage. On the other hand, he offered, "If you think I can be more helpful by having a public position and influence . . . to do some things worth while for myself and you and yours, I will pay you $5,000 per year, in March each year, so long as I am in that public service." Through the beneficence of the Republican party, something very much like this happened: one of its representatives, perhaps Albert Lasker, gave her $25,000 ($20,000 plus a monthly payment while Harding was in office) and boat fare to leave the country with her husband, Jim, for a nice long trip to the Orient during the campaign.[138]

Florence stood by her husband through this humiliating episode; it could not have been easy. Such fortitude "gives her memory an almost noble quality, as compared to the calumnies it suffered in the years after her death," one historian has observed.[139] With Carrie disposed of, though, there was still the "black blood" issue. Harding's background in Blooming Grove, an abolitionist stronghold, as well as his relative open-mindedness on race relations, had caused his enemies to identify him as racially African. Harding's campaign had also worked to ensure greater black participation, including among women, an effort Mary Church Terrell helped to orchestrate.[140] William Allen White described Harding's complexion once as "dark waxen," although he makes no mention of Harding's racial makeup.[141] It was a history professor who made the most frequent and noisy claims about Harding's African background: the Amherst and Harvard Law–educated Wooster College teacher William Estabrook Chancellor, who put together a compilation of "evidence," along with the recollections of "certain mysterious home folk," in his brief.[142]

Nasty slurs soon appeared: "Keep the White House white! Vote for a real Nigger!"[143] Harding had first wanted Chancellor to come to Marion and "confront him personally," but then he thought better of it. He refused to dignify the charges with any response, even though consensus in the party was for outright denial.[144] Some of his supporters defiantly declared he came from New England "blue-eyed stock."[145] Harding's father put together a family history for public consumption that turned up no connection to an African American ancestor—if much underground railroading. But Harding did not endorse his campaign's joining this pedigree palaver, and he privately noted that the charges might even be true. Who knew? It was impossible to deny or disprove it "completely."[146]

To friends who worried about the implications for the campaign as Chancellor grew ever shriller shortly before the election, Florence was stalwart. She told Evalyn and Ned that she was indeed "a conservative woman" who "did not want to make claims that might be regarded by anyone as extravagant" regarding their prospects. Nevertheless, she insisted, "we are wholly secure. I believe that nothing can change that." As if to underline her assurance of the other side's panic, she slammed the rumors as "last ditch, desperate propaganda. We are going to win." Similarly, Florence told her friends the News, "These wild tales have been circulated before, but never so bad as in this campaign, probably because they have never been quite so desperate. . . . We are going to win—and BIG!"[147]

Still, the Hardings were rattled. Kathleen Lawler and Mrs. Harding made sure that a black man, William H. Proctor, a "scullion" in the House of Representatives who had been invited to a party at the home of Senator Joseph France's, was disinvited in order for the Hardings to attend the same party.[148] The rumors lived on. In 1922, Kentucky Democrat Robert Young Thomas wrote to one of his daughters that he would not let her accept an invitation to the White House, "because, as I well know, Harding is one-eighth 'nigger,' and I would not want you to attend such a place."[149] Nearly five decades later, during the height of the civil rights movement, historian Francis Russell could not resist reviving the story by calling his book *The Shadow of Blooming Grove*. In 1988, a Connecticut African American group, the WGH Memorial Foundation, celebrated the fact of Harding's reputed black ancestry.[150] Twenty years later, a first-term black senator from the Midwest was elected president—and in a parallel to Harding's experience, faced rumors about his ethnic and religious background.

ELECTION

Florence was too nervous to sleep much the night before the election; as Lawler recalled, she kept getting up, checking on things, remembering a telegram that had to go out at 3 A.M., for instance, and at 4:30 alerting someone else who needed to be woken up. The morning of November 2 dawned "cheerless": rainy and windy, with trees and branches leaning horizontally—not an auspicious day for a good turnout. Florence lay in bed as the day began, feeling a nasty cold coming on, but it is unlikely she could sleep much even then, as flowers for Harding's fifty-fifth birthday (which coincided with Election Day—an auspicious omen!) started to arrive at 8 A.M., and continued to fill the house, as did the smell of 139 cakes being unloaded, all needing interment, of course. But it could only have been a thrill for her to go to the polls and cast her first vote—for her husband!—at 9:45 that morning.[151]

Soon, friends came bearing more and more gifts, which were then surreptitiously—and sometimes unblushingly—lifted by the visiting public who, as the overwhelming victory became apparent, began to fill the house, even stealing Kathleen's prize 1912 elephant collection. Florence remained cautious despite the trampling disciples: "let us be sure before we jubilate too much," the "Doubting Duchess" declared. Once the magnitude of the victory became crystal clear, she could still only say, "I still feel that I am in a dream."[152] Her husband would win a smashing victory, 16,152,000 souls choosing him against the 9,147,353 who picked Cox, with 404 electoral votes on his roster (127 for Cox). He won thirty-seven states; in Ohio, where he had once struggled, the president-elect got a 350,000 majority!

Many apparently agreed with George Harding Sr. that Harding "looks the senator and well he would look the president." The power of the Ohioan's looks and stature has been pointed out by writers such as Malcolm Gladwell, who cites his victory as the first example of a "Harding error," a term Gladwell uses to designate unthinking decisions based on attractiveness, or as he calls it, "the dark side of

*Florence voting for first time, November 2, 1920.
Courtesy of the Marion County Historical Society, Marion, Ohio.*

rapid cognition."[153] As so many others have been, Gladwell is too dismissive of Harding. He was both personally popular and blessed with a lackluster opponent, a man saddled with the unpopular associations of Woodrow Wilson, especially Wilson's controversial legacy of internationalism and wartime sacrifices. So, sitting with the boys from Western Union, charting the returns on a map on his table, Harding was ready, around midnight, for a "good ol' homey celebration," Sawyer recalled.[154]

The Secret Service came at midnight, surprising the Hardings, and Florence told them they could go home in the morning. Only they couldn't, and eventually she made sure they had a house to stay in for the long interregnum—until March 4. A little later in that evening, the Hardings' beloved Columbus Glee Club came to sing for them, and Florence was literally carried over the crowd to hear them at headquarters next door. After their performance, she called out to her husband to come and speak to the throngs in front of the porch. The Hardings shook hands with perhaps 5,000 people before the crowd dispersed at 4 A.M.[155] Florence told the movie men there they would not be welcome at the White House, but she soon forgot that pledge.

It was a thrilling victory, and Florence's role was widely recognized. As the *New York Times* noted the following week, "even more than her husband, Mrs. Harding is a leader. She likes to sway the crowds." The paper predicted, "Responsibility for the White House, politically as well as domestically, will rest on four shoulders during the next four years."[156] Indeed, it did, except tragedy intervened after less than two and a half.

With four months to go before Wilson left office, the Hardings were going to celebrate in full style. It being late fall, they were headed south, to Texas, Panama, Jamaica, and Florida. In Pt. Isabel, Texas, Scobey, the McLeans, and Albert Fall joined them at the home of R. R. Creager, where Harding canvassed with his friends on his Cabinet. Although he made some regrettable choices (Albert Fall as secretary of the interior, for instance, and Edwin Denby as secretary of the navy), he also picked some of the best and brightest in his generation, including Herbert Hoover, for commerce, and Charles Evans Hughes, for state. As he wrote Jennings of this difficult process, "I find I am called upon to be rather impersonable about it and put aside some of my very intimate views of the man and give some consideration to the public estimate of available timber," no easy task for a politician who so valued his friends.[157] Florence undoubtedly served as a consultant here. She certainly assisted with the ill-fated choice of Charles Forbes for the Veterans Bureau.

After Texas, the Scobeys and the McLeans went on with them via New Orleans to Panama. Florence gushingly likened herself to "Cinderella" on this trip—and commented on having her "prince Charming with me."[158] Instead of pumpkins, they were charioted on United Fruit freighters, the *Parismina, Atenas,* and *Pastores.*[159] Florence also had the opportunity to ride in a small plane at the Panama Naval Air Station. It was her first flight, and she found it "perfection."[160] On December 4, a month after the election, the Hardings returned to Norwalk, Virginia, and thence to Washington, to stay with the McLeans.

Truly Florence was happy in this period—excited, busy, gratified, challenged, and amazed. Back in the capital, she certainly was not to have the "quiet month" that her Senate friend, Mrs. Hale, had prescribed for her.[161] Instead, she would first experience "two memorable, heart-gripping history making days" in Washington. First, she

*Florence prepares to take her first plane ride in Panama.
Courtesy of the Marion County Historical Society, Marion, Ohio.*

saw her husband give a speech to the Senate at its opening session, the first sitting senator and president-elect to do so. She raved to Evalyn, "Mr. Harding was splendid. His own instincts are right, because they are good!"[162] In anticipation of the transition, Mrs. Wilson invited Florence to tea on December 6. With Lawler, they had tea in the Blue Room, visited the state dining room, and had an extensive chat about White House "domestic machinery."[163]

The next day, Florence also had lunch with some of the Senate ladies in her old group. It was a most happy reunion. She was reassured that all was made whole again after the election, despite the demise of the presidential hopes of others, including some senators. She sighed, "the manifestations of genuine friendship on all sides . . . brought to me a sense of security, and a comfort that nothing else has approached" after the divisive campaign; it brought "tears . . . and [a] lump in my throat." She looked forward to continuing her association with the Senate ladies "in the same old sweet way." And she did.[164] Later that day, she and Lawler got on a train for Marion, but a wreck delayed their arrival until the afternoon of the following day, December 8.

Florence also reached out to Grace Coolidge, the vice president–elect's wife, at this time, looking forward to being "shoulder to shoulder with our husbands in the tremendous undertakings which lie just ahead."[165] The Coolidges would come to Marion in December and be warmly welcomed by Florence and her husband. They would soon take the de facto vice presidential quarters at the Willard, at $8 per day, in the rooms occupied by Wilson's vice president, Thomas R. Marshall, and his wife, Lois. Knowing almost no one, the governor's wife from Massachusetts was happy that the Democratic vice lady introduced her to the senate wives as one of her last official acts. Like Florence, Mrs. Coolidge soon found her life one mad whirl of social engagements, leaving no time to "talk and darn socks."[166]

Once back in Marion, Florence collapsed from exhaustion, and Sawyer ordered her to bed. He was one of the few who could do so. Lawler remembered a morning some weeks later when they were packing up the Marion house before the move to Washington, when Florence was particularly worn out amid the intense timetable they had to keep, and Sawyer put a hand on her arm, gently said, "a little less strenuous this morning, if you can," and left. Florence turned to

Florence and Evalyn McLean at the Senate Ladies Luncheon. Courtesy of the Library of Congress.

Lawler and sighed, "I must calm down. I owe my life many, many times to Dr. Sawyer. I could not live and keep house without the Doctor and Mandy," his wife.[167] Indeed, her reliance on Charles Sawyer was deep, and they would see even more of him in the White House than they had in the Senate. He was given an important medical post in the new administration, as well as a new title, and moved to Washington—although he continued to make regular trips back to his sanitarium in Marion.

Florence did not just lie docilely in bed, though, especially not after someone brought her the Cleveland *Plain Dealer* and she read a headline that stated, in so many words: "Harry Daugherty Made President Harding." Waving the paper at Kathleen, Florence struggled to get out of bed in her outrage. She was keen to dictate a furious letter to the author. "She was at fever heat," Kathleen recalled. "Her eyes flashed fire as she read what she had dictated." She barked too at Harry Daugherty, who did not appear to have encouraged the piece, and later that day, having had a chance to calm down, explained, "People may say what they please about me . . . but when anything derogatory of Warren Harding is said, I see red . . . it makes me wild." Kathleen, fortunately, had not sent out the note, and Florence, to her credit, was greatly relieved. "What we need here more than anything else is brains," she said.[168]

Despite such lapses in judgment, it was Mrs. Harding herself who deserved overwhelming credit for the victory, this "dynamo" within "a cloak of merriment," as one observer noted, who never sat still. Her husband agreed: "whatever of honor has come to me this day I owed to Florence." Of course, she demurred immediately, insisting the stars were responsible: "Destiny has marked you for the man and so you are chosen."[169]

With destiny in mind, Ned McLean was planning a big do for the inauguration. Florence, too, believed it was what Americans would want, especially "after the terrible war." But her husband felt differently. He wanted to get to work, and he believed the people, suffering as they were in the postwar depression, would be angry to see an ostentatious display.[170] He was also annoyed about the way that it has been pushed forward by McLean, and others, like Daugherty aide Jess Smith, who was gleefully predicting it would be the "biggest in . . . history." Jess, rough-edged and pushy, was rather an unfortunate addition to their circle, but he quite insinuated himself into their lives before he took his own in 1923.[171]

With the large inaugural in the offing, Grace Coolidge wrote Florence in January to see what kind of gown she would wear for the inauguration—"Court train?" But trains were soon derailed; the inauguration was instead scaled down to fit the times and Harding's wishes. Florence wrote to Grace in a state of some confusion: "Everything in the way of ceremonies and functions having been declared off, I shall have nothing in the way of an inaugural gown." She would soon go to New York "to work out the dress problem definitely." Meanwhile, she welcomed the change in plans, or at least rationalized it: "it does simplify for us, doesn't it?"[172]

Florence needed a little simplification in her increasingly complex life. Shuttling between Washington and Marion, she was in the throes of readying the Washington house for sale (which paid back those renovations with a $30,000 profit) and again renting out the Marion house, spending $600 there to fix the bathrooms. She was desperately ready for their next trip, to Florida, and told Evaland Scobey, "th[e] vacation will be merited with a vengeance!"[173]

Florence now almost always used a secretary to type her letters, even personal ones. In December, she still felt she had to apologize for this: "You will not mind that I send you a typed letter; you . . .

know what a help it is to me to dictate my letters," she wrote Evaland.[174] But the continued pressures made it a necessity, which upset her friend Catherine New, who thought such dictated personal notes a "monstrous breach of etiquette." By January, Florence was done with apologizing: "You are crazy! I have no time to write . . . pen letters." As a compromise, her friend asked that she at least handwrite the envelopes.[175] Florence shrugged to Mrs. Hale: "You see I am quite confirmed in my role of 'dictator'. . . , there is no other way for me."[176]

Indeed, in giving up one life and taking on a much bigger one, she had had to learn to multitask at a new level, as she wrote her niece Louise in January: "I am about the busiest mortal today on this globe." She listed her skills: "my dear, I can dictate now while doing a dozen other things," including offering herself to "my face artist, hair lady, [and] manicure performer," even as she was "interviewing the cook, holding telephone political conferences," and preparing to go out. Her face artist could transform her, Florence confirmed, forwarding a picture to her niece: "you will not recognize [it]. . . . neither do I, but it is a fine example of what can be done in certain directions."[177] According to Clinton Wallace Gilbert, becoming first lady was a powerful beauty treatment in itself. Florence, who had been "up til some fourth of March an elderly county woman grown dull in the monotony of village life or worn with the task of pushing an ambitious husband forward to power [and looked] her most natural . . . in the frankness of early morning unpreparedness," now appears "to the awed eyes of Washington Women, quite 'beautiful.'"[178]

Perhaps he was a disappointed office seeker. As future first lady, Florence was besieged, just as her husband was, by requests; thus, trading on her connections as a fellow Senate wife, Mrs. Henry Cabot Lodge wrote Florence with a recommendation for social secretary.[179] But Mrs. Harding would soon find her own secretary: the smart, sensitive, and indispensable Laura Harlan. But she had other needs, too, and a black dressmaker, Laura Havis of Macon, solicited Florence directly; she wanted to work in the White House even "if you already have a white dressmaker," since as Havis said, she could "see after your laundry." She provided her weight and skin tone. Another woman, Mrs. R. Reynolds of Wayne, Michigan, wrote Florence asking for clothes for *her* children.[180]

Florence was rarely left alone even back in Marion. One day, with her hair in a towel as she was cleaning and packing up at Mt. Vernon, some men stopped by hoping to stand on the famous porch, and thought she was the cook! She said, tartly, "I *can* cook and have cooked many meals for my husband, and am proud of it, and just let me say to you that he likes my cooking."[181] Florence's big treat in January would be a New York trip for shopping and shows with Mrs. McLean and Mrs. New. They traveled stylishly in Evalyn's private car. As Florence got ready for the sartorial junket, Lawler noted, "she looked beautiful, regal and handsome," adding that Florence would be a much anticipated "ornament" for the White House. But she would be far more than that.[182]

Florence had a marvelous time with her two intimates in the glamour of New York's boutiques, many of whom sent representatives to her apartment at the Ritz Carlton. She "dismissed" the more outrageously expensive items.[183] A. P. Moore, Pittsburgh newspaper publisher and husband of actress Lillian Russell, coordinated the army of reporters and movie men who crowded her suite to interview her on this occasion. As usual, she insisted that she couldn't give interviews and restricted herself to pleasantries. She refused to divulge her inaugural garb, but assured them she was buying "100 percent 'American.'" She would not wear "imported models."(Mrs. Wilson had bought French clothes when in Paris in 1919.)[184] She was also not buying anything too flashy, either—her gowns were "sleeved," with "conservative décolleté," and skirts to the ankle.[185] Despite her posh tastes, she did not burn her bridges with her old pals in humbler circumstances. She had spent many Senate recesses in Ohio, and she looked forward to having friends like Mary Broadfield Meek and the rest of the Columbus Bridge Club to the White House. As she noted in her diary, for a woman especially, being friendless was about as bad as it got, and Florence intended to keep hers.

Returning to Washington from New York, she had a relapse of her old illness, "inevitable," Lawler thought, given the pace she had been keeping since the election.[186] But she recovered and was off to St. Augustine on February 10, for a real rest, joining Warren, who was already there. Some were offended that the president-elect and his wife were in Florida while so many Americans still suffered economic difficulties, so the sensitive Hardings' solution was not to have any pictures taken!¹⁸⁷ After their rest, they returned to Marion one last time, launching their new lives from its train station on March 2 by climbing aboard the "Inaugural Special." Standing side by side on the rear platform, they greeted crowds at every station going east. Once they had arrived at Union Station, they were whisked out a special exit and off to the New Willard, to await the inauguration, their new life, and more—so very many thousands more—waves and handclasps.

CHAPTER 3

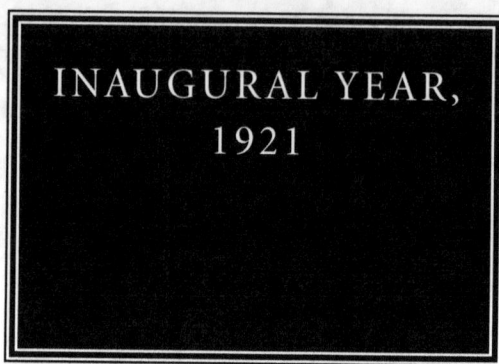

INAUGURAL YEAR, 1921

INAUGURATION

The Hardings and their party, including the Sawyers, Dr. Harding, his brother, George Tryon, and his sister, Abby, arrived in the city quietly, slipping through a private gate at the station and thus disappointing the thousands awaiting them on the tracks. At their hotel, the New Willard, they again escaped the crowds and were quickly hidden away by ushers. It would be one of their last opportunities for peace and solitude in the days ahead. Five gleaming new cars would later arrive to take them to the White House.[1]

On a glorious March 4 morning, the Hardings drove up in their shiny cars to the executive mansion, and after collecting the Wilsons, took a short drive to the Capitol, witnessed by 100,000 people. The ailing president joined Harding in his car; the two men's wives followed in a separate vehicle. There was no parade, just a small band and military escort for the presidents. In acknowledgment of the continuing economic straits after the war, as well as the illness of the outgoing president, original plans for an elaborate inauguration had been scaled down, then eliminated. Still, there was certainly celebration. As one reporter noted, "it was a bright and fair world" that day, under a crisp "Harding blue" sky.[2] In a sign of the modern age, Harding gave his inaugural address echoed by amplifiers for the first time. He had changed his speech in line with Florence's preferences;

as always, she was his trusted editor. She too was in "Harding blue"—the color of the embroidery on her gray turn-back collar, which, along with her pearl necklace and her ever-present "black velvet band with jeweled ornament," bedecked her neck. Her gown was "blue charmeuse with steel bead trimmings," and she wore elbow-length white gloves, a black lace hat with trimmings, and a wrap with chinchilla fur.[3] Her New York shopping trip had been a productive one. She made a fitting companion for her husband, described as "probably the most attractive man in the long list of presidential residents at the White House."[4]

Frustrated at seeing the Spartan official ceremonies, all the same, Ned and Evalyn McLean decided to do up the inaugural right, with a ball at their place that evening. There were three tables of a hundred each, with gold service; they served champagne (no doubt purchased before Prohibition), and an orchestra offered dancing. The Coolidges—who were the guests of honor—attended, as did the Cabinet, Supreme Court justices, and the diplomatic corps. This was only one of two "brilliant" balls the Hardings skipped that night, including the benefit Child Welfare ball at the Willard, which was open to the public. To avoid offending anyone by accepting an invitation, they stayed home and played bridge—and poker.[5]

The Hardings were no doubt most happy with that choice, as they were very comfortable enjoying favorite pastimes with their old friends, whom they really could be "just folks" with, regardless of their "elevation" in station.[6] Mark Sullivan criticized Florence for this, suggesting, "It is rather pathetic the way she clings to her former friends, the effort she seems to make not to let her position as mistress of the White House separate her from the rest of the world." There she was, consorting with the likes of Mrs. Miles Poindexter at the Senate Woman's Luncheon Club, "a woman of her own sort, a friendly companionable body." But Florence cherished her old friends, and moreover, she was keen to skip formalities and made it a practice whenever possible to reduce punctilious protocol.[7] Her approach also brought the contempt of their Secret Service agent, Starling, a veteran of the more buttoned-down Wilson White House, who compared them to a couple of local yokels: "Joe was an amiable fellow who hates to get dressed up and whose greatest joy is the Saturday night poker game at the country club.... Susie likes to

Outgoing and incoming first ladies share a seat, March 4, 1920. Courtesy of the Library of Congress.

play bridge . . . spends a lot of money on her clothes but always manages to look a little dowdy around the edges," he smirked.[8]

Actually, Americans welcomed the lack of pretensions of the first couple; as the *New York Herald* noted, "Their humanness is the Hardings' most appealing quality."[9] Of course, it was hard for Florence not to seem approachable when compared with the secretive second Mrs. Wilson, who had earned sharp disapproval for her imperious assumption of virtual executive power during her husband's incapacity, and who had essentially locked down the People's House. Sullivan and Starling both underestimated the Hardings. Certainly, they brought several of the Marion flock to Washington, including nonveteran Dr. Charles Sawyer, who infuriated some by acquiring the title of brigadier general of the Army's Medical Reserve Corps and became a paid U.S. official—coordinator of hospitals—while he continued as the Hardings' personal physician. Their old friend and neighbor, George Christian Jr., was named Harding's secretary, and turned out to be a very good one. More problematic was Ora "Reddy" Baldinger, former *Star* newsboy, who became Florence's all-around factotum and took his elevation in station as a justification for pushing others around. Another young male assistant, Harry Barker, her Secret Service detail, also had "dictatorial" tendencies, according to Boone, "taking his job too seriously." But Florence apparently liked to have eager young men working for her, as she had at the *Star*.[10] Despite the evidence of their provincialism, the Hardings also enhanced the country's welfare with an impressive team of "best men" who did not come from Marion. Along with Hughes at State and Hoover at Commerce, there was Henry Wallace at Agriculture and Andrew W. Mellon at Treasury. More ill-fated appointments, along with Fall and Denby, included Harry Daugherty, who became head of the Justice Department, and Charles Forbes, at the Veterans Bureau.

Although she was no appointee, Florence herself was of immense importance to the president. Whether from her longtime focus on her husband's needs, or with her clear understanding of what exemplary service in the position demanded—especially in organization and public relations skills—she would be an influential member of the administration, and as such, a transitional first lady.[11] As this and the next three chapters will show, she took the first lady post in different directions than her modern predecessors, including the two Mrs. Wilsons, Nellie Taft, and Edith Roosevelt.

Edith Roosevelt, for instance, while the first to hire a social secretary, Isabella "Belle" Hagner, was a very private person who liked to keep herself and her family out of the limelight. She did hold musicales in the White House, emulated by later first ladies, but she did not like to see herself covered extensively in the newspapers, as Florence did. She was furious when the press picked up on her thrifty recycling of clothes, necessitated by her husband's losses in Western herds and on expensive safari trips, as well as his own ample White House entertaining.[12] As her sister-in-law, Corrine Roosevelt Robinson, noted, in contrast to Mrs. Harding, "very few people ever heard about her. She always kept in the background and allowed 'Teddy' to do the talking."[13] Nellie Taft took on a more visible role as planter of cherry trees, creating the annual glories associated with Washington's springs to this day and indelibly linking first ladies with environmental beautification. Unlike her predecessor, she was willing to speak to the press, and she gave an interview to *Ladies' Home Journal* that got her in trouble because she noted that she would have a spiked punch bowl on offer at White House dinners![14] Sadly, a stroke in just her third month in the White House silenced her for a year, and the public was completely left in the dark about her condition. Her daughter, Helen, became acting mistress of the White House. By contrast, Florence's illness of 1922 was widely reported, as she had wanted.

The Wilson women, Florence's immediate predecessors, were more visible. Ellen Axson Wilson, for example, was the first to campaign with her husband, in 1912. She continued the horticultural interests of her predecessor and planted the Rose Garden. Reluctantly, she gave interviews to female reporters, at publications including the *Ladies' Home Journal*, the *Independent*, and *Good Housekeeping*, which required an expanded workload for her secretarial staff when piles of letters came in.[15] She also was a keen adherent of assisting Washington's poorest and most benighted. Unlike her husband, she wanted to help African Americans, and she pushed for cleaning out the Washington slums in which many of them lived. Her work on the Alley Bill, an effort she was happy to see publicized, finally saw fruition when she died. She also pressed for washrooms for female postal employees, who had none. A Progressive who had encouraged her husband in more socially conscious directions, her work was sadly cut short after just eighteen months in her post, when she died of kidney disease in August 1914.[16]

Unlike Ellen, or Florence later, Edith Bolling Galt, whom Wilson married in December 1915 after a quick courtship, had no causes to speak of, and was in some ways traditional in her lack of activism. But she still had much to do, especially when her husband became incapacitated. As his closest confidant, with whom he shared secrets of the highest wartime importance, she soon drove out other intimates like Colonel Edward M. House as well as Wilson's close woman friend, Mrs. Mary Ellen Hulbert Peck, whom Ellen had tolerated. Edith was also secretive, especially after the president suffered two debilitating strokes in September and October 1919. The White House became a fortress, and its grazing sheep served to keep away visitors. Suffrage activists demonstrating in front of the White House, too, were shooed away—or arrested, in the case of Alice Paul, Lucy Branham, and others, and sent to the Occoquan Workhouse in Virginia. Wilson favored suffrage on a state-by-state basis (his wife voted in New Jersey), but he did not support a national amendment, and neither did Edith—indeed, the protesters seemed to have made her even more intransigent.[17]

The lockdown underlined the growing reclusiveness of the Wilsons and allowed Edith Wilson to take the first ladyship in directions it has never gone, before or since. She essentially became an unelected president in the time of her husband's illness. In her powerful position, many historians believe, she convinced Wilson to refuse any compromise on the League of Nations. Few knew at the time how ill he was; his doctor, Cary T. Grayson, told the press the president merely suffered from "nervous exhaustion," and as more information leaked out, Grayson blatantly falsified the situation. Of course, even the president himself may have never accepted how ill he was. Meanwhile, the nation suffered as appointments remained unfilled, decisions were left unmade, or worse, made by Edith, and advisors were shunned. "No one should have played such a role of surrogate president," John Milton Cooper Jr. aptly observes.[18] Edith Wilson crossed a line, and as Kristie Miller writes, "in some ways [she] came to define the limits of the role of first lady."[19] Given such a predecessor, one might have expected Florence to be cautious and diffident in her position, but fortunately, she recognized the anomaly of Edith's role and was secure in her own abilities to balance her activism with the prerogatives of her husband in the institution of the presidency, which she never attempted to undermine.

Florence was smart, skillful, assertive, and discreet in her role. As she said on coming into the White House as first lady, "I have not come here to play." But she did not take herself, a mere newspaperwoman, as she always put it, too seriously. "I hope the world will not expect too much from me. . . . I am just an ordinary mortal."[20] But these self-deprecating words mask her impressive record in the White House. Florence was an activist—for veterans, animals, and the oppressed of all kinds, especially women and children; she was also someone who welcomed the celebrity culture of her age and made active efforts to cultivate it, inviting Hollywood personalities like the Gish sisters and D. W. Griffith to the White House—and Einstein, too. Unlike her immediate predecessors, she wanted to make the White House a "destination" for the public, offering much greater access to herself and her husband than the Roosevelts, Tafts, or Wilsons had done. She and Warren connected with the American people, and they welcomed tourists' visits on the grounds and in the house. They complemented each other; while he may have been the more lovable of the two, she was the more tireless in this effort.

Her first act set the tone for her enhanced position as a transitional first lady and was greeted with jubilation. She would open the White House and its grounds after the long months of President Wilson's confinement and remove the sheep that had been grazing on its lawn—a holdover from the war's economies, but also a symbol of the peoples' exclusion from the White House.[21] Florence herself remembered walking by the mansion and its barnyard during the Wilson years, facing a policeman with an uncomforting rod and staff shooing away the public, urging onlookers to move on. One cold, wet day after being so harassed, Florence slipped and fell into the mud.[22]

After Harding's nomination, she had vowed to open the grounds if he was elected.[23] This was one of her most important initiatives, and it brought a million people to the White House during President Harding's tenure. White House gardeners planted masses of crocuses in the lawn, to replace the bulbs the sheep had shredded. Florence also put out bird boxes; she not only wanted to protect birds, but also to nurture squirrels![24] The grounds were filled with throngs of walkers; cars also drove by, eager to press close after four long years of being kept away from "the big front door."[25] The curmudgeonly Professor William Chancellor snapped in response, "the common people do not like a man who tries to please them . . . opening the White House front lawn to the run of everyone, [and] professing to wish to keep open house . . . do not 'get' him anywhere."[26]

But of course the American people loved it. Citizen James Williams had written the *Washington Post* shortly after the election in happy anticipation: "speed the fourth of March! Let the people once more come into their own! . . . We need a home-loving, neighborly mistress of the White House and such we are sure Mrs. H will prove to be." Another man wrote, "Hats off to Mrs. H! . . . Out with them [the sheep]. . . . Let us have the gates thrown open, and the men and woman who make up the great body of the nation given a show."[27] *Show* was the right word—the Hardings were indeed celebrities with their new policy of openness. As journalist Evelyn Hunt noted two weeks into the administration, "The grounds are constantly filled with people hoping to catch a glimpse of the Chief Executive and the First Lady" while their "popularity . . . is growing by leaps and bounds."[28] Accordingly, Florence instituted marine band concerts on the south portico on Saturday afternoons. This access was fitting for a woman who believed, as Florence did, that "The more I live, the more faith I have in the common people and the greater my affection for them."[29]

In her new role, Florence would have many chances to develop her affection for the masses. That very first day in the White House, 300 Ohio visitors showed up for a reception, and the receiving only continued. In one two-hour span that first month, they shook 3,200 hands in succession.[30] To keep things manageable, when they were at home, the Hardings set aside the period after lunch for receiving. At the appointed hour, the first couple stood together behind a rope of blue velvet, hands outstretched, with Florence's new secretary, Miss Laura Harlan, and an army and navy attaché alongside, the Secret Service standing guard.[31] In what passed as a security measure in those days, everyone had to have a letter of introduction from either a Congress member or someone with standing to wait in line. On any given day, 1,000 or more would stop by. Florence offered more than a perfunctory palm press to her visitors; she had a word and a generous smile for all of them.

Admonitions about the potentially exhaustive effects of this practice were met with a scowl from the grateful president: "It wasn't long ago that I was out . . . asking people to vote for me. Now when they come to Washington . . . the least that I can do is to shake hands with them."[32] This approachable man loved this part of the job, pointing out, "the only bright spot of my day is seeing those admiring and kindly faces. I love to meet them. They have nothing to ask." Florence, Edna Coleman writes, agreed with him, and thus "their social regime was planned to give the greatest pleasure and include . . . as many people as the size of the house would safely admit."[33] Yet her private correspondence reveals that the first lady found the endless round of greeting in general exhausting, even if she felt it her duty to accommodate the visitors as custodian of the People's House.

SETTLING IN

Their first Sunday in the White House, March 6, they relaxed with old friends, including the Scobeys, Creagers, Jenningses (who were staying with the McLeans for a few days), old Doctor Harding and the Harding sisters and their families, and of course the Sawyers. Reminisce about the days of old happily, they did—but it was soon clear that their former life had vanished. Two weeks in, Harding wrote Jennings, "I do not think I can half convey to you the enormity of the task which I have undertaken."[34] Florence felt the same. As she wrote her Ohio friend Mary Lee, she and the president were just overwhelmed. "Really, it is a tragedy when one stops to think how little time one can have to himself in this place.... It is just one mad rush all the time, and delegation after delegation ... coming in on us."[35] But Mary was welcome any time, even if Florence could not spend much time with her. She hoped that things would calm down later and she would have more time, although this was a vain wish—it was only to get busier. Indeed, it would take a severe illness for her to get some quiet at last. Florence would thus find it impossible to take advantage of the kind offer of Malcolm Jennings to find seclusion at his home in Columbus.[36]

Because of her fragile health, Florence started her appointments after 11 A.M. Her doctor kept her in bed (or at least on her "downy couch") every day until close to noon. But Florence still worked, even in bed, dictating to Miss Harlan "while still recumbent." Once vertical, she saw many people throughout the day. Thus on Friday, March 18, a not untypical twelve-hour day began with old friends Evalyn McLean and Catherine New visiting at 11 A.M., followed by guests at lunch and all afternoon, and after a ride in the Laudalet, their town car, the Hardings hosted dinner with the commerce secretary and his wife, Herbert and Lou Henry Hoover, and then had a late visit with their old friend Harry Daugherty at 10:45 P.M.[37] Journalist Daisy Ayres worried that Florence would overwork herself, not only by holding all the meetings, but also because in them, Florence would often take on the burden of conversation.[38] She managed her meetings by keeping them short, 10 minutes at most, and in these short visits, as one journalist noted, could stay "in touch with what many different sorts of people are thinking about, which makes profitable subjects of conversation with her husband."[39] Of course, this meant many long, busy afternoons, with up to three dozen meetings daily, as well as regular teas and receptions too.

The president's days were even longer, beginning at 7 A.M. and ending with a visit with Florence before bed. Breakfasts were a highlight of the Hardings' day, if a threat to the president's arteries. He loved waffles, which he ate two to three times a week, often with dry beef gravy and any kind of warm bread, from muffins to biscuits. These would be accompanied by fruit, bacon, sausage, eggs, and coffee. After a look at the newspaper and a smoke, he would go over to the executive office building, just a few steps away, to be joined by Christian and Rudolph Forster, his executive clerk, and the White House's first female stenographer, Eva B. Uhl, who would take his dictation. Secretary Hughes would often visit, followed by Hoover, and then a long line of supplicants.[40]

Florence accompanied her husband at breakfast, and then turned to her mail, with correspondence coming from everyone ranging from office seekers to charities to morals enforcers, before her meetings began at 11 A.M. She loved to do her mail; it was one task she was loath to give up even when she was ill. She often joined the president for lunch, along with his other guests, and thus participated in discussions where "very many of the great and far reaching policies of the Nation are determined."[41]

On Sundays, there was church, usually at Calvary Baptist, Harding's denomination, but she also attended the Methodist Church as well. Florence was often the motivating force in getting him to services! She also liked to spend part of her Sundays visiting patients at Walter Reed Hospital. Outside of work, the Hardings especially liked to have friends and family visit, and they hosted a near-constant stream of visitors. In the evenings, there were regular entertainments, including performances at Keith's theater, movies at the White House, and intimate dinners.[42] Most often in their company were the News, the Weeks, the Fletchers, the Frelinghuysens, the Hales, the McLeans, and of course the Sawyers and Christians.

All of them were old friends from Senate days or Ohio friends. Some were Cabinet members as well, like New and Weeks. Hughes, Hoover, Mellon—perhaps the best minds in the Cabinet—were not their intimates. As Florence noted, "One has 'acquaintances' everywhere, but very few real close old-fashioned friends."[43] And friends she needed, to unwind with after the stress of being "on" so much with strangers, who mostly wanted favors.[44]

With her friends, though, she could be herself, serving comfortable foods like "pumpkin and mince pies, spare ribs, corn on the cob, corn bread, ginger bread, Boston baked beans."[45] The White House kitchen staff, black and white, made these delicacies, and many more elaborate spreads. Until Florence got ill, there were also frequent formal social events, including posh dinners for dignitaries and huge receptions. If not actually preparing the food, Mrs. Harding was intimately involved in planning these occasions, orchestrating them with her staff.

For a less dignified, but definitely cuter, set, she also hosted the first White House Easter Egg Roll since the war began. Fifty guests joined the Hardings on the South Portico on March 28, including Cabinet members and close friends like the Christians and the McLeans, to watch the tiny thousands below, baskets in hand, rolling their eggs, with Laddie Boy joining in the fun. It became an annual custom, and Florence loved seeing the children. She and her husband got out and mingled with them happily.[46]

In planning such affairs, and so many other details, Florence had much important help from her secretary, Laura Harlan, the daughter of the late associate justice John Marshall Harlan (he is perhaps most famous for writing the dissent in 1896's prosegregation decision, *Plessy v. Ferguson*). Laura Harlan had formerly worked for Mrs. George Wickersham, the wife of President Taft's attorney general. She also had been an assistant to Lady Geddes, wife of the British ambassador, and Mrs. Norman Davis, whose husband became Harding's secretary of labor. With this background, reporters recognized, she "knows official life and all of the intricate problems," as well as Washington social life. She was an efficient, discerning, "broad-minded" professional, who was well paid in the White House, earning from $4,000 to $5000 per year.[47] She and Florence spent many hours huddled together, and Miss Harlan, as she was always called, felt close to the first lady, who was not so much older than she. With her mother and father both deceased, her home was the White House, although her nights were spent mostly in the dwelling she shared with her unmarried sister, Ruth.[48]

Easter Egg Roll, April 17, 1922. Courtesy of the Library of Congress.

Although some thought she was merely a social secretary, an office that Edith Roosevelt had pioneered during her years in the White House, Harlan was really an executive secretary. She read and responded to mail, knew how to answer each request for support, made sure that only the most personal mail went to the first lady, and set up Florence's meetings. In short, she was indispensable. She had help, too, including William Rockwell and R. W. McGee, who ran the social bureau at the White House.[49]

Women's suffrage had made a position like Harlan's much more important than before. With so many diverse delegations of women visiting the White House, the first lady had now to play a much greater role in receiving them. Florence needed to handle female visitors carefully, too, because these women's causes often had political implications. As one journalist noted, "A misstep on her part very easily might do serious damage to her husband's political fortunes"—and of course, the reverse was also true.[50]

Florence's aides, including Baldinger, as well as her Secret Service man, Barker—the first assigned to any first lady—were also important adjuncts facilitating her busy life. Like her newsboys at the *Star*, these young men were essential to efficient operations. Upon hearing that one attaché might be reassigned, she wrote Secretary Weeks of the War Department: "I am not making suggestions but am merely anxious to know if these men can be kept nearby."[51] No doubt he took the hint.

Baldinger was assigned to the president, but as Ike Hoover, White House usher, observed, "Mrs. Harding... adopted... [him] as her own. She had him assigned to her and he acted as messenger, special watchman, general handy man, and at times almost as a lady's maid." Florence did have a real lady's maid, Katherine Wynne, and, after her illness began in September 1922, a regular nurse, Ruth V. Powderly. And of course she had her two doctors, including Sawyer, who had watched over her for years, and Joel Boone, who began working for the Hardings in 1922. The White House staff thus grew under their administration.

HOUSEKEEPING

Mrs. Harding, despite her freewheeling spending at Wyoming Avenue—or perhaps because of it—was more circumspect in her White House purchases. Now she was dealing with other people's money, and the country was still suffering from the postwar depression. She wanted to set an example and show that she, too, shared in this straitened atmosphere. The Wilsons had taken much of their furniture away, leaving the White House "bare and chill." Congress had appropriated $10,000 for her to fix up the house, but she declined it; instead, she decided to use her Wyoming Avenue furnishings, some only a couple of years old, at least until the country was back on track. But there were still many household expenses. The Hardings' vision of the White House as an open space meant that money would need to be spent to keep it presentable, especially on the first floor. Flowers were the answer, and Florence put them in all the rooms visitors generally saw: the East Room, with its busts of Washington, Franklin, Jefferson, and Lincoln; the Blue Room, which had Lafayette's gold clock (from Napoleon) and a lacquer cabinet of Japanese origin from the Buchanan administration; the Red Room, graced with Washington's portrait saved in the War of 1812 by Dolley Madison; and finally, the state dining room, with its heads of game animals (which Florence had removed because of her concern about animal suffering)—all were softened and brightened by floral decoration.[52]

{ *Inaugural Year* }

Flowers were Florence's passion. She loved them and used them with abandon; she arranged them, and rearranged the work of others.[53] Fortunately, the White House had greenhouses, as well as a separate flower room where the bouquets were prepared: every morning, 300 roses were distributed through the house, filling sixty vases.[54] Although she would claim that the hothouses—sixteen of them—actually saved money, since for a few hundred dollars they grew flowers that, if purchased, would cost tens of thousands, the expenses overall were growing at the People's House. For one thing, compared with the ailing Wilson administration, also constrained by war, the Hardings were doing "a lot more entertaining," and not everyone thought Florence was being as frugal as she might be. Colonel Clarence O. Sherrill of the Office of Public Buildings and Grounds delicately told Congress that "a lady does not appreciate how much money is involved." Florence's obsession with flowers left Sherrill a bit wilted: "I am criticized if I do not provide all of the flowers and decorations called for. It does not make any difference whether I have the money or no. I have got to get the flowers, that is all. So, sometimes we have had to send fifteen or twenty miles out in the country . . . [for] leaves and branches of trees and so on." Besides the flowers, the influx of visitors had taken a toll on the mansion, where the budget had increased almost 50 percent since 1919 because "the walking-through of the public causes wear and tear on the different fibers, the walls and the upholstery, so that the items of upkeep are very much larger than they were before," noted Sherrill.[55]

The staff was another expense, and also under Mrs. Harding's charge. She at first thought she would fire Wilson's Secret Service chief, Edmund Starling, having heard that he was not only a Democratic Southerner, but also inclined to be officious. She was mistaken about the latter, as she graciously admitted: "we were given information about you which was entirely untrue. I am sorry for that." She asked him to stay, an excellent decision; even if he was not exactly fond of the Hardings, he kept them safe.[56] Florence also had planned to send housekeeper Elizabeth Jaffray packing. Hired during the Taft administration, Jaffray ran her regime from her second floor living quarters, with eighteen servants under her. Nellie Taft had given Florence a mixed report: "Mrs. Jaffray was a capable[,] intelligent[,] and agreeable housekeeper in my time but I always did the ordering for all meals and entertainment myself."[57] But Mrs. Harding soon realized how vital the housekeeper was to the operation, and they developed a respectful, if sometimes volatile, relationship.

In Mrs. Jaffray's recollection, Florence was often mercurial, and her temper could flare, as it did when she misplaced valued items, like her favorite velvet collar with the diamond decoration. Jaffray noted that "she had about as little reserve as any grown person I have ever met." Another difference they had was over Florence's emphasis on keeping household bills down, which made Mrs. Jaffray's work subject to unwelcome oversight. Once, when Florence demanded that she make sixty cups of coffee from a pound of grounds, Mrs. Jaffray left in a huff of exasperation. She then returned quickly, asked for a kiss, and was instantly granted it![58]

Nevertheless, despite her issues with Mrs. Harding and her "badly controlled temper," Jaffray's judgment is revealing: not only was Florence "a trifle unconventional," she was also "honest, fearless, and in her own way very kindly, and she tried to do what was right." Indeed, this often critical housekeeper, who had been on the verge of leaving Florence's employ "many times," praised the first lady's "rugged honesty and sincerity" and declared that she was "especially dear to me."[59] Despite her sometimes maddening nature in the house, Florence earned Mrs. Jaffray's respect. Grace Coolidge did fire her, however.

In addition to the housekeeper, the Harding White House also had three cooks, who worked in a relatively modern kitchen, with its "electric dumb waiter" and "electric plate wamer."[60] The mansion had almost 7,500 pieces of china and glassware, and Florence was frugal here as well, insisting on using the Wilson administration's set, thus saving thousands of dollars.[61] She kept close track of spending on household items, and in 1923, she cut back on sugar consumption when price gouging became widespread.[62]

FIRST YEAR AS FIRST LADY

As these practices show, Florence was intimately involved in the workings of the White House. But as a transitional first lady, she was also not content merely to housekeep or to hold teas. Florence had always been coequal with her husband, and life in the White House would be no different. As Joel Boone observed, "Mrs. Harding was always very much interested, and showed it, in politics."[63] One newspaper observed, "She had no hesitancy in expressing her mind with vehemence and with a positiveness . . . she had what one would call a "'man's mind.'" Adding to the masculine portrait, contemporaries sometimes described Florence's frank approach that verged on abruptness, and her vigorous handshake. Florence was fully connected with the political controversies of her day and was known to be "at home with any group of men" who were similarly engaged. Indeed, her private conversations with these men often took place without her husband's involvement or knowledge. Writing to ambassador George B. M. Harvey in London, in response to his description of a recent stimulating dinner he'd attended, Florence expressed her wish to have been with him: "I should like most to have been present visibly or invisibly . . . to listen to clever men's talk of world affairs."[64] Kathleen Lawler confirmed: "she liked above all others the game of politics."[65] Her friend Mary Lee, a Republican activist from Westerville, Ohio, certainly recognized that, keeping Florence up to date on the state's developments, including a four-page summary of issues in the Ohio house of representatives.[66]

As she shared Harding's political life, Florence did not hesitate to give her husband advice, as his cabinet secretaries knew. As a result of her "special interest" in maritime issues, for example, Edwin Denby, the secretary of the navy, asked for her views on matters in his office.[67] She helped scout out people for posts, too; in June 1922, for instance, Columbia president Nicholas Murray Butler wrote Florence in response to her request for him to think about a suitable candidate for customs collector at the port of New York.[68] Florence also named a woman to the position of receiver of public moneys in the United States Land Office, a "coveted job."[69] Her action here was controversial, and one paper felt compelled to defend her by stating, "When the people elect a President they at the same time elect a Presidentess."[70] In another case, Florence received a request from a child welfare organization for assistance in the naming of a new officer for child welfare, with the proviso that a woman be named to the post.[71]

How far did Florence think her influence extended? Ike Hoover declared that she had boasted she had "made Warren Harding President," but this seems an unfair jab, and it is not clear that even Florence believed it. It is more likely instead that, as Warren himself observed, "Mrs. Harding wants to be the drum major in every band that passes."[72] Sometimes, when her husband would find fault with her advice, the conversation would become heated, and he would "scowl, shut his mouth tight and leave the room where they had been holding their discussion," Dr. Boone related. But he never yelled at her.[73] He would instead joke about the exceptionally few times that he got his own way in their marriage.

But Florence never crossed the line that her predecessor had; she did not attempt to speak for her husband. Though in the White House her "scepter [was] supreme," as one paper noted, she "observed punctiliously the proper distinctions between her own place and her husband's" and did not enter the president's executive offices.[74] She had her sphere and her own cabinet: there was Mrs. Jaffray to handle the meals and help with purchasing; Miss Harlan to assist with correspondence; friends like Catherine New to provide aid with seasonal changes in the home's draperies and furniture covers; and Evalyn McLean and Beatrice Fletcher to assist with her clothes.

Despite all the help, she was very busy. In those early months, visitors rained down on her. Often it was women's groups: the League of Women Voters, the Ohio DARs, the Federation of Women's Clubs, the League of American Penwomen, and the National Society of the Daughters of 1812, among others. Despite her "masculine" demeanor as noted above, one paper reported that she "likes to meet women and she is particularly a woman's woman, holding and interesting them with her consummate talent for things literary, political, domestic, and what not." But these meetings were not coffee klatsches; Florence had a political aim in mind. As she told a reporter, "we women have so recently attained suffrage. I want to help the women of the country to understand their government.... I want representative women to meet their chief Executive and to understand the policies of the present administration."[75]

She also planned escapes from work as often as was feasible. For instance, she ditched the National Congress of Mothers and Parent-Teachers Association's visit on April 27 to go on the *Mayflower*. This luxury yacht, built in 1894, was maintained and run for the White House by the navy.[76] It became a regular refuge for her at the White House. Her first trip occurred less than two weeks into her tenure as first lady, with her good friend Catherine New, on March 15.[77] She took people out much more than any of her predecessors had, and those on board enjoyed teas, dancing, and dinners; sometimes they even stayed on board overnight.

They also got to mingle with the ship's dashing crew, including the courtly and athletic Dr. Joel Boone, who joined the ship as medical officer in 1922. He was a good dancer, if not such a great bridge player (he recalled his "pathetic" involvement in many games with Mrs. Harding). Still, he wouldn't dance with all the women; this unostentatious Quaker found Evalyn "showy and jewel bedecked—unattractive."[78]

In addition to a gracious staff, the ship's naval auspices gave the trips some pomp. Every time the *Mayflower* passed Mt. Vernon, for instance, the marine guard stood at the rail with their rifles and saluted, playing "The Star-Spangled Banner" and taps, and dipping their flags.[79] Other areas the *Mayflower* visited had less appealing rituals, including its dockage on the Anacostia River at the navy yard. Boone noted that one hot May night, his men leaped overboard there to swim. But the landing was an "open sewer," and Boone recommended any further strokes be stopped. As he observed, the "odors were perfectly awful ... flies were unbearable.... They blackened the underside of the canvas awning which was stretched across the deck.... I knew we were getting a great deal of infection into our food," he reckoned. He did finally get the dump removed.[80] All the same, the *Mayflower* food, infected or not, was delicious and plentiful.[81]

The Hardings had always loved traveling, even if it was only to the mouth of the Potomac River. They also loved receiving interesting guests. In April Albert Einstein came to visit on his way to the National Academy of Sciences. Harding confessed he, like many others, did not understand the theory of relativity.[82] The Hardings also hosted Marie Curie on May 20 and gave her a gram of radium worth $100,000, which a group of American women had purchased on her behalf, an effort in which Florence had joined. The following day, Harding had a much sadder duty to perform when he gave a speech at Hoboken, New Jersey, upon the return of 5,212 bodies of soldiers and sailors from overseas. Their disabled brothers soon became a focus of Florence's attention; she held regular parties for them and frequently visited them in the hospital. The late war was a preoccupying presence for both Hardings. In the wake of the United States' decision to stay out of the League of Nations, the president badly wanted to be seen as a promoter of international peace, and later in 1921 he would sponsor the Washington Disarmament Conference.

That conference would provide a rationale for some of the most glittering evenings ever seen in the capital, but there was still a hot Washington summer to endure first. Lacking a vacation White House as some presidents had enjoyed before them, the Hardings escaped as often as they could to visit friends. They had a cool respite at the Frelinghuysens' estate in New Jersey in early July; golf was the aim, but when the Senate unexpectedly approved the peace treaty with Germany, Harding signed it at his friend's home on July 2. Florence, who was not feeling well, stayed upstairs for the signing, but she joined her husband on the Fourth of July to shake the hands of 3,000 visitors; they then came back to the White House the next day, when another throng came to see them. Even the sometimes xenophobic Florence found it illuminating: "they were all such new types that in spite of the heat I got a good deal of interest out of it. They were mostly from the factory population, foreigners or Americans in the making," she told Ethel Jennings.[83]

With an acrimonious Congress sweatily arguing over contentious issues like the bonus, farm relief, tariff reform, railroad strikes, unemployment, budget concerns, and lynching legislation, the Hardings were unable to leave Washington for long that summer or the next. Florence followed these developments closely, and the Hardings' dinner guests discussed them frequently around their table.[84] Harding expressed his opposition to the bonus bill at a congressional session on July 12.[85] Jennings urged the president to show more leadership of this kind, even though "I know this is distasteful to you," as Harding did not feel he should trample on the legislators' turf too freely.[86] Yet William Allen White, influential editor of the *Emporia Gazette* in Emporia, Kansas, was impressed with the president's leadership. Florence thanked White for an article he wrote at this time, which he had sent along: "It is indeed gratifying to us both to read such expressions of good will as yours, and we thank you warmly."[87]

Harding managed to escape later in July on a camping trip with Thomas A. Edison, Harvey Firestone, and Henry Ford near Hagerstown, Maryland, a trip that has become legendary. Florence, recovering from ptomaine poisoning from chicken salad and then further complications from "fire brand" taken to treat the problem, could not join them. She had few regrets. "In my present state of mind, [I] am not quite sure what my attitude might have been toward 'that Henry Ford.'" (He had opposed U.S. intervention in World War I.)[88]

The trip involved a horseback ride over a stream, and an impromptu outdoor service with 300 "country folk," and hymns played on the camp pianola by Mrs. Firestone along with a sermon thumping the virtues of the United States staying disentangled from foreign ties. Starling, along to protect the president, thought the camp was atrocious. Not only was it situated on a road, low down next to a "sluggish" river and saturated with flies, but it offered no hot water for shaving on an extremely humid weekend.[89]

Florence had recovered sufficiently to join Warren on a *Mayflower* trip to New England on July 30, their first real vacation that summer. In their absence, they had the White House painted, but the first lady insisted that tourists could still visit for guided tours.[90] Their New England trip took them first to Plymouth, Massachusetts, for its tercentenary, where British and Dutch representatives also arrived to greet a crowd of 100,000. The *Mayflower* next sailed north to Portland, Maine, where it moored so that the presidential party could visit Secretary Weeks's summer home, The Lodge, in the White Mountains at Lancaster, New Hampshire. On the way, there was "an orgy of golf and doughnuts"—the golf played with tennis balls!—and visits with hospitalized veterans in the nearby town of Gorham.[91] They also stopped in Poland Spring, Maine, for lunch at the home of Senator Frederick Hale and his wife, who was on the trip with the Hardings along with the Christians, Senator Frelinghuysen, Harry and Catherine New, and Dr. Sawyer. Rounding out the group, Harry Daugherty and his friend, Jess Smith, came by as well. Daugherty's wife, Lucie, was confined to bed at home, so Smith was Daugherty's regular companion; they lived together, first at 1509 H Street, in a house belonging to Ned McLean, and then at the Wardman Park Hotel. Smith, an unsavory character, carried a gun as protection against the sort of men who threatened his role as an enforcer of Prohibition, though these crooks also included bootleggers who paid him "protection money." Florence too relied on Smith, whose connections in the "dry goods business" allowed him to secure bargains for her.⁹²

Despite Smith's corrupted enforcement and Daugherty's flawed judgment about him, these two characters should not be seen as typical of the Harding set. Most of their friends were solid and decent citizens, like Harry New and George Christian. Malcolm Jennings, for instance, a kindly and astute Columbus businessman, was one of the president's closest confidants; "short and rather rotund in the middle and bowlegged" with thick glasses, he made a comic contrast with Harding.⁹³ He was no fan of Daugherty, and when Harding ran the attorney general's recommendations on postmasters past Jennings, his friend usefully pointed out that some of Daugherty's people would be considered "political."⁹⁴ Jennings always offered his frank opinion of Harding's actions, such as his boldly pardoning Eugene Debs.⁹⁵ Overall, however, his close friendship blinded him to what indeed would be his dear friend, the president's, undoing: "the impression rather sedulously cultivated, I think by your colleagues in the Senate . . . that you were a genial, harmless creature fashioned of potters clay and plastic in the hands of your friends and fellow partisans." Of course, this was an exaggerated portrait. But Jennings believed it was completely wrong, when indeed it was just this trust in his "friends" that wrecked Harding's reputation later.⁹⁶

But all this was far in the future. Meanwhile, there was another *Mayflower* cruise to enjoy at the end of August and into Labor Day, which traversed the lower Chesapeake and went as far north as Atlantic City, where rough seas prevented landing.⁹⁷ Similarly tumultuous labor trouble in West Virginia, however—described as a "strike war"—did not stop the party from golf in Norfolk on their return.⁹⁸

Plans for yet one more late summer *Mayflower* trip, this one to take them as far as Bar Harbor, Maine, were changed, and the Hardings and their friends instead set out on a driving vacation in September, which took them to Atlantic City for the city's first beauty pageant, as well as some golfing stops. They stayed in the resort's posh Ritz-Carlton, taking up the entire fifth floor. The presidential couple occupied an ocean-facing suite, with an orchestra, gold dinner service, and special roller chairs, though the Hardings refused the gold plates and other deluxe treatment. They enjoyed the movies of the pageant in their rooms, along with newsreels of themselves, however.[99] After golf at the Seaview Country Club, their vacation continued north with a 2½-hour slog to the ferry in South Amboy over 110 miles of slippery dirt road (their era's New Jersey Turnpike). Autograph seekers swarmed them, celebrity style, as they embarked for New York. In the city, they reveled in cultural offerings, including a musical as well as a movie, *The Affairs of Anatol*, at their suite in another Ritz-Carlton.[100] The trip concluded with more tee time on the slopes of the notoriously difficult National Golf Links of America course in Southhampton, Long Island, with its marshes and high wind. Florence played lots of bridge in the club house during these golf games, joining the other women, and secretaries Hoover and Weeks. They returned on the *Mayflower* via West Point, under a full moon.[101]

A lovely respite it was, but now Florence faced her inaugural social season that fall, and the pace of life rapidly intensified. She was cheered in this effort by their new dog, a bull terrier named Oh Boy, born on March 4, like the presidency, a new friend for Laddie Boy.[102] Charity groups began making their pilgrimages and dinners began filling the calendar; the White House sponsored a Supreme Court breakfast on October 2 and a big dinner for senators on October 7.[103] To assist her in her receiving duties, the Masons of St. Louis had purchased for her a $2,000 seal coat. No one, certainly not she, then thought it at all inappropriate—either as a gift or as an animal's skin—and she got herself measured for it that fall. She picked up her luxurious garment on October 22, just in time to receive the ladies of the Senate and Cabinet, who came to tea to meet each other. In bringing them together, as noted earlier, Florence had saved them from troubling with the antiquated custom of leaving individual calling cards at each other's homes. It was an "inspiration," said Antoinette Hughes, wife of Charles Evans Hughes. In November, she did the same with congressmen's wives, bringing them to meet the Cabinet ladies at the White House. Florence's history as a Senate wife herself, someone who had had to go through the card-calling exercise numerous times, made her sensitive to her former colleagues' plight.[104] Any invalids left at home, of course, would have to wait for visits.

Later in October the Hardings went to Birmingham, Alabama, and then to Atlanta, returning at the end of the month. Harding gave a speech in Birmingham on race relations that was not only progressive, calling for legal equality (including political and economic fairness), but also politically risky, especially given the locale. One Mississippi senator called it "a blow to the white civilization of this country." The president was undeterred. Though the speech did not call for social equality (indeed, he argued against it) and in the end did little to change the oppressive conditions in which many blacks lived in the 1920s, his approachable and open manner was heartening to African Americans all the same. Harry C. Smith, editor of a black newspaper, the *Cleveland Gazette,* later concluded: "As far as our race is concerned, President Harding is our real friend and we have only to wait a few more months, . . . to have a full and complete realization of this fact." Sadly, this was on May 29, 1923, and Harding had less than three months to live; he did not fulfill such hopes.[105]

The signal event of that fall and winter was the Washington Conference, set to start in November. Just before it opened, the recent war occasioned another ceremony, the first Armistice Day in Washington on November 11, with a parade of 50,000 soldiers honoring the Unknown Soldier, held in an unmarked coffin just shipped back from France, down Pennsylvania Avenue. The procession then traveled to Arlington, where the president dedicated the monument for this cause, known to this day as the Tomb of the Unknowns. Florence left a white rose, and Harding's speech was broadcast to the entire country for the first time on an AT&T public address system.

The next day, the conference opened, and Florence was there, along with 1,300 others. This was the first international conference devoted to disarmament and was Warren G. Harding's chief contribution to world peace, serving as an alternative to the spurned League of Nations. Joel Boone averred that Harding, who saw himself as an "apostle of understanding," called for the conference to show not only that the United States was *not* retreating from the world after rejecting the league, but also because he believed that "if nations would take the trouble to learn what their rivals were really thinking" and were thus enlightened that they were "working for understanding, [and] willing . . . to live together in harmony," wars would be unnecessary.[106] The conference had first been spearheaded by one of Harding's old colleagues in the Senate, William Borah, who had urged the incoming president to call such a meeting to discuss naval limitations with Japan and Britain.[107] Indeed, by limiting expenditures on naval weaponry, the conference would serve another of Harding's goals: to bring the budget back to "normalcy."

So important was the conference to both of them that Florence missed only one open session from her special box, where she was often joined by other women, including Mrs. Coolidge, Mrs. Taft, Mrs. Gillett (wife of the Speaker of the House), Mrs. Frank B. Kellogg, Mrs. John W. Weeks, Mrs. Edwin Denby, and Florence's friend Princess Cantacuzene—Ulysses S. Grant's granddaughter, Julia Grant, who had married a Russian prince. With such a glittering international gathering, there were numerous dinners, receptions, and ceremonies, including a tree planting at the Lincoln Memorial, where Florence brought in a trowel to help throw the first earth for two Ohio elms in honor of the Allied armies and navies.[108]

The first dinner for the conference delegates was a luminous affair, with ninety in attendance, representing almost half as many nations. The luminary dignitaries included Sir Auckland and Lady Geddes of Britain, David Balfour, Premier Aristide Briand, Ambassador M. Jusserand from France (Florence's favorite, who escorted her after she and Warren descended the stairway), Marshal Foch, General Armondo Vittorio Diaz from Portugal, and Prince Tokugawa of Japan. Florence doubted "there will ever be a more notable collection of people around the table here." She dressed for the occasion in "a plain gown of white satin, embroidered with crystal," with a long train. Her throat was decorated with her usual black velvet band with its diamond slide, and she carried an ostrich feather fan.[109] Five hundred more came to the reception later. The men were eye-catching, in their diplomatic and dress uniforms, their chests glittering with buttons. As was her forte, Florence managed to maintain a simplicity and dignity about the evening, despite its coruscating glamour. As was also her aim, she used White House events like this as a way to connect with the larger public, underlining her sense of the celebrity culture of the White House and the importance of its visibility during such spectacles. She thus invited in society page journalists to see the decorations beforehand, as well as her dress, "chatting with them intimately," a consideration which these women reporters most appreciated.[110]

After dinner, the guests enjoyed a musicale with soprano, violinist, and two piano players. They could look out the windows and see Pennsylvania Avenue at the moment when the president pressed a button to flood the street with light to start the conference. Florence was justifiably proud, telling her friend, the ambassador to England, Colonel Harvey, "it was most successful"; indeed, it was "beautiful and brilliant."[111] As Starling noted, this was "the honeymoon period of the Harding administration," and many more social delights awaited.[112] Florence told Esther, "Washington has not been so gay for many a year as now." Having been there since 1915, she knew what she was talking about.[113]

Around this time, Ned McLean gave also her a beautiful sorrel mare named Lady, to her great joy. She was ready to don her new skinny riding outfit and go with this new mare, and be "the first wife of a President to indulge in this form of outdoor sport" in the memory of people then alive. Unfortunately, she did not get to ride Lady that fall. Dr. Sawyer told her she mustn't ride, as her physical condition would not stand for it. Meanwhile, Sawyer got to ride all the time, often going with Boone to Rock Creek Park, on the White House horses.[114] She complained bitterly to her daughter-in-law: "My! Was I disappointed. I was going to ride astride . . . because I thought it would be better for my kidney."[115] Two months later, when Harvey Firestone sent her and her husband another pair of "fine riding horses," she lamented afresh about her inability to go on horseback.[116] Recalling her childhood passion, she had hoped to ride from the beginning, visiting the White House stables and their "beautiful mounts" her first month in the mansion, looking for the right horse.[117]

While her precarious health prevented her from doing much riding anymore, she did find a happy escape behind the wheel of a car, out driving with her friends. Florence often enjoyed taking drives with Evalyn. This treasured friend was perhaps the person with whom Florence had the most fun in those years; her letters are full of gossip and jokey asides, which Florence loved, living as she did in an often stultifying bubble. In those early days, the Hardings also had time to play golf together, at the Chevy Chase Club.[118] But mostly that was Warren's refuge. In the early months of his administration, he went there almost every afternoon for his eighteen holes; it was cooler than Pennsylvania Avenue. Starling noted that the golf was usually accompanied by bets, which Harding often lost, always graciously. As he wrote Evaland Scobey, "I am so out of patience with my own game that I extend expressions of sympathy to every player who draws me for his partner on the foursome. Once in a while I break under fifty.... Still, it is lots of fun. I do get the exercise and the life out of doors."[119]

After playing, they would retire to the special club house reserved for the president for drinks, though Harding generally had only one highball, according to Starling. George Christian Sr. recalled that the president had doubted the wisdom of "absolute prohibition," and Starling suggests "plenty of liquor" was served in the White House, indicating quite a stockpile had been ordered before Prohibition's restrictions came into effect. Starling spent many hours with the president and was often biting in his observations, so his assessment of Harding's moderation must be taken soberly. Florence was also not so keen on Prohibition, but she told her complaining Aunt Carrie, "it is a law and the law must be obeyed." The president at last committed himself fully to the cause on the eve of his Alaska trip in 1923, no doubt aware of the temptations that would ensue on a long journey.[120] Yet the legend of his boozing lives on: a recent book declares that Harding was "among the capital's heaviest drinkers," but this assertion seems mostly based on the partying of his friends, like Nick Longworth, who liked to guzzle at the White House. He and the Ohio congressman may have shared drinks, but their taste in alcohol was very different.[121] Indeed, Harding urged friends like Scobey to join him in refraining from excessive consumption of cigars, and he also wrote Scobey, a serious imbiber, "You are a joy to me when you have the candles lighted but you do not fit the Marble Room of the Capitol appropriately under a complete lighting up, and it was for that reason I felt it necessary for both you and me to send you into retirement to the Committee room." These cautionary words do not sound like the words of a man with a drinking problem.[122]

Golfing and card games, not alcohol consumption—or women—were Harding's favorite pastimes. Starling, who spent many, many hours with the president, was "certain" that Harding did not "get into trouble with [women]" at the White House. "He preferred the company of men," as Starling shows, citing the many poker evenings Harding shared, either at the club, with the McLeans, or with other friends.[123] After these games, which could last into the night, Warren would always have Starling call Duchess to tell her he was coming home.

Florence, for her part, loved her girlfriends, but home in Washington was feeling a bit empty that late fall of 1921. She missed the old folks at home, and especially with the holidays approaching, she keenly felt the separation from her grandchildren. Esther and her new husband, Roscoe Mezger, a grocer in Marion, had just had a baby, a little sister for Jean and George, Helen Elizabeth Mezger. Florence looked forward to seeing the new arrival, whom she heard was "too sweet for words," although she didn't know when. She sent them all a picture of Laddie Boy and promised that one day, "'Goggy' is going to send you a picture of herself on her new horse." Apparently, it did not occur to "Goggy" to invite her grandchildren to the White House for the holidays, though earlier that year, she chided Roscoe for not showing up with a group of visiting Masons at the White House.[124] Thanksgiving was at least enlivened for Florence by the Navy Relief Ball at the New Willard.

It would be a quiet Christmas, too, with "no little folks like you about," she told her grandchildren. She sent them $5 each for the holiday—in addition to the $33.35 she sent Esther each month for Jean and George. She urged them to help their mother with baby Helen: "Jean, you certainly must by this time have grown to be quite a woman. If you are anything at all like your 'Goggy' you are amounting to a great deal these days and of very great assistance to your mother."[125] While this last comment reveals a prideful streak in Florence, of more significance is the way this letter shows her desire to have a warm relationship with these children and how she identified strongly with them, although she seems not to have wanted them to be a visible part of her life.

She kept her focus instead on national affairs, like the naval conference, which continued to provide excitement and interest to her. By late December, she thought France was acting like "a capricious prima donna."[126] On the whole, she was grateful that she and Warren were happy and healthy; Florence told Mary Lee as

Christmas approached that "Mr. Harding is in fine form, notwithstanding many, many anxieties and annoyances he is obliged to face every day."[127]

In the quiet of the White House that holiday, Florence had time to reflect on her first year as first lady too. One newspaper had characterized the position as "the hardest 'Woman's Job' in All America." Although she, unlike many other first ladies, had been living in Washington for years and knew its ways, being the president's wife was still a great adjustment. It was life in a bubble, her every mannerism and style of dress inspected. Moreover, she felt a duty to protect her husband from the troubles of the office, a task that was, because of her attention to detail, a particular encumbrance for Florence. As a result, her life was intense, "very interesting, but very strenuous."[128] At the same time, the holiday brought out how lonely it could be at the top. As she wrote Lee, Christmas had been "one of the great events in my life, but down here it is different."[129] Her husband felt just the same, writing Mrs. Christian back in Marion, "I suppose most people think me the most fortunate man in the world, but . . . the exclusion from the happiness of home-kin folk and life-long friends at Xmas time" was one of the major drawbacks.[130]

Even with that seasonal emptiness, Florence didn't have time to do much relaxing reading, though she loved novels, and the White House library had lots of books, including classics like the works of Dickens, Scott, Lowell, Emerson, Irving, Longfellow, and Pope, as well as plentiful general history and biographies.[131] She had been sent a book for holiday reading about Queen Alexandria, but like her husband, she mostly only had time to read newspapers and magazines, so as to keep up with political developments.[132] The events of the dawning year, of course, would make all such leisurely pastimes even more infrequent. Florence had to get ready for her first New Year's reception, the first held in the mansion since before World War I, and nearly 7,000 people would be coming.

CHAPTER 4

DEFINING THE JOB, JANUARY–AUGUST 1922

SOCIAL ROLE, CELEBRITY CULTURE

Not only was Florence Warren G. Harding's wife and business partner, but now she was also the top organizer of official social life in the nation's capital, with a responsibility for elaborate formal entertainments. Although these social responsibilities, long characteristic of first ladies, did not define Florence's role in the White House—she made too many other contributions for that—they still consumed a huge amount of her time.

Though she did not, as some papers asserted, go directly from a "quiet Ohio home" to the "sumptuous affairs of state in the executive mansion," compared to her life as a Senate wife, she was now required to accomplish far more work in a much more visible way, in an environment daunting for anyone, especially a sixty-year-old woman in uncertain health.[1] But she had dealt with severe challenges before: she had picked up the pieces after a bad marriage left her a single mother and broke; she had gotten the *Star* off the ground when her more relaxed husband had run it into debt; and she had tolerated infidelity in Harding, a man she could usually dominate, pushing herself to focus on the larger enterprise they shared: his political career. Florence quickly saw the needs and opportunities her new post presented. And she was able to maintain her lifelong "ease and gracious womanliness" despite the new pressures.[2]

This quality served her well in the White House. So, too, did her thrill to be there—she loved it—the old manse and its attendant baggage, the other Washington institutions like Mt. Vernon and Arlington Cemetery, the Lincoln Memorial, all of it. Moreover, she had a capacity for passionate interest in many of the affairs that came to her attention, which only enlivened things for her. As one newspaper reported, "She has a characteristic attitude when intensely interested. She crosses her knees, clasps her firm and capable hands, leans forward slightly and never misses a word, intonation or gesture."[3] Thus, despite her "busy, busy life," she told her close friends, "there is always so much of interest that it makes up for the fatigue of it all."[4] And journalists picked up on her engagement. As Dolly Madison, the pseudonymous *Philadelphia Ledger* social page writer, wrote: "Mrs. Harding certainly is a wonder. She is not well. But no one would ever guess it, and she works harder at her job than any mistress the White House has ever had."[5]

Sometimes, however, the fatigue could be overwhelming, as Florence found with the demanding social agenda of her job. She assisted her husband greatly by filling this active social role, not only in meetings with varied constituencies, but in splashy entertainments, like those associated with the Washington conference. She saw hundreds by special appointment at the White House, but she met thousands and thousands more in impromptu gatherings and formal receptions. Florence did what she had to do, and did it well—though she found much of it bone-wearying.[6]

Perhaps the biggest single social event of the administration was the New Year's reception of 1922. It would be the Hardings' first and only such reception; their next New Year's came in 1923, in the midst of Florence's convalescence. Befitting the Washington hierarchy, members of the Cabinet arrived first at 11:00 A.M.; they descended the White House stairs with the president and his wife to greet the diplomatic corps, including Austrian and German representatives who had not been welcomed in the mansion since 1917. Senators and congressmen arrived forty minutes later, army and navy staff ten minutes after that, and other officials kept coming—the librarian of Congress, tariff commissioners, and even members of the Federal Board for Vocational Education! Veterans came too, and then the public—an enormous throng—from 2 to 4 P.M. The masses perhaps

Line for New Year's reception, January 2, 1922. Courtesy of the Library of Congress.

enjoyed it more than anybody—all 6,576 of them. Mostly women and children attended, it being a weekday; they had begun lining up at 10 A.M., bundled against the cold, some standing on carpet remnants to keep warm.[7]

This popular custom itself had started under Abigail Adams. The *Baltimore American* noted with approval Harding's restoration of this ritual. Wilson, as the paper noted, "did not care for public commingling just for the joy of the thing. Mr. Harding . . . does." How did Mrs. Harding feel? She was as gracious as ever, dressed in a gown decorated with skunk fur—but by the end of the ordeal, she may have felt as ripe as this rodent, despite her diamond neck clasp and brooch preserving a semblance of cool glamour.[8] In five hours of shaking, Florence's right hand became so swollen with welts that it went numb, and she had to switch to her left. Meanwhile, her discolored gloves required changing several times. Observers attributed her grasp of the task to her piano playing and horseback riding skills, which had developed her digits prodigiously. She apologized, however, that she was out of practice since the campaign, when she was "never tired."[9] Boone remembered the crowds extending to the State-War-Navy building (later known as the Old Executive Office building); he had wondered how the president could stand it for so long.¹⁰ He was less worried about Florence; she seemed to handle the "handshaking ordeals" better than some in her audience, "smiling, alert, and as fresh as the roses about her," while those in line "leaned on their escorts, or complained of their shoes or tired feet; . . . slunk into chairs and . . . shifted their weight from one tired foot to another."¹¹ But of course, she had a soft carpet to stand on, and they had only remnants!¹²

With so many in line, the marine band played marching tunes to keep things moving—unlike the more majestic music provided for the dignitaries earlier in the day. Police stationed every 10 yards watched the comers closely, keeping them from making any "rehearsed speeches," and many citizens cooperated by holding out empty hands. Any who had hidden theirs in pockets or in muffs could be ejected from the line.¹³

Some days later, when she next had energy and a working hand again to write, Florence told her friend Mary Lee, "Our New Year's Reception was very interesting and an experience never to be forgotten. It sent me to bed for a couple of days before getting ready for it, and put me to bed for forty-eight hours afterwards, with my right hand very much swollen and very sore." Still, she pointed out, she had been showered with appreciative letters, and "when I think of the great line that stood for hours I feel more than repaid."¹⁴ She expressed similar, conflicted feelings to her friend Evaland Scobey: "the official season is on full blast, but I am enjoying it immensely. . . . there are times when I am worn more or less to a frazzle, but when the eventual day or night arrives I seem to arise to the occasion."¹⁵ She also wrote Esther after a day lying horizontal: "It was a very wonderful experience but I went to bed as soon as it was over and remained there until 7:30 this PM," she noted. She had another reason to resent the reception: "My how I hate to write 1922. Time goes altogether too fast and it makes me sad."¹⁶

Kathleen Lawler insisted, all the same, that Florence "loved society," and "had her health permitted, her brief reign in the White House would have been gayer and more brilliant than any the stately mansion had ever known." Yet Florence told Lee how her days were "very strenuous," and she wrote Lawler that "If anybody thinks this is just one lovely bed of roses, I can tell you that person is greatly mistaken."[17] Despite her mixed feelings and her less than perfect health, Florence worked tirelessly to expand the access and visibility of the White House. She would be a part of people's lives in a way that her predecessors had never approached. One observer noted that the Hardings had made Washington "gayer than at any time in 7 years." Indeed, the *Louisville Courier Journal* attested, after "six years . . . of wartime worries and other vicissitudes . . . the lid is really off the White House and we are in this winter for the highest of old-time times." Florence's "old fashioned early Victorian set up" struck this author as "so Old World and delicious." Florence might not have appreciated the description of one of her recent outfits the paper gave: "a brown, filmy slip-over thing, just like yours, you know . . . really a very simple little proposition," but she would have appreciated that the dress, like her, had "no pretentions."[18]

Other journalists saw that the Hardings' "high times" came at a high cost for the first couple. "They are putting so much energy and good will into occupying their position . . . that one wonders whether they will not end in physical bankruptcy," wrote Jean Eliot in the *Washington Times*. Not only was there the "social game" of receptions and entertainments, but they had guests nearly constantly as well, and "probably six days in the week they have people in informally at luncheon or at dinner, or both," in addition to Florence's frequent afternoon teas.[19]

That January there was not only the New Year's reception, but numerous formal state dinners and other affairs, as well as balls to attend: a continual blitz of sociability. Still, President Harding thought his wife was thriving in this hectic environment, and he told her daughter-in-law so a few days after the New Year's reception: "Mrs. Harding is surprisingly well under the circumstances, and seems to enjoy her tasks immensely."[20]

But medical professionals worried that the constant greetings, especially the handshaking, could affect the Hardings' health.[21] The National American Institute of Homeopaths contended the couple could pick up a disease from this practice, and of course, they were right (although Florence's gloves likely helped her, as long as they stayed intact!). Fifteen hundred members of the group thus passed a resolution that at their upcoming visit to the White House, they would only "bow to the President when welcomed by him." However, they then reconsidered, thinking it "presumptuous," and instead shook hands, concerned they might offend the Hardings!

While the New Year's reception was largely for the hoi polloi, the next affair was much more high-powered: the diplomatic reception on January 12, the first since 1914. Florence worked on this with her husband's military attaché, Colonel C. O. Sherrill, and as with all her events, it included lots of natural decoration. Guests were treated to a very special evening, with flowers and decorative lights, thanks to Mrs. Harding's oversight. This reception, planned to honor forty-four heads of state, soon mushroomed into a huge affair, with innumerable attachés and other officials, as well as their family members. In fact, 3,000 people turned up. Despite the planning, glitches could not be avoided. Some invitees had handed off their cards to friends, so unfamiliar faces were also in the crowd. People were "packed in everywhere like sardines, and it was most uncomfortable and . . . undignified," one paper sniffed.[22]

Despite the sweaty intimacy, it was a beautiful scene in the Blue Room, with the Hardings beaming. Ancient trumpeters, playing "Hail to the Chief," announced the arrival of the president and his wife as they came down the marble stairway into the room at 9:30, under a "bower" of palms and ferns, with Cabinet members following them through the thicket of flowers and potted plants arranged on the steps. Some of the musicians then retired their instruments, Mrs. Harding having stipulated that only nonbrass instruments be played during the reception to keep things audible. There was no attempt to provide serious food to the hordes; instead, the Hardings, and Hughes, shook hands in a receiving line for two hours.[23] The diplomatic dinner was a more controlled affair on the 19th; a more exclusive group ate at a horseshoe-shaped table with the Dolley Madison china, as well as a profusion of the White House's own flowers, including "splendid yellow and pink chrysanthemums, pink roses . . . romainina hyacinth in mounds and feathery masses of farleyense fern," as one paper reported.[24] It was events like this that led journalists to praise Florence for creating "a finer social atmosphere" than any ever before witnessed in the White House.[25]

Society page contributors were thrilled to be included in these events, which in January and February happened nearly every week, and Florence happily invited them, eager for the positive coverage.[26] She was rewarded by columns like that of the *Philadelphia Ledger*'s Dolly Madison, who reported: "The president looked proud of his attractive wife, and he had reason to be. She looked the part of the first lady." At the diplomatic reception, Florence was beautiful in "a gown of white panne velvet heavily embroidered with silver and jet and trimmed with ermine." As usual, her gown was accented by her black velvet neckband with its "exquisite pendant of diamonds."[27] The ubiquitous neckband was used to hide the swelling her illness caused her, about which she was self-conscious, although "Miss Madison" was delicate enough not to mention that fact. Florence, too, almost always wore bodices with tops, and elbow sleeves or some kind of arm veiling to cover up the bloat affecting her arms, and she underemphasized her feet and ankles for the same reason.

As her care for these personal details shows, Florence was sensitive to how she was seen. She was also interested in what others were wearing, and she documented all these affairs in the White House with a huge file of society page stories, nearly all extremely positive. At the same time, she chided those who sent her unflattering clippings, asserting that "a great many of these newspaper articles had to be taken with a large grain of salt."[28] Her practices do betray a certain insecurity about her looks. She wrote next to one photo of herself, "Awful! Who is it?—I don't know!"[29]

Mrs. Harding played well her ceremonial role as the president's domestic ambassador: she became commander of the Girl Scouts, and he took the same role with the Boy Scouts. She attended charity fund-raisers like the Children's Hospital Ball on January 9.[30] On January 22, she went to the ball for the Society for Southern Relief, which benefited pensionless Confederates, as well as one for the Garfield Hospital Nurses Home Fund on the 25th. The Garfield ball was a glittering affair, one of the "gayest balls of the winter," and the Hardings "contributed in no small measure" to its success. At the end, Florence walked out on Warren's arm to her favorite song, Carrie Jacobs Bond's "The End of a Perfect Day."[31] Their presence at such balls helped raise thousands of dollars for the organizers.[32]

Perhaps the biggest event that season, in prestige if not in size, was the Congressional Club reception.[33] The Congressional Club was composed of Capitol Hill wives, and with their old friends all massed together, it was a great evening for the Hardings, Florence gossiping with her old friends, and Warren "jollying all the girls." Dolly Madison wrote flatteringly that "Mrs. Harding, with her beautifully puffed silvery hair, looked like a French marquise of the Watteau period."[34]

And it was not only the privileged few who got to see her in this capacity. On January 23, 500 "dirt farmers," as Florence called them, came to Washington for an agricultural conference, and were welcomed at the White House.[35] A more darkly cloaked crowd came on January 26, when Florence and Warren hosted another huge reception, this time for Chief Justice Taft and members of the Supreme Court, as well as the federal judiciary; with military aides and other hangers-on, it would be another night that topped 3,000. On the day of the jurists' visit, an exhausted Florence lay in bed, dictating a letter to Laura Harlan for Mary Lee, "with a neck so stiff that I want to shriek with pain every time I turn, and still I have to go on." She complained that it "will either cure my neck or break it, I do not know which." In the same letter, she also urged Lee herself to cut back on her political work and its required socializing: "I warn you ... you and I are getting to that time of life where we have to have a care and consideration for ourselves and our strength." Ruefully, she added, "If you were here, no doubt you would say: "physician, heal thyself." Lee, sympathizing, wrote back: "It's mighty hard to keep a stiff upper lip and a smile when suffering acute torture as I know you must have suffered." She reassured Florence, "You are doing so splendidly, winning so many friends, restoring the customs that our people like." Lee had heard this confirmed in "effusive" reports from Ohio friends who had visited Washington recently. Florence was surely happy to hear her friends' warm words: "the people . . . say that the President is the greatest President in our history. They say that you are a wonderful First Lady." Nevertheless, Lee noted worriedly, "it is about killing you."[36]

Reporters noticed her tenseness, even as she put on a good front: "a smile is never far behind her rather firm-set lips," noted one paper.[37] But she was determined to transcend her challenges, and to assist her, she regularly employed her hairstylist, Jules, and face artist, Vern. Her housekeeper, Elizabeth Jaffray, was impressed at the time Mrs. Harding spent with these assistants; they came almost every day, often spending more than an hour with her.[38] Her use of them led the White House usher, Ike Hoover, to describe her as "very fixy" in her style, "so much so that she always looked artificial."[39] Edmund Starling, as well, pointed to her "marcelled" hair—even if she did not take out her gray.[40] But one person with a keen eye for the visual did not think her "fixy" at all: film director D. W. Griffith, who suggested in January 1922 that "the three most beautiful faces I have seen are the faces of mature women," among them Mrs. Harding's. This "plain Ohio woman . . . has the nobility of the [dowager] queen [Alexandria, whose biography Florence had just read] . . . and she has that sturdy humanity of the charwoman . . . a union I think could only exist in America." It was the "character" in her face that Griffith was drawn to.[41] This character was a product of a life that had had its share of challenges, yet would not succumb to them.

One artist whom she thought best captured her character was Philip Alexius Laszlo de Lombos, painter of popes and countesses, whose last White House portrait was of Teddy Roosevelt.[42] One of Florence's friends told her Laszlo's work was a great success: "the portrait is delightful—the artist has caught the spirit of your personality in all its womanliness and has not attempted to portray the role which for a time it is your part to assume. He is . . . like a Rorincy or Reynolds."[43] His would be her favorite painting of herself.

At the end of January, a disaster befell many whose features were less known in Washington, when a record snowstorm (total accumulation 33 inches, still the highest on record) split open the roof of the city's newest movie theatre, the Knickerbocker, killing 98 people and injuring 133. Out of respect for the victims, a number of events were postponed at the White House, including the army/navy reception. Nevertheless, the arms conference was back in full swing for its concluding meetings in early February, and Florence braced herself for her next big function, the Supreme Court dinner on February 3, when eighty came to the White House, including a number of senators. They would be treated to a musicale with a tenor, Vladimir Rosing, and a cellist, Miss Rozal Varady.

She was back at the conference the next morning, with her old friends and associates, including Mesdames Coolidge, Taft, Gillett, Weeks, Denby, Kellogg, and Princess Cantacuzene. Women made up perhaps half of those in the audience of the sessions, sharing a

Laszlo's painting of Florence. Courtesy of the Library of Congress.

passion for the international spectacle and its demonstration of American importance.[44] The meetings finished on February 6, and Florence heard her husband's closing speech; four days later, she would accompany him when he presented the peace treaties to Congress. The Hardings were thrilled with the conference, which led to arms limitation agreements between the United States, Britain, and Japan, as well as France and Italy.[45] Despite her full box that final day of the conference, Florence had missed Evalyn; she boasted to her, "'that man Hadin' didn't do so bad." Evalyn would join her in late March for the Senate vote; Florence would spend "several hours" listening to that debate.[46]

In the meantime, Mrs. Harding could content herself with seeing her friend's baby—Florence's new goddaughter, Emily (later also Evalyn) McLean, and telling Evalyn, then down in Florida, all about it. Florence recalled visiting the baby and her nurse one snowy day, when "Emily was having her airing, all dressed up in pink, lying in her carriage, with the windows all wide open, taking in the good fresh air." Florence had more opportunities to see this girl than her own stepgranddaughter, also a newborn in Marion, and she possibly spent more time with Emily than Evalyn, down in Florida that winter, did.[47]

On February 7, the Hardings hosted another enormous reception, this time for Congressmen, their wives, and friends. With 2,000 in attendance, Florence's right hand in its "long white gloves" soon wore out.[48] Close on the heels of the congressional reception was the dinner for Frederick H. Gillett, the Speaker of the House. The winter social season was at a fever pitch—"Washington is still very gay," she told her daughter-in-law—and it all tired out Florence considerably. She especially missed Evalyn and her advice on invitees. She told Esther, "My days are so full I don't know which way to turn." More visitors had descended on them, she noted: "Stranger, strangers, most of the time—but it's a great life 'if you don't weaken.'" She was glad when Lent finally arrived, allowing for a reprieve and "a little chance to enjoy my friends." She pined to see Evalyn—and was frustrated that the Hardings' planned winter vacation to Florida would now be delayed again.[49] She urged Mac Jennings to visit, as the Scobeys soon would; and she sent Esther her monthly check—but did not mention *her* coming. Esther had had her baby recently, of course, but certainly,

Florence's keenness to be with grandchildren was less pressing than her desire to see her old friends.

Catherine New was one of these very close friends, Mrs. Harding's "most intimate," according to journalist Daisy Ayres. The Hardings saw the News regularly, another sign of their close identification with their old Senate life. Harding had also to deal with the Senate as a whole, so these meetings with old friends from the Hill were often discreetly held: it was the Hardings, "little private, happy, homey time with old chums, that they never let on about," said one paper.[50] Cabinet members were considered more appropriate company for the Hardings.[51] Florence, nevertheless, much looked forward to the Congressional Club breakfast on February 27. This all-female gathering featured a skit, said to be "humorous in the extreme," called "The Mirrors of Washington," about the servants who worked in the capital. In it, two congressional wives put on blackface to pretend they were gossiping about their bosses.[52]

More tastefully, Florence sent her husband flowers on their first anniversary in office. He responded in a note, touched by her concern—he was just getting over an illness. He "hope[d] to see you very shortly to tell you how much pleasure your thought gave me this morning."[53] This anniversary also marked their sixth year in Washington, but the Hardings had not forgotten their hometown roots and Marion's own anniversary: the town was turning a century old. They decided to go that summer, making their first and only trip back home during the presidency. Having heard of the trip, Mary Lee wrote from Westerville, eager for them to visit. By way of an anniversary present, Lee sent maple syrup for the president's favorite breakfast and wrote Warren fulsomely of his wife: "I know of no woman who has so met the expectations and realized the hopes of a nation as she has. . . . No seeking after gallery applause. Just sweet, noble, intelligent womanhood and the people like it. I hope it won't shorten the years too much," she wrote.[54]

Mary Lee's letter had reminded Florence of "the great many experiences that have come into our lives the past year," experiences she appreciated, but still, Florence sighed, she could also count "a great many more gray hairs in my head." Sadly, Florence doubted they'd have enough time for a visit when they were in Ohio. She wasn't even sure if she'd have much time to visit with Lee if she came to D.C. This was a contrast with a year earlier, when she'd urged her friend to come.[55]

With the onset of Lent, the gala evenings were out, and Mrs. Harding took advantage of the respite in the social schedule to take some drives through Washington's parks. This was one of her favorite activities, but despite its essentially private nature, even in her car, she had to think about her clothes.[56] Sometimes she picked people up on these drives, like the disabled soldier she once saw on Sixteenth Street.[57] Visitors continued to come to the White House, of course, no matter the season; on March 7, for instance, they had a few college presidents for dinner, including Harry A. Garfield of Williams College and A. Laurence Lowell of Harvard. The following day, the Hardings finally got away for their long-awaited trip to Florida, where they stayed for a week with their friends. It was a welcome break. Warren looked forward to golf, Florence to relaxing with Evalyn. They enjoyed a boat trip and a visit to St. Augustine on this short trip, as well as some "good bridge" with the Weekses on the way back in the train. Rather than lose, as her husband had expected, Florence ended the game with a "stand off," she proudly told Evalyn.[58]

When they returned, one of their visiting groups included the Ohio DAR. Among the Daughters was Alice Roosevelt Longworth, who enjoyed the crowd's warmth at her witty repartee. As gossip columnist Dolly Madison wrote, "It goes without saying that Mrs. Longworth was the center of attraction," but that was only "until Mrs. Harding . . . came in and joined the party, chatting animatedly with the guests over her own tea cup. . . . the crowd gathered around her, and those on the outskirts were full of admiring comments. She is a gracious, attractive hostess, and she looked as fresh in her afternoon gown of delicate periwinkle blue, as if she had not been on her feet for hours."[59] Alice must have chafed at the competition!

Along with old Ohio friends, the Hardings also hobnobbed with Hollywood stars that month, when D. W. Griffith and the Gish sisters, Lillian and Dorothy, came to the White House.[60] The Hardings liked celebrities and had welcomed them to the Front Porch. The Gishes and Griffith brought the glamour and excitement of the movies, which the Hardings also loved. With warm hugs from the president ("Darling!" he greeted each of them), the sisters spent the day, which featured lunch and beautiful flowers picked by Florence.[61]

Not long after their visit, the first lady invited for tea a young doctor who would become a more permanent member of the White House family, Lieutenant Commander Joel Boone, along with his wife, Suzanne. Dr. Boone was being reassigned from his position as director of the Bureau of Naval Affairs at the American Red Cross to serve as medical officer on the *Mayflower,* so the Hardings had to find him shipshape. They saw right away what a trustworthy and capable man he was. The young doctor was also a highly decorated veteran of World War I who had been commended for his many brave acts in assisting the wounded in makeshift outdoor mobile hospitals from Belleau Wood to the Argonne Forest. Boone would soon be unusually intimate with the Hardings as a result of Florence's fragile medical condition and her husband's more occasional illnesses. He would remain associated with the White House in a medical capacity until the Roosevelt administration.[62] Sawyer, too, had to approve him, and did expeditiously—although later he would resent the younger man's strong appeal to the Hardings and Coolidges.

Around the same time that this valuable doctor joined the White House entourage, another more damaging member was first exposed, when reports surfaced that the secretary of the Interior, Albert Fall, had leased part of the Teapot Dome Reserve in Wyoming to oilmen Harry Sinclair and Edward Doheny with no competitive bidding. Fall's denials of any wrongdoing kept the crisis at bay for a time, although Senator Robert LaFollette spearheaded an investigation with a critical resolution attacking the Interior Department's "sluiceway for . . . corruption" on April 28, 1922.[63] Fall would resign the following January for other reasons, long before the full story came out; when it did, in 1929, he was convicted of accepting nearly $400,000 in bribes from Doheny. The Harding administration's reputation suffered a blow from which it has never recovered, though the president had not known of Fall's schemes.

As spring approached, Florence made it a point to get away for more motoring expeditions in the late afternoons, often with Evalyn, watching the cherry trees and magnolias burst forth. She contributed to the splendor by planting a large magnolia tree on the White House grounds with the aid of actress Lillian Russell.[64] As Florence told her friend Mary Lee in April, "from now on Washington is a pretty nice place to be, hot though it is at times."[65] Florence looked forward to attending an amaryllis show, where a species of the "pure white" flower named after her would be first displayed. She had no lack of namesakes: a New York flower show had named a rose after her, and John Philip Sousa had dedicated a march in Florence's honor, "Keeping Step with the Union."

On April 12, she would be honored yet again by an even larger crowd, 25,000 at the Washington Nationals' season opener, where the home team won, 6-5, against the Yankees. She clapped nonstop. Although her gloves may have suffered from the beating, her head was also at risk from the crowd who by the ninth inning were hurling cushions in excitement at the field. Many were landing on those in the prized lower seats.[66] Florence saw more crowds at the White House a few days later for their second Easter Monday egg roll, and then on the 19th, they hosted the army and navy reception, put off after the Knickerbocker disaster, with 2,498 guests and dancing. Two days later, the DAR brought another 2,200 visitors. Smaller numbers of the Daughters of the War of 1812, the Dames of the Loyal Legion, and the American Pen Women also visited that week. Florence was in her element, entertaining like a celebrity herself.

All the same, she was enthusiastic to make a rapid getaway with friends on April 26, this time for a short trip to the Grant centennial in Point Pleasant, Ohio. This trip, on the War Department tug *Cayuga*, was enlivened by the appearance of a Dickensian stowaway, especially interested in the food—"turkey, hams, enormous cakes, all kinds of sandwiches"—on board. After a quick scolding, Mrs. Harding "petted the boy laughingly and ordered that he be well fed."[67]

Another boy was not so lucky on board the *Island Queen*, the steamer on which the Hardings were supposed to have traveled to the centennial—along with any other ticket holders who wanted to join them—until Starling intervened, fearing their security on such a public tour. He could not stop the *Island Queen* from shadowing them, however, and when the passengers all rushed to one side to gape at the passing presidential party, the *Island Queen*'s upper deck collapsed under their combined weight! A young band player was among the many below crushed by this incident, fortunately not fatally. Made aware of his injury, Florence wrote to him in the hospital and cheered him up immensely: he then "chatted gaily and strummed a gay tune on his cloak of plaster."[68]

When they returned to the White House, Lord and Lady Astor came to visit on April 29, and a fired-up Florence later told her friend Ambassador Harvey that she wanted to take issue with the American-born expatriate lady on "three points." Whether these included her Christian Scientism, her role in the British parliament, or perhaps her support of imperialism, was left unsaid. Florence told Harvey, "I could not forget myself . . . to a stranger within our gates, and so she will never know how near we were to a debate!"[69]

The Hardings took another little jaunt in mid-May, this time to New Jersey, with friends including the Weekses, the McLeans, Sawyer, Daugherty, Frelinghuysen, and Christian. Harding gave some speeches, including a suffrage talk to a woman's group. Their final destination, however, was the Seaview Golf Club, where they had gone the previous September.[70] While the men golfed, Florence and her female friends headed for the beach. Although she no doubt enjoyed the relaxation, getting ready for these trips could be taxing. Florence complained to Esther that "I could go to France with much less trouble than start on a trip like this." But on the whole she was grateful for these breaks. As she told George Christian Sr., her "weekend expeditions save the day for us. We always come back refreshed and it seems to be the only way to escape from interruptions of all kinds."[71]

Shortly after their return, she and Warren went to the circus with Evalyn and Ned as guests of John Ringling, who escorted them across the arena. Florence was thrilled as the crowd roared about her, and interestingly, did not seem to have worried about the animals' treatment; a few weeks later, she enjoyed the National Horse Show as well.[72] She had even more fun on her first cruise of the season on the *Mayflower* with seventy-nine Senate ladies on May 19, with tea, dancing, and music.[73] Three days later, the Hardings hosted their last big formal feast that season, the judicial dinner, and Florence was no doubt beside herself to have Carrie Jacobs Bond, lyricist of her favorite song, "The End of a Perfect Day," as well as the most successful female songwriter of her generation, in the room, accompanying herself on the piano with a baritone and a cellist. A skilled pianist herself, Mrs. Harding very much enjoyed concerts of this kind. Although few have credited her with the cultural tastes of, say, first lady Jackie Kennedy, she often attended musical performances, including engagements of the Philadelphia orchestra or the New York symphony with her friends. Still, compared with the Coolidges' salons, the Hardings were philistines. Mrs. Coolidge seems to have had Sergei Rachmaninoff anytime she wanted him![74]

Despite such cachet, the rumor was that Florence and Warren looked down on the Coolidges. Even though Harding invited Coolidge to attend Cabinet meetings—the first vice president granted this honor—he also called him "the little fellow" and planned to drop him in the next election. Mrs. Harding showed her condescension toward the couple when, according to an oft-repeated story, she declared that there should be no congressional bill passed to allocate funds for them to live in their own house. The proposed home was once owned by a senator from Missouri, John B. Henderson, and known as Henderson Castle. Perhaps its grandiosity was the rub for Florence. According to Nicholas Murray Butler's 1939 recollection, Mrs. Harding said to him, "Not a bit of it, not a bit of it. I am going to have that bill defeated. Do you think I am going to have those Coolidges living in a house like that? An hotel apartment is plenty good enough for them."[75] Despite its delightful pungency, the accuracy of the quote is questionable. Mrs. Harding was generally friendly to Mrs. Coolidge; she was not a snob. She refused to stand on ceremony and shrugged off with humor the occasional moment when Grace was standing on the "wrong side" of her in "precedence."[76] Indeed, Mrs. Harding lived in the Coolidges' hotel herself after leaving the White House.

The first couple ended the month of May with a three-day cruise with friends to Annapolis. They had a grand time, were saluted by a British ship, the HMS *Raleigh*, and saw the navy beat the army, 8–6, at baseball. They returned in time for the dedication of the long-planned Lincoln Memorial on the 30th, joining 100,000 others for a moving ceremony. Supreme Justice Taft chaired the program, and Harding and Dr. Robert Moton, president of Tuskegee Institute, made addresses. Robert Todd Lincoln, Abraham Lincoln's surviving son, was also there.[77] Florence herself had a passion for the sixteenth president and had tried to secure for his White House bedroom as many authentic pieces as she could.

Perhaps her daughter-in-law got to see some of those items when she came to the White House on June 5 to stay for a week. There is no evidence, however, that Esther Mezger was invited to any of the Harding jaunts in early June, including several on the *Mayflower*—Florence doggedly kept her personal life very private, and was gratified, it seems, that her previous life remained mostly unknown. It seems unlikely, for instance, that Esther would have joined a group of congressional wives on a cruise the day after her arrival, or even that she would have gone to Princeton on the 9th for the dedication of a Revolutionary monument and golfing at the Frelinghuysens. She was not mentioned, in any case. Frelinghuysen had the wealth to live on some lovely links, but one critic cracked that he was not as well endowed upstairs; the senator "recognizes that literature has its place, on all four walls of a large room, and bought in sets." Be that as it may, his friend and former Senate colleague, Warren Harding, used this occasion to speak at a place of extremely lofty brows, Wilson's alma mater of Princeton, and pick up an honorary doctor of laws degree there.[78]

On June 24, Florence was delighted by the visit of a female delegation from the Philippine Parliamentary Mission, even if she did not necessarily agree with their goal of seeking independence for their country. The newspapers were mostly interested in the "native costumes" of the "pretty ladies" in the party, including Mrs. Jaime C. DeVeyra, wife of the Filipino delegate to Congress. Whether Mrs. DeVeyra appreciated being seen as a "native" while she was seeking independence was not recorded. Certainly Florence enjoyed hosting these women and having pictures taken with them on tour.[79]

STYLE AND CLOTHES

The visit of the Filipino women was just what Florence loved about her White House duties, offering her the chance to be both the gracious hostess and to be engaged in issues. As she would tell reporters the following summer, "It's a fascinating game, this being a President's wife. Hard work, but I love it."[80] This was about as much as she would say on the subject for the record, since she refrained from giving interviews at the White House, despite her affinity for journalists of all sexes. She was happy to talk to reporters but insisted they "please don't quote me," since "I do not want to embarrass the president, and something I might say could be twisted to hurt him or his friends." But as she well pointed out, even without

Florence being photographed with Filipino guests.
Courtesy of the Library of Congress.

interviews, she provided "plenty of 'copy.'" She certainly met with reporters regularly, published letters in major newspapers, and appeared in newsreels and thousands of photographs with and without her husband, and in this way "engaged in some unorthodox behaviors for first ladies."[81] Still, not everyone was happy with her approach. Journalist Marcia Forbes complained, "Any attempt to get information about national or personal matters" went nowhere; "all you get is a lovely smile."[82] Florence, an old hand at the newspaper business, well knew what to say—or more accurately, what *not* to say, when journalists were near, as a *New York Times* columnist noted.[83] She was so skillful that at her death, her hometown newspaper spoke approvingly of her "aversion to publicity."[84]

But just as the Filipino women must have, Florence too could not have helped noticing that often, all the press cared about was her clothes. Sometimes their attentions were insulting. At one reception, a columnist clucked that Florence's dress "suggested the modes of about a decade ago," and where was her fan? Yet at the Supreme Court dinner, another paper declared that if her black-and-white dress was made of a "heavy creamy white satin . . . which would stand along in our grandmother's day," she still wore it in an updated way, "supple and clinging . . . in the new draped effect."[85] They noticed her jewelry, to the extent she must have felt like a pincushion: "her décolletage is filled in with pearl embroidered tulle," one paper reported, as were her sleeves; accented with "silver slippers, with rhinestone buckles, and . . . jeweled pins in her beautifully coiffured hair." She was likely gratified that someone noticed at least that "she is not given to boudoir caps and frizzly hair with a curl paper showing here and there."[86]

According to the unsentimental Mrs. Jaffray, Florence Harding was "the best dressed First Lady of the Land." Even compared with Martha Washington and Dolley Madison? Perhaps this was a way for Jaffray to snipe at Edith Wilson![87] But the housekeeper had a point. Despite later reports of her as "sexless," Florence could look quite "chic"—and indeed, the attention paid to her clothes was in large part her own choice because she made herself and her parties accessible to the society journalists and their scrutiny. Her care in saving their articles shows that she relished this attention, most of the time. She put care into her outfits, feeding the curiosity of the public and sustaining the celebrity culture of the decade. On one occasion, she wore this confection: a dress of "sparkling white sequins in an elaborate massed pattern," topped with a "luxurious evening wrap from . . . finest Russian ermine . . . with collar and cuffs of white fox, trimmed with ermine tails and lined with white roman crepe over Harding Blue chiffon velvet." But because of her animal rights consciousness, there would be no peacock feathers for her![88] Florence had an abundance of accessories, far more than any "need" dictated. Her gloves came in many styles: lavender kid, pearl, jabot, rhinestone, and long black-and-tan suede ones. She had numerous hair veils too, black and white, and party bags. She had many, many shoes, from white lace high boots to bronze slippers to black jet buckled heels. Underneath it all were crepe de chine corset covers and itchy Scotch wool ones.

Then and now, one of the chief desiderata of an active social life is the proper attire, and Florence knew this. With the social obligations to set for the entire country and an increasing sense that she too was a celebrity, she had to accumulate a vast wardrobe. Nevertheless, she claimed she cared little for clothes "or styles."[89] Certainly, had she wished to snub convention, as Lou Henry Hoover did, she could have shunned the frill and frippery. But she lacked Mrs. Hoover's confidence to comfortably shrug at such things, and no doubt felt it proper, owing to her very public presence, to give the people the kind of first lady they "expected" and wanted to see. More than that, she enjoyed the attention. Still, she had mixed feelings; she liked looking good, but she also found all the changes a great bother. "How I hate clothes and how I have to be dressed up most of the time," Florence complained to Esther, who might have had a hard time relating to this problem. "It seems I have to spend half of my time changing my clothes," she added, yet she remembered that she once had thought this would be glamorous: "Strange how one always wants to be doing the 'other thing.'" And the quantities needed were daunting: "about the time I get my winter duds in order I find spring has arrived."[90]

During her first fall season in the White House, she wrote her daughter-in-law, "You have no idea how many [clothes] I have to have[,] especially evening things. Many a day I change from three to four times a day—So does Mr. Harding. My big dinners are coming fast now."[91] Esther could be forgiven for not feeling properly sorry for her. The clothes prevented Florence from doing more for her grandchildren, after all. When she sent $50 toward Jean's summer camp in 1922, the first lady lamented her financial limitations. Her excuse was the cost of her wardrobe; she had to "look my best" to meet the people's expectations of this most visible first lady.[92] With couture coming directly from Paris (she did find its fashions irresistible, after all) and New York to the White House, they were not cheap. When an old friend complained that his suit had cost $160, Florence jested, "Don't let a thing like that worry you. . . . I've got on $800 worth today, myself."[93] Indeed, bills for garments purchased in

May 1922, for instance, include $150 for a gown from Nickson Inc., and another $150 for a dress from Stein and Blaine.[94] These last two would be well over $1,000 in today's dollars, each.

As first lady, Florence had little time to shop on her own. Instead, designers, importers, and friends brought her clothes to the White House.[95] And Mrs. Beatrice Fletcher, her friend and the wife of the ambassador to Belgium, ordered clothes from Paris direct, but this had its risks: the sizes might not fit.[96] Evalyn sent her clothes as well, from posh shops in Palm Beach. A package from her dear friend could send Florence into raptures. "Oh, Evalyn, I wish you could have been here when I opened that wonderful box. I think I shall wear one gown to the Speaker's dinner—the others I shall await your coming . . . because I want your opinion on one of them particularly. And say, Evalyn, that wrap—well it is so wonderful that it beggars description."[97]

Fortunately, she was a wealthy woman for her day, thanks to her inheritance and savvy stock purchases, so the dressing up was not a hardship. The Hardings continued to receive their dividends as president and first lady, and unlike today, when officials in their position are obliged to put their money in a blind trust, they knew where their money was coming from and were friendly with its sources, like the Wrigleys.[98]

Like them or not, it was hard for Florence to avoid a focus on clothes when no matter what women were meeting about—politics, civic affairs, welfare, literary subjects, charities—it was their dress that demanded attention.[99] Noted the *New York Herald,* "Oh, but I can almost hear your reproach that I haven't told you what Mrs. Harding had on for her one appearance at the horse show. Nothing very revolutionary." And a visit of French diplomat Marshall Joffre to the White House was once again an occasion to remark on her dress: "Mrs. Harding's gown was one that any woman would have looked at twice," said one column, it was " 'Harding' blue—a strong, rather bright blue."[100] First ladies, and first lady hopefuls, are still defined by their dress. In 2008, Michelle Obama's striking purple sheath, which she wore the evening her husband, Barack Obama, claimed the Democratic nomination, got almost as much attention as a defining hue of their potential administration as did the tenor of her husband's speech.[101]

With all this fuss about clothes, it was a relief for Florence that she no longer had to worry about Warren's as she once had to in Columbus. Major Arthur Brooks, valet to every president since McKinley, was "the final arbiter in matters of dress and social adornment to the President."[102] As we will see below, he was instrumental in foiling wardrobe malfunctions.

The attention paid to Florence's clothes, hair, and makeup was not entirely her doing—women have long faced obsessive attention to their clothes—but there seems little doubt that she cultivated this attention as well, even when she did not enjoy the necessary fuss and expense. She did so because she anticipated that her look was important to the public; she was a celebrity, not unlike the Gish sisters. Florence was no movie star, of course, but her visibility—generated by the Hardings' willingness to open the grounds, to meet so many people personally, and to maintain their close relationship with the press—made them both accessible to a much wider public than their predecessors. People saw her in the newspaper, in movie theaters on newsreels, and if they came to Washington, they had an excellent chance of shaking her hand. Conscious of this prominence, if not of her pioneering legacy, Florence played a starring role.

CAUSES AND CONCERNS

More lasting as a legacy of Florence than her attire was her advocacy. She was closely concerned with her husband's business, and she was an especially strong activist for those who could not speak easily for themselves. Among her causes were the comfort and assistance of disabled veterans, the protection of animals, and the promotion of humane conditions for female prisoners.[103] Indeed, she was deeply concerned about women, incarcerated or not. She was also passionately interested in foreign affairs, as demonstrated by her effective pressuring of her husband to remain aloof from the League of Nations (not that he needed much convincing) and her close interest in the progress of the Washington naval conference of 1921–1922.[104]

Florence's strong convictions about women's political agency were influential here. The aftermath of suffrage presented a brief but golden opportunity for women activists, and growing numbers of them gained regular access to the executive branch. Florence saw this as an exciting turn, and she urged women to become engaged in political life, as she was.

Disabled Veterans

Mrs. Harding was passionate about supporting the wounded veterans of the world war. She realized how quickly they had been forgotten in the rush back to "normalcy," but she was even more motivated by something closer to home: "My own illness has been so trying that I have great sympathy and understanding with those who have to experience suffering," she reflected. She went often to Walter Reed Army Hospital, with its numerous wards of disabled vets, and sent flowers weekly to veterans' hospitals, recalling, "I was in a hospital for eight months with an open wound that had to be dressed twice a day, and I know what hospital life means to a patient."[105] Her sympathy for the war's victims did not extend to support of a bonus for all veterans in general; she agreed with her husband on vetoing the bonus because it appeared to threaten sound fiscal policy. Nevertheless, where the disabled were concerned, she was always moved to assist.[106] Less publicly, she also supported the Cincinnati Tuberculosis Sanitarium in memory of her son.

She invited veterans to the White House for parties each summer, visited them regularly at their hospitals and homes, and sought out their creative work.[107] In May 1922, she joined Lou Hoover and Mrs. Geddes, the British ambassador's wife, at Mt. Alto, where they hosted a garden party for the veterans. Many of them came "in their chairs"; some of these disabled men were blind, too, and some had wives and babies to take care of.[108] The following month, she brought 1,340 of these veterans to a garden party at the White House, where they met General Pershing, the Coolidges, and Teddy Roosevelt Jr.[109] Young Teddy was impressed with the kindness of the Hardings in this effort, and the soldiers' appreciation.[110] The "chair cases," along with the ambulatory soldiers, were showered with music, roses, handshakes, and refreshments under "brightly striped marquees."[111] The men ate ice cream and chatted with young women from the Veterans Bureau. When Florence couldn't fit her signature on their admission cards, she got their addresses and promised to send her autograph along. She allowed the blind veterans to feel her face, jewelry, and clothes.

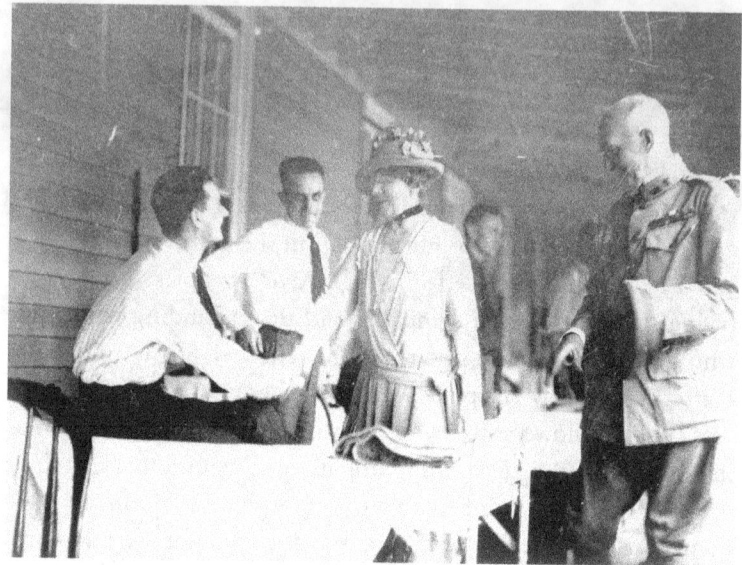

Florence Harding visits a disabled veteran. Courtesy of the Library of Congress.

Her sympathies were not confined to veterans of the Great War. She hosted aging Confederate veterans and staff from the Jefferson Davis Confederate Veterans' home, despite her strong Republican background. And she did more than lift morale. Florence attempted to intervene on behalf of aggrieved veterans too. Just two weeks into the administration, she wrote Secretary John Weeks, asking him to consider an honorable discharge for a soldier who had been, she thought, peremptorily imprisoned for deserting, when he had had a solid record of two years' service in the war. She gently ribbed Weeks that she was giving him "a warning that if you are amiably disposed in helping me handle such troubles as this, I shall take occasion to send more."[112]

Her concern for veterans was well known. Watchmen at the patent office, complaining of new management rules that were compelling them to stand for eight hours a day, pointed out to her in an appeal that some of the men were crippled war veterans.[113] With the first lady's sympathies in mind, Stella Marks at the Veterans Bureau asked if Florence would mind lending her name to a seaside cottage that would serve as a retreat for the "boys" at Walter Reed. Florence thought that was just fine.[114]

Pleas for financial assistance got less of her sympathy, such as the request from Civil War widow Mrs. Elizabeth Noblett of Detroit for a hike in her monthly pension from $30 to $50 for the "very short time" she had left after spending much of her life in a vain attempt to save her husband's, a victim of the Andersonville prison. Florence assured her that Congress was looking into such matters, but "it would be a very unseemly thing for the wife of the President to . . . recommend to the Congress what its duty is in matters of legislation." But she did exactly that when she thought the cause meritorious, of course—as with the Mt. Weather prison for women. Mrs. Noblett probably didn't appreciate hearing Florence lecture her that Congress was already busy dealing with the claims of World War I veterans who also "crave more assistance."[115] Indeed, one of these wives of the recent wounded, Mrs. A. A. Carter, wanted more than her $95 per month allotment while her husband was in the hospital. Florence had supported Mrs. Carter's initial appeal, which presumably had helped her obtain the $95, but now felt uncomfortable lobbying more on her behalf: "I must ask you to excuse me from further appeal, where I really had no right to interfere." According to Florence, her husband did not issue executive orders to enhance pensions.[116]

Her interest in veterans' affairs led her to tour Walter Reed with Colonel Forbes, head of the Veterans Bureau, in July 1922, but she picked up as yet no inkling of Forbes's kleptomania. She might have been more attentive because reports were already circulating about abuses in the hospitals. For instance, 3,500 mentally ill vets were said to be sleeping on the floor, "like cattle," while their hospitals were making a $300 profit on each one of them.[117]

While Forbes remained unhampered in his greed, the administration of veterans benefits was already haunting Dr. Sawyer, the chief coordinator of the Federal Bureau of Hospitalization, who was hearing a number of these negative reports. Sawyer had other problems as well. He had received an appointment as a brigadier general in the Officers' Reserve Corps "to give him an official status," and was then assigned his new post at the bureau. But of course he was no military man; he was Harding's friend, and this became a weakness and an increasing distraction. In August 1922, the American Legion demanded he step down from his post because his White House priorities were leading to his neglect of the overcrowded conditions, they alleged, assuring "hundred of chronic insane" veterans rather than "cured and useful citizens."[118] Sawyer also became the target of furious veterans upset at Harding's opposition to their bonus. With information coming out about how well both labor and business had been compensated during the war, and with a sharp postwar depression lingering, veterans groups were "aggressive, almost savage" in their demands, Boone noted. For the old doctor, the attacks were "scarring."[119] Veteran activists continued to be critical of the Harding administration, especially after Forbes's scandalous thefts were exposed in 1923. In 1924, Congress finally passed a bonus for the veterans over President Coolidge's veto, to become due in 1945. It was this promised sum that served as the impetus for the bonus march of 1932, when 15,000 men marched on Washington demanding payment without delay.

Animals

Florence avoided such controversies in her ministrations to the suffering veterans. Similarly, she also won plaudits for her work on behalf of another underprivileged group: animals. She was "militant" in her concern for them.[120] Humane groups knew they could count on Florence's regular assistance and endorsement for their activities, special weeks, and benefits.[121] After all, she said, "I long to see societies organized all over the country for this purpose, and to have these principles taught children in the schools."[122] She even made sure that the animals lost in the war, including mules and horses, were not forgotten—she attended a tree-planting ceremony in their honor in October 1921.

Laddie Boy also did good work on behalf of his furry friends, attending bridge parties for the benefit of the Animal Rescue League. Laddie, of course, was not just any dog. He was the White House Airedale, and had a special pedigree; he was the son of champion Tintern Tip Top of Toledo.[123] Although Florence loved pets, and she and Warren had had a series of dogs and horses, she told an interviewer that she just couldn't have another pet after Laddie. "I love them so much that I can't give them up and if anything happens to them, it just makes me sick."[124]

For her, animal protection trumped any brief pleasures enjoyed by others at the creatures' expense, in similar fashion to those today who shame friends who eat veal or foie gras. She wrote Evalyn a little sheepishly about her outspoken criticism at a rodeo performance they'd attended in May 1922: "I hope you did not think me too abrupt about the wild west show.... I fear I am apt to be a little too emphatic." Still, while Evalyn had assured her that cowboys "really love" their horses, Florence could only think of the animals' fright.

Her passion for pets affected her husband as well, who intervened to stop the shooting of Dick, a St. Bernard–mastiff mix belonging to Russian immigrant Jacob Silverman of Lansdale, Pennsylvania. His owner was an "alien" and thus not permitted to own a dog, according to Pennsylvania law. Florence urged Warren to prevail upon Governor William Cameron Sproul, a family friend, to prevent this travesty. The newspapers loved the story, and Dick lived—only not with Mr. Silverman, who had to get his citizenship first.[125] Florence also helped keep a dying horse, fifty-one-year-old Clover, from going to the knackers. His owner, a poor preacher, had sought help to keep the horse alive, a "noble struggle," according to Florence, who said she was "deeply moved" by the "sacrifice" the preacher was making. She sent him $100. This proved an embarrassment for her, however; cartoons made hay of this generous subsidy for a horse when railroad workers, among others, were being asked to take a pay cut.[126] Her love for animals also got her an offer of a German police dog direct from the Argonne Forest. It is not recorded that Laddie Boy ever kept company with this war refugee.[127]

Florence worried, too, about creatures farther from home. She was particularly upset to learn that seals off La Jolla, California, were being killed by fishermen because they ate desirable species of fish. She decided to do something about it, and she wrote wildlife commissioner Henry O'Malley in order to know the particulars so she could "make intelligent reply" to these fishermen, adding "it is difficult for me to believe that the protection of the fish requires the sacrifice of these seals."[128] Apparently, she was less worried that one way or another, the fish were not going to be protected, but eaten!

Federal Prison for Women

One of the most important struggles that Florence joined was the attempt to build a federal prison for women. This was the first time that she actively tried to influence policy, as opposed to simply lending her support. Her sister-in-law, Carolyn, was instrumental in sparking her activism here, and she appealed to the first lady to press her influence in passing legislation, HR 13927, for this "urgent need," writing, "I will appreciate deeply the help you may be able to give in securing its early consideration by the House of Representatives."[129] As this effort shows, Mrs. Harding was considered a first lady of some political power.

The prison drew Florence's strong enthusiasm because it tied together the differing strands of her political outlook, including her progressive values, her concern for women's rights, and her humanitarianism. Many women's groups were involved in the effort, from the DAR to the League of Women Voters to the American Association of Collegiate Alumnae. In the early 1920s, there was as yet no adequate federal prison dedicated to female inmates outside California, and the conversion of an existing former weather observatory near Bluemont, Virginia, offered an attractively priced means of creating one. For about $125,000, backers had learned, such a prison could open within months, with a hospital attached (because "a considerable percent are infested with one or more venereal diseases"). It would not be for "hardened offenders"—they would continue to go to the inferior state institutions—but instead would be designed for those female felons with "most hope for successful rehabilitation."[130] Although the local community supported the idea, as did the judiciary committees of both houses of Congress, the area's congressman, Robert Walton Moore (D-Va.), was holding up progress owing to the complaints of "six summer residents . . . one of them being a cousin of Mr. Moore," according to Mrs. Harding's source.[131]

The bill did not pass during the short-lived Harding administration, but thanks to Florence's efforts, and those of other activists like Eleanor Roosevelt, Alderson Federal Prison Camp was established in 1927 in Alderson, West Virginia, and still operates today. A recent inmate was Martha Stewart, whose moniker for it, "Camp Cupcake," recalled Florence's humanitarian ideals.

Women

As her efforts on behalf of the prison show, Florence cared deeply about women's rights. She was, indeed, in many ways a feminist: she always used her maiden name, she worked full-time in her husband's business, and she was for a time a working single mother. She was enthusiastic that women's roles had "greatly changed even in my own generation," and she was eager to see all young girls being prepared for these roles by developing their physical capacity in such groups as the Campfire Girls and the Girl Scouts.

She was especially thrilled that women were politically active, not only as advocates for change, as they had been in the Progressive Era, but also now genuinely influential, both by voting and being elected to office. As she affirmed, "I am always anxious to know what the women are thinking and the President is ever eager to be responsive to their wishes whenever it is consistently possible."[132] She strongly agreed with Mrs. James D. Tillinghast of the Republican Women of Massachusetts "about the importance of [organizing] work among the women, . . . [women] *are* in politics, and it is their duty to make their participation effective and of real service to their country." Nevertheless, she showed some doubts about the commitment of her sex, noting "much and aggressive work is needed to maintain their interest."[133]

In the immediate wake of suffrage, Florence was all in favor of women being directly involved in party affairs, favoring the idea of her friend Mrs. George H. Lorimer, wife of the editor of the *Saturday Evening Post,* who wanted to activate a network of organizations of Republican women in her home state of Pennsylvania. Florence believed that women, with their "training" in benevolent and philanthropic enterprises, were suited for "a part in political affairs which need be in no wise subordinate to that of men." Of course, she hoped women would get involved through the Republican Party; she had little faith in such groups as the National Women's Party, which she opposed for what she saw as its narrow "species of political solidarity among the women."[134] She would have argued that the Republicans, having supported suffrage more consistently than the Democrats, were the party worthy of women's support, although they did not support the ERA, as the NWP did.

Putting teeth into her statements for women's partisan activism, Florence planned to attend a luncheon hosted by the National Republican Club at the New York Biltmore in January 1922, along with 1,000 other women, at the invitation of Mrs. Arthur Livermore of the club's executive committee. It would be "one of the few occasions on which she has attended any women's political affair since she became the first lady," papers pointed out.[135] But she did not attend, cancelling at nearly the last minute. It was, of course, the height of the Washington social season, and she had reason to be overcome with exhaustion.

As she told Mrs. Livermore apologetically, "the strain of the last few days, culminating in the Diplomatic reception last night," had worn her out. "The stress of these recent duties, and the imminence of others hardly less demanding, compels me to beg the Club to excuse me," she wrote. She was very disappointed; she had wanted so much "the opportunity to express to you my hearty sympathy and appreciation for the splendid work your organization is doing."[136] The *Washington Herald* speculated convincingly, though, that there might be another reason: her attendance "would have established a precedent which might have proved embarrassing."[137] If she had come to New York's gathering, how could she turn down others? Florence telegraphed Ruth Hanna McCormick, wife of Senator Medill McCormick (R-Ill.), something very much along these lines: "my common sense tells me that I would do more harm than good (stop) So please leave me out of the plan without overlooking the fact that I . . . appreciate the really magnificent work that you are doing."[138] Florence was a pioneer in her activism, but she could not be reckless. Mrs. Coolidge went in her stead, and, always more circumspect than Mrs. Harding even when she was first lady, was careful to keep her own counsel at the affair.

Although she did not attend, Florence nevertheless eagerly embraced the issues at hand. She was a long activist in politics, having played a key role in her husband's campaigns, and she did not shrink at expressing her views and her party loyalties. She wrote a three-page letter to the club to be read to the assembled ladies, "believed to be the first political document ever issued by the wife of a President of the United States."[139] She made a strong pitch for party involvement: "If I did not feel that the nation could, and in the long run must, be served through parties I would not be a partisan Republican." And she made the usual nods to "organization, education, and advancement" of causes among the women.[140]

Although Florence did not attend the meeting, her interest in this group's work, and the publicity that her activist role generated, underlines not only her concern for women's political agency, but also her position as a transitional first lady. She had no qualms about being visible where her beloved party, and its women, were concerned. The National Republican Club women, in turn, responded with enthusiasm to her, taking up Mrs. Harding's call for partisanship and bashing the nonpartisan League of Women Voters, the newly formed successor to the National American Woman Suffrage Association. "No man [sic] can serve two masters," partisan and nonpartisan, declared the only congresswoman in attendance, Alice G. Robertson (R-Okla). For Ruth Hanna McCormick, a former member of NAWSA herself who had tried to stop the formation of the league in Illinois, "The time is passed now for a separate women's organization," whether LWV or NWP. She declared, "we have no need in this country to draw the sex line. The parties here are open to us and it is incumbent upon us to prove that we do not lack decision as individuals." Another woman, Mrs. John T. Adams, wife of the chairman of the Republican National Committee, asserted, "there is about as much logic in women forming a political party . . . as there would be in having the green-eyed, the red-haired, or the bald-headed people set themselves up as a political party."[141] But one difficulty with this rigid pro-partisan stance on the league was that it risked driving out progressives from the Republican ranks who favored the league's work—women like Mrs. Harriet Taylor Upton, vice chairman of the Republican Executive Committee and a friend of Florence's, who had worked with the league on social reform and other pressing issues.[142] Florence did not entirely reject the organization. She welcomed an LWV delegation at the White House in March, when they met with the Pan American Conference of Women.[143]

Nor did Warren G. Harding refuse to assist the group. Republican women were furious to learn later that he had lent the league a "helping hand" by laying the cornerstone of their new building in Washington, "on a par with a policeman's hob-nobbing with a gun man," Mrs. Charles E. Broomfield spluttered, again questioning how one could be both a partisan Republican and nonpartisan together? Florence assured her that "an embarrassed" president remained committed to "his position that women's highest usefulness may be exercised within the political parties."[144]

Yet the partisan approach overlooked an even more important consideration. The Republican Party was not ready for an influx of women activists and placeholders—and neither was its rival. In early 1923, with only a year or so to go before the primaries, Florence's Youngstown friend, Mrs. David Todd, grew concerned that no women were yet on the Republican National Committee, and Florence reminded her that only at the 1924 convention could a new slate of members be named at the states' recommendations. Women's "entrance . . . in the political world was so sudden we must be willing to bide our time a little."[145] The biding was not so short as she had hoped. Much of the political process on the federal and state levels remained a male bastion for decades, and not until 2008 was a woman a strong contender for nomination for president in either party. Of course, there were exceptions, like Oklahoma's congresswoman, Alice G. Robertson. But likely many women were turned off by party politics. The Republican-controlled House was a less than inspiring sight in the early 1920s: "Congress is absolutely discredited. Lack of leadership, lack of discipline, lack of vision and the total inability to institute or adhere to a constructive program have been obvious and fatal to party prestige," Mack Jennings noted. Even Harding's friends, New and Frelinghuysen, were "powerless," he pointed out.[146]

Although Mrs. Harding did not travel to New York, the Pennsylvania Republican Women's Club hoped she would come to their meeting in April 1922. Mrs. Lorimer's connections with the 2.25 million readers of the *Saturday Evening Post,* and Mrs. Barclay Warburton's with the large John Wanamaker department store, were certainly inducements, but Florence wasn't coming. Not only did she want to avoid setting this sort of "precedent" again, but the Philadelphia society dames were feuding.[147] Still, Florence was happy to publicize the success of these women, speaking about the accomplishments of their organization for the newspapers.[148] And behind the scenes, her advice and input were much sought after.[149] When Florence learned in 1922 that an Ohio women's group had named her woman of the day, she took some time to reflect on what this meant, and though it is unclear she ever sent her drafted response, her sentiments reveal the nature of her feminist views. She wondered whether she was "entitled" to be "woman of the day," since she had "certain ideas about the relations of women to society and particularly to its economic organization, which some people perhaps do not regard as entirely up-to-date."[150] She did not object to the "so called woman movement," she stressed, but nonetheless she thought it would be better off with "conservative influences." She professed herself a conservative, if a "moderate" one. Such views might make it seem, she knew, that she shunned "controversy" and held back from setting an example "for American femininity."[151] But she happily looked to others to set this example: "I have such great faith in the women of America that I think it is through them that order will come about after the chaotic condition . . . of the war."[152] Despite her demurrals, she was no namby-pamby—no stranger to controversy; she held her views passionately. She did not, however, seek to force them on others without careful deliberation, knowing the weight of her position and not wishing to take undue advantage of it unless she thought the cause merited such influence.

On the issue of women's economic equality, she was unequivocally in favor, though she believed that "one 'career' is as many as a single family should undertake." Perhaps, as customary, she noted, it would be the husband's, and the wife would "merge" hers into his, as Florence had done. But it could also be the wife's, as she was sure in the future it would be "in an increasing proportion of cases," when "with no sacrifice of self-respect or of recognition by the community," the husband could "permit himself to be the less prominent and distinguished member of the combination." She urged that a "woman who has some special talent or capacity . . . in literature, or in science, or in art," should be supported and enabled to develop her talents. There should not be a trade-off, marriage *or* career. To her, women, even "genius" ones, should enjoy a "rounded and satisfactory life." Madame Curie, for instance, was such an example. She and her husband, like George Eliot and Mr. Lewes, had the kind of exemplary relationship Florence extolled. In the case of George Eliot, she "was the great genius of that combination . . . but . . . her genius would never have bloomed . . . had it not been for the inspiration which she derived from her husband's companionship," Florence aptly noted.[153]

Favors

Besides her work on behalf of women, veterans, and animals, Florence faced constant pressure to assist people with help from the government. Marionites, for instance, importuned her for jobs. She had to turn them down, mostly, although she might contact a congressman on their behalf, especially if an ex-soldier was involved.[154] Her husband had to think of "other localities," she pointed out.[155] Laura Harlan informed supplicants, moreover, that such recommendations could get Florence "mixed up in political entanglements."[156]

All the same, good old friends, like Mary Lee, especially counted on Florence for help. In May 1921, Lee was pursuing two jobs, one as state librarian, another as a local postmistress. Florence liked the idea of her friend becoming a librarian; she wrote that it would "give you [the opportunity] to get sound conservative literature before schools and clubs," and she urged her friend to "go ahead."[157] All the same, she had to remind her that Warren could not press anything on the Ohio governor, though he could put in a good word. A year later, when Lee thought of working in Washington, Harding offered her a position in the Department of Commerce at $1,800 a year, with the promise of a quick raise to $3,000.[158]

Many believed Florence could also effect federal appointments. Federal Prohibition Director J. E. Russell wrote her regarding the posting of Alfred A. King of Lorain, Ohio, to be a Prohibition agent, urging her to have her secretary call on one of the federal Prohibition commissioners in support of King's appointment.[159] In another case, Mary C. Wiggin, of the Joint Committee on Industrial Conditions for Women and Children in Massachusetts, called on Florence to see that Miss Mary Anderson was reappointed as director of the Women's Bureau of the Labor Department, again with the assumption that Florence had the ability to do this. The first lady wrote back encouragingly, in this case: "You may be sure of my interest in the betterment of conditions among women in all departments of industry.... I will be pleased to call the President's attention to what you have said."[160]

Florence also helped her husband find suitable people for positions; thus, in June 1922, she asked old friend Nicholas Murray Butler to help identify "the best possible" man for the position as Collector of the Port of New York. He recommended Lafayette B. Gleason, a Yale graduate, an "admirable lawyer" and "a warm personal friend of mine."[161] Charles Dewey Hilles of the Republican National Committee also wrote Florence about "our talk on the subject of the head of the Federal Reserve System" and gave her some names.[162] Florence's influence in shaping the administration's personnel was not negligible.

In addition to making efforts to assist such already advantaged persons as Mr. Gleason, Florence was "always pleased to take an interest in the unfortunate," as she affirmed, and she regularly used her power to intervene on their behalf. She had an especially soft spot for young men in trouble—which perhaps had led to her marriage to DeWolfe long before! Thus, she defended Winfield Scott Walters, in prison at Eastern State Penitentiary on larceny charges, who had had the temerity to send her a gift package via his sister in Atlantic City, which was "contrary to the regulations." Florence wanted him not to have to serve additional time for this infraction.[163] She also helped a young man return to France who was being held in Blackwell's Island in New York for cadging a free meal and was in the midst of serving a two-and-a-half-year sentence for this. Florence personally paid $103 for his return home.[164] She also wrote the governor of Georgia about a former caddy who was now in a state prison and who had written her for help; she hoped, if he had been "sufficiently punished," that he might then be pardoned.[165] Although many know of first lady Eleanor Roosevelt's efforts on behalf of African Americans and others mistreated in the U.S. judicial system during her husband's administration, few are aware that Florence Harding also intervened with the Justice Department for the same purpose. In the summer of 1922, she attempted to stop the execution of Ephram High of Bibb County, Alabama, for stealing $59. Just as Mrs. Roosevelt often was, Florence too was unsuccessful in this effort. Harry Daugherty informed Florence that the federal government had no jurisdiction in the case, and the Alabama statutes did indeed permit "death" as a punishment for robbery.[166] In another case, the first lady was more successful. She pressed Daugherty's office to review the evidence in a West Virginia post office robbery case that had led to sentencing a group of boys (the youngest was just seven) to five years of penal servitude. Her efforts led to her husband's pardon of three of the boys. An investigation showed that not only had third-degree methods had been used to "wr[i]ng" out their confessions, but also the chief evidence against them was supplied by a pack of bloodhounds who followed a trail to a steelworkers' camp in the woods. Dog lover that she was, Florence was rightly skeptical of relying on such methods.[167] Florence also tried to save the life of a woman, Mrs. Hattie Dixon, who was sentenced to be electrocuted in New York in June 1921. A judicial official told her that "careful thought will be given to" her statements.[168]

At Lee's request, Florence also intervened to help the Kohns, a Jewish family who were attempting to bring a relative to the United States despite a filled quota. Still, Florence revealed her stereotypical views of Mrs. Kohn by feeling the need to introduce an irrelevant detail, her "soft and pleasant" voice.[169] While Jews faced difficulties in Europe, others were struggling in Marion, including a man who had lost his job at the Huber steam shovel company. Florence wrote a friend in Marion to see if he could hire this unfortunate fellow.[170] Farmers throughout the country were in particularly bad shape in the early 1920s, and Florence heard about that too. She wrote Mrs. Brink of Warren, Ohio, of her concern, assuring her that the president keenly felt his responsibility "to do everything in his power" to alleviate these conditions. She added, rather gratuitously, "you may be sure that suffering and misfortune have not come to any single class of people . . . the men entrusted with National leadership and responsibility are not blind to these things." Still, considering her husband's difficulties with Congress, it is questionable that she truly believed legislators "are working, sincerely, earnestly, devotedly" on the farmers' problems.[171] She couldn't help everybody, of course. Sometimes she claimed not to be "sufficiently informed"; other times it was "an impropriety" for her to act.[172] Assistance was needed in many quarters. In January 1922, a delegation of West Virginia members of the United Mine Workers, along with a miner's widow named Alice Underwood, came to see the president to complain about the lack of work and frequent evictions that union members faced, a prelude to that summer's coal strike. Mrs. Underwood brought her two girls with her, Dorothy and Hallie, aged ten and twelve, respectively, and told Harding that she had two sons blacklisted for union activity—they couldn't even get highway jobs. They, along with her other four children, lacked food and clothes. The president gave Hallie a $5 bill to buy "candy and nicies" and told Underwood and her committee to confer with Davis, the Department of Labor secretary, about the "alleged blacklist," but later strife suggests that little improvement occurred for the struggling miners.[173]

Florence did her part to help other poor people in the South. For their wedding—perhaps the most glorious to take place during the Harding years—Florence gave Miss Catherine Hughes (daughter of the secretary of state) and Mr. Chauncey Lockhart Waddell beautifully designed muslin bedspreads made by women from North Carolina's mountains who were in a cooperative called the Southern Industrial Association, which assisted these isolated women to sell their work. Florence was the charity's honorary president.

Florence did not get involved in all causes. Although she and Warren sponsored a child from war-torn Armenia, she would not lend her assistance to Near East Relief in general, despite the difficult conditions there.[174] Owing to her "personal situation" as first lady, she pointed out, her involvement would only lead to "embarrassment . . . on consideration of the various diplomatic and international aspects which are involved," she told the relief agency.[175] Florence also would not lend her support to an antismoking campaign. Miss Harlan wrote Louise H. Rumpf, an antinicotine activist from Evansville, Indiana, that although "Mrs. Harding does not smoke and does not commend it, . . . she knows a goodly number of people do." She was supportive of Miss Rumpf's "motives," but the Hardings could not possibly join all the associations that asked them to. Of course, Harding himself chewed tobacco freely, but that emitted no smoke![176]

LAST SUMMER IN THE WHITE HOUSE

Nineteen twenty-two would be a hard summer for the Hardings, who were stuck in Washington for most of it, although they had earlier hoped to make it their summer for an Alaskan trip. With a railroad strike and a coal strike underway, they did not think it prudent to leave, except for some short *Mayflower* jaunts and a few other getaways. There were three such river trips in June, two of which included her old friends, the congressional wives. The Cabinet was mostly gone, though, as Washington's steamy season approached, and the diplomatic corps too—so at least there was less entertaining.[177]

Railway shopmen were on strike in protest of a wage cut, and eventually nearly half a million men walked off the job. The railroads hired strikebreakers, yet even though train operators and conductors remained on duty, the lack of machinists and other shop workers led to dire conditions by the end of July. Florence, who lived and breathed her husband's job, could not separate herself from these issues. She reflected to Lee, "It is most trying, and a very, very serious situation.... There seem to be a great many misunderstandings on both sides. And as to sleepless nights—I know all about them too."[178] Florence received suggestions from her contacts on the Republican National Committee and in the business world about ways of reconciling the warring factions.[179] The president was showing the strain by not eating well and forsaking his beloved golf. Florence could see "his jaw closing tighter each day." Harding wanted to "put federal troops in mines and on trains," a highly controversial proposal.[180]

He made an ineffectual stab to bring the two sides together, offering the preservation of seniority rights to all workers, which the railroads rejected. His friend Jennings then called for him to stiffen his backbone and adopt "stern determination to use the force of the Government to keep trains in operation and to repress disorder."[181] The nonconfrontational Harding waffled, encouraging his attorney general to step in, which he did, most heavy-handedly in the infamous Daugherty Injunction. This made the strikes illegal—and more than that, its gag rule provisions made even *discussing* strikes against the law. Things remained testy throughout the summer, and the railway workers, who eventually returned to work, got no raise until the eve of World War II. Coal miners were also striking, if less damagingly; the United Mine Workers had called a work stoppage against both wage cuts and the issue of union recognition.

These troubles meant that Congress's work went on into a summer session, with "rather heated scenes," no doubt exacerbated by the lack of air conditioning. Reading of these angry debates, Florence reflected, "when women come into what some of them feel is 'their own,' I wonder if they will work off their nerves on such occasions by a tear or two!"[182] Tears, not swears! As for herself and her husband, she wrote her daughter-in-law, "Our hands are full but I think it's all going to come out right."[183]

They did get to the McLeans' country home in Leesburg, the old Robert E. Lee mansion, at the end of June.[184] Such a weekend was a pleasant diversion, but Florence ached to get away, she told Mary Lee, "for a complete change."[185] They very much looked forward to their next summer trip, even if it would be to a familiar clime. They were going home for Marion's centennial. Not only was this a chance to show off her hometown to some new friends and pal around with old ones, but it was also an opportunity for Florence to drive fast, as she loved to do—even on the nascent roads of the era, steep and narrow as they were. George Wharton Pepper (R-Pa.), who joined the party, connected this with her "highly nervous organization," and certainly, their caravan sent the dust flying along the Lincoln National Highway at 50 mph.[186] Not only were the roads bad then, but cars were also rather unreliable. As Starling reported, "tires blew out easily, axles broke, things happened to the motors."[187] Fortunately, the weather was on their side, and they got safely to their first stop, Gettysburg, to watch a reenactment of Pickett's charge, camped out in tents in the rain. After several more stops, they joyfully arrived in Marion at 10:30 P.M. on July 3. Marionites were thrilled to see the first couple process down Main Street, Harding lifting his hat and Florence waving, a joint exercise that they would repeat endlessly the next summer in cities across the nation. Their old friends in the Columbus Glee Club had even written a song in praise of the first lady in celebration of her return, "Flo. from Ohio."[188]

The Hardings saw old friends and family, they visited the *Star*, and they attended an American Legion reunion and a pageant. Harding golfed a good bit, and, complete with tobacco in cheek, worked on an issue of his paper.[189] On their way back, he picked up an honorary doctorate from Muskingum College, which had taken over his alma mater, Ohio Central College, in New Concord; they also stopped in Uniontown, Pennsylvania, for an evening of dinner and dancing at a posh hotel.

Although her grandchildren lived in Marion, and she was there for several days, Florence didn't see them. She regretted this, as she told Evalyn—no time, she said.[190] But it doesn't seem that she made much effort; she certainly didn't mention her upcoming visit in a letter she wrote Esther in June.[191] On the basis of Harding's plentiful hours on the links, Florence likely had the opportunity. She took time to hear the Columbus Glee Club and go shopping, after all. To be fair, she didn't go and see her good friend Mary Lee; but had she held back from seeing the Mezgers because it might have drawn attention to her past—a past she had insisted be left out of the presidential campaign? In Marion, her history was not unknown. Yet she may have worried about the national attention. She rarely acknowledged this part of her life, suggesting the stigma it still carried for her years later.

The Jenningses were there to greet them when the Hardings got back to the White House on July 8, and life was pleasant those next few weeks of July despite the labor troubles, with visits, movies, dinners, and bridge at home, matinees at Keith's, occasional breaks for golf at Chevy Chase for Warren, and frequent lengthy car rides with Evalyn for Florence.[192] The McLeans did not leave for Bar Harbor until later in the month. The unsettled national situation prevented the Hardings from joining them there as they had hoped, however.[193] Evalyn commiserated with her friend's plight of being stuck in Washington and missed her. She hoped, at least, that Florence would use Ned's horse, and take daily drives. The Hardings did not get in the saddle, but they did take the car out regularly.[194]

Florence got a bit testy having to miss her usual quotient of *Mayflower* trips in July. If the railroad situation worked itself out, she was ready to "close up the White House entirely, and go for a little rest."[195] She did at last get the chance in the middle of the month to take out some newspaperwomen on the vessel, with a number of friends and associates, including Sawyer, Grace Coolidge, some Senate wives, Miss Harlan, and Ned McLean. As one reporter noted, "Mrs. Harding made everyone feel at home," shaking hands "in the most *informal* way."[196] As journalist Marcia Forbes wrote, "Her ease of manner puts every other person in the same happy frame of mind. Therein is her wonderful popularity."[197]

One way that Washington might have been more bearable for the presidential couple would have been a summer White House, as Grover Cleveland had created in his time at Cleveland Park. Florence did look around for one; earlier in July, she and Evalyn had visited a house on Conduit Road (now McArthur Boulevard) in a pretty part of Washington called the Palisades, near the Little Falls of the Potomac. She hoped that the owners were in no hurry to sell because she would not get time that summer to pursue her purchase.[198] Meanwhile, Evalyn invited them to stay at her delightful home, Friendship. It would have been a well-guarded summer executive mansion, behind an iron-topped stone wall and delightfully situated next to the Grasslands country club. But they did not take it.

In part, this was because Florence was finding her own amusements on the White House's beautiful grounds. She decided to use the enforced confinement in the capital to discover her own backyard, literally, and she did more walking than she ever had on the grounds that summer. These walks were her break; as she wrote Esther: "we have no plans for a vacation—not even weekends."[199] This was not idle strolling; she was launching a scientific study. On July 20 she inspected trees and shrubs on both the South and North Grounds for nearly two and a half hours with two government experts, including the aptly named Mr. Hemlock and an associate, Dr. Taylor, chief of the Forestry Bureau in the Department of Agriculture, making note of the horticulture. She was pleased to notice how her gardens were colorful and full of good smells, and the rest of the summer, she continued inspecting on her own every day. She told Esther, "I am trying to get all I can out of life."[200]

Of course, most of Washington's populace was in the same boat, and they had to find their amusements in the capital too that long, hot summer. In addition to parks, they sought relief at the city's bathing beach, now slightly less crowded by the hoi polloi than it had been in the "extreme democracy of the war summers." Indeed, "perfectly good people" go there, according to Dolly Madison of the *Philadelphia Ledger*. Of course, elected officials could use the Senate office building's pool, and others of means could apply to do their laps in the Wardman Park's waters.[201] As for Laddie Boy, he couldn't have been happier. He was given a four-layer dog-biscuit cake for his third birthday that summer, and he remained in the good hands of the White House master of hounds, Wilson Jackson.

By August, Florence was doing little besides her walks. Her days passed pleasantly with casual entertaining of old friends and some jaunts in the car; she also celebrated, as it turned out, her last birthday in the White House on the 15th, with Jennings and old friend Governor Sproul alongside. Despite the heat, one reporter noticed,

Laddie Boy's third birthday, July 25, 1922. Courtesy of the Library of Congress.

"Mrs. Harding is one of those women who can give the impression of trim coolness even when it is physically impossible for her to be feeling that way."[202]

With the railroad strike more or less settled by August, life was increasingly languid in Washington, and thus news from 807 South Prospect Street affected Florence with greater force. On the 19th, she heard of little George's fall from a tree—breaking both wrists—and Esther's mother's death. She wrote: "Tell George Goggy is very sorry to hear he has been hurt and hug that dear little baby for me. It seems to be part of a *real* boy's life to have so many falls and so many hurts and so many broken bones before he is fairly launched." She fretted, "I feel so sorry for him. . . . I cannot help being interested and I wish I were there to help alleviate his suffering if it were possible." Of course, she had entirely missed the chance the month before to see him when he was intact! To the larger issue of her daughter-in-law's recent bereavement, Florence was patronizing: "It's all very sad Esther but remember you have a wonderful husband and a nice little family to live for." She wrote again two days later, happy to hear George was getting better, yet despite such expressions of devotion, Florence proved unwilling to do those things that would have helped Esther much more at that moment, either by sending additional money, or—better yet—coming to lend a hand with the baby.[203] But of course, she couldn't—she was too busy, even as the country got back to normal: "Think we are tied for the rest of the season right here. Our days are full [of] anxieties and many are the nights I sleep but very little. My housekeeper is now away and Barker is just returned so I find plenty to keep occupied."[204]

They apparently weren't *that* busy, it seems, because Teddy Roosevelt Jr. remembers playing card games with the Hardings, along with Alice and Nick, the very day she wrote her first letter. Mrs. Harding and a few others played bridge, he recalled, and everyone else played poker.[205] The summer continued pleasantly; the press followed their parade of visiting company, including family members like Miss Daisy Harding and Mrs. Votaw, and old Ohio friends like Mrs. Boyd and Mrs. Christian. And nearly every night there were dinner guests: the Hugheses and the News, the Weekses, Daugherty, Gillette, and Lasker, among others. Any one of their friends unfortunate enough to find themselves back in the capital for some of the dog days of August knew they could find a home at the Hardings. And it was finally slow enough for Florence to plan a getaway.

Late in the day on August 26, Boone was called to duty on the *Mayflower*. Mrs. Harding wanted a little trip, as she hadn't been able to enjoy since the jaunt with newspaperwomen in mid-July. It was only a two-day trek, down the Potomac to Chesapeake Bay; nevertheless, the trip was still planned as a "working" one, with the "Strike Cabinet" in full force to discuss the remaining issues affecting the railway situation, as well as "the Red danger," which for many, like Hoover, seemed alive and well with that summer's labor strife. Along with the secretary of commerce on the *Mayflower* were Fall, Daugherty, Lasker, Senators Cummings and Kellogg, and Christian and Sawyer. The ladies included Mrs. Kellogg, Miss Daisy Harding, Mrs. Christian, and Mrs. Boyd. Working or not, this was a long-overdue vacation away from the White House, and they were going to do it up right. Boone noticed that even as they boarded, "Christian showed evidence of having been drinking." The trip was meant to be relaxing: the passengers watched movies on deck, projected onto the fantail. If it rained, they could go down into the presidential quarters, where on Saturday evening they saw *The Prisoner of Zenda*. Florence missed the movie that night and dinner beforehand, however; she didn't feel well and stayed in her stateroom.[206]

Friends later said they believed that her close following of the "acute industrial situation" had weakened her, and certainly it had been taxing, although the last month had been much less stressful.[207] No doubt the many tasks associated with her work, including the heavy social component, all contributed to wearing her down—but of course, her illness was chronic. Its return, if not its timing, was predictable. What no one could have foreseen was how much worse it would be this time.

CHAPTER 5

CRISIS AND CONVALESCENCE, SEPTEMBER 1922– JUNE 1923

CRISIS

That last *Mayflower* cruise brought to a close the longest span of normalcy in the Harding administration. Florence had become seriously ill, and when they returned at 8 A.M. on August 28 to Washington via the Navy Yard—close by the appalling smells of the Anacostia dump—she went right to bed.

Later that morning, she decided she had recovered sufficiently to walk with her recently arrived houseguests, the John Woods, on the West Terrace before lunch. But Florence's health was precarious, and another trip on the *Mayflower* on Labor Day was looking doubtful. She was soon back in bed, and the papers reported that she suffered from a severe cold.[1] As her condition began to appear less like a cold, Dr. Sawyer guessed indigestion, but knowing Florence, he probably had an inkling of what was going on. On September 6, with her final houseguest gone and with just hours remaining before she succumbed to the furies of her ailment, Florence expressed a last vain hope for a summer vacation in a note to Evalyn: "I have been really under the weather ... and am not able to follow my usual routine, which alone is irksome to me, and with everything so unsettled we have been obliged to forego any plan making." A plaintive handwritten note added, "Was taken sick on ... our second trip this year, for a weekend. I doubt very much my being able to leave home.... I do long to see you all."[2] On the 7th, as her illness became more pronounced and Harding became increasingly more worried about her, James S. McCandless, imperial potentate of the Shriners, helpfully distracted the president with his plans for the order's next meeting, a giant extravaganza in the capital.

Still unaware of the first lady's condition that day himself, Dr. Boone called Dr. Sawyer to join him in a horseback ride.[3] Sawyer responded that Boone should come to the White House immediately instead. The old doctor had never fully shared the first lady's medical history, but he needed advice now. Boone was informed about Florence's periodic attacks in more detail. Her condition, known as nephritis, was caused by excess fluid collecting in her kidneys, the result of a blockage in the flow of urine between the kidney and bladder. Sawyer was unsure exactly why Florence was so susceptible; it could have been a "floating kidney," described as the movement of the organ in such a way that it blocked the necessary waste passage, or perhaps a crystallized stone was the culprit, but either way, the condition was incredibly painful and potentially fatal. Left alone, fluid accumulation would lead to toxicity or death.[4] Boone approached a number of medical experts in the navy, in part to secure the use of the navy's lab and dispensary for the first lady. However, his most important acquisition from the service was navy dispensary nurse Ruth Powderly (a relative of Knights of Labor head Terence Powderly), who came to the White House that evening of the 7th to care for the first lady.[5]

President Harding met Boone as he arrived that evening and urged him to visit Florence. At first, the young doctor was reluctant, pointing out that Mrs. Harding was "Gen. Sawyer's patient," and she had not invited him. Waving off such protests, Harding took him upstairs, and the first thing that Boone noticed was her terrible suffering, despite the $\frac{3}{8}$ gram of codeine she had taken. Kathleen Lawler well described the "fragile, courageous, cheerful Duchess writhing on a bed of pain, valiantly beating back the grim reaper," while Warren read her the 121st psalm.[6]

Thus began two frightening weeks in the Harding administration as Florence, near death, struggled in and out of consciousness.[7] Sawyer recognized the situation clearly, and he dropped any proprietary rights over Mrs. Harding, telling Boone that he "wished me to help him in every way possible."[8]

The first priority was more expert help. Sawyer and Boone called in Charles Mayo from Rochester, Minnesota. Since Mayo could not get there immediately, they consulted Dr. John M. T. Finney of Baltimore. Finney arrived at 9:30 P.M. on the 8th and advised surgery.[9] Carl Sawyer also came. That night, others, too, stayed late with the Hardings, including the Christians, Mandy Sawyer, D. R. Crissinger, and Cabinet members Denby, Davis, Wallace, and New. Harry Daugherty, as was his frequent custom, slept over. Florence had a fairly "comfortable" rest that night, although her husband got very little sleep.[10] During her illness, Laddie Boy shared the president's vigil. Harding would sit outside her door, Laddie Boy's head on his knee or his feet, or else move into her room.[11]

Boone was eating dinner at the Army and Navy Club later that evening when he learned that the president wanted him back at the White House. He set himself up to sleep on a large red couch he had pulled across the hall from Mrs. Harding's room. At about 2:30 A.M. on the 9th, Boone spied a fully dressed Harding coming out of the study down the hall. He urged Boone to get off the couch and go to bed, pointing out that "this would not be a short illness," so he might as well get comfortable.[12]

The president took Boone to the Pink Bedroom first, but finding it too big for the diminutive doctor, took him to a cozier room, where he "pulled down the covers of the bed, stuffed up the pillows" and pointed out, kindly, "You're a little fellow." Then, realizing that Boone hadn't brought any sleepwear, he went off for those too, returning with "a very beautiful pair of blue-striped [silk] pajamas." Then he went into the adjoining bathroom and turned on the tub. Boone was greatly affected by this solicitousness, which no doubt made much more palatable the prospect of residency in the White House, where the young doctor would spend much of the next four months, instead of at home with his wife and baby daughter.[13]

Meanwhile, the Harding medical team awaited Mayo's insights about an operation. Florence was not responding to the application of "heavy blankets and hot towels" to her fevered body, to flush out waste through her pores that could not get out through her renal system—a punishing cure indeed in the heat of a Washington summer! Her fever continued on the 9th, reaching 102 degrees; she frequently drifted in and out of consciousness, sometimes "tug[ging] nervously at the bed clothing."[14] Fearing septicemia, a potentially fatal condition, Boone ran frequent blood tests. He noted, "I had seen her looking terrible, at times . . . almost completely unconscious without any interest whatsoever in her appearance because of her weakened condition and her suffering."[15]

Notwithstanding such moments, her "tremendous pluck and fortitude" and her "optimistic nature" were instrumental in bearing this toxic infection and crippling pain.[16] As she told her aide, Barker: "Don't worry, Harry. I will get well alright."[17] She could see the worry in Warren's "beloved face," as well, despite his attempts to mask it. As Lawler wrote, "in the agonies of excruciating pain, with her temperature at 105 degrees and the end momentarily expected," she looked at him and said, "Don't worry, Warren, I am not going to die."[18]

"On that bed," said one reporter, "was a determined soul." Rather than let herself slip into a coma, she forced herself to remain awake for 10 hours or more. She drifted while still conscious, "as if she was on a moving platform, with voices in the distance at the foot of the bed, which was gradually fading farther and farther away. She clenched her little hands with determination" and did not let go.[19]

Florence later told Evalyn about this "out of body" experience, noting that she could feel Warren's presence while it was going on, and had to come back for him. She also told some of the newspaperwomen who came to see her when she was recovered enough to have a visit that the president and her doctors "seemed to swim before her eyes . . . [she remembered] that her father had during his last illness sunk in to a comatose condition and died." Vowing not to do so herself, "she . . . purely by strength of mind kept herself from sinking into unconsciousness." She had adopted this practice of using her mind to control her body from her readings of French healer Dr. Emile Coué, a practitioner whose theory of training the mind included repeating the mantra, "Every day in every way, I'm getting better and better," to solve one's illnesses. Mrs. Harding had read his book, *Self-Mastery through Conscious Autosuggestion,* just out in 1922, and had him to the White House when she was convalescing, thanks to Ambassador Jules Jusserand.[20] His writings had convinced her that the mind could be trained to counteract unhealthy developments in the body. Boone was amazed at her strength, both of will and of physical being: "This very kindly lady, as I found her to be . . . demonstrated that, when death was on the threshold for her, she kept herself from dying truly by pure willpower." At one point, despite her drifting grasp of consciousness, she took Boone's hands and "squeezed [them] so firmly that I cut the palms . . . until they bled."[21]

For the first time since the Hardings entered it, the public was barred from the executive mansion that weekend. Nevertheless, the grounds were still open, except in the very early morning hours, and were filled as usual with strollers.[22] These numbers would dwindle as her illness quickly became known.

On the morning of the 10th, at five past midnight, Evalyn Walsh McLean rolled in to the White House.[23] Her presence over the next day did much for Florence's spirits, and the following evening, she reported that "Mrs. Harding is better. . . . She has quieted down and is going to sleep now. I think there is good hope for her recovery."[24]

As Mrs. McLean was waking in the White House on the 10th, a police escort was rushing Dr. Mayo and his wife to the mansion, with a movie crew at the front door waiting to record the renowned doctor's entry, suggesting by its presence the Hardings' role as public personalities. Sawyer took Mayo immediately to the sickroom.[25] The house was filling up; Harding's brother, George, a cardiologist, his sister, Mrs. Votaw, and Florence's brother, Clifford, all came that day, and many other friends stopped by.

The medical team spent several hours analyzing the results of Florence's blood tests. Even if they showed that the levels of poisons were down, the next likely outcome seemed to be surgery, a procedure of "tapping and draining" her kidneys.[26] Florence actually seemed improved with Mayo's arrival; the visit with Evalyn, no doubt, had been a boost as well. She slept better, her pain abated, her temperature dropped to 100, her pulse to 102, and she ate a little.[27] Because of her unexpected rallying, the surgery sparked a lively debate. Adding to the intense atmosphere, President Harding also spent three hours with the doctors as they mulled over the decision.[28]

Sawyer strongly opposed an operation, believing "she could not survive one." He was convinced that "the mental and physical shock," combined with "her temperament and her nervous system . . . and her dread of operation," would make it a catastrophe. Her

Florence's physicians. Courtesy of the Library of Congress.

trepidation stemmed from her first operation—when she had had a displaced kidney that had to be surgically anchored.[29] Physically, too, her heart was not strong enough for such a procedure; but above all, Sawyer expostulated, "if we operate the Duchess WILL die. I know her. I know her history and . . . I cannot . . . agree to it."[30]

After seeing his wife, and talking with Boone, who also opposed an operation, the president declared there would be no surgery that day.[31] The navy doctor recalled in his diary, "I thought I never should have voiced an opinion and that I had ruined my professional career." Awake at 4 A.M., Boone saw Mayo come down the hall "all dressed," and his words only confirmed Boone's fretful thoughts. "I have doubts in my mind and feel we erred," Mayo said. Yet Boone and Sawyer had made the right call. Though still in critical condition, Mrs. Harding began to recover.[32]

With the surgery canceled, Finney returned to Maryland and Mayo to Minnesota. Florence continued with the hot applications and the opiates, and improved, almost miraculously.[33] Her temperature and pulse fell,[34] and the president took this as an opportunity to go outside for a two-hour walk on the White House gardens with "Big Bill" Hays, former chairman of the Republican

National Committee and postmaster general, and Ed McLean.[35] Supportive friends poured into the White House in an "endless stream"—the McLeans, the Scobeys, Lasker, and Jesse Smith, among them, providing comfort. As the president told one of his friends, "I have been going through a period of very great anxiety, but I think Mrs. Harding has passed over the critical period and is quite certain to make a good recovery."[36]

PUBLIC REACTION

Florence Harding's Coué-trained will was keeping her alive. But another element was the combined prayers of the entire country—prayers that had been encouraged by the administration's own openness about her illness.[37] After the reports of her "cold" proved unfounded, the public learned of the real reason for her sickness on September 9, her worst day, in an announcement where Sawyer intimated that her recovery was "uncertain." "Boys, Mrs. Harding is in a very critical condition," Harding told newspapermen, and he let them know she'd been sick for 10 days.[38]

The administration's openness was as remarkable as it was unusual, and was exactly appropriate in acknowledging "the intense popular interest in the President's wife."[39] President Woodrow Wilson's first wife Ellen's own fatal kidney ailment was a close-held secret—as would his own condition be after his stroke in 1919. And when first lady Nellie Taft lost her speech after a fall on the *Sylph* in 1909, the public only heard that she was ill, or at the most, she'd had a "nervous breakdown," but never that she'd had a stroke.[40] By contrast, Florence's candid approach garnered her an enormous outpouring of concern, as measured by ceremonies and services, editorials, personal letters, and White House visitors. The capital's churches, the Masons, and 171,000 disabled veterans were among those who joined in prayer. The *New York Tribune* noted that the most important reason for this was "the genuinely democratic attitude she has held at all times."[41] Mrs. Harding's health was the nation's—and the president's—concern, as May Warner of Seattle, wrote: "None needs the gracious ministry of woman more than the man who is our chosen head."[42]

Florence herself urged Warren to play golf and pressed him to go to the office. But mostly he stayed close by, either outside her bedroom in a big chair or at her side.⁴³ Indeed, the *Times* noted, "he is pathetically importunate in his questions of physicians and nurses . . . and looks eagerly for any ray of hope."⁴⁴ Harding tried to keep a positive presence in front of his wife, yet while he flitted back and forth from her room to his office, he was unable to work in those early days.⁴⁵ Instead, he paced, as one paper said, "a man broken by the grave anxiety of her condition; his hair, whitened by problems . . . blends in to the pallor of his countenance."⁴⁶ Whatever their issues, Harding loved Florence dearly. He could not imagine living without her. She wasn't just the Duchess; Warren affectionately called her the "best Scout a fellow ever had."⁴⁷ If nothing else, this illness showed the closeness of their relationship.

The *Philadelphia Public Ledger* praised the administration for keeping the public informed, noting how this contrasted in "striking" fashion with the previous administration's approach, when "Washington scarcely knew of the fatal illness of the first Mrs. Woodrow Wilson until she was at the point of death."⁴⁸ Moreover, Florence's near-death experience underlined for many her important role in the White House. "She has been closely associated with the President in all his work and it is known that her counsel has aided him in many different problems," noted the *Washington News*. That very work—or an excess of it—had likely brought on her illness, the *Ledger* suggested: "perhaps no wife of a president . . . has entered into the White House duties with more energy and zest than Mrs. Harding." She had traveled with the president on all his trips, and had become involved in all the social season's engagements—including the endless "handshaking ordeals" which brought "welts between her fingers." It had all been too much: "Perhaps it is impossible, even for a woman, to be the idealized and ethereal personality whom we imagined to exist in Mrs. Harding," the *Ledger* noted.⁴⁹

The White House's openness allowed for speculation about her condition. Some believed that "there seems to be very little chance for her recovery." Others opined that the sweating treatment was working, but worried that the case's severity, and her age (sixty-two) would complicate matters.⁵⁰ Regardless, the country was informed about and engaged in the issue thanks to the policy of candor, and this very involvement brought the power of prayer on her side. As the *Post* reported: "thousands kneel as ministers call for divine aid."⁵¹ Indeed, hundreds came to Keith's Theatre on September 13 for such a vigil, a place where Mrs. Harding had often enjoyed performances.⁵² VFW members meeting in the capital honored her with a two-minute standing prayer. In Marion, of course, the appeals came thick and fast. Crowds of people waited at the *Star*, hoping for news. But the effort was nationwide, including a concerted effort to pray by four million members of the Christian Endeavor society. This most public first lady had made a striking connection with the American people.

THE TIDE TURNS

The petitions seemed to be working; the signs grew encouraging. Dr. George T. Harding Jr. noted that Mrs. Harding had asked for food on the 11th, the first time since she'd gotten ill, and in a stronger voice than any had heard for some time.⁵³ Even if her organs were only working "partially," Sawyer noted, "the increased elimination has given us a sense of relief."⁵⁴ Florence was still receiving hot applications and opiates, and she was too weak for a full examination of the kidneys to be sure what was happening. Nevertheless, surgery was now a worry of the past. The *New York Times* predicted that Mrs. Harding's recovery needed only "days," an overly optimistic projection.⁵⁵ Still, on September 18, Boone went home for the first time, and Harding felt she was well enough that he could play golf with Senators Kellogg and Hale, and the assistant secretary of the treasury, James Wadsworth. No doubt they discussed the veterans' bonus bill, which Harding would veto the following day. He considered it a "Treasury raid."⁵⁶

Florence, meanwhile, was getting much better, and well aware of what had been going on during her dark days. She had not forgotten Boone's sacrifices—including no tennis for three weeks while she was most ill. She encouraged him to use the White House courts with his friends, and she sent flowers at least twice a week from the greenhouses at the White House to Mrs. Boone and their daughter, Suzanne. She arranged for "a car, chauffeur and footman" for the Boone girls to take driving each week in Rock Creek Park and other places while their man stayed at the White House. This included Florence's "much prized landaulet."⁵⁷

Laura Harlan's diary identified September 24 as the beginning of "recovery" for Mrs. Harding. Still, she suffered from "piles and bladder tenesmus," the latter a "distressing but ineffectual urge to evacuate the rectum or bladder."[58] Harlan told a family friend that Mrs. Harding "is still too ill to see her mail," although she "is full of courage, and her recovery seems to be only a matter of time.[59] President Harding agreed, and the following night, Boone slept at home for first time since early September. Despite the stresses of the past month, it had been "a very, very privileged opportunity to be a member of the President's and First Lady's family" all that time, he noted. On October 10, as he returned to the *Mayflower*, Florence urged him "to always consider myself as 'one of the family.' "[60]

As October began, the White House was reopened for tourists.[61] The downstairs visiting areas soon filled again. The justices of the Supreme Court came on October 2, after their first day of the fall session. The Daughters of American Revolution visited as well, with a "monster bouquet" to Florence.[62] It is unlikely that Florence actually saw these groups, but she was certainly taking a greater interest in the world. She was in good spirits, as evident in a letter she dictated for Laura to send along to Evalyn, thanking her friend for a basket of fruit and two flower arrangements. She joked about Mrs. McLean having just been "lolling in the lap of luxury at the Ritz," and she fondly remembered their earlier "great shopping expedition" with Mrs. Frelinghuysen and Mrs. Weeks to New York.[63]

On the afternoon of October 16, Evalyn saw Florence for a brief visit, and the first lady sat up for a half hour. Other visitors that month were mostly the regulars: the Sawyers and Christians, Daugherty, Smith, McLean, Lasker, and Cressinger. Dr. Mayo and his wife came back on the 29th and stayed for dinner with Harding, Sawyer, and Boone. But their social life had definitely become quieter since Florence's illness.

On November 2, Harding turned fifty-seven, and Boone reported him to be in "very good, jolly spirits," reminiscing about his youth. He and Florence had less reason to be happy a few days later when some of their Senate friends were defeated in midterm elections. As Harding told his shocked wife of Frank Kellogg's loss, she reared off her pillow and sat straight up. "Warren Harding, I just do not believe you! Frank K cannot be defeated. He is one of the stalwarts of the Senate."[64]

Boone came frequently to attend to Mrs. Harding, and she liked it that way. When the *Mayflower* went down to Norfolk for repairs in November, she insisted he stay in Washington, in case Sawyer couldn't attend her. Harding then actually ordered Boone not to go to Norfolk. The young doctor obliged; he worried that the stress of looking after his wife, as well as all the other details of the presidency, were wearing out the president. Boone's proximity gave him a full picture of developments at the White House, and now with less preoccupation with his patient, he thought it a somewhat strange environment, where "everyone seems suspicious of everyone else." Florence's "boys," especially, had become officious in the discharge of their duties, taking advantage of her reliance on them. Baldinger, for instance, was intrusive, insinuating, and uncouth, "a vicious sort of person . . . [with] a way of getting out of line and getting into people's hair." He would "station . . . himself just outside her bedroom door in earshot" when friends visited her, which disgusted another Secret Service man, Harry Barker. Yet Barker himself haunted Mrs. Harding's door "practically all day long." This was what Florence wanted, apparently; she was "very attached" to Barker, and "because of certain suspicions"—or even superstitions—kept him posted like a sentry. This infuriated the head usher, "Ike" Hoover, who didn't like anyone to get between him and the first couple. Hoover spent nearly fifty years in the White House, where he "required and demanded that things be run punctiliously, uniformly, and with exaction."[65] That suited Florence very well too.

Weeks went by, and her condition, while still critical, did not worsen. As Warren wrote Mary Lee, "I am glad to tell you that Mrs. Harding continues to improve, though she is not yet able to leave her room."[66] On November 11, Veterans Day, Harding went to Arlington to place a wreath on the Tomb of the Unknown Soldier, and at home, Florence had a large contingent of visitors: Senators Edge and Kellogg, Mrs. Todd, Secretaries Mellon, Weeks, and Daugherty, and Ned McLean among them. More followed in the next few days, and on November 14, Laura Harlan recorded that "Mrs. Harding is now receiving." Florence saw her visitors in her wheelchair; she was not yet strong enough to stand long. She was thus limited in her travels and unable to sit in her box for the joint session of Congress on November 21 to hear her husband's address. Evalyn sat there instead with some other friends, including Sawyer, Mrs. Taft, Mrs. Denby, and Boone, at Florence's behest, and told the first lady, "I missed you so, and the place seemed so queer without you . . . do hurry up and get well."[67] In December, Florence heard Harding's address to an unprecedented fourth session of Congress on her Radiophone, because for the first time in history, the presidential speech was broadcast.

Mrs. Harding came downstairs the day before Thanksgiving, November 29, and on the holiday itself dined downstairs for the first time with her husband, the Christians (Jr. and Sr.) and Harry Daugherty.[68] It was her first meal downstairs in three months. Old Mr. Christian recalled, "Florence was almost a child in her expression of delight" at being at dinner."[69]

Journalist Mark Sullivan sent her a leg of venison, which was a great treat, and Harlan wrote him appreciatively on behalf of the first lady, noting that Florence hoped to see him when she was better. Her daily routine of "two hours of sitting up, and [a] walk about her room" were rapidly restoring her.[70] On December 7, Mrs. Harding felt strong enough to see an important state visitor, former French prime minister Georges Clemenceau, thanks to Boone, who persuaded her and her husband that she should and could. Clemenceau and his party came up to her bedroom hall to visit, and she was nervous; she "did not have a good hold on herself," Boone reported. All the same, "she had gotten herself pretty well primped up and her hair nicely set, had a beautiful negligee on and looked really very well . . . very pretty really in blue in her wheelchair. I thought I had never seen her looking so well." Ambassador Jusserand, a most delightful man, showed *his* nervous delight by rubbing his hands together incessantly, so charmed was he to see Mrs. Harding. Unfortunately, Boone was not so honored, because Mrs. Harding forgot to introduce him to Clemenceau, much to his embarrassment and her later mortification; she blamed her illness. A few days later, an apologetic Florence made a point of discussing Boone's position at the White House, reminding him that they wanted him to have "the run of the house at all time[s]."[71]

Florence saw more visitors in early December, and came down for dinner again with her father-in-law, Dr. George T. Harding, on December 10. A few days later, she received eleven journalists from the White House newsmen's association. With Christmas approaching, she sent checks to Esther, $5 for each member of the family, "Not much I know but it takes with it my very best love to you all." She noted that while she knew that she was "doing well," still, "it seems very slow to me." Christmas 1922 was more crowded than the previous year. Because of her illness, friends clustered around, among them Daughterty, the News, the senior Christians, and the McLeans, as well as Boone and his father.[72]

Sawyer was away over the Christmas holidays in 1922, so Boone had to be at the executive mansion at least twice a day. One Sunday he noticed the president reading to Mrs. Harding. As he read her letters from their old Marion friends, inquiring after her health, she began to cry, so he turned to other reading matter. In this way, he often soothed her to sleep. How did Florence deal with this long period of convalescence when her husband could *not* be near? Did it offer, as her friend Mary Hutchins Drake suggested, valuable "mental repose"? Or was it more of a sad burden? As she wrote her daughter-in-law in early January, "Some days I am very much discouraged—guess I don't yet realize how desperately ill I have been."[73]

Overall, Florence was recovering well and taking more and more interest in affairs of the White House and the outside world, but she would not be well enough to have a White House reception. Instead, the Coolidges would hold a smaller gathering, while Charles Evans Hughes hosted the diplomats. Florence was also too ill to attend Evalyn and Ned McLean's jaw-dropping ball on New Year's. Their house on I Street and Vermont Avenue had a ballroom big enough for a Baldwin locomotive to drive into, and they did justice to its size, with two large orchestras for dancing, and "liquid and solid food" in abundance (Boone did not specify what kind of liquids were served). All in all, it was a "land of fantasy" to this Quaker.[74]

President Harding wrote to Evalyn on New Year's Day, reporting that Florence was moving about a bit more on the upper floor of the executive mansion, although she was not yet getting dressed.[75] Evalyn had remembered her friend with an attractive set of rose bed covers that, Florence joked, "will make me want to stay an invalid!" The first lady also reported that she was pushing herself more each day, augmenting her "sitting up program" with walks to the study and back three times daily, finding enough energy to clean the "numerous trophies" lining the study walls, and, with joyful anticipation, examining her *Mayflower* suits for their fitness for wear with the help of her maid, Catherine Wynn. "Mr. Harding has been going about beaming ever since on account of this energy," she told her friend.[76] Her next goal was to take her wheelchair to the South Gallery and sun herself, if the weather held up. But she had also been chatting with George Harvey, the ambassador to Britain, and catching up on stories from the Court of St. James.

Florence also felt strong enough to write a long letter to Esther and her husband, thanking them for a "beautiful" gift of handkerchiefs. She was mostly interested, however, in making suggestions on her granddaughter's clothes. Florence, despite her own fancy wardrobe, did not like the idea of Jean being dressed "too much in silk and satins." She declared, "when I look about and see the children of today dressed better to go to school than I did to go to church . . . I think it is a great mistake, because there is nothing left for them to anticipate in the future." Being dressed as "simply as possible" was best for the girl, noted this fuddy-duddy grandmother. Not surprisingly, given her own silks and satins (or rhinestones and ermine), she had yet to see anything in *her* wardrobe "suitable" to be redone for Jean, but sent enough gingham to be sewn for Jean's dresses. Sounding a bit defensive about her level of financial support, Florence told her daughter-in-law that she did "always . . . keep her in mind because I do know how all these things help," but lectured Esther that with "care and good judgment" she could dress Jean and her brother, George, "on their little income that is theirs, at least for a time." Florence felt she could be frank with her daughter-in-law about her health, telling Esther, "I do not mind saying to you quietly, [I am] very much discouraged. What is the use of having a good looking automobile if the engine won't run?" She noted, too, it would be six months in March—and even if her husband was encouraged to see her cleaning the bric-a-brac, "my convalescence seems very, very slow . . . I have gotten where I can walk around the room at least six times without sitting down, but then after that I have to rest for an hour." By way of advice, she urged Esther to "get about some because I think it is so essential not to get in a rut." She could have been talking to herself—fighting ruts even when doing the "convalescent stunt."[77]

To prepare for a late winter trip to Florida, and in hopes of finally making their summer trip to Alaska too, Mrs. Harding was getting herself out to the South Lawn every day in her wheelchair, well wrapped. She was no longer using a cane, as she had earlier in her convalescence. Though Florence was getting healthier, not everyone believed it, as she herself knew, and she asked Laura Harlan to find out from Florence's close confidant, Kathleen Lawler, the source of rumors that the first lady was a "skeleton." Lawler quickly told Harlan that it was the misapprehension of a certain Mrs. Marye, who "is telling around that poor Mrs. Harding is in a dreadful state . . . that she has seen Mrs. Harding . . . lying on the top of the bed . . . her hair was braided in two braids, and . . . Mrs. Harding is not this size"—a finger span less than nine inches in diameter. Lawler reported she was "astounded" by these reports: "someone is romancing." Indeed, Lawler learned Florence was now 140 pounds, 2 pounds more than was normal for her height "according to the technical scale," a sign of "substantial, steady, permanent improvement," she declared. Florence, indeed, was worried about putting on weight, lacking much exercise.

In late January, Florence fretted that her further progress was at a "standstill."[78] She wrote her friend Ada Denman, "I can only sit up about 4 hours a day, and I can assure you that some days the morale in this room . . . is very low," although she tried to be optimistic.[79] Things seemed even worse when her husband, too, sickened that month, struck by the grippe, an attack so violent in its early phase that Boone was up every two hours with him. Major Brooks had already reported that Harding wasn't sleeping well: the valet reported that "he has to be propped up with pillows and he sits up that way all night. If he lies down he can't get his breath." Starling thought Harding's "high stomach" was a sign of the troubles.[80]

In times like these, Florence looked to the stars. In her bond book, for example, she had pinned an astrological reading from sometime in late 1922 or early 1923 that predicted his attack: "The President is coming under some very powerful influences and needs to safe-guard his health[,] and he will have a *narrow* escape from some personal danger. The planet Mars—ruling fire-arms—presages some trouble may arise through some 'crank' so the President should be careful not to put himself in any place as a *target*." The crank seems to have been Colonel Forbes. Fortunately, though, her notes continued, "Venus is approaching the place of Jupiter at his birth which *may* mitigate the evil." All the same, "The opposition of the Moon to the Sun and Saturn in his horoscope shows that he cannot depend upon his friends. He should be suspicious of the ones he *should* trust and *trust* those he *should* be suspicious of."[81] Interestingly, the piece concluded, "If he can "pass" the sudden evil threatened ... until the spring of 1923 he will prove not only a great benefactor to his own country but with the world in general."[82]

Oblivious to the stars, except as an aid to navigation or romance, but attentive to his patient, the devoted homeopath Boone settled in once again in the small northwest bedroom with its bath en suite to help Harding recover. The grippe became a bad cold that "lingered," and Boone found Harding's patience and gratitude as a patient endearing: "He was a very lovable person ... he always gave of himself freely to other people. He just loved people." With Florence's illness persisting and the president ailing as well, it was a good thing that Sawyer renovated a linen closet to replace the minimalist "medicine bag" as the White House health facility. If it was not the dispensary that Boone hoped for, it at least had shelves, a folding table, and an overhead light.[83]

As the stars had hinted, Harding had other reasons to feel unwell that January. Boone recalled that Florence had "championed" their old chum, Charles R. Forbes, in his original appointment as director of the War Risk Insurance Bureau and then the Veterans Bureau, but by January 22, "she seemed to have had her eyes opened" as perhaps "one of the biggest scandals in government history" unfolded.[84] Florence had heard reports as early as December 1922 from a California friend in hospital administration that there were financial and other "irregularities" around the construction of a veterans' facility in Livermore, although her source held onto the hope that Forbes would not "violate the confidence that you and the President have in him."[85] But indeed Forbes had done exactly that, repeatedly absconding with bureau supplies for the disabled veterans and selling them for his own profit and that of favored contractors, according to the director of the Secret Service, William J. Burns.[86]

Forbes's pilferage was centered at the Veterans Hospital in Perryville, Maryland, where "surplus stores," including handmade items such as 98,000 pairs of pajamas made by Red Cross women, were essentially given away to favored dealers to sell them at their own price. The gloves, for instance, left for 30 cents each, and sheets that cost the government $1.25 were let go for 20 cents each, with Forbes taking a percentage of the earnings his purchaser netted from each phony transaction and resale. In addition to letting things go cheap, the bureau bought them high! Thus, it paid $35,000 for floor cleaner, which was not only expensive, but amounted to enough for 100 years' worth of scrubbing pleasure—and was a fire hazard to boot. In all, Forbes's malfeasance cost the nation as much as $200 to $250 million. And that was not all. At the bureau, there was "a room . . . fitted up with cocktail shakers . . . to make the dull hours pass faster, " and "girl clerks of the flapper type are reported to have the right of way over the older and more experienced women in promotions," leading to a "demoralized" staff.[87]

As the evidence accumulated, Harding was slow to act, "loath to believe anything ill of his fellow man," a blind spot for him.[88] The president had been charmed by Forbes, a "'good fellow' type" whom they first met in Hawaii when Harding was on a senatorial junket to Honolulu and Forbes was the commissioner of public works there. Although he had won the Croix de Guerre and Distinguished Service Medal in World War I, Forbes had no experience with running a budget of $500 million and overseeing 300,000 veterans. Yet he had hoped to run the shipping board, or even take over the Department of the Interior after Fall's departure. Florence had helped promote him, and her influence would be key now in ending his malevolent presence. Consequently, one of the chief officers of the Veterans Bureau contacted Mrs. Harding to see if she could get her husband to have Forbes removed. It was understood that her intervention would be necessary, underlining once again her key role in personnel decisions.[89] The president, furious at his old friend's betrayal of his trust, at one point forcefully shook him. He at last forced Forbes to resign, accepting his resignation by telegram when Forbes was in Liverpool, en route to study veterans' problems abroad, so that he could not return with his title.[90]

FLORENCE'S RECOVERY

Forbes's unhealthy presence was gone, but another member of the administration soon sickened. On January 26, Dr. Boone found

Harry Daugherty sprawled in bed at his apartment at Wardman Park, having experienced a cerebral hemorrhage. Boone now had another patient who needed him almost daily. Daugherty also urged the doctor to look at his friend, Jess, but Boone, who had never been fond of Smith, was dubious; he didn't think the overweight, diabetic Smith would follow any advice, and he was right. Smith had already had abdominal surgery, but he liked to eat well and thus did not make any attempt to control his condition.[91]

President Harding, meanwhile, was mostly better by the end of January, but he never completely recovered, remaining susceptible for the attack he would have in July. Florence wrote to Evalyn that "the aftermath of grippe is far more annoying than the disease itself," telling her friend about Warren's still "wobbly" legs.[92] His midwinter illness was a setback for Florence, as he was less able to care for her, and she lost 2½ pounds in a week. She determined she had to do more to get better. As she wrote Evalyn on February 5, "You were the last caller I received in a social way, because I finally decided there is only one way to get well and that is to stop seeing people."[93] While her heart was still "uncertain," she was very excited finally to be getting to Florida with Evalyn the following month.[94] She added, wickedly, "I remember you asked that Miss Harlan might drop you a line every now and then, but I thought I would like a little gossip myself. The pity is the things I would like to say cannot be put on paper!" But self-doubt also crept in: after seeing pictures of the social scene in Florida, she wondered if she could be "dressy" enough in her current condition.[95]

Evalyn soon wrote to reassure her in a breathless, gossipy letter from her "little cottage . . . larger than the one we had last year," at the Breakers in Palm Beach.[96] The houseboat they would use was two times as big as their last one, she told Florence, and she and Ned were very much looking forward to having the first lady and their other friends, especially Weeks and Daugherty. "I can't tell you how much I miss you and how anxious I am to see you," she gushed, pointing out how restful it would be for her still-recovering friend.[97]

Catherine New could confirm that she had not seen Florence for about six weeks after the first lady's pledge to have no social calls. But on February 20, the News were invited over for dinner and movies, and she noted to Evalyn how well Florence looked, in a "very becoming pink velour tea gown," with her hair done.[98] Boone, at the same evening, confirmed that "Mrs. Harding looked beautiful and so well."[99] Others described her in those days wearing a "robe d' interieur"—certainly much more elegant than a bathrobe—looking "softer and more fragile" without her glasses.[100] Boone thought such meetings with others were important just "to bring her back . . . to the world of reality."[101] With the news, she had also been treated to a special viewing of African wild animal footage.

The Woods, their old friends from Norwalk, Ohio, also showed up in February, and Florence joined them for lunch. When they first arrived, she was "simply but becomingly gowned in some sort of a silky negligee" on her couch; later, she joined them "wrapped in a huge motor robe spread over her chair." It was quite a cozy scene, as they sat eating around a large round wooden table decorated with doilies, with "two colored boys in wine-colored uniforms" looking after their needs, a fire burning brightly, and Laddie Boy poised to catch every scrap. Harding encouraged all to feed the Airedale: "every family should have a baby, and we have never had one. So Laddie Boy's the baby of the family." The food was comforting too: hard-boiled egg with cream sauce, lamb chops, potatoes, spinach, brown bread, and a peach tart. Mrs. Harding, taking new interest in the food offerings, announced that they would have "creamed codfish" the next day. Although one observer suggested that "it was a great disappointment" for Florence that she could not carry out that winter her "formal program and gayeties of the usual White House social season," it is not clear that this was the case. These intimate affairs occasioned by her illness suited her very well.[102]

The slower pace was helping her recover, and now it looked as if the Florida trip would really happen. Warren thought it would be good for Florence, as he told Mary Lee, now postmistress of Westerville: "I am hopeful that the out of door life and change of scene and climate will greatly accelerate her complete restoration."[103] Florence was also convinced the trip to Florida would assist her health. All she had seen was "the four walls of one room" for months, "my life . . . a matter of getting up and going to bed, with the emphasis on the going to bed where I spend the largest part of the 24 hours."[104] According to one reporter, when out of her rooms, she "passed much of her time in the President's study, seeing virtually no one but him." The president himself hadn't been out of his study much, owing to his care for her, and his speech at a dinner for Lincoln Memorial University on the same day was one of his first public appearances in "months."[105]

Florence was definitely feeling better; "I had a shampoo yesterday and my hair up again," she wrote happily to Evalyn.[106] She was paying more attention to her appearance; she had not realized, she wrote another friend, that W.G. (as she often called him in letters) "hated my boudoir caps," and now, he was telling her, "I look twenty years younger with my hair up." She wasn't sure about that, but she did enjoy looking at gowns which Harry Collins had brought over for her to decide on, giving her something to look forward to—dressing up!—after her six months' convalescence. She did not comment about her fondness of the canary that been given to her as company in January, which could start and stop singing on command.

She focused herself on getting outside for at least fifteen minutes every day that it was nice enough to do so, and on February 12, for the first time, she emerged "bundled in furs" at noon and *stood* on the South Portico.[107] The Florida trip would help her husband, too; he still experienced some shortness of breath and took a short nap after lunch each day. Florence remained concerned about him: she urged him to get in more golf, and on one occasion in January, she broke up a meeting between him and Christian that was getting Warren agitated. "She left her wheel chair and . . . expressed her opinion in direct and candid fashion." Christian left, and the obedient president was back on his couch, "resting quietly and emitting not a murmur," joked a Cincinnati paper.[108]

As part of her recovery, Florence began attending dinner downstairs in the state dining room each night, and on February 26, she hosted her first reception since her illness, with female journalists and other friends. As Laura Harlan poured tea for the thirty in attendance, Florence openly discussed her convalescence, pointing out the absolutely essential importance of the "prayers of the people" in this process.[109] She was dressed becomingly in "a tea gown of stately linen, fashioned of coral red velvet . . . worn over a frilly dress of silver-color chiffon, showing lace and shirring and an appliqué of dainty pink roses just across the top of the square neck bodice." One of the visitors noted that she was "becoming herself again," with "that old familiar gesture with the index finger, and the vivacity and charming sparkle in her eyes . . . even when she looked the convalescent, quite girlish in braided hair reclining on a couch, restfully, sickroom pallor slightly evident, and a little lace cap all suggesting the high school miss recovering from a siege of pneumonia."[110]

The reporters were excited to be taken into the upstairs "sanctum" of Mrs. Harding's sitting room, "with its piano, its great comfortable chintz covered chairs and davenports, and the books, photographs and shaded lamps which speak so insistently of home." On the walls were several portraits, including Florence's favorite one of herself by Laszlo, as he was known, above the chimney. This room had been used by Margaret Wilson as well, and Florence had done little to change it. Nonetheless, her stamp was apparent, with ferns, flowers, canaries, and goldfish. She noted, poignantly, that there had been a "blessing" in her sickness, since it had brought her and her husband closer together. "Before . . . there was not a minute of the day that either of us was free. There was never a meal when we were alone. I can tell you it was a treat to be able to take advantage of my condition and sit upstairs here in the evening and talk to my husband." The reporters also noted that she had made a reentry into public affairs, with her work to get a federal prison for women "drug addicts" in the Blue Ridge Mountains pushed through Congress, including her petitioning Republican leader Frank Mondell, though so far, efforts had been "blocked."[111]

THE FLORIDA TRIP

Along with Florence's improving health, Congress's adjournment—for nine months—helped make the Florida and Alaska trips possible. The Hardings were keenly looking forward to their first real vacation since the inauguration, and their first trip away from Washington since going to Marion the previous July.[112] Harding was annoyed at Congress for failing to pass many measures he had proposed, including a bill for the merchant marine. "He was frankly sick of the job," the *Washington Post* surmised.[113] Indeed, he was not well, the *Marion Star* suggested. "He is physically and mentally tired." And although he was advised by doctors "to lead an outdoor life as much as possible," he had also been derided for playing golf, as people thought he was slacking off. Indeed, as work piled up, he played less, and his health suffered—leading to his extended recovery from "a slight cold"—the winter grippe.[114]

Florence did think the trip would help her health, and her husband's. It would also be good for their ailing friend, Harry Daugherty. With all of them recuperating, it was only natural that the president and first lady urged Boone to come too, and he obliged. Florence found it taxing to prepare herself for the trip, writing Esther on February 28 that the packing was particularly daunting; she had not worn "real clothes" for half a year.[115] She chided Esther for not writing her: "I suppose you are too busy?" But even Florence wasn't sure she would have time to stop in Marion on their return from Florida—and they did not visit there. But if the family front in Marion once again got neglected, she carefully made arrangements for Washington affairs before she left, making sure that flowers were regularly distributed in her absence to hospitals and charity events, as well as her friends, and that the White House would remain open.

Florence must have been excited, or else horrified, by the Florida social scene as Evalyn described it: "Mrs. Hearst is here . . . looks lovely and her clothes are beautiful." She had heard, as well, that William Randolph Hearst was dying and Mrs. Hearst seemed "very pleased"! Evalyn went on, "I saw Sen. [Emile] Dupont . . . he is still up to his old tricks. He leaves Mrs. Dupont in the hotel and he runs around with lovely young girls! There are a lot of 'Follies' girls here and they are wonderful." One was "hitting the high shots—she drinks like a fish and never gets to bed until daylight." Everyone, it seemed, had their "beau" and "you must never be seen with your husband."[116]

With excitement—or dread—at such a scene, Florence and her husband left the capital on March 5, 1923, at noon, by train, arriving in Ormond, Florida, twenty-four hours later. On board with them was a large entourage including the Christians, Sawyers, Boone, Daugherty, Jess Smith, the Frelinghuysens, the Weekses, Secretary Davis, Senator Fred Hale, and Albert D. Lasker, as well as ten members of the press. Despite the escape, Harding was reminded of the previous summer's troubles when the train passed Rocky Mount, North Carolina, where former striking railroad workers were out to greet them. The *Washington Herald* noted there was "little handclapping and less cheering" among the men. Upon reaching Florida, they stopped in St. Augustine, where some of the party got off, including the Frelinghuysens and Weekses; Mrs. Harding stood on the rear platform for the first time, to greet well-wishers. Largely quiet on the trip, she now "radiated happiness." At their next stop, Ormond, the Harding party, and others, including Christian, McLean, Dawes, Sawyer, and Lasker, got on the McLeans' houseboat, *Pioneer*. Boone, who had seen Florence every day for the past six months, would now be leaving her temporarily, staying on the train for the rest of the trip. The president and his buddies played some golf in Ormond, too, the first of the 553 holes Harding would play over the next month in Florida.[117]

The *Pioneer* was a hulking boat; while only about 150 feet long, it was almost as wide as the *Mayflower*, at 321 feet long. The four-day river trip was meandering, with no set plan and lots of stops for golf and handshaking along the Indian and Halifax rivers; the Secret Service followed in both a yacht and a car. Mrs. Harding enjoyed the stops; she and Evalyn stayed aboard and had peace and quiet while the men were off on the links.[118] And when she chose to greet people, she was well received. As one observer noted, she "had the warmest of handclasps—the kind that comes straight from the heart . . . [while] sweetly attributing much help in her regaining her strength to the Florida sunshine."[119]

One of their first stops was at Clifford Kling's home, Rockledge, one mile south of Cocoa Beach, where the Hardings were given a plot of land in honor of earlier visits they had made to nearby Merritt Island. Florence took the deed, shaking hands with fifty people. They were next off to stops including Daytona, New Smyrna, Hobe Sound, Palm Beach, Ft. Lauderdale, and Miami. Arriving in Palm Beach, Florence walked firmly down a wobbly gangplank, according to the *Washington Post*, dressed in "white pumps and white stockings, a pleated white outing skirt, a white blouse with a black silk necktie and a black and white sport hat."[120]

During this trip, according to Evalyn's later recollections, Harding took advantage of a golfing stop one day to visit with some women. He and Ned returned at 4 p.m., "whooping and yelling," she writes, "and the Duchess was furious, and raging." Evalyn continued, "They went downstairs and you can say they had a bitter disagreement in the stateroom because you could hear it all over the boat."[121]

Evalyn reported on more shenanigans later at Palm Beach, claiming that her husband, Ned, introduced Warren to some of the local beauties, including Mrs. E. Clarence Jones and Maizie Haywood (Bill Haywood's wife), while pretending they were at a golf game. To facilitate this, Evalyn took Florence on a long ride, and rather foolishly drove past Mrs. Jones's house—and saw Starling, the Secret Service man, out front. Florence grabbed Evalyn's arm: "I am black and blue for days," she complained, and Florence demanded, "Whose house is that?" Evalyn explained she had no idea, and back at their cottage, "the top was . . . blown off" when the men returned. According to Evalyn, Harding came in and said, "We-e-ell, Duchess, you look beautiful tonight." She said, "Warren, go upstairs this minute. I want to talk to you . . . you have been drinking. . . . Where have you been? Out with a lot of hussies." His reply, in Evalyn's words: "Now, listen, I am President of the United States. You think you are most of the time, but by God I am tonight," whereupon he "poured himself a whale of a drink." While Florence scolded her husband for his misbehavior, she was hypocritical about her own, Evalyn asserted, since Mrs. Harding insisted as the boat passed under bridges that they cover up their card playing, in case people looking over the side thought it was gambling.[122]

How reliable are Evalyn's tales of men, women, and their games? Not only do the outbursts she describes seem completely out of character for the mellow Warren, but so too do the indiscreet comments by Florence in front of others. It is not unlikely that Harding had a good time with his friends in Florida, and that women were even present; Mrs. Harding was no doubt concerned about appearances. But as to Harding's drinking or carousing, this is much less credible. According to George Christian Sr., "During all the years of our close friendship with Mr. and Mrs. Harding . . . there was no alcoholic liquor of any description kept in or about the house. Whatever liquor was indulged in was . . . along social lines . . . [and] of the most moderate character."[123] Of course, Christian was a loyal friend and neighbor. But Starling, no Harding sycophant, provides similar reports of the president's moderate consumption. Moreover, Evalyn's quite nasty portrait of Florence seems too jarring, considering their warm friendship then. She had written Florence in February that "I miss you so and will be so happy when I see you."[124]

The previous summer, too, when gossipy stories circulated about their friendship—heightened by the "celebrity culture" that cast a certain glare on both women—the heiress wrote her friend, "Of course they are only trying to make trouble between us and I should think after trying so hard and for such a long time they might realize by this time it is no use! . . . Dear Mrs. Harding don't worry about the horrid newspapers! . . . You know I love you, and I can't begin to tell you how proud I am of you."[125]

Evalyn's snarky comments later were probably connected to both the decline in the Hardings' reputation by the time she was recording her memories in the mid-1930s, and, perhaps even more, to Evalyn's own descent into morphine addiction, which had likely distorted her outlook on the past. Even more telling, her original manuscript was deemed so bad that George Lorimer of the *Saturday Evening Post*, who planned to serialize it, demanded she—or rather her ghostwriter, Boyden Sparkes—revise it, because "as it stands, the book is thoroughly out of balance." Her agent, Charles Baker, agreed that the manuscript's last 30,000 words were in "exceedingly bad taste." Evalyn defensively asserted that "I would never consider for an instant having it published the way it was," undermining the veracity of her own words. Still, Evalyn doubted that Sparkes would revise it properly, "because he is in an antagonistic frame of mind toward her."[126] So here we have a manuscript that is tainted by Evalyn's illness, her ghostwriter's animus, or some combination—all undermining its credibility.

In any case, the reliable Dr. Boone can tell us little, as he had stayed on the train with Daugherty, his nurse, and Jess Smith; their train would meet the president's boat in Miami.[127] They got to that city's luxurious Flamingo Hotel ahead of the riverine group on March 7, taking a large fifth-floor suite on its gorgeous grounds. Joel and Jess had to share a room, much to the doctor's discomfort. Smith liked to talk on the phone much of the time, and loudly. "Jess Smith's way of living and my way of living . . . were almost the opposite," Boone sighed. Indeed, Boone liked him less and less, resenting him as a "bumptious" attention seeker.[128] Still, with swimming and golf abundant and free, Boone could not complain for long, although he was often busy dealing with everyone's ailments.

Conditions were also trying on the *Pioneer,* indeed, "strenuous and hectic," because the boat ran aground on sandbars on several occasions and its close quarters put everyone on each other's nerves. Boone thought that the boat trip had been rather stressful for Florence; despite having mostly been on the deck, she looked less well than she had at the start of the trip. She and Mrs. McLean would now rest up in their little bungalow at the Flamingo, meeting with friends like Mrs. Isabelle Firestone and Mrs. Cyrus H. K. Curtis of Philadelphia. Warren, on the other hand, was determined to get everything out of this long-delayed vacation, as Boone noted, and "kept them following a terrible pace."[129] As if to make up for lost time, the president immediately was off on a speedboat to the Cocolobo Cay Club, from which he and his friends would take a deep-sea fishing trip. It would be his and Florence's first separation since her illness. Florence saw him off, taking the longest walk she had yet taken in her convalescence.[130] But Harding actually returned the next day when a strong wind prevented the trip.

On March 17, Florence made her first social call since becoming ill, going to Harvey and Isabelle Firestone's for lunch with Warren and the McLeans, and letting herself be photographed. She and Evalyn departed the following day for Palm Beach on the McLean train, the *Enquire.* There, she shook hands with 100 people. Harding went north by car, and they all then boarded the *Pioneer* in Palm Beach for a harrowing trip north. If not for the "giant Negro pilot," George Williams, they would have surely been stuck in the sandbars. Florence mostly rested again, while Harding stopped for frequent golf.[131] On March 26, he played thirty-six holes, the equivalent of eight miles, while Florence and Evalyn took a ten-mile drive. They next visited St. Augustine and the deluxe Ponce de Leon Hotel. Florence's room looked out onto its lovely courtyard, filled with flowers and birds; the famed Alcazar gardens were across the street.[132]

While at the Ponce de Leon, the Hardings and their friends saw a new film, *The Message of Emile Coué,* at Florence's suggestion, and lightened up with a Charlie Chaplin movie as well.[133] Florence also held her first "authorized" interview since her illness. She told columnist Edith C. Dunton on March 27 that she was going to Alaska that summer with the president. It was actually the first "positive official statement" of this western trip; she looked forward to being on trains and in coliseums with him, "just as she always has." The Florida trip had, despite Boone's worries, on the whole restored her; she could now walk easily and was strong enough to withstand the longer venture. Mrs. Harding told Dunton she believed that the reason she had gotten ill (and the president too, with grippe) were the pressures and stresses of the Washington Conference and its associated entertainments. While they had valiantly worked "to bring . . . foreign nations . . . into touch and association with every element of American life and into a common understanding," these worthy goals, and the enormous social engagements needed to make this understanding possible, had worn them out. Her revived health was owing to the "prayers of the people" and Florida's sunshine. She was happy she now could be involved again in causes that mattered to her, especially, "the service men of the country."[134]

Florence did not overlook her grandchildren in the middle of her merrymaking, either—even if she thought that her daughter-in-law was in danger of forgetting *her*, complaining that Esther never wrote. Of course, Esther's new baby, as well as two young children, might have explained her inattention! But Florence could not resist chiding Esther that she had not noticed her mother-in-law's checks had come three months in advance. She sent the money, Florence noted a little peevishly, because "I thought it might make it easier for you," especially when new clothes might be needed for the children. She was happy to report at the same time that she had done well on the trip, even if she rarely left the boat or the hotel, and now she could walk better and even stand the crowds. Though she thought home was the best place to recover, as she noticed others, like Mrs. Sawyer and Mrs. Christian, all "having a good time," she was ever more convinced that "one of these days I will be a new woman too."[135] Florence was nothing if not determined.

She had to be, with so much going on in St. Augustine. The Miami group's train arrived on the 28th, and the addled attorney general soon announced, publicly and with no provocation, that Harding would run again and be renominated![136] Sawyer was appalled by Daugherty's recklessness, and he complained to Boone that this was not only premature, but evidence that the attorney general "at times overestimated what he had done in the President's behalf." If so, many agreed with such conceptions and pestered the attorney general constantly, thinking he was the president's "oracle," as Boone put it.[137]

As Sawyer, Boone, and no doubt Harding feared, a number of papers were critical of this precipitous announcement, although by today's standards, it was not *that* early. More sympathetically, the *Philadelphia Public Ledger* put it down to the fact that the president's vacation after a hard year, and the frightening sickness of his wife, had readied him for a new challenge. Harding declared, however, that he was not announcing anything yet. He was angry at Daugherty, but in his typical nonconfrontational way, he avoided direct conflict, likely blaming his friend's illness for the blunder.[138] Harding continued to play golf and avoid all the political talk. If anything, he seemed to be making other plans, when a few days later papers announced he had bought his birthplace, situated on 265½ acres in Mt. Gilead, Ohio, where he would build a new house and a golf course, to enjoy his time after leaving the White House.[139]

The Hardings arrived in Augusta to spend a week of more golf on April 1; 200 were waiting for them there at 6:30 A.M. Florence went right to the Hotel Bon-Air, exhausted. Despite temperatures in the 40s, her husband played for hours. The Boone/Daugherty party, meanwhile, was off to Grove Park Inn in Asheville, North Carolina, for several weeks, to give the attorney general more time to recover—he still had sometimes slurred speech—and Daugherty kindly paid for a visit from Boone's wife and daughter. Daugherty wrote to Florence on April 11, appreciating the rest if feeling homesick. "I always consider you no matter how brutal you are," he joked.[140]

RETURN TO THE CAPITAL AND PREPARATION FOR ALASKA

Back in Washington, Florence now felt strong enough to walk through the station to her car, which she hadn't done on the way south. But columnist Jean Eliot wondered, as did others, whether she would be having parties anytime soon. Parties were happening, nonetheless—the Easter Egg Roll on April 1 had brought 5,000 to the White House. Meanwhile, Florence had not forgotten her garden, with spring busting out everywhere. She was planning to have some vintage flowers planted in the south lawn, including hollyhocks, asters, foxgloves, wild violets, and hyacinths. By May, the grounds were "lovelier than ever," with songbirds drawn by new fountains and birdhouses.[141] Florence was building here on the work of Edith Roosevelt, who had created a Dutch garden on the grounds, as well as Ellen Wilson, who created the Rose Garden. While Florence lovingly ministered to the White House's exterior, the administration's secretary of the interior, Albert Fall, had quietly resigned, claiming his business interests—in the oil industry, ironically!—needed his attention.

Unaware of Fall's financial finaglings, President Harding returned happy, noting how good the trip had been for both of them, and vowing to get out to a golf course three times a week for his health.[142] Alas, the demands of his Washington life made this impossible before leaving for Alaska. Florence, too, was upbeat, writing Mrs. Jennings that the trip had been salutary. "I can see no reason now, if I exercise my judgment at all and have common sense, I should not get perfectly well." She was back in the swing of things; that night they would see Al Jolson in his new play.[143]

But as she also wrote another friend, she still felt she had to be careful and not "overdo."[144] She echoed this theme in a letter to Esther later in April: "while I look much better I am only about 75% to the good yet. Seem to have no endurance. Maybe that will come a little. The weather is lovely but I don't get out to ride or walk. Have been to church twice [and] the theatre three times."[145] Her first lady duties, like "receiving diplomats," were also "very trying, for being shut up so long ago I have lost 'my stride' to speak." She told Esther, "one does not realize how many changes can take place in six months." That night, she looked forward to "sup. with Stella," a Marion friend, where they would "have a nice little visit and talk about you all back home."[146]

Until she was fully herself, Florence felt compelled to travel with Warren only "unofficially," as she did in a "hectic" trip to New York from April 23 to 25. Nevertheless, she still joined him for most of the activities there; she saw him speak to the American Society of Newspaper Editors about the World Court, and she visited the new plant of the *Herald Tribune*, where she started the presses. They attended a Music Box review, and Florence went clothes shopping too.

She was most visible and socially engaged her last day, when she hosted newspaperwomen in the reception room at the Waldorf Astoria, her first day fully "back," as she put it.[147] She treated the journalists to her observations of "human nature." Impressed by her vivacity, they listened intently to her analysis, and her conviction of the relative importance of "features," starting with the mouth, then the ears, and then the eyes as the most revealing human characteristics. One young reporter's aural organ drew Florence's inspection, and she declared it "a nice ear . . . artistic," and wondered why the journalist was covering it up, "rashly." Indulging in a little psychoanalysis of her own, Florence speculated, "you don't take up for yourself, do you?" And what about hands, this young woman wondered. "I have large hands," said Florence. "I studied music and . . . I have always driven fast horses. Those things increase the size of hands." Lawler too, had noted Mrs. Harding's hands: "unusually large, strong, powerful, crushing . . . did not fit her delicate body." Reporter Ruth Dayton was quite taken by Florence's performance at this reception, and perhaps even more by the first lady's own renewed appearance: she was "tall and slender, her gray hair was in waves and done high. Her famous 'dog collar' that she always wears . . . with its mass of diamonds, was about her neck. A long clinging real lace evening dress was draped about her, over black satin, and seemingly tied up on one side with a large bow of orchid and black ribbon. Black hose and black satin slippers with brilliants ornamented her feet." Her clothes were an indication of her vigor. Florence told the gathering, "It is my first real day back in the world after my illness and it feels good. I am talking to you because I am interested in women. I like to see women succeed," she said.[148]

On the way back from New York she caught a cold, and she could not get out of bed for two days. Rumors flew that she was "seriously ill."[149] She was not, and recovered quickly. She wrote her friend William Wrigley that she now was 85 percent to the good, and she intended to continue to care of herself, so she would enjoy Alaska.[150] When Boone and Daugherty returned in early May from Asheville, she told the doctor he needn't come twice a day anymore to check on her. Boone felt she was brusque in this instruction, which he thought was "unintentional"; she was probably trying to save him trouble. Still, her "attitude" struck him.[151] Perhaps Sawyer had been attempting to reassert himself as Florence's chief medical adviser. In any case, her health really seemed to be improving, as she continued her activities in May, attending a horse show at Arlington Park and a vaudeville performance at Keith's. She frequently invited people over to the White House to see movies, too, and clearly had no animus against Boone, inviting his sister, Marjorie Hood, to a showing of *The Bright Shawl* on May 24. The film featured Dorothy Gish, a White House habitué. With old friend and former postmaster general Will Hays, now the first president of the Motion Picture Producers and Distributors of America, the Hardings had a conduit for movies. A guest at one of her evenings observed, "Her color, buoyancy and old-time vivacity have all returned. Many think she has grown perceptibly younger in looks." Florence took it upon herself to do all the preparation for these gatherings, including flower arrangements.[152]

In the meantime, her still fragile health prevented her involvement in any large receptions. Thus, when the Hardings opened the White House grounds to large groups like the Girl Scouts that spring, only the president received them. Nevertheless, Florence made herself visible from the South Portico, where "hundreds of eager-faced scouts gaz[ed] up at her with respect and affection" and sang to her, while her husband shook their hands.[153] Similarly, he grasped the proffered palms of 5,000 social workers, members of the Big Brothers and Big Sisters organization, who lined up by the South Portico to hear a personal greeting from Mrs. Harding and a short "maiden speech," her first since her illness, where she told them she "was a Big Sister herself—and would like to be one to the whole population."[154] Her passive but intent involvement in civic affairs continued as she lent her name to events as patroness or "honorary sponsor," even if she did not attend them, such as the League of American Pen Women's fete on May 14 and the American Women's Legion garden party on May 24. She also subscribed to the first ($50) bond to construct a home for the Women's National Republican Club, thus assisting in the raising of $100,000 for the home, called a "milestone in the history of feminism in this country."[155] Florence, despite her continuing convalescence, was once again engaged with many of her former passions.

On May 22, Boone learned that he really was indispensable after all; the Hardings wanted him to go to Alaska. His medical abilities, and his navy connections, made him a vital presence on the voyage. They would be taking the naval transport *Henderson* for the leg from

Florence greeting delegates to the National Conference of Social Work with Ora Baldinger and Laura Harlan. Courtesy of the Library of Congress.

Tacoma to Alaska, as well as for the San Diego–Panama–Newport News return. Boone knew this ship, having last been on it during his tour to France in 1917. He knew some of its personnel as well, and he was most concerned that the ship's medical staff be fully appraised of the first lady's health—because unlike the train, the ocean voyage would take them far from necessary medical facilities. Although Florence was no doubt better, Boone worried that frequent changes in climate, summer heat, changing foods, and "nervous, emotional and great physical strain" could create hazards.[156] He arranged for navy nurse Powderly to come with them, and he took it upon himself, "very secretly," to make sure that there was a surgeon on board; finally, and most quietly, he planned for a coffin to be placed on the ship. A morbid plan, but a necessary one, he felt: "The casket . . . was, I thought, foresighted action on my part should Mrs. Harding again be gravely stricken and succumb."[157] Florence knew nothing of this, but was sad for another reason: Evalyn would not be joining them. Her friend had had a goiter operation in May and would need weeks to recover. On May 16, Miss Todd, Evalyn's secretary, thanked Florence for a flower arrangement she'd sent. Evalyn had yet to sit up, but when she did, "I am sure you will be the first person, she will want to see."[158]

The president's health also seemed fragile just then. As Florence wrote her daughter-in-law on May 27, "Was up until three this morning with Mr. H. A case of indigestion. I have *no* use for that trouble." Continuing the medical focus, she urged Esther to get Roscoe's ulcers x-rayed and to protect George from the ills of summer camp until at least puberty: "He is not strong enough to stand that *out of door* exposure," she opined, although Jean was perfectly suited for it. On a cheerier note, she told Esther of some recent White House delights: outside, there had been the lit-up vista of Pennsylvania Avenue for the Strangers in Our Gates festival, and within, the house has been "full of people," including old friends like the Christians for movies in the East Room. Mostly, though, she told Esther, she was busy getting ready for Alaska, which would be "hectic" and "require a good deal changing clothes." Because her maid was ill, she was glad to have the invaluable Ruth Powderly. But, she worried, "I must have more care and am afraid she can't do it all." In the end, Catherine Wynn recovered enough to come.[159]

In the midst of these preparations, the Harding household was hit with a bizarre shock. On May 30, Boone got a call at 6:30 A.M. from the manager of the Wardman Park Hotel, where Smith and Daugherty shared an apartment, urgently asking him to rush over. Daugherty was sleeping at the White House that night, and Smith was alone in the apartment—or what was left of Smith. As Boone soon saw, Daugherty's aide had shot himself at close range, and lay doubled over on his bed. The doctor immediately called the president, and when Harding told his houseguest, Daugherty, appalled, "leaned way over toward the floor with his head in this hands" and kept asking himself, "Why did he do it?"[160] There were any number of reasons, of course, including Smith's selective and legally questionable enforcement of Prohibition while working for Daugherty; he had long been an unsavory character, as Boone noticed. Missed by few, Smith's death left an indelible mark on the administration, a harbinger of the trouble to come later. The attorney general, still infirm, would suffer the most for having allowed such high jinks to go on.[161]

The following day, May 31, saw the Hardings, or at least a number of their tiniest fans, almost undergo the same fate—involuntarily. It was Washington's music week, and Florence and her husband attended a concert of 8,000 singing children at American League Park. The trouble started when five-year-old Helen Briggs, after singing a song with several hundred other kindergartners, called out to the president, "Will you come today and play with us?" Harding could hardly say no, and took Helen into his arms and the box. But his kindness only incited the other little ones, who stampeded the first couple in a rush of excitement, pelting the president with flowers (each child had a bouquet), and grabbing and tugging at his clothes. Harding then grabbed the littlest children close to him, pulling them to safety in his box, as the organizers began playing loud music to distract the other hordes of youngsters, and the marines standing guard reestablished control. This frightening episode, which came close to being tragic, serves as further indication of a warmth and approachability that made the Hardings hugely appealing public personalities, though it much taxed the president and his wife.[162] After the near trampling, on June 4, the Hardings led another major public event, laying the Zero Mile Marker in Washington, the "Hub of [a] National Highway System," to serve as a guide for distances from Washington, D.C., to other cities. It was also a testament to the Hardings' passion for driving. As S. M. Johnson, general director of the Lee Highway Association, boldly declared: "We have taken our stand for a paved United States." Unfortunately, all the pavement in the world could not stop a low-flying airplane from marring the ceremonies, interrupting the president's speech with the roar of engines.[163] No matter; as if to underline the importance of the marker, the imminent arrival of the National Shriners Convention made possible "the greatest assemblage of automobiles in history" in the nation's capital.

The four-day Shriner fest would only complicate the Hardings' lives as they attempted to plan and pack for Alaska, contributing to much extra hoopla and resulting exhaustion. The benevolent order's Washington visitors began their proceedings with a four-hour parade, including 25,000 "nobles of the Mystic shrine" and 110 bands, under a punishing sun that had transformed Pennsylvania Avenue "into a heat radiating mass of asphalt." From their box, the Hardings, along with 200,000 others, watched the joyful members of this "bizarre" ensemble, where "the men looked rather foolish in their very glad rags," as one columnist snickered.[164] But Florence and Warren, a thirty-third-degree Mason himself, didn't just watch. They saluted each time the Stars and Stripes passed, and over the course of two more parades, including a pageant parade and a 3½-hour-long evening procession lit up by batteries in the Shriners' sleeves, she and her husband jumped up 1,500 times, just about every third minute. Other women saw Mrs. Harding and decided to emulate her, which she approved wholeheartedly. "Why shouldn't the women of America pay the same respect to the flag as the men do? . . . I propose hereafter, as long as I live, to salute the American flag."[165]

The next day, a thousand of the Ohio contingent and their wives came to the White House for a reception, among the 50,000 who would come to the White House for tours during the Shriner festival (including 20,000 on June 7, a one-day record). The latter were admitted in groups of 1,000 and given free range on the first floor, reminiscent of Andrew Jackson's inauguration. They brought with them blocks of ice—which likely caused more mess than coolness—and purchased pictures of Laddie Boy to take home, to benefit the Animal Rescue League (Florence was enterprising, as usual). Harding did not greet all of them—only about 10,000. Meanwhile, he and Florence were entertained by the members of the Aladdin Temple of Columbus, Harding's home temple, who sang "My Hero" to them. The Baghdad temple from Montana, meanwhile, appeared in blackface with a portable piano. Trying to recoup her strength, Florence stayed on the portico, calling down to friends, trying to direct the band, clapping, singing, and cheering loudly. Her doctors had forbade her to mingle, although she finally did, with the Hawaiian Shriners.[166]

Exhausted after this huge affair, Mrs. Harding rested for a day, but only in preparation for their next Masonic engagement. They left the morning of June 9 with friends for a trip on the *Mayflower* ending up in Milford, Delaware, where President Harding would be initiated into an elite Masonic tribe, the Tall Cedars of Lebanon. The first stop was lunch in Wilmington with a group of Young Republicans, followed by a forty-car motorcade to Milford, with stops in Dover and Newark for speeches on the way. After the two-hour induction, with 5,000 Cedars in attendance, they headed for Lewes at midnight to board the *Mayflower* home, and were nearly mauled there by a group who swarmed their limousine, as if they were movie stars.[167] By the time of his speech in Lewes, Harding's seventh in eighteen hours, it was close to 2 A.M., and his voice was hoarse. As they waited to embark on the *Mayflower*, Mrs. Harding narrowly missed being hit by a steel cable. No doubt they were all relieved to reach Washington the next morning.[168] But after this gauntlet, how could Alaska faze her? The *Washington Post* noted with approval how well she had withstood the strain of this short but packed weekend.[169]

Mrs. Harding wrote to a friend that the trip to Delaware was "extremely strenuous, especially after the excitement of the Shriner week," and she told Esther that the trip had just "about finished me, but I am still here."[170] With Alaska ever closer, she had even more to pack in—her clothes. How would she finish filling the trunks, what with all her interruptions, and houseguests, and her maid, Catherine, still ill? But she did, somehow, and was ready to depart for the biggest, most ambitious journey of her life. In her sixty-three years, she would never have so much happiness, so much excitement, as the trip to Alaska brought. Yet at the same time, neither did any journey ever leave her so heartbroken.

CHAPTER 6

CROSSING THE COUNTRY, JUNE–AUGUST 1923

ALASKA JOURNEY

Mrs. Harding did not have to go with Warren to Alaska, of course, but not only was she very interested, she also felt it her duty, as one newspaper put it, owing to "her high estimate of the importance of her role" in the relationship—a not unmerited reckoning.[1] She had wanted to go to Alaska for half a dozen years, and finally her doctor was going to let her. But she was still upset that Evalyn would not be along. On the eve of her departure for Alaska, Florence wrote a heartfelt letter to her friend: "I am just distressed beyond words that we have not been able to break bread together before my leaving." Dr. Sawyer had forbade her to meet with Evalyn in those remaining days, worried she might be "worn out" by additional socializing and thus lose her strength. Perhaps he worried it would tax the recovering Mrs. McLean as well. What a "disappointment" the last year had been, Florence sighed: "between my condition and yours we have not been able to have our usual good old times." Eerily, she added, "Should I live to return from the trip I do hope this fall we can be more together, and again cannot refrain from voicing my regret that you and Ned cannot be members of our party." She sent her love along with "a parting kiss to little Emily."[2] Her husband perhaps had a premonition of his own, because shortly before their departure, he sold the *Star* for about $525,000, making him the richest occupant of the White House up to that time.³ Despite their divestment and the new owners' stake, Florence continued to believe that the *Star* was invested with "a moral public ownership . . . its interest and goodwill held by Marion and Marion County and the people therein."⁴

For some, this seemed to confirm Harding would never return to Ohio after leaving the White House but would settle in Washington. Or did he have some sense he might not return from Alaska at all? The irrepressible Gaston Means would have argued he had good reason to feel that way, since Florence had planned the trip to Alaska as a way to do away with him! Following Madame Marcia's predictions that she was a "Child of Destiny," Mrs. Harding had to rid herself of her husband, so that "the greatest, richest . . . most powerful nation on earth shall know the rule of a woman." (One might argue that it had already known it, in the previous administration.) Florence, an "unhappy and dishonored woman," who was now "half-mad, fanatical," Means declared, would be no Josephine to Warren's Napoleon, no "discarded wife."⁵

But Harding was more worried about his advance man's planning killing him than he was about Florence's plotting doing so. Harding complained to Starling that Walter Brown had made "a circus out of the trip . . . he has booked me from 8 to 10 hours of constant activity every place we are to stop." Harding concluded, rightly, "I won't get a minute's rest." As Starling discovered, Brown had arranged things so that the president would pass every factory owned by local Republican committeemen, and be subject to their long-winded speeches, and forced to make many more of his own! It was the first time Harding had ever asked for a break of this kind. But the busy spring, Smith's death and Forbes's resignation had exhausted the president, the Secret Service man guessed; "he looked more weary than I had ever seen him."⁶

Yet Harding does not seem to have gone to Alaska to "ponder his troubles," as one recent author has suggested.⁷ First of all, the trip was a long-planned one, not occasioned by "troubles." Second, Harding didn't really have any "troubles" in June 1923—he had fired Forbes, Fall had resigned, and nothing yet of his malfeasance, or Daugherty's, had been connected with the administration. Jess Smith's suicide certainly left a pall, but his demise hardly merited a trip of such ambitious scope! Herbert Hoover, however, believed

Smith's demise was the reason an "exceedingly nervous and distraught" Harding invited him to come to his cabin as they steamed for Alaska, where Harding asked the secretary: "If you knew of a great scandal in our administration, would you for the good of the country and the party expose it publicly or would you bury it?" Hoover stoutly replied that the president should "Publish it, and at least get credit for integrity on your side." He recalled that as soon as he raised the issue of Daugherty's involvement, Harding dropped the matter. This story, timely as it sounds, rings somewhat tinny. Smith had not killed himself "just before" the trip, as Hoover said, but nearly a month earlier, an age in politics. Moreover, Harding didn't really like Hoover, so it's not clear he would have unburdened himself to the secretary.[8]

The trip, in any case, was pared down. Although they would still cover close to 25,000 miles, Harding planned only to make twenty formal speeches en route.[9] Florence, meanwhile, ordered Starling to keep Boone and Sawyer close by, in adjoining suites, if possible. Starling, foresightful man that he was, also made sure that the San Francisco hotel rooms were ready from mid-July on, in case they were needed ahead of schedule—as they unfortunately would be.[10]

ALASKA JOURNEY

As the first president to visit Alaska, Harding had hoped to reform the territory's administration, encourage more immigration, and bring in experts who could speak to the more efficient exploitation of its resources and the development of transportation networks, in a territory where, though a billion dollars' worth of resources had been extracted since 1867, "the surface has hardly been scratched." Yet just as today, there were concerns then about conservation of these resources. The situation was complex, and the president soon realized it might take two generations before it could be sorted out.[11] Nevertheless, the trip was a beginning toward a greater connection with that vast territory, and was aptly called the "Voyage of Understanding."

Their journey would cover 5,000 miles by train, the other 20,000 by an ocean-going vessel. The naval transport *Henderson* was thought to be more relaxing for Florence, and Warren, than a reverse cross-country rail tour.[12] Their return would go back through the Panama Canal, a jaunt Florence was anticipating as a long rest and as a sweet reminder of their joyous postelection trip. After Panama, there would be stops in San Juan, Puerto Rico, St. Thomas, Virgin Islands, Newport News, Virginia, and finally, New York City, on August 28.[13] Florence later reflected that while she knew her husband was not entirely well beforehand, she hoped the Panama cruise, at least, would revive him.[14]

At precisely 3:45 P.M. on June 20, a quarter of an hour before their train was ready to leave Washington, "five or six, alert, athletic young men" of the Secret Service came to escort the Hardings down to Union Station. Valets had already taken their bags. Once at the station, crowds pressed upon them, the police struggling to hold the people back. The Harding party had to rush into the station through the President's Room. They boarded their luxurious train with its six compartment cars, a diner, two baggage cars, and of course their coach, the *Superbe*. There was a large observation platform in the rear, equipped with amplifiers for making speeches. The *Superbe*, at the end of the train, also included a combined observation and drawing room car with "cool green" upholstery. The car had four sleeping apartments, for the Hardings (two), Sawyers, and Works, and a kitchen. It also had a chef, H. W. Smith, a porter, and a waiter. All the waitstaff were not only Pullman's best but models of "masculine pulchritude."[15] Not looking so bad himself was Arthur Brooks, Harding's valet, a major in the colored division of the District of Columbia's national guard, and a most excellent judge not only of clothes but of all the needs of his client, as he had been for every president since William H. Taft. Chef Smith, who had been in presidential service since the Grant administration, noted that the Hardings liked "plain things," like "cereal, fruits, bacon and eggs, toast and coffee."[16] Still, variety was available if they wanted it: in Pocatello, Idaho, for instance, the president got not only 150 pounds of trout, but a case of new potatoes and four cases of Idaho lettuce.[17]

Also along for the trip were friends, politicians, and administration members including the Christians, Sawyers, and Jenningses; Frederick H. Gillette, Speaker of the House; publicist Judson C. Welliver; and Major Baldinger, Dr. Boone, and Secretaries Work and Wallace and their wives.[18] Members of the press had joined them too, of course, as well as telephone men, to connect the correspondents with their home offices. Radio men operated the amplifiers for Harding's speeches; these would be rigged for national broadcast as well.

All told, eighty-five passengers embarked for Alaska on that hot June day. Among the most eager of them was Florence, the first first lady to make a trip of this magnitude. She was very much in charge of the trip's program. If changes were to be made, she was the one to consult, the "social as well as the political center of the expedition."[19] She would be visible as well, and would give spontaneous speeches and interviews with reporters, and energetically greet crowds from her train.

The weather stayed hot through St. Louis, their first major stop, where they attended various functions, including a visit to the International Rotary Convention, a reception at the Statler Hotel, and another address at the Coliseum, plus a theatre performance, *The Prince of Pilsen*. After this, they were on their way to Kansas City at midnight. As the Hardings exited the train the next morning, they were greeted by 1,800 people—more than a third of whom were on the reception committee! Standing by to keep the hordes at bay were representatives of the police, the military, and the Boy Scouts. As they always did, the first couple greeted each visitor personally. Concerned about such exertions in the heat, Boone and Sawyer were trying to get Florence to stop this practice, but she refused and would continue it through many more parades, receptions, and banquets on this trip. As she insisted, "I don't get tired, because I have such a good time doing it." Boone was amazed at her performance.[20]

Following the handshaking, the Hardings joined a parade of 200 cars in front of an assemblage of 200,000 Kansas Citians.[21] This was followed by a reception at the posh Muehlenbach Hotel (where they were nearly stampeded), some golf, and more greetings, this time with Boy Scouts and war mothers. Florence coped by fanning herself constantly, but Warren's lips got sunburned and swollen, so he went to bed. At dinner, Emma Fall, wife of the former secretary of the interior, Albert, came to join the Hardings and their friends at dinner, and rumors have flown ever since that it was on this occasion that the Hardings learned of the oil scandal in which Fall was later implicated. No, Mrs. Fall insists, and Christian, who was also there, backs her up: indeed, she could not get a moment alone with the Hardings for any such intimate discussion.[22]

Florence, meanwhile, drew much favorable attention on this visit. She was, one paper reported, "the center of as much, if not more, interest than was the president." A reporter commented flatteringly on her hair, "a golden brown, slightly streaked with gray," and her clothes, including her dress, a navy blue flowered crepe, cut slightly low in the neck; her accessories, including her black velvet choker and long white kid gloves; and the "daintiness" of her shoes in graceful gray suede, high-heeled strap pumps with cut steel buckles.[23]

The following day in Hutchinson, Kansas, the heat was even worse. After a long and sweltering parade, the Hardings went to a farm, where the president operated a tractor and stacked wheat "quite successfully and skillfully,"[24] even though he had had little direct contact with grains for years, except in his cereal bowl. Unfortunately, he also got a horrific sunburn. Nevertheless, waking up the next morning in Colorado Springs to a Sunday crowd at 6:57 A.M., the president gave an inspiring sermon on the tracks. He rued the decline of religiosity over the last half century, and he lamented America's "sordid" obsession with "material existence."[25]

In Denver later that morning, greeted by 10,000, the Hardings' main goal was rest — after church and lunch with Senator Lawrence C. Phipps and his wife, and a visit to Fitzsimons Hospital. Florence was, as always, in her element on that hospital visit. She did not ask about injuries or simply offer sympathy, but instead "laughed with [the patients], joked with them, made them forget [their] hips were in casts," the *Denver Post* noted. Although the rest was meant largely for Florence, she seemed "the life of the party" in Denver.[26]

One female journalist was wowed to meet Mrs. Harding, with her "democratic" manner. Frances Wayne was pleased to note, too, that "there is nothing of the invalid" about her, but instead "enthusiasm, the bright eyes, the smiling lips, the brisk, free walk of youth."[27] As Boone observed, Florence "took part in everything," operating almost on some drug of her own body's making.[28] She was unquestionably having "the time of her life."[29] Poor Miss Wayne was unlikely to learn much from Florence or the other women of the group beyond their views of the weather, however, as the Harding administration's "unwritten laws" made them unavailable for interview. "We might say too much or not enough," Mrs. Work said, "and so the best way is the silent way." Another in the party agreed: "Anyone who has read history knows what ducks and drakes women have played with men's affairs."[30]

After her return from the hospital, Florence went off to bed. But that evening, the trip's joy was blighted by the deaths of three journalists in the party, in a car accident in Bear Canyon. Harding was crushed by the tragedy, thought to have been caused by a broken gear on the steep slope, which had sent the newsmen crashing below. One man, amazingly, survived. Harding pulled himself together and the next day, after a huge parade, he gave a stern speech on Prohibition—his most adamant ever—urging people not to drink, even legally, from old stores of booze. According to Boone, this seemed to underline that Harding had become a "total abstainer," and indeed, except for a small drink when he was very ill, which his doctors urged upon him, he held off completely for the rest of his days.[31] The *New York Times* remarked on his speech on the Volstead law: "Mr. Harding stated his position in such a way as to show a belief in the virtues of prohibition and indicated confidence that [it] had come to stay and ultimately would be observed." The *Times* attributed his emphatic tone to Florence's influence.[32]

Such observations imply that this was a change from Harding's earlier patterns in the White House, an assessment in which Mrs. Jaffray, the housekeeper, would have concurred. During Prohibition, no drinks could be served at state dinners, whether of store or new liquor, she notes. Nevertheless, "on occasions when he entertained his most intimate man friends," she asserted, he "would serve a cocktail in the library or in his study" before dinner, or afterward, over cards.[33] If Alice Roosevelt Longworth is to be believed, Harding's "study was filled with cronies . . . the air heavy with tobacco smoke, trays with bottles containing every imaginable brand of whiskey stood about, cards, and poker chips ready at hand—a general atmosphere of waistcoat unbuttoned, feet on the desk, and the spittoon alongside."[34] Smoking, drinking, and card games may well have transpired, but as mentioned earlier, Harding's intake of liquor was generally moderate, and it is not clear that the whiskey was illegally obtained; its provenance was not revealed by Mrs. Longworth.

The Hardings were in Cheyenne on June 26, where the president gave a coal speech in that mining center, before pushing on to Salt Lake City later that day, passing thirty-seven miles of people en route from Cheyenne. There was a parade, a reception, and golf in Salt Lake, followed by dinner and a visit to the Mormon Tabernacle. The following day, at the urging of Utah Republican Senator Reed Smoot, the Harding party visited the newly proposed Zion National Park, no easy trek. First, they traveled nearly 300 miles over a brand-new railway, to Cedar City, Utah; there, they were met by seventy-five Plute Indians in full paint and regalia. These bucks, squaws, and their papooses looked forward to shaking the hand of "heap big man of United States," as Captain Pete, chief of the tribe, called the president.[35] Six thousand whites were also waiting to meet him there. The Harding entourage then continued by automobile for four more hours of dirt roads, stirring up clouds of dust in their wake, and in their throats. At the end of this second leg, the male members of the group got on horseback to ride up the dry Virgin River bed. "He made a very picturesque figure wearing leather chaps, blue flowing neckerchief, and large Panama hat," noted Boone of President Harding. Their ride eventually took them to water, where they become muddy indeed. As Harding rode his "fiery" steed, he found himself needing to stand up in the stirrups. His hemorrhoids had become painfully inflamed, and, as Boone grimly observed, "the saddle acted almost like a file on his rear end." No one knew of his difficulties except his doctors, who heard about it later in "good frontiersmen's language."[36]

The next day found the Hardings and their associates in Idaho Falls and Pocatello, after a speech in Brigham, Utah, where Harding addressed an early morning crowd in a bathrobe. After a particularly exhausting round of parades, receptions, and speeches in the two Idaho cities, the party slept peacefully on a siding. It must have been delicious, especially after a day of intense handshaking.

In Butte, where the noise of the Anaconda Copper Company reminded Florence of the *Star*'s machinery, she especially enjoyed meeting the miners; she reached out for their grimy hands, despite some of the men self-consciously holding back. Florence actually preferred shaking men's hands to women's: as she noted, "It is a terrible confession for a woman, [but] we can pass from 1500 to 2000 men in an hour—but never more than 1000 women. The reason? Well, every one of them has a neat little speech prepared to make to the president."[37] Florence seemed to be holding up better than her husband in these marathons, and in Butte, he dropped plans to give a speech and let his wife wave at the crowds. Perhaps he was depressed by what he saw. Nearly devoid of trees, Butte "was the most drab looking community," Boone recalled.[38] Not only was it not green, it was also "red," and extra Secret Service men were called to duty to protect the president from restless radicals. The Buttites, though, were ever generous to their guests, with the *Daily Post* observing, "Mrs. Harding is far better looking than her pictures . . . her smile is the essence of sweetness and graciousness, while her photographs often give her the appearance of sternness." They noticed that she looked "frail" next to her "stalwart" husband, a misconception held by many.[39] Others more accurately saw her strength, or at least her ability to "play the game," better than Warren. On one occasion during a long, hot parade, she sent her wilted husband back to the hotel for ice water and a fan while she continued on without him.[40]

After the pain of Zion, Yellowstone on June 30 and July 1 was a welcome reprieve, with spectacular scenery, breakfast at the Mammoth Falls Hotel, geysers to gape at most of the afternoon, and an evening at the "big rambling fire-trap sprawling" Old Faithful Inn.[41] But on July 2, they returned to their routine, arriving in Spokane for another broiling, ninety-minute parade, Harding bowing and smiling all the while. Despite the heat, the party's women looked "trim and smart," coming out "fluffily" from the train, privileged to have a private car where they could "carry fresh frocks" for every stop.[42] There would be a reception for 1,000 at their hotel (ballooning by a factor of three from the original estimate, a common occurrence), a banquet, a visit to the Columbia River Basin, and a speech at the armory. Once again, the papers noticed Harding's "power" and "geniality," but also raved about Mrs. Harding's "vividness" and "the humanness . . . that adjusted itself to each person" whose hand she shook.[43] She had a quality handshake, according to one observer: "hers is no cold, limp, fin-like nonchalant gesture."[44]

It was an exhausting full day in Spokane, and the next morning, after visiting a memorial for four Legionnaires who were killed by IWW militants in Centralia, Washington, they spent a packed thirteen hours in Meacham, Oregon, including a twenty-one-gun salute, a reception with surviving, pre-1853 pioneers, a historical pageant, and the dedication of the Oregon Trail monument. Local

Indians treated the party to a grand powwow and a peace pipe ceremony as well, followed by a reenactment, complete with cavalry rescue. The Hardings delighted in the spectacle.[45]

They went south again to Portland for the Fourth of July, for another thirteen hours of activities, including a parade, a reception, a major address (30,000 heard Harding's call for the "deportation or imprisonment" of all immigrants who "seek to break down American institutions," which the president credited Florence for writing), as well as a hospital visit. The two-mile parade drew a boisterous and ebullient crowd. No doubt, they had been whipped up by an offshore twenty-one-gun salute from the British cruiser, the *Curlew*, honoring Independence Day—and even sending armed sailors to march in the parade!—as well as by circling army planes, which dropped rose petals on the Rose City. At their reception at the Multnomah Hotel—then the Northwest's finest—there was another huge gathering to greet. Ten thousand people awaited, and the Hardings shook hands with almost half of them.

As always, the crowds were well stocked with police and secret agents, 200 all told at the various appearances that day. One inspector stopped an IWW member who got as close as fifth in line from the president while brandishing a flyer calling for the release of "war prisoners."[46] Authorities also spotted a "woman fanatic" who seemed to be following Harding around during this Western trip, a "bad actor" who was spotted in the huge throng at the hotel.[47] Boone remained astounded at Florence's staying power. Except for the horseback ride in Zion, indeed, she had missed nothing. "She went from one activity to another like a steam engine."[48] And she looked great, as the *Portland Oregonian* noticed: her hat, "golden brown lacey straw, and just piled thick with soft fluffy fronds of ostrich feathers," and her dress, "a summery, silken affair, with a hint of the last King Tutankamen in it[s] Egyptian coloring and pattern." Still, the paper said warmly, "she is just home folk . . . exactly the type of home body you'd take over a jar of your strawberry preserves . . . or the kind that would come in the middle of the night bringing turpentine and encouragement if the baby choked up with croup."[49]

Indeed, she could not have been happier. Another paper noted that she "has more ginger at the end of the day than any other member of the party . . . [she] is always on the dot."[50] Her husband,

Harding addressing crowds. Courtesy of the Marion County Historical Society, Marion, Ohio.

meanwhile, despite his "good humor," nevertheless showed for those who looked closely "the grimness of responsibility."⁵¹ Of course, for Harding, the schedule never stopped. He had to make major speeches in the evening after greeting people all day, and he was expected to be ready to pop out on the train platform for other extemporaneous talks at 4 A.M., as well.

Their next city, Tacoma, would host the grand send-off to Alaska. After another large reception on their hotel veranda (5,000 people—and many more were turned away) and an additional hospital stop, Harding gave a rain-soaked speech in Tacoma's seaside stadium that contrasted sharply with his Red-baiting one of the day before. Here, he called for an eight-hour workday, cheering the demise of the twelve-hour one in the steel industry—even as he endured similar days himself, repeatedly! After the presidential party left the stadium to board the *Henderson*, the 35,000 souls in the arena stayed in their seats in the drizzle for ninety minutes, just to see the Hardings' ship pass.⁵² As Boone recalled, their voices could be heard through the rain singing "God be with you till we meet again."⁵³ A poignant au revoir, considering how the trip would end.

The departure for Alaska carried great anticipation for those on the *Henderson*. Yet despite his tan and "powerful muscular shoulders," which so impressed Tacomans, Harding was tired.⁵⁴ He asked

Walter Brown again to cut back his engagements, at least after the Alaska leg, or "it will kill me. I just cannot keep up such a pace."⁵⁵ The *Henderson* would prove a welcome respite for them all. Nearly 500 feet long with four decks, this modern ship included a staff of more than 600 sailors and marines, including a 55-member navy band, and it would all be at their service for the rest of the trip. Florence took advantage of the break in scheduling, and slept the entire first day on the boat. They enjoyed a delightful coastal voyage. Each morning, after having breakfast in their private quarters—the marine colonel's digs—the Hardings usually joined everyone for meals, with a navy band entertaining at dinner.

Their first stop was Metlakatla, Alaska, an Indian reservation, on July 8. After a sermon to the Native Americans about the "mollifying, uplifting and refining influence" of Christianity, Harding and his Cabinet men met with Indians regarding resource issues, including their protest against canneries taking much of their needed salmon.⁵⁶ Upon hearing that a "college graduate" had suggested the Indians "should blow up the canneries" to stop white men's work there, Florence lashed out: "And is that all they get from a college education?" Holding herself in check, she added, "If I were just an ordinary citizen ... I would have a few things to say to you from the heart."⁵⁷

After a stop in Ketchikan, by which time they were already 836 miles from Tacoma, they went to Wrangell for a parade and speeches. The party arrived in Juneau, the capital, on July 10 at 10 A.M., and joined a procession to the home of Governor Scott C. Bone, followed by speeches, a conference, and a reception. Juneau's mayor, Isadore Goldstein, declared the day a holiday in his city. They sailed out of Juneau at 2 A.M. the next morning, spent the next two days relaxing at sea, and on the 13th, arrived at Seward for another day of parades and speeches. In their honor, Governor Bone renamed the entrance to Resurrection Bay the "Harding Gateway," a name it still bears. The Hardings departed Seward that day on a nine-car train bound for Fairbanks, 467 miles away, on Alaska's recently completed railroad. Florence rode some of the way in a construction car, a Dodge automobile that was attached to the rails to ride like a train. The Alaska inland tour was most enjoyable, giving Mrs. Harding a chance to enjoy even more the peoples of that territory, and especially their "Americanism."⁵⁸ They visited

Hardings on the Henderson. *Courtesy of the Library of Congress.*

coalfields, saw huskies, and ate huge meals from graniteware place settings. They saw the summit of the Alaska range, at Mt. McKinley National Park. The first couple even took over the train at Wasilla, and with Harding at the throttle and his wife next to the fireman, they steered the train for 26 miles in 51 minutes, breaking 11 cups in the dining room![59] In Nenana, Harding drove the golden spike joining the northern and southern sections of the Alaska railroad (and the Pacific and Arctic Oceans) near the road's 700-foot single span bridge at the Tanana River. By now, though, Florence was wearing down—she had masked her fatigue, Boone noted, "admirably but threateningly"—and went to bed.⁶⁰

Her old illness had returned. When they arrived in Fairbanks—the most northern point reached by any first lady, ninety miles from the Arctic Circle—she left the train only to go directly to her hotel bed, surrounded by her doctors and nurses. Well cared for, she did return to her active life within days, thanks to her physicians' "restoratives," Ruth Powderly's nurturing attention, and her own will—unlike poor Mrs. McKinley, another first lady who became ill in 1901 during an earlier presidential cross-country trip, which led to the abrupt ending of that tour in San Francisco.⁶¹ To assist Florence's recovery, Boone, Sawyer, and Powderly urged the cancellation of their next leg, a planned motor trip on the Richardson Highway, and instead, the party headed back down to Seward immediately by train, two days after their arrival in Fairbanks.

Sawyer and Boone, in concert on Florence's treatment, had more differences over the treatment of another patient on this trip. When Harding got an infection in his finger and wanted it lanced, Sawyer, "because of [his] poor vision," couldn't do it, so Boone did. Sawyer was furious at Boone's treatment without his say-so, and the younger doctor defended himself as "subject to the President's orders." While nothing else was said, Boone would regularly find himself uninformed as to Harding's daily condition, as Sawyer played a dangerous game of one-upsmanship with the president's health.⁶²

From Seward, they boarded the *Henderson* for their last Alaska city, Sitka, in the southeast, and Florence again went right to her rooms. The ship stopped on the way at Valdez and at Cordova, to visit the Childs and Miles Glaciers. There, Harding rather recklessly requested one of the Secret Service men to blast his gun at a glacier wall, setting off twenty-one spectacular ice explosions into the river below. At Cordova, the party picked up canned crab that, when consumed, later sickened several on the *Henderson* and became a suspected cause for the onset of Harding's fatal illness.⁶³

Florence, however, was feeling much better by the time they reached Sitka on July 22, joining the party for dinner and a movie. She also was busily making plans to have several types of Alaska flower seeds sent back to the White House for cultivation in its greenhouses. The president continued the relentless round of receptions

*Hardings and party with Great Alaskan Totem Pole at Sitka.
Courtesy of the Library of Congress.*

and visits in Sitka, leading Boone to conclude that he had probably touched the hands of one-third of the population of Alaska![64]

After two weeks in Alaska, and a last push of nearly 1,000 miles from Sitka by vessel, the presidential entourage reached Vancouver, British Columbia, at 10 A.M. on July 23 to a twenty-one-gun salute, and another twelve hours of parading, speeches, receptions, golf, and formal meals.[65] It was the first visit by a sitting president and first lady to the neighboring country, and Florence was feeling well enough to receive a group herself. The Vancouverians were enthusiastic about her, noting she was "full of the joy of living, liked to see those about her happy and contented . . . she was very democratic and always pleased to chat with poverty-stricken people." Florence was no doubt sympathetic with all comers. Whether she also "relish[ed] being amongst them, greeting them by the hundreds and hundreds on single occasions" was another matter. As we know from her letters to friends, despite her devotion to the practice, it exhausted her.[66]

PRESIDENT HARDING BECOMES ILL

It was at Vancouver's Shaugnessy Heights Golf Club that it first became apparent to Boone that the president wasn't himself. Harding told the young doctor, "I just can't get on my game today. I don't feel too well." After a round on the links, he complained of a "gastrointestinal upset," and Boone urged him to go to bed and stay there, but this was impossible, with another reception, speech, and dinner that day.[67]

In the evening, Harding's valet came to Boone, and told him that he and Sawyer "must hold the president down or 'He will break. He is hurrying too much.'" Boone respected Major Brooks's opinion greatly—he knew the president well. The physician, too, became convinced that they had to slow Harding down, but it was too late. They did not know it, but the president's own constitution was giving out.[68]

On the *Henderson* that night of July 26–27 as they approached Seattle, all seemed quiet until they hit blinding fog, and the ship's horn began blaring. There was much stopping and starting in these conditions, and Harding got sick as a result during the night. In the morning, the mist only got thicker; their two destroyer escorts nearby were invisible despite the daylight. Even more scary, the Pacific Fleet was also in the sound, with large numbers of ships, because Harding was supposed to review the fleet!

Meanwhile, back in the States, other clouds were brewing. The *Denver Post* contained a cartoon that week that lampooned "Harding's Old Guard Administration" and "Teapot Dome Cabinet Trouble." Yet despite the ongoing Senate investigation into Albert Fall's Wyoming dealings, the scandal had not yet caught the public's attention. Harding, moreover, had only positive words for his former secretary.[69] So did Florence. Mrs. Fall averred that the first lady had written her in January 1923 with sadness upon hearing of Fall's imminent departure from the Cabinet, "because the administration needed him so badly and he was so loyal in his friendship."[70] Other storms, closer to the Hardings, were more threatening. The president was about to have one of his most exhausting days yet, and it would take a tremendous toll. Although no one yet knew it, Seattle would be his last visiting day. It began suitably violently.

At 7:55 A.M. on July 26, off Port Townsend, the *Henderson* crashed into a destroyer, *Zeilin*, from the U.S. Pacific Fleet and damaged it so badly that it had to be towed away by three destroyers, listing forty degrees to port. It could have been far worse; the *Henderson* was traveling at only one-third its normal speed owing to the fog. It was the third near-miss on water for the Hardings. Both previous times, Stirling had saved them. At the 1922 Grant centennial, he stopped them from boarding the rattletrap steamer *Island Queen;* and in 1921, on a trip to Atlantic City, he prevented their disembarkation from the *Mayflower* onto a small boat for the trip ashore, owing to turbulent surf.[71]

Saved he may have been, but Harding came out of his cabin that morning not looking well. The crash and its aftermath would delay their entry to Seattle by four hours, and George Christian accordingly tried to reduce the day's schedule, but the boosterish mayor would not hear of it. Everything already planned, and more, would be crammed now into the afternoon!

Nevertheless, Harding's illness during the night was enough for Florence to urge him to stay on the ship for the day. Standing on the bridge holding his arm, as Boone observed, she "looked at him and felt a deep concern, and said to him, which I overheard as I was standing near them, 'Oh, Warren, please cancel our going ashore. You are not physically up to it.'" But Harding only saw all the people awaiting him, as Boone too noticed them, "on rooftops and all the windows that we could see, along roads and docks." The president turned to his wife, and said, "Of course . . . I would not disappoint them for anything, Florence."

They would go ashore, even if it was going to kill him. His doctors could not dissuade him either, so off he went, into the parade in an open car for another lengthy procession, doffing his hat constantly to left and right.[72] It was sweltering by afternoon, but there were more outdoor activities, including a gathering for 15,000 to 20,000 girls at Volunteer Park, among them two lucky ones who got to present Florence with a boa of ostrich feathers and delphiniums, and a huge Scout picnic—30,000 boys—hosted by the Elks in Woodland Park, where the president led the crowd in the Pledge of Allegiance as thousands of energetic scouts, all stuffed with "bags of candy . . . peanuts, ice cream bars and hot dogs," had the time of their lives.⁷³ This was followed by an address at the University of Washington stadium in front of 40,000 people. Florence sensed something was off at the stadium. She watched him closely, and as one paper reported, "She arose from her chair several times and straightened her dress in a nervous manner."⁷⁴ Boone, too, could not miss how tired the president was getting, that he lost his place in the talk, and that his voice was weaker than usual. Later, Florence told Lawler that indeed, it was at Seattle where she first realized how undeniably ill he was: "I never expected to get him out of there alive. I never permitted my eyes to leave his face during that time in Seattle."⁷⁵

There was one last speech at the Seattle Press Club, and he could not miss that, not with his comrades in arms from the printing business. But when he got back to his quarters on the train at 7 P.M., the president threw his hat across the room and collapsed. His stomach bothered him greatly, and the papers reported that Boone and Sawyer persuaded him to stay in bed through the following day, the 27th. In actuality, Boone learned nothing about Harding's having had a bad night after the Seattle ordeal *until* the next day. Sawyer once again peevishly kept him in the dark. It was Florence who told him then what was going on and begged the young doctor to stay the whole night with her husband, as she had the night before.⁷⁶

Oregonians noticed something was wrong when at 8:25 A.M. on July 28, the train stopped once again in their state, in the little town of Roseburg, and no Harding appeared on the platform. Secretary Work came out instead. Florence herself would frequently appear in the next few days at the back of the train too, attempting to fill his shoes. At Eugene, the state's two Republican senators, Charles McNary and Robert Stanfield, hoping to meet the president, got in his place an audience with Florence. The public, wondering where the president was, learned that Harding had sickened from Alaskan crabs that the party had eaten on the *Henderson* before going to Vancouver, poisoned from copper in the cans. This was Sawyer's theory, cemented when several other passengers, including Christian, got sick as well.⁷⁷ The president's condition was called a "slight illness" that had only caused the "postponement" of their planned Yosemite visit. The papers reported he was "recovering nicely" from the poisoning and overexposure to heat. Yet that night, as Boone watched him, he detected the president's enlarged heart.

Florence and the doctors abandoned their stop in Yosemite. Instead, they went straight to San Francisco so he could rest at the Palace Hotel. Starling's prescient planning meant the suite was available, and they arrived there on the morning of Sunday, July 29. The president would rest that day and Monday, and then "resume" his schedule Tuesday morning. The San Francisco "Harding fete" included a review of the merchant marine in the harbor by ferry, a hospital visit, a reception and a speech at the Presidio, meetings with various groups including women and clergy, a tree planting, and the bestowal of "the largest bouquet of wild flowers ever picked" by the "girls of Marin" at the civic center. After an address there, he would return at 10 P.M. to the Palace. Harding was sure it would all happen; he would be able to quash his illness. Florence, meanwhile, was reported to be "very anxious that nobody become unduly alarmed over the President's condition."[78] The party insisted all its subsequent plans were still on, including visiting San Diego and the Panama Canal.

Boone was very concerned about the president's heart, however, and wanted to get an ambulance to pick him up when they arrived. Harding would not hear of it. Instead, he got dressed with Brooks's help and snapped, "Don't think for a minute that I am going to receive the Governor of the Sovereign State of California and the Mayor of our host city . . . in pajamas. . . . I will not be carried off this train!"[79]

Brooks and Harding often had sartorial scuffles, which enlivened their special friendship. As Boone recalled, "they kidded and joshed each other and Brooks . . . [was] perfectly at home with Pres. Harding . . . one morning when Brooks had laid out [a] very plain tie and the cufflinks in a white shirt, as was his custom daily, he found the President had gotten up . . . and dressed himself. He had put on quite a colorful shirt which he had specially made with starched cuffs . . . [a] blue, wide blue striped shirt, and quite a gay tie." Brooks was annoyed, holding up his preferred white shirt, and insisting the president change. Despite Harding's protests, the valet said, "A president cannot wear anything but a white shirt and the plainest kind of tie, no gaiety." In the end, it turned out that Brooks liked the colored shirt "very much," they were the same size, and Harding gave him the shirt! So did the valet save Florence all kinds of trouble, and dressed her husband impeccably.[80]

This time, there was decidedly less joshing about Harding's desire to dress himself, but Monsieur Coué would have commiserated with the president. Harding was determined to walk unassisted off the train in his chosen clothes, brave and smiling, warmly shaking the hand of Mayor James Rolph before getting into the mayor's car. Florence and Herbert Hoover waved to the crowd, and Florence posed for pictures with Hoover. But there was no parade this time. Instead, they went as fast as they could by a back way, and entered the Palace Hotel from a side entrance. The party walked through the lobby, which the Secret Service had cleared of people, thus purposely missing the 1,000 waiting out front. They took the elevator to the eighth floor, Harding panting by now, and he immediately "threw himself" on his bed, a large one of solid walnut. His doctors discovered his temperature was 102.

The comfort of the Palace and its suite on the sunny southwest corner of the hotel must have been reassuring. The presidential suite included five rooms; there were three bedrooms (Florence's was in mahogany, with gray tapestries; Boone was in the third) and baths, a dining room, and a living room. Sawyer and his wife were in an adjoining suite. Ornaments bespeaking the importance of the guests were in abundance, including a big Japanese screen in the main room and Versailles-type paneling of circassian walnut, although Florence would probably have objected to the deer heads on the wall. She no doubt appreciated more the abundant flowers, as well as the eight canaries and two lovebirds hanging in cages in the ivory-finished reception room's ten windows. Only three others had ever stayed in the suite at the fifteen-year-old hotel: Presidents Taft and Roosevelt, and Belgium's King Albert.

Right away, Boone and Sawyer set up Harding for medical exams, and just as they had done with Florence in 1922, they arranged to bring in more expertise on the case, including Ray Lyman Wilbur, a former professor of internal medicine and a specialist in gastroenterology at Stanford Medical School who had also served as president of the American Medical Association, and Charles Minor Cooper, a cardiologist. Interior Secretary Hubert Work, who was also a doctor—a psychiatrist—was enlisted as well. A former AMA president himself, he had not seen patients for years; Cooper was the only expert who was in active practice. The doctors consulted on Sunday night for two hours, concluding at 1:30 A.M. They attributed Harding's troubles to travel, to all the human contact (speaking and handshaking), to the crabmeat, and to the subsequent purgatives he had been administered, which, while designed to drive out the poisons, had probably weakened him considerably. They soon diagnosed him with "general toxemia with fever and leucocytosis" along with pneumonia.

Florence, too, had worried about the burdens of travel on his condition, and the next day, with his condition worsening, she convinced him to cancel the rest of the trip. Because many would be coming from far away to see him on his planned stops, it was important that they be given enough notice to avoid an unnecessary journey. The president's gallbladder became inflamed on the morning of the 30th; the doctors soon discovered his heart and lung also looked worse as well. That day, his doctors and valet kept him in bed, not even letting him use the bathroom. At one point, Boone had to assist Harding in lessening the swelling of his hemorrhoids. "He became very, very embarrassed that I did so. He said it chagrined him to have me do such menial service for him, adding that he was just a common citizen and I was a naval officer and a government official. I assured him that I was merely a physician performing a service . . . as I would to any other patient under similar circumstances."[81]

Though Sawyer still continued to think the "unwholesome crab" was the culprit, whether from the cans or perhaps from mineral deposits near the crab breeding grounds, the president's worsening condition indicated something else was likely going on. After all, no one else in the party had gotten so sick. Still, the old doctor insisted they would not leave the hotel, where they had everything they needed, including two oxygen tanks, just brought in that morning, and an x-ray machine. Moreover, said Sawyer (who likely wished this *was* the sum of Boone's medical training), the young doctor's presence meant "we have a lab technician of the highest qualifications."[82]

There was no attempt to hide the president's condition. The public would be told the full story, as the doctors understood it. Two evening bulletins were issued on the 30th, one at 5 P.M. and another four hours later, and these were "frankly pessimistic." Boone declared: "We freely admit the situation is grave. The President is fighting pneumonia."[83] Harding, too, quipping "I have nothing to conceal," called for an x-ray. To facilitate the spread of information, as well as run the country's business, the Palace Hotel for these days became the western White House, with phone and telegraph lines connected to Washington. Visitors, journalists, and others congregating on the eighth floor, meanwhile, were held back by detectives, who kept them 200 feet away from the Hardings. There were sixty police in the hotel keeping tabs on security. No one, except very close family and friends, got to the president.

Outside the suite, fifty newspapermen hung out, waiting for developments, in an atmosphere redolent of cigarette smoke. The hotel was not a hospital, and music and dancing could be heard from the lower floors. Perhaps this cheered Florence, even as she tried to catch up on sleep she missed the night before. Her strength was continually remarked upon by the papers; she was "keeping her head up and her eyes dry and facing all the cold medical facts. . . . She knew the fight her man was facing . . . and that all she could do was to pray and smile," one columnist said.[84]

The dire prospects on Monday meant that the president would return to Washington as soon as he was strong enough to do so. In a trip one-third as long as expected—8,000 rather than 25,000 miles—he had still made sixty-seven speeches, more than three times the number he had planned. Florence, who was responsible for canceling the California tour, remained hopeful about his prospects, staying near him, reading to him. She told the entourage, "Don't look so gloomy, gentlemen. The president is going to be all right, of that I am sure."[85] It seemed she had reason for her optimism. If Monday was a rocky night, Tuesday was better. The pneumonia patches were not spreading, his temperature was down to 99, his pulse had lowered to 114, and he was reading the paper. And even when ill, he was "never peevish."[86]

With this better news, Florence felt her prayers were working, and her "cheerful spirit," too. She took the opportunity to meet with a group of San Francisco newspaperwomen she had had to put off the day before. They found her "dressed simply," in a black silk crepe skirt, a black-and-white blouse with gray shoes and stockings, and of course her diamond neckpiece, and noted that "She appeared the dignified, tastily clad leading lady of America . . . masses of light brown hair, interspersed with white, framed her set, motherly face."

In the midst of the tense situation in her husband's quarters, she remained "calm and unruffled."[87]

Florence told the women, "I am so glad to have this opportunity of meeting with you and chatting with you!" She confided, "I like the job of being the President's wife. It's a bit strenuous on trips like this, and occupies all one's time, but I love it." Florence was popular with the members of her former profession, and appeared all hope and smiles. She said of her present work, "It's a fine job. I like it. I don't resent the fact that we have little private life." One of the men who had been with her from the beginning of the trip told the San Francisco "girls" that "Mrs. Harding is the best little sport in the world. . . . she's a game little traveler."[88]

A journalist in the group asked her, "Mrs. Harding, you are a firm believer in your own sex, aren't you?" After her most emphatic nod, the woman continued, "What do you think about women in politics?" She answered measuredly, "I believe it's a good thing under certain circumstances." But she would not venture further to discuss the feminist movement when asked her opinion of it, demonstrating that she was not an outspoken first lady, even if she was an active one, and harked back to her "no interview" rule. "Now, girls, I'm glad to chat with you, but you must not question me like that. I never give out interviews. That part of our family life is left to Mr. Harding." She reverted to pleasantries.[89]

The president continued to improve, and by the morning of Wednesday, August 1, Sawyer remarked that the "crisis" had passed. Harding's sister, Mrs. Elton E. Remsberg, came up from Southern California to visit her brother early that afternoon. Though she stayed with him for just five minutes, she was gratified to see his renewed strength, as he ate his milky toast and greeted her in a "cheerful" manner. He was enjoying the eight canaries and two lovebirds that trilled in the Harding suite, and his doctors, too, were singing an optimistic refrain, their task now chiefly "'standing by' while nature, largely unassisted, performed the work of healing."[90] Florence stayed nearby, eating well (the Palace food was delicious), taking care of some letters, and holding herself together well.[91]

The next morning, August 2, papers were reporting that the "Recovery of President Is Now Certain" and "President Harding Out of Danger," based on Sawyer's reports the previous evening and at 9:45

that morning.[92] Harding had had his second full restful night, and was "officially out of the woods," his old doctor said reassuringly. Sawyer cautioned, however, that "the road to convalescence is a long, tedious one." He added, "we are likely to have our ups and downs, and anything is liable to happen."[93]

Later that afternoon, at 4:30 P.M., the doctors again had good news for the press: Harding had had "his most satisfactory day since his illness began." While all five of the medical men signed this statement, Boone noted that save for Sawyer, their optimism was "cautious." Still, even Boone had said, "Things look mighty good." Sawyer was positive enough to say they could leave for home as early as the following Tuesday, August 7.[94] Boone celebrated by taking his first bath in five days. He, like some others, thought Harding could recuperate well at Catalina, William Wrigley's beautiful island paradise. Wrigley had hoped to see them on their West Coast trip, and Boone was happy to oblige.

In any case, things looked good enough for Dr. Wilbur to plan to return to his interrupted fishing trip in the High Sierras, and Cooper to go back to his office, although they had not left before the evening's dramatic turn of events. Sawyer was now more worried about Florence. As the urgency passed and her husband was "out of the woods," she was showing signs of exhaustion. She had been giving her all to him, but tragically, that would not be enough.

CHAPTER 7

HARDING'S DEATH AND ITS AFTERMATH, AUGUST 1923

HOUR OF DEATH

By August 2, Harding seemed to have markedly improved. Dr. Sawyer was using the term *convalescence* to describe his condition. Joel Boone, too, was now saying how "splendid" Harding looked.[1] He was eating, even with some indigestion; his lungs seemed better; his temperature was back to normal. Their plan now was to leave for Washington the following Tuesday. Sawyer optimistically declared the "fire is out," though he also cautioned that Harding "still is a very sick man." They would now focus on "the slow, gradual, and we hope, uninterrupted process of rebuilding the exhausted system of our patient."[2]

Florence, however, had her suspicions. That morning, when as was her custom she went in to groom him with comb and washcloth—"He always liked me to do that for him"—she caught her breath. "I was horrified. Death stared back at me; looked me in the face." There was "a decided change for the worse." Even as Sawyer and Boone "tried to reassure me, telling me I was over-anxious and overwrought," she saw something else. "I knew he was going."[3] Malcolm Jennings picked up a similar sense of things when he talked to the president on two occasions that day. Harding, despite his recovering appearance, told his old friend, "I am so tired, so tired," even as he clung, nonetheless, to the thought that he was "out of the woods."[4]

After his long-anticipated bath that afternoon, Boone went into Harding's room as the evening came on. He sat down, joining Sawyer, who was on the bed near the president's feet. Nurse Powderly sat on the other side of the president, while Florence was next to him, reading aloud.[5] As the president listened contentedly, she read him an article about himself entitled "A Calm View of a Calm Man."[6] Suddenly, Harding abruptly stiffened, with a look of fear. He went pale and began sweating profusely. As Sawyer took his arm to find his pulse, Boone recalled, "Miss Powderly and I jumped up and moved close to the President. His pajamas were wringing wet." Coming slowly back, Harding told them he had been afflicted by a "very strange, sinking feeling that I have never experienced before." They all urged him to keep calm and still. He snapped, "But I'm so damn wet!" With a minimum of fuss, Nurse Powerly undressed him, dried him, and put him in new pajamas. Feeling more normal, Harding reassured them, "I don't know what happened to me . . . [but] now I feel perfectly comfortable." He wanted Florence to continue reading, but she was too agitated and could not pick up the article. She became more relaxed as she saw the color slowly returning to his face and his breathing became more even, and she and the others talked quietly to him. At that moment, perhaps around 6:45, Boone asked if it would be all right if he went outside—he had not done so since they arrived four days before.[7]

No one had any objection, so Boone strode out for a short walk. He made a few jokes with the remaining journalists loitering in the hall—the rest of them, along with the presidential party, were out enjoying what seemed like a positive turn in the president's condition—and Boone did not mention the seizure, which seemed now to be quite over. After a short walk on Market Street, where he thirstily drank in the fresh air, he turned to go back. But he had gone up the wrong street, and it took him perhaps ten minutes to get back to the hotel. Or perhaps he just wanted the walk![8] In any case, as he went back up in the elevator, he heard his name, or what he thought was his name, echoing eerily through the elevator shaft above. When he got out, he recalled, "a newspaperman appeared from nowhere into the hallway, and I heard somebody say, There is Doctor Boone, there's Dr. Boone!" As he rushed into the president's room, "Mrs. Harding grabbed me hysterically, shook me by the shoulders, looked me in the eye with a very startled expression, and said, 'Dr Boone, you can save him, you can save him! You can bring him back! Hurry, hurry, hurry!'"

Sawyer and Secretaries Herbert Hoover and Hubert Work were also in the room by this time, and Boone tried to be calm. But as soon as he looked at the president, the doctor knew he was dead. To offer some comfort to Florence, he put his fingers on Harding's eyes and closed their lids. As he stood up, the usually formal Mrs. Harding, showing her clear shock and devastation, rushed into his arms, wailing, "No one can save him, no one can restore him to life. He is gone!" Fighting this natural emotion, she cried, "I can't realize it. I can't realize it. Still I've something to do." Her head dropped onto Boone's shoulders as she heaved with sobs. Mrs. Hoover and Mrs. Wallace, who were also there, then helped take her gently off Boone and led her back to her own room, "biting her lips and clenching her hands" to hold herself in check. Nurse Powderly followed them, and calmed the first lady with sedatives.[9] She went to bed at last at 1 A.M. and "slept fitfully."[10]

Perhaps only Lou Hoover, who soothed Florence that night, along with Ruth Powderly, who stayed over until morning, knew how close the first lady came to crumbling that night. Her kind nurse commented, however, that "Mrs. Harding has borne the shock wonderfully well." She saw the true agony Florence felt, of course, but Powderly insisted that the first lady had not broken down: "There is nothing like a collapse. She is going to be terribly upset if she sees the newspapers that said she collapsed."[11] Indeed, Florence was sharp enough in mind to reject such speculations the next day. Her mantra remained, "I am not going to break down," regardless of how exhausted and overwhelmed she seemed.[12] Some saw her strength drawing from her Christian faith. "She knew, to whom to turn in her sorrow."[13] Faith no doubt helped, but chance was nonetheless fickle. After all, it had not been so long before that she had been at death's door herself. Despite her strong affirmation of her intact mind and body, the papers could not resist emphasizing the pathos of it all. "The nation's heart aches for [her]. . . . President and Mrs. Harding . . . were helpmeets and companions in the highest sense. They worked together in the upbuilding of their newspaper and counseled and watched over each other in the White House."[14]

Sawyer also insisted that there had been "no collapse, no hysteria. Just a brave rally to face her sorrows and duties at this hour."[15] Boone himself felt inadequate. The junior doctor in the entire assemblage, and the most idealistic, he felt "It was just incomprehensible that President Harding had died and I as a physician had no power to restore his life to his country, or his countrymen, wife, family." It was a memory he never forgot: "It has always been hard to bear that Mrs. Harding in her great hour when her husband was so stricken . . . that she had confidence in me . . . to bring him back to life. Would that I could have had such power!"[16]

What happened in the interim is still the subject of debate, but it seems to have gone something like this. After Boone had stepped out for his little walk, Sawyer also went to his room in an adjoining suite for a little break. Feeling at last relaxed enough to start reading again, Florence took up the article once more. As she read to her husband, Captain Sue Dauser, the night nurse, came in to take over from Powderly.[17] With both nurses present, the president urged his wife to continue: "That's good; go on, read some more." Those were his last words. Within moments, he threw up his arm, one paper later reported, "as though he sought to ward off the blow which death . . . had aimed with unerring directness at a vital spot, went limp, his body quivered, shaking the bed, and the color drained from him." Mrs. Harding, aghast, flew from the room, screaming over and over again, "Get Dr. Boone! Get Dr. Boone! Get Dr. Boone!"[18] It is not clear why she called for him first, and not the old faithful friend from White Oaks Farm next door. He, of course, rushed in, as Florence cried, "Do something for him, give him something!" Sawyer grasped a hypodermic syringe and injected the president with "a stimulating liquid," and he urged Powderly to bring hot water bags, which she quickly did. Sawyer too began calling for the other doctors. Dr. (and Secretary) Work was first to arrive, at 7:26; then Dr. Wilbur, then Dr. Cooper.[19] Commerce Secretary Hoover and Secretary Wallace also came in.[20] Finally Boone came. Called away from dinner, Secret Service agent Edmund Starling recalled seeing Florence by the bed, saying, "Warren, Warren, Warren."[21]

Sawyer, along with the other four doctors, attributed the death to "apoplexy or a rupture of a blood vessel in the axis of the brain near the respiratory center"—in other words, a stroke.[22] Their diagnosis was no doubt hastened by the fact that Harding's sister had died of the same thing. Of course, there were unique complications. He had a "gastro-instestinal infection including cholecystitis and bronchopneumonia." Moreover, his systolic blood pressure had been high, around 150, for some time, and doctors believed this was connected with arterial sclerosis, heart enlargement and even defective kidneys.[23] These heart troubles, especially, were disregarded, and they were likely the cause of death, not a stroke. Several historians have suggested Sawyer was to blame for missing this problem.[24] Robert Ferrell agrees that it was the president's heart that had attacked him, not his brain. As he shows, Harding had a myocardial infarction—a constriction of the blood vessel leading to the heart by a clot. Such an attack kills instantly; a stroke can take ten minutes at least. The misunderstanding of his illness as digestive had only made things worse as he had been moved about from Vancouver to San Francisco. Yet none of the doctors, except Cooper, changed their minds even decades later.[25]

What had weakened Harding's heart? He had no doubt undertaken a trip that was terribly taxing. Just like Wilson, who was stricken himself on a cross-country campaign for an "understanding" of a different sort, some contended that "Warren Harding was a martyr to this country as truly as if he had fallen on the battlefield in its behalf."[26] Even before the journey, he was wrestling with a workload that had expanded greatly since Teddy Roosevelt's day. Eventually, the call for more "competent assistants" in his office would be heeded, but too late to help Harding.[27] Yet Harding had not been completely healthy for some time; he exercised too little and ate too much. Even when on vacation, he barely got a rest from demands for speeches and "face time" on the golf course. Unlike Wilson, though, he had at least *been* a physically active man, "adhering to . . . golf and his recreation despite the sneers of the thoughtless who envision the President of the United States as a slave properly chained to his desk," as one paper put it.[28] Yet Harding had done less of his favorite activities, including golf, handball, and horseback riding, in the latter part of his term. Indeed, he had stopped riding horses almost entirely in the White House, finding it too much fuss to dress himself and the horse.[29] Even when he golfed, he rushed, as his Florida games showed. There was little time for just relaxation and sleep.

Still, he was considered "physically more fit than most men of his age," Boone noted. Neither Boone nor Sawyer had expected the *president* would be the trip's casualty.

Perhaps they could have pressed him harder to slow down, and trimmed the ceremonies, speeches, and handshaking marathons beyond those already taken out of Brown's packed schedule, but when they suggested it, he refused to listen. As one newspaper noted, he "wanted to be friends with all men." His death, while no doubt due to natural causes, had in part been accelerated by his indiscriminate friendliness to others, many observers thought.[30] And Florence's still-recent illness had made things even more challenging. As Boone well pointed out, "The First Lady is an essential requisite to a successful Presidential Administration." Both depended on one another "for the success of each in his and her spheres of individual activity." Florence's importance to her husband was unusual for any first lady, and her long convalescence had made life doubly difficult for the president leading up to the trip.[31]

Of course, some have gone even further in finding Mrs. Harding culpable for her husband's death. Gaston Means, in *The Strange Death of President Harding* (1930), helped to spread the scurrilous tale of her designs on Harding's life, popular in the 1920s—especially as the Harding administration lost its glow in the light of subsequent congressional investigations—and long after.[32] Means was a criminal himself—he infamously extorted $100,000 from Evalyn McLean in ransom money in order to rescue the Lindbergh baby in 1935. Sentenced to fifteen years for grand larceny, it was not his first such shakedown: in the 1920s, he had fleeced sources as an informant for the Department of Justice.[33]

Means charged that Florence had poisoned her husband, and despite all the evidence against it, most clearly her obvious devastation at his death, this theory has held its following.[34] Even in the scholarly community, which does not consider anything as crude as poison to be likely, she is held culpable in other ways. Carl Sferrazza Anthony suggests that she did nothing to stop the bungling efforts of an incompetent medical team, and moreover, she pushed her husband to his limit on the trip out West. He further adds that she "became an accomplice to his negligent homicide" because she refused to allow an autopsy. She was thus part of a "conspiracy" to cover up the doctors' ineptitude in misdiagnosing Harding's heart troubles.[35]

Certainly, Florence wanted to keep her husband's body intact; here she anticipated the wishes of millions of Americans who also wanted to see him as his train steamed back East, and later when his casket lay in the rotunda. His physicians may well have overprescribed purgatives that shocked the president's weak cardiovascular system, and were mistaken in attributing the death to a brain hemorrhage rather than a heart attack. But to expect life-saving competence in fighting heart disease from practitioners of 1920s medicine seems overly optimistic, since even with today's advanced medical treatments, myocardial infarctions still kill close to 300,000 people every year.[36] More importantly, Florence loved her husband. She did not want him to die, and she would not have tolerated any medical malfeasance had she known it to exist. Her deep grief at her husband's death, and her trust in the same doctors, confirms this.

Indeed, a month later, she would move to White Oaks Sanitarium to be closer to Dr. Sawyer! Mrs. Harding thus bears no respon-sibility for her husband's death, unless she can be blamed for ac-quiescing to his hectic schedule. But then neither his valet nor his doctors were able to stop him. She had tried on the bridge of the *Henderson*, as they approached Seattle, but he had refused to listen. Harding died of a heart attack brought on by overwork and, no doubt, preexisting conditions, and it's hard to imagine what any doctor could have done with such a patient in those days, never mind a very upset wife.

His untimely death at the relatively young age of fifty-seven came as a great shock — "an electric current of alarm" to those at the hotel. "He just went like that," Boone said, snapping his fingers. All had seemed normal; two little girls had just come with flowers to the sickroom. The few newspapermen still in the hall stood stunned. The other members of the party, eating downstairs, "stood up sud-denly from half eaten dinners, indescribable horror and unbelief blended on their faces," one paper reported.[37]

Should Florence have been so shocked? After all, her savant, Madame Marcia, had predicted the death of Harding once he was in office. The astrologer asserted, however, that Mrs. Harding, although she well knew of this "destiny," nevertheless had railed against it while her husband was still alive: "Power—glory—they make us slaves, Marcia—slaves! They are killing my husband—they are killing me! The price is too great, Marcia, too great, too cruel for us to have to pay!"[38] It seems Florence never accepted the psychic's prediction, despite her apprehension that it was all too true. Madame Marcia, meanwhile, stuck to her story. Even when Harding appeared to be improving in San Francisco, she did not see it that way. "It is the end. He will never recover. The crisis will come Thursday night. He will be dead by Friday," she predicted on Monday, July 31.[39]

Marcia was not the only one to sense this fate. Harding's father, too, had had a recurring dream since 1920 predicting his son's death, and Florence herself, even before the inauguration, felt sure that "something will happen to one of us" if he went to the White House. She had visited Madame Marcia in the spring of 1920, when the psychic had predicted she would be first lady; later, Marcia had forecast a "sudden, if not violent" death for Warren G. Harding.[40] Even Harding himself may have known. One paper speculated earlier that "he himself had warning, a strange foreboding that he was nearing the end and would not live long enough to return to his post at Washington."[41] Did that explain why he had made his will, sold the *Star*, and had even handed over the title of the Blooming Grove property to his nephew before the Alaska trip?

Whatever the harbingers, his death shocked the nation. At a vaudeville show in Santa Ana, California, the audience learned of the death at the end of the first performance on August 2. They took the news "in awe . . . [and] solemnly moved to the exits. There was no talking. Those present declared they never had seen the attitude of a crowd change so quickly."[42] Those who mocked the prevailing mood paid the price: when inmates at the Lisbon, Ohio, jail cheered at the death of the president, their matron fed them only bread and water for two days until they apologized![43]

Despite the prisoners' cheer, Harding was held with almost universal affection. As the *Dallas Journal* well noted, "Warren Harding was not a great President. He was a growing [one] . . . in utterance and in stature. . . . Harding as a *man* was what the people loved."[44] Another paper echoed the sentiment: "His gentle and friendly personality made a very strong impression upon the whole public . . . and created for him a vast fund of affection."[45]

The loss of such a man was especially painful to one woman in particular. With Harding's death, Florence was said to be "the most lonesome widow the world has ever known."[46] Journalist Estelle

Lawton Lindsey wrote: "to every woman who loves a man she is the chief figure in this national calamity, for we all know the colossal tragedy that has come to her and if we are women we must stop for one moment to whisper: 'God help her.'"47 Yet Florence was stoic in this moment of grief. She declared grimly, "I will not break down." The *Los Angeles Record* quoted her saying on August 3: "I will be brave—I shall not collapse." Other reports noted with amazement her "control of herself as [the] trying day wore on. . . . She seemed to have her nerves under constant and unceasing grip. The doctors . . . marveled and shook their heads. 'It's wonderful,' said one. 'I only hope it can last.'"48

This view of her self-control as "wonderful," and her desire to assert it, underline the times in which she lived. Sigmund Freud's psychological theories were ascendant. She wanted to avoid what he and his followers would call a "pathological" response to her grief, characterized by "hysteria" or some kind of "anxiety state." Even today, such reactions to death are considered by some a form of mental illness.49 Likely she felt too that her insistence of stability was needed to quell the rumors swirling around predicting her imminent collapse or even death. Yet it was others who could not focus, actually; "She gently directed, when others were too stunned to move," one paper observed. Sawyer added: "She always has been a wonderful woman to meet an emergency . . . one of those creatures who shows up best under fire." Of course, he added, when Harding died, "she was shocked . . . and at first unable to realize that she had lost the husband who had made up all the interest in her life."50

But Florence had always had other interests beside her husband. She was also perfectly capable of thinking about the suffering of others at this time. She worried in particular about George Christian Jr., who had gone to Los Angeles to deliver the scheduled speech there that Mr. Harding was too incapacitated to give, and who would find out about Harding's death alone.51 She was thinking too about Harding's legacy. She asked newspapermen to look at his still warm body: "I know what some of his critics were saying. They charged that he was weak. I want you to look at those firm lips of his and see. I look at them and know they show he was not weak. I know that he had strength and courage."52 How could such a woman ever have consented to an autopsy?

Some needed little convincing of his courage even beyond the grave. Sir Arthur Conan Doyle, author of the Sherlock Holmes stories and himself a noted spiritualist, pointed out that Harding's last speech—the one delivered by Christian—was "deeply religious," suggesting Harding's spirit's ascent to a "higher" plane. He believed the president could yet appear through a medium with a message for the new president, Calvin Coolidge.[53]

But perhaps Coolidge had already heard Harding's celestial voice. In any case, he was fully aware of his new responsibilities. He had taken the oath of office on his Vermont farm early in the morning of August 3, heading off immediately for Washington, because, as one paper noted, "the business of the state cannot wait for more than a moment of sorrow however great the loss."[54]

THE COUNTRY MOURNS

The state may not have been able to wait, but the rest of the country desperately wanted to. When a national leader falls, especially a popular and well-loved one, Americans conduct elaborate rituals to commemorate the loss. And though Warren G. Harding's death occurred nearly a century ago, his funeral rites were very much like those still observed for prominent state and civic leaders today: the deceased's body typically lies for some lengthy hours in the Capitol Rotunda, as Rosa Parks's did in 2005; there are also separate funerals in different locales, such as were held for Ronald Reagan in 2004. Reaction to the death of the beloved Harding was not that different from the official mourning associated with John F. Kennedy, who, like Harding, was also struck down in the third year of his first term, in 1963—although of course, in a much more shocking way. Another tragic assassination, that of his brother, presidential candidate Robert Kennedy, five years later, also included a funeral train like Harding's, and in the late 1960s, just as in the mid-1920s, thousands waited to see a stricken leader pass. Harding's body, which traveled much further than Kennedy's, and in two different directions, was seen by perhaps three million people.

This trip and its rituals were made possible by the work of skilled morticians, who for six hours labored over Harding's body, finally finishing their embalming at 3 o'clock in the morning on August 3.[55]

Harding's funeral train, August 1923. Courtesy of Mike and Linda Perry.

Back in Ohio at the same time, residents of the small town of Fremont awoke to the pealing chimes at St. Joseph's, St. Ann's, and St. Casimir's churches and even the city fire bell at 1 A.M., pouring out their sad sounds. In Coshocton, the post office flag mysteriously dropped to half mast by itself![56] While the campaniles clanged, most Americans were quiet in their mourning. As Joseph De Barthe, a contemporary author, recalled, there was "awe-inspiring silence — . . . almost uncanny quietude — that pervaded the nation, even to its remotest sections. . . . A grief so profound, so heart-felt, that human faculties were numbed. . . . people went about their wonted tasks and pursued their favorite phantoms, *listlessly.*"[57]

Florence, too, was numb, even as she and the rest of San Francisco awoke to a thirteen-gun salute from army and navy guns that next morning, a barrage that continued every thirty minutes for the rest of the day, ending with a last salute of forty-eight guns as the funeral train departed east in the evening. The firing likely little disturbed her with so much on her mind already. She managed to choke down some warm milk and a soft-boiled egg for breakfast, and she received a number of visitors during that long day before their train left the station, timed to assure an early afternoon arrival in Washington on the 7th. Captain Allen Buchanan of the *Henderson* stopped by and was impressed with Florence's "great bravery and courage." Colonel George Filmer, a former "potentate of the Mystic Shrine" and a San Francisco Mason, came by to pay his respects too, and saw "only . . . a few tears."[58] She also spent time with close friends and family like the Christians, her sister-in-law, Mrs. Remsberg, and Harry Daugherty. In the late afternoon, she had arranged for a brief service in the presidential suite at the Palace Hotel, where she joined fifty people in the sunny, flower-choked drawing room, including many weeping newspaper reporters.[59]

She entered this gathering after everyone else, wearing a full-length black cape and a veiled, wide-brimmed black hat. Mrs. Christian led her in, and Florence stood with the Christians over the open, glass-covered steel coffin lined with white silk, looking down on her husband in a black coat and black-striped pants.[60] She listened to the comforting words of James West, a Baptist clergyman, during the brief ten-minute service. Hearing West's description of her husband, she began to sob at one point, and grabbed Christian's arm. He quickly took her around the waist, while his wife gave her hand a squeeze. All around her were her old, dear friends and family, and she quickly regained her composure. At the end, she spent a few minutes alone with her husband and said quietly to West: "I want you to look at his face. It was magnificent in life but is more wonderful in death."[61] The glass was gently lowered on that face as the afternoon drew to a close.

Her strength drew wonder, as newspapers like the *Los Angeles Times* speculated how long she could hold on in the "long, dreary days ahead," dreary days because "her chief mission in [life] is gone," said the *Washington Star*.[62] Still, her breakdown would happen, Estelle Lindsey was sure: "She is too stunned, the thing that has happened is too big, too terrible to be realized just yet. But . . . the sense of loss will lie like a canker in her aching soul . . . she will learn how brief is fame, how fickle the mob . . . In those days she will break down." If no one else, Laddie Boy would bring on her collapse when he nosed his way into her lap looking for Warren, Lindsey suggested.[63] Yet this "mob"—the American people—remained devoted to her and her husband's memory that evening in San Francisco, as the casket slowly paraded past them to the train station in "a stunning silence."[64]

THE FUNERAL TRAIN

The 1923 transcontinental journey would be, as one paper wrote, "a nationwide funeral, lasting four days and four nights, stretching over 3,100 miles."[65] It was no doubt a moving sight, and it inspired a maudlin poem by Harold Alexander Leon De Aryan, "The Funeral Train."[66] As De Aryan's poem suggested, speed was of the essence. Harding's body had to be back in Washington as soon as possible for burial to take place in a timely and seemly fashion, so the body would not wilt as crowds flocked to see him one last time in Washington and Marion. Fortunately, the morticians had done their job well. The body arrived in "excellent condition."[67] The ferns and cypresses adorning the *Superbe*—symbols of immortality—and the white asters hanging from its roof were more withered.

At 5:00 P.M. on August 3, Harding's body left the Palace Hotel carried on the backs of four young marines in full dress and black crepe-draped swords. The procession, including many of the Palace Hotel party, made its way slowly down Market to the Southern Pacific Railway Station, to the strains of band members playing "The Star-Spangled Banner" and Harding's favorite hymn, "Lead Kindly Light."[68] Airplanes from Crissy Field flew over the procession, trailing black streamers and dropping roses on the train.

At the station, the coffin was lifted through the car windows. Daugherty, one of the pallbearers, watched, "sobbing and repeating brokenly phrases of sorrow," while Florence, under tight control, gripped Christian's arm.[69] As the train departed, the San Francisco mayor called for an hour of silence in his city. Still, rumors flew. When Florence did not come down with the hearse, the story spread that her doctors had forbidden her from joining her husband on the train owing to illness. But she had only decided to take a separate, shaded car with the Sawyers and Jennings to avoid the crowds.[70]

She went to her room as the train left the station at 7:10, and her nurse settled her down for sleep. First, though, she checked that her husband's casket was secure, and that the guards were given comfortable chairs and not made to stand all night, as had been previously suggested. If she peeked out a window, she would have seen that people lined the tracks for twenty miles. Passing the crowds, the train began to build up speed, up to 55 mph or more, and reached Tracy, California, at 9:40. Thousands met the train there, which rocketed on, getting to Sparks, Nevada, at a very early hour. Here another crowd waited, and as would become a frequent custom, a visiting delegation, including the governor, came on board to present a wreath.

The train would take the central route: Reno, Ogden, Cheyenne, Omaha, Chicago, and thence to Washington. It would stop only for needed water or fuel.[71] But the people in the hinterlands, with no chance of getting to the nation's capital or even to Ohio, were not going to let the train just rush by them. Thousands stood along the sidings under the searing sun or in the darkness of the early morning, hoping for a long, slow look at the president in his bronze metal coffin.[72] No matter what time it was, people turned out, as Starling recorded. This was especially moving in the wee hours: "from either side of us out of the misty night would come the flicker of white garments, then the low, rolling tones of thousands of men softly singing *Lead Kindly Light* or *Nearer My God to Thee* . . . rising up and washing over our train like a tide."[73]

Wisely, Mrs. Harding decided that they should not be disappointed. Despite initial hopes that they might break a record in their speed, the train slowed down to ten miles per hour when crowds were present, so that the president could be seen through the window.[74] As Judson Welliver, a Harding speechwriter, described the practice in a crowded, black-draped station, "At snails' pace the train passes through an unending line of humanity; motionless, uncovered. The viaduct over the tracks is swarmed; and the roofs of nearby buildings. But there is not a whisper. . . . every eye is on the last car, where all can see plainly the bier, the flag-draped casket, the military guard."[75] They lined the tracks in tiny desert towns like Fernley, Hazen, Desert, Lovelock, and Imlay, Nevada, "a reverent people . . . pay[ing] homage in the only way they could . . . silent, respectful, saddened."[76]

Harding would not see the onlookers, but his wife did—and their concern and sympathy was poignant to her.[77] Like Florence, Americans who stood along the rails for miles to witness Harding's passing (both by them, on the train, and from them, into the next life) were reminded of pieces of their own lives now broken away with the end of his era. Florence was moved by the response of those outside the train, including a farmer who turned his plow animal's head toward the train and then reverently faced it himself.[78] "I can understand what a shock my husband's death has been to the nation," the *New York Times* quoted her. "I read genuine sorrow in all those faces. It is comforting."[79]

That first night on the train, warmed by the night vigil outside, Mrs. Harding slept better, and she was still asleep at 8 A.M. Apparently, she had at last let herself collapse in a cathartic "flood of tears," which one paper contended served as "a help rather than a detriment." She stayed in her compartment for a full fifteen hours, until she called for her maid at 11 A.M. The train soothed her, as did the peace of acceptance, as the *Philadelphia Ledger* suggested: "her lonely hours in the rear car riding across the most desolate section of the American continent" allowed her to face her situation. Her husband was dead, but she could be near him. Of course it was very hot, and her fragility remained a worry. Powderly, Sawyer, and Boone kept a close eye on her. No doubt conscious of their gaze, she kept up a good front, sharing a box of chocolates with the journalists on board, and turned her attention not on herself but on the wishes of the people outside, and their desire to see the body.

She received a number of visitors that first day on the train, including the Sawyers and Christians, and Boone. She wanted to hear her fellow travelers' stories about her husband, too; she invited them to come to her room to share these. The journey thus served as a sort of traveling shivah or collation.[80] Florence left her quarters only to visit the casket, down a narrow corridor to the observation car, ten feet away. There, she might say a word to the soldiers, who every two hours relieved each other at the bier.[81] She was not the only one bound to her room; Harry Daugherty lay low as well for most of the trip. Daugherty, along with the Remsberg family and Pershing, were the only passengers on the funeral train who had not been to Alaska. Florence refused to entertain all other offers of visitors who wanted to join them for the trip back east. But she did not reject the rapidly accumulating mounds of flowers, and in Iowa, another train had to be added to take on the profusion of floral offerings, already up to the knees of the guards. Mrs. Harding stayed in her room as the train went through the Cornhusker State on August 5, and observers continued to worry that she would have enough strength to carry her through the ordeal; she ate little.

When it could, the train attempted to make up time at the then "terrific speed" of 60 mph.[82] But to no avail. In Omaha, Nebraska, where the president's train arrived at 3 A.M. on the 6th, 40,000 were waiting to salute. As one paper observed, "The crowd stretched into the darkness as far as one could see . . . out of the darkness loomed masses of flowers, seeming to move by themselves and hiding their bearers."[83] The train had to slow down, and Florence watched in silent appreciation from her berth. The police could not hold them back—men, women, and children, in the dark or under broiling sun. The *Cleveland Plain Dealer* noted, "There have been other sorrowful progresses of dead presidents, but never one so long . . . to wait for long hours in the heat of the day or in the dead of night merely to catch a glimpse of a passing train cannot be the result of morbid curiosity . . . there is something unmistakably genuine in the people's grief."[84] With the advent of the telegraph and the railroad, Lincoln and McKinley's deaths reached more people than those of Presidents Harrison and Taylor; the untimely loss of Lincoln drew 120,000 to see his body in New York's City Hall, even more than those who came to see Harding's in Washington. Still, the superior communications and transportation of the 1920s made it possible for a vaster crowd to see the funeral train cross the country.

As the locomotive crossed the Mississippi River into Illinois and on to Chicago, progress was often completely stopped. "At Glen Ellyn, Lombard, Melrose Park, Maywood, River Forest, and Oak Park throngs surged along the right of way, virtually blockading all traffic in either direction," the *New York Times* reported. In the Windy City itself, the crowds were so thick, up to possibly one million in all, that they completely overran the tracks in places. The Kedzie Avenue station was impassable. Yet as Boone noted, "there were no pulsing movements, there was no crowding, no pushing."[85] The train itself could not move, all the same. People hung on buildings, scaffolding, bridges, phone poles, railcars, anywhere they could get a closer look—and the crowds went on for fifty miles.[86]

Soon, though, the anxious, waiting people grew restive. Not even an intrepid Methodist minister, E. F. Miller, could bring order to the throngs then. His timely sermon was instead "drowned out by the tumult." The huge crowd began to surge, "jostling, shoving, jumping up." At the Wood Street yards, a lone flagman walked ahead of the train, beating back the mob, ten or twenty deep, as they surged forward. It must have been scary for him, and those inside. The people called for Mrs. Harding to come out, and a few would not be put off. The mayor's committee, with aldermen, "swarmed aboard," even though they had been told specifically that Mrs. Harding was not available.[87]

Still, she never forgot the importance of allowing the crowds to see her husband, and the train was kept at a slow pace through the most packed areas. Somehow, they got through Chicago.[88] Then there was Ohio, whose well-organized crowds could not be slighted. Florence only slept four hours during the night they passed through her home state, and she awoke on August 7 to cross the river into Pittsburgh, where the appreciative steelworkers, who had her husband to thank for ending their twelve-hour day, stopped their noisy labor on the river front, and "in their soiled clothes and besmeared faces and hands," bowed their heads as the train passed.[89]

By now it was clear the party would never reach Washington by daylight on the 7th; they hoped to get there at least in time for Florence to get a good night's sleep, so the train rocketed through Pennsylvania and Maryland.[90] In the end, the hot and exhausting journey took ninety-six hours—or four days—much of the time going at a speed of less than ten miles per hour. It was thus nine hours late reaching Washington. The delay made Florence anxious. They did not arrive until 10:22 P.M., and previous plans for an East Room reception had to be scrapped. This was not necessarily bad; the delay had allowed so many more to see him who otherwise might not have. But the slow arrival had also occasioned further rumors about Mrs. Harding as well. Had she died on the train, possibly?[91] She had not. Instead, she had taken herself immediately to the White House, arriving there at 10:50 P.M. in time to receive her husband's body at 11:10, joined by Grace Coolidge and some of the Cabinet wives.

But first, a procession of cars, beginning with Coolidge and finishing with William Howard Taft—the current president and the oldest living one—and current Chief Justice—met the train, along with Cabinet members (the entire Cabinet was being retained by Coolidge) and congressional leaders, at Union Station. There were also 75,000 Americans who had waited to see the arrival. Harding was placed on a caisson with cavalry and field artillery. There was a "terrible, terrible stillness as we walked into the White House," Boone recalled.[92]

WASHINGTON FUNERAL

In Washington, the rituals of mourning attained a grand scale, with thousands upon thousands participating in the funeral processions, memorial speeches, prayers, and vigils by the body. Florence played a large role in planning the entire endeavor, and the War Department and Washington police forces worked out the details.[93]

There would be 300 marines for crowd control at the Capitol, where the funeral and viewing would be held, while the police would monitor the crowds back and forth from Union Station and from the White House to the Capitol. Secretary of State Hughes announced that government offices would close, beginning a half-hour before the body arrived until Saturday, the 11th; the Lincoln Memorial and the public bathing beach were also closed. Formal visits would not be accepted at the White House until September 3, following a thirty-day national mourning period. Business as a whole would shut down on the 8th and the 10th for the funerals in both the District of Columbia and Ohio. All government-owned merchant vessels would also pause on the 10th at 3:00 P.M.

Harding rested in state in the East Room, following others who had died in office before him: Lincoln (1865), Garfield (1881), and McKinley (1901).[94] For Florence and Warren, the night of August 7–8 would be their last in the White House together. At 1:15 A.M., after everyone had gone, Florence visited him, praying silently with the guards for a half hour, and choosing some of the multitude of flowers along the walls to be placed next to him. While she did so, a most beloved visitor arrived. Evalyn rushed in from Bar Harbor at 1:30 A.M., and she joined Florence with the corpse. The late president "looked perfectly lovely," Evalyn recalled, despite being nearly a week old. Florence talked to her late husband for an hour and a half, "a very womanly thing" to do, her friend observed. Florence seemed to draw a compelling energy from her husband—perhaps owing to her own mystical connections, the dead man gave her an infusion of his life. Evalyn was amazed. "I never saw Mrs. Harding shed a tear, never broke—she had great gameness, that woman."[95] Florence went to bed well after 2 and rose the next morning at 7:45, somewhat rested, and shared her breakfast with their dog, Laddie Boy, brought in by servant William Jackson at her request. Laddie Boy had missed her. She had not seen him since before the trip to Alaska. She urged Jackson to bring him in to Warren as well. Florence would later give the dog to her guard, Harry Barker.

There was one more small service at her husband's side, with Christian and Sawyer, Coolidge, the Cabinet, and Supreme Court justices in attendance, before Florence and the others went over to the Capitol. The procession to the state funeral would be huge and elaborate, fitting the occasion, with thousands of eyes on her. But in the intimate East Room, she could rest her eyes on the flowers, including a six-foot-high anchor of white and purple asters, decorated with orchids, and the many more flowers outside the window. Geraniums "flamed" on the parapet, near the "prim" bay trees on the terrace; nearby, White House roses, and "long beds of phlox, like mounds of snow, lie at the gates," as one paper noted. There were helenium and plumbago, too, and crepe myrtle by the railings. Florence had loved that garden, visiting it every day when she could. She would miss the flowers perhaps more than anything else about the White House, and she probably hated to pull herself away for the trial of the enormous public funeral.[96]

Heavily veiled, she dutifully left the White House with Sawyer, Baldinger, and Barker, her oft-present protectors, and got into her limousine behind the horse-drawn caisson with Harding's body. Inside the car, she remained invisible behind tightly drawn curtains, hearing only the four black horses clip-clopping ahead of her and the drums of five bands beating out their slow tattoo. Behind her, there were other dignitaries in automobiles; above, a black-draped plane slowly droned. There were another 2,000 marching in the procession, some in front, some behind, including military, political, and civic groups. The horses' funereal gait set the pace for all of them; caissons have long signaled the deliberate speed that mourning rituals require. The single mile from the White House to the Capitol was thus slowed to an hour-long procession—so long and so slow that the civic groups were still in formation at the White House by the time the VIPs had reached the Capitol. This pace allowed the 200,000 in the streets to observe the procession closely in the sweltering heat. They had already been waiting for hours for this passage, and they would wait hours more to visit the president's body in the rotunda. The *Philadelphia Ledger* saw the ceremony as especially fitting for after all, had Harding not prevented a "tinseled procession" for his inauguration? Now, "he had in death the stately procession he declined in life."[97]

Leading the march was World War I general John J. Pershing, along with numerous other representatives of the armed forces, including six generals, six admirals, and sailors, marines, cavalry, infantry, and field artillery. Behind them, and just in front of the caisson and casket, was Parade Marshal Henry Cabot Lodge, leading a civic procession headed by clergy and Harding's doctors. Seven senators and congressmen were next, the honorary pallbearers at the caisson, followed by Mrs. Harding and the Harding families behind the casket. Then came Calvin Coolidge, William Howard Taft, and other Supreme Court justices, the Cabinet, the chairman of the Federal Reserve, former president Wilson and his wife, congressmen, governors, ambassadors, lesser diplomats, and citizens' groups. Some of these included the Daughters of the American Revolution, the Women's Christian Temperance Union, the Red Cross, the Colonial Dames, and the League of Women Voters (despite their controversial platform!). Of course, there were plenty of men's groups too, like the American Legion, the Knights of Pythias, the Sons of the American Revolution, and the Knights Templar.[98]

After arriving at the Capitol Plaza, the troops arranged themselves exactly at the spot where Harding had been inaugurated just twenty-nine months earlier. They then carried the coffin up the steps to the marine band's rendition of Chopin's funeral march. In the rotunda, whose last funeral had been for the Unknown Soldier on November 9–11, 1921, the men laid their burden on a catafalque originally built for Lincoln. The doors opened at 10:00 A.M. in the rotunda. It was two-thirds full within a half-hour, including the entire Senate. William Tyler Page, clerk of the House, supervised the screening of the more than 1,000 attendees, who also included diplomats, governors, and Cabinet members, along with the Secret Service. There were just about enough flower arrangements for each of the guests, had they wished to take one home.[99]

Florence and the White House cohort arrived late after the long procession, delaying the services forty minutes, or until almost noon.

Funeral procession, August 8, 1923. Courtesy of the Library of Congress.

She stepped off the rotunda's elevator under her veil on Christian's arm, at the same time her husband's body came through the rotunda doorway. The "firm lines of her mouth indicated she retained complete control of herself," one paper noted, as did "the erect manner in which she crossed the stone floor." She would not sit until the coffin was in its place. She tucked herself away unobtrusively a few feet from her husband's casket, which was "heaped with red, yellow and white gladioli." A male quartet from Calvary sang "Lead Kindly Light," and prayers included an Old Testament verse from Micah 6:8, which the president had kissed during his oath of office in 1921. The final selection was a comforting one from Revelation 22:1–5: "on either side of the river, was there the tree of life, which bore twelve manner of fruits . . . and the leaves of the tree were for the healing of all nations . . . and there shall be no night there." The funeral finished with "Nearer My God to Thee," a favorite hymn of Harding's, sung by 2,000 children all dressed in white.[100]

It was over in twenty minutes. Mrs. Harding went out, again on Christian's arm, and "sank limply" into a White House car.[101] She was so exhausted—or grief stricken—that Christian had to carry her back into the White House when they arrived. She tried to step down, and instead fell forward into his arms. He and Sawyer took her to her room to rest. After lunch with family members, she had also to greet visitors, including Mrs. Coolidge and some Cabinet wives, before getting much time to herself. As the *Washington Post* said, "It has been a day that tried her very soul."[102]

Back at the rotunda, the mass of flowers cramming the room made for a scent that was "almost overpowering" and soon after the funeral ended, would mingle with the smells of the thousands of men, women, and children who came to see the president's body lying in state all afternoon. The heat rose off the pavement in waves, and the crowds had to wait nearly an hour for the military representatives and the members of the funeral procession's various civic and fraternal groups to get the first look. Once the crowds had been unleashed, they came quickly, passing at "the rate of 100 a minute" or 15,000 an hour in two lines, one on each side, or about 100,000 persons total. By comparison, 130,000 had passed the tomb of the unknown solder in 1922, and 85,000 had passed McKinley.[103]

Reverently, they gazed at the coffin with its glass lid revealing the head and shoulders of Harding, resting under the Freedom Statue. A varied group—old, young, and of all colors—passed; veterans, Masons, nuns, housewives, Girl Scouts and Boy Scouts, too—and nearly three dozen photographers, who at some points stopped the procession to take pictures. By 3 o'clock, the line of shuffling witnesses snaked around the Capitol to the Peace Monument. Possibly as many as 40,000 of those lined up under the broiling sun waited in vain, for at 4:30, the rotunda was closed to the public. The crowds were held back as the body was placed on the caisson to return to Union Station for the overnight trip to Marion, Ohio. The sweating multitude was denied a final look.

President Coolidge, Chief Justice Taft, and other dignitaries took the casket back to the station for its final trip to Marion, following the marines carrying the bier. Meanwhile, at the White House, three cars filled with family and friends pulled up just before 5:30 to take the exhausted Florence separately to join her husband on the funeral train. She came out of the house resting on Christian's arm. He and Sawyer assisted her into the McLeans' automobile, where she joined

Line to see the president lying in state in the rotunda, August 8, 1923. Courtesy of the Library of Congress.

Evalyn and Dr. Sawyer.[104] After she said a final word to Evalyn, Christian helped her onto *Superbe*.[105] She stopped to see her husband as she entered, crying, "Oh! You poor boy!," and then took some newspapers with coverage of the funeral to her compartment in a separate car belonging to the McLeans, who had attached it to the train for her use. On the trip to Marion, she was, as ever, conscious of the people and their wishes — and ordered the train to slow down once again when crowds gathered, such as the large throng in Johnstown, Pennsylvania, at 3 A.M.

What is amazing is how Florence stood it all, certainly "a week of such pain and suffering as would overnight whiten the hair of an ordinary woman."[106] In short order, she had not only lost her husband but had to arrange separate services in three different cities. It took all of her strength — indeed, an "iron will" to endure all this as well as to organize such a complicated operation.[107]

MARION FUNERAL

Coolidge had declared August 10, the day Harding would be laid to rest in his hometown of Marion, Ohio, an official day of mourning and prayer. The new president urged everyone to drop their daily business, and "to assemble on that day in their respective places of divine worship, there to bow down in submission to the will of Almighty God and to pay out of full hearts homage and love and reverence to the memory of the great and good president."[108] Florence was no doubt heartened by his call. Realizing that she could do little to keep the Washington ceremonies small, she had already resolved that the Marion funeral, at least, would be a simple one. She thus instructed that the body would rest in Harding's father's modest house, with no military cortege or caisson, nor a huge civic procession, either. "I want Warren buried as a distinguished citizen of Marion, not as the President," she said.[109] She wanted to avoid "any suggestion of circumstance or display."[110]

Delayed once again by crowds, the train was over three hours late reaching Marion Thursday morning, arriving at 12:40 P.M. For those on board, it would be the last trip with President Harding after so many weeks together, from Washington to Alaska to California, then back to Washington and to Ohio. The windows came out of the observation car for the last time to enable the removal of the flag-draped coffin and its placement in a gray hearse.[111] His body was taken to his father's house in a procession led by the Ohio National Guard and the officers who had been with the body since Washington. The Cabinet officers, Hughes, Weeks, Work, New, Daugherty, Wallace, Denby and Hoover, followed the hearse in full formal dress of long coats and silk hats. Florence, too, was once more in a funeral procession, and "not the smiling and cheerful woman" the town had once known. She was in her dark mourning clothes in a curtained car.[112]

The town was already swollen with 100,000 people, or some said twice that, who had arrived in Marion in the previous twenty-four hours. It was like the Front Porch, but without the frivolity. The visitors could find no place to sleep, except for their cars (if they were lucky enough to have them), in ditches, or in parks; nor could they find enough places to eat. The dignitaries, of course, had no such problem; they stayed at the Hotel Marion, Clifford Kling's establishment. To keep the famished, sweaty, patient throng in order, Marion's sixty blocks were transformed into a military zone with 3,000 patrols, keeping the men and women moving. But no one would be denied the opportunity to see the casket for as long as time allowed. It sat in the bay window of Dr. Harding's narrow house at 498 East Centre Street. Florence was there already, sitting upstairs after making sure everything was properly arranged. As the hours passed, she felt the vibrations from 20,000 pairs of feet coming through the front room and the hushed chatter of half as many outside hoping to join them. She saw a few friends during the day, to whom she intimated that after tidying up her affairs in Washington, she planned to stay in Marion with her brother, Clifford, for some time, allowing her tenants to stay on Mt. Vernon Avenue.[113] The mourners kept coming until 10 P.M. Mrs. Harding was loath to turn them away. With 15,000 still waiting, she said, "Don't stop the line, let them come until daylight."[114] But she and the doctor needed to sleep, so the house was closed until 9 A.M. the next day. She would spend that last night with her husband's body at his father's house, comforting, and being comforted by, the old doctor.[115]

She invited some of the *Star* employees for a special viewing the next morning at 8:30; she would also welcome President Coolidge and the others in his party, including Chief Justice Taft, whose eleven-car train also arrived at 8:30. When Coolidge and Taft showed up at the house, she came down to meet them on the arm of Christian. "Mr. President, I greet you," she said with all the force she could muster, and wished Grace Coolidge "success as the new mistress." But when Secretary Hughes stretched out his hands, she could only say, grasping his hand, "Mr. Secretary." She became teary, as did he and Taft. She recovered quickly, took one last look at her husband, then went upstairs with Christian and Sawyer, concealed from the street by a window shade. She insisted that no additional person be turned away until the absolute last minute. Fully 20,000 remained in the street, disappointed, when the doors finally shut to visitors at 1 P.M.[116]

After the house was closed, a small, abbreviated funeral service led by Reverend George King, of Columbus, former pastor of Trinity Church, took place there with the Coolidges, Taft, the Cabinet, and some relatives in attendance. Extracting themselves from the house proved difficult with the crowds still packed outside. It took half an hour for anyone to move in any direction whatsoever.

The presidential party traveled along Center Street, with 4,000 to 5,000 Ohio guardsmen leading them en route to the cemetery on Delaware Avenue, where around 2:30 P.M., the invited guests began to arrive, assembling in a roped-off area under birch, oak, and maple trees. This quiet spot, clogged with sweet-smelling flowers, included, disconcertingly, the "fiery cross" of the KKK in red tiger lilies, carried

Florence and Warren's final journey together, from Dr. Harding's home to the cemetery, August 10, 1923. Courtesy of Mike and Linda Perry.

from Doctor Harding's lawn with all the other bouquets. The service took place at Harding's ivy-clad, iron-barred vault, near the graves of his mother and sister, Mary Clarissa Harding, and other Marion friends. The simple ten-by-fifteen-foot vault was crowned by a cross and framed by six white pillars topped with eagles and laurel leaves.[117] General Pershing was at the vault, and so too was the "Camping party" from the previous summer, including Thomas Edison and his wife, Mr. and Mrs. Henry Ford, and the Harvey Firestones and their sons. Numerous senators were there, along with a choir in black and white.

The crowd on the road to the cemetery, as opposed to the dignified group in the vault area, were held back with ropes and military personnel. Wanting to get a closer look at the oncoming celebrities, at one point they lurched forward and broke the restraining rope; several men fell into the street. But a quick-witted army lieutenant stopped the rushing by invoking Florence's name, and the rope was tied back together.

Those who waited were soon rewarded with the sight of a sailor bearing the president's flag. An entourage of clergy, soldiers, admirals, generals, and cars full of family and friends followed. As they arrived, Florence left her screened-in car, escorted once again by

Christian, and she stood, "drawn and still," on the other side of President Coolidge. In that stiff company, old Dr. Harding was the only one to weep openly. Florence stood motionless, "as firm as if she had been carved out of the rock itself."[118] As for the attorney general, Boone noticed that he looked "old and very sad and drawn."[119] An era had ended.

At 2:50 P.M., some short rites were read, and just ten minutes later, military and naval aides carried President Harding in the door of his simple vault as the Trinity Baptist Church choir sang "Lead, Kindly Light." Only once did it look as if Florence would crack—when her old friend Reverend Swank offered her words of comfort and consolation during the service, and she sobbed briefly before getting herself under control once again.

The brief services concluded with a final benediction, and then a military escort took the coffin into the vault's inner sanctum. After the sounding of taps, Mrs. Harding went into the vault on Christian's arm. No more than sixty seconds passed before she reemerged and with a "brave, certain step" walked toward the cemetery's entrance, head at first raised to the sky, then lowered. As Starling recalled, when she came out of the tomb, "her face was lifted, and her eyes shone with a light I had not seen in them before." She had again received a mystical sustenance from her dearly departed. Waiting a moment to follow her from a respectful distance, the Coolidges, and Taft, walked after "the proud lady . . . [who] was passing from the national picture."[120]

The entire country was with her at that moment. Traffic, on subways, trains, and vessels, stopped in many cities for several minutes. Communication ceased too; Western Union and the postal service each observed similar pauses at two minutes before 5 P.M. EST.[121] (Marion was two hours behind the East Coast at that time.) The U.S. merchant marine, long a pet of Harding's, also stopped for 120 seconds.[122] In New York City, cars, trains, and boats all halted from 5:00 to 5:02 P.M. in honor of the vault being closed on former President Harding.[123] New York's example was followed by many other cities from Boston to Juneau, where industrial activity stopped and offices closed during the Washington and Marion funerals. Thus, in Philadelphia, "Traffic on hundreds of streets came to a dead stop . . . like a mechanical carnival run down. . . . A throng . . . stood in

Independence Square with heads bared and eyes upraised to the belfry, where sorrow spoke in the tone of a bell clapper."[124] Prisoners at Eastern State Penitentiary ceased their drills; in Columbus, swimmers and baseball players canceled their meets.[125] Similarly, the vaudeville circuit went dark Friday afternoon, only opening after 6 P.M.; by the evening, however, Broadway and other amusements were wide open again, and the streets were clogged.

Florence left her husband in the capable hands of twenty-five soldiers who would watch his grave for six months, until the planned mausoleum was built (she knew nothing yet of the glories of the later shrine to be built by the Harding Memorial Association!). She went back to Center Street for one last visit to Harding's father and to see a few more friends before joining Sawyer and Christian to return to Washington at 7:00 P.M. on the train—one car short this time—to empty out the White House.[126] The Cabinet secretaries and others who had been with her since June were also on this train, many of them still wearing their ribbons announcing "The President's Alaska Party," now stained with travel. As they neared the capital, she asked all the veterans of the Alaska trip to come to her stateroom for a final word.

BACK IN WASHINGTON

The Coolidges had graciously invited Florence to stay in the White House "indefinitely" while they remained in their rooms at the New Willard Hotel, urging her to use anything she needed, cars and employees included. Coolidge's personal staff, in the interim, was working without pay. Along with the entire Harding Cabinet, the new president had also retained both Dr. Sawyer and Dr. Boone. Sawyer served as White House physician until July 1924, but well before then, undeniable friction (as well as Coolidge's low estimation of his competence) had undermined his position in the White House, and Boone supplanted him.[127] For some time, however, at least until she got very ill, Florence maintained her friendships with both doctors.

Florence knew she had to vacate the White House quickly. She "was too practical and too well versed in the proprieties to take advantage of this presidential courtesy" for any longer than she needed, as Lawler writes.[128] Florence did not want to be a hindrance.

Instead, she planned to move to her friend Evalyn McLean's mansion, Friendship, for a few weeks. Evalyn was then in Maine with her children. After that, Florence's plan for the next six months was to rest and "be very largely in seclusion from the large circle that knew her" before figuring out what she would do. She would live for that time in Marion, just as she and Warren had planned. Still, being a single woman complicated matters; alone, Marion held less appeal. She could not long resist the call of Washington, as it turned out.

When Florence arrived back in the capital at 9:20 A.M. on August 11, she was greeted at Union Station by Coolidge's military aide (and Harding's former one), Colonel O. S. Sherrill, who promptly insulted her with, "Mrs. Coolidge and the ladies of the Cabinet will be pleased to meet you," even though Florence was still, technically, mistress of the house—and would be for nearly another week. Sherrill added injury to insult by then chatting up Major Reddy Baldinger, her personal aide, whom Sherrill had already sacked from White House service.[129]

But she did not have time to fuss over Sherrill's impertinence. Christian and Sawyer were ready to escort her to the White House, where Mrs. Coolidge waited to give her a friendly welcome. After Grace left, Florence rested until noon, and then worked straight through until 5:30, sorting her husband's papers and effects, including furniture, clothing, and gifts, with the help of Christian and executive clerk Rudolph Forster.[130] Sawyer also stopped by, and that night she had another friendly visit from the new first lady. They "clasped hands and tenderly and affectionately kissed one another" while Florence told Grace about the ways of the house and her new responsibilities, just as Mrs. Wilson had done for her. Papers reported it as "a most human and touching scene. . . . there was no mistaking the depth of friendship" of the two. If so, this was a departure; they had not been supremely close before.[131]

Florence was undoubtedly grateful to the Coolidges, who enabled her to spend nearly a week at the White House, an unprecedented stay in such circumstances, not seen again until Jackie Kennedy stayed in the White House after her husband's death, and a surprise to many who though she would not be comfortable sleeping there alone.[132] There was no provision made for a White House widow at that time; she had effectively lost both her husband's paycheck and her housing on August 2, but for the graciousness of the Coolidges. Florence had much to do at the White House. Fortunately she had help, including Laura Harlan's, with answering condolence cards and gathering the voluminous papers of the administration. The packing job was yet another "ordeal" for her to endure.[133]

Although she occupied the White House for a week and spent two more at Friendship, this was less than a month for Florence and her assistants to sort through an entire presidency. Working with Harlan and Baldinger, Mrs. Harding herself took on the "private office" material. On the first day, August 11, she was in the executive offices, a place she had barely frequented during her husband's term, looking for these personal papers. Anything incriminating was apparently burned, either at the White House, at Friendship, or back in Marion. But there was much she saved, and much more she did not find or have, and thus could not burn.[134]

Then there were all their belongings and effects and furniture to sort through. Florence would keep her husband's beaten-up desk, and his office and Cabinet chairs, and give away to friends his campaign and other souvenirs from his study bookcase, like the Indian peace pipe and the gold horseshoe. Their horse, Harbel, ridden only a couple of times, would go back to Harvey Firestone. The Firestones needed Harbel, as they were soon off for another camping trip with the Fords and Edisons. They wished that she might join them! In exchange for the horse, Firestone offered to have his secretary fix her car with "air cushion tires . . . wonderful riding tires . . . [to] save you from jars and jolts." She happily accepted the tires.[135]

The work was trying and at times overwhelming, and on Sunday, August 12, she took a "complete rest," no doubt under Nurse Powderly's kind care.[136] Reclusive she may have been, but she was remembered in church pulpits all the same her first Sunday back.[137] On Monday, she worked until 10 P.M., and started her slow, sad work again the following morning. On Tuesday, she would once more work late into the night.[138] She had so much to sort—bric-a-brac, much of it, but also, most poignantly, her husband's elaborate and extensive wardrobe, and her own, with its many dresses, gowns, and hats, most of which she would never wear again. Despite the short tenure of their stay in the White House, these effects were "voluminous" in contrast to other first couples.[139] All the same, Florence complained that she had had only "one little black dress" for the funeral, and had had to dye two others, including a yellow-and-red one, which "saved me quite a bit."[140] Her bulky items would mostly go to Clifford Kling in Marion, but some would stay in a Washington warehouse, including her piano.

At least she felt well; it seemed to give her a boost to have this job to do. And the work kept expanding. But one chilly mid-August evening, Florence Harding was finally ready to leave the White House for the last time. She had packed until late in the day with Christian and Baldinger, and then Mrs. Coolidge came to pick her up and take her to her temporary home at Friendship. After a final look over the house and a half-hour visit with the new first lady, Florence strode calmly across the portico with Grace and Christian on August 17 into the dusky, dreary gloom. At 6:40 P.M., she joined Barker and Jim Haley, Mrs. Coolidge's Secret Service man, in a waiting car.[141] Laura Harlan and Ruth Powderly followed them. There were only three newspapermen there to notice her exit, and some White House policemen. What a contrast to that glorious March day when she had entered the White House not quite two and a half years before! One paper noted rather melodramatically that she had thus descended "the crowning height of a useful and energetic life."[142] Florence looked around at her beloved grounds, with their dripping trees and bent-over flowers, and settled into the car. Her two female assistants followed in a second vehicle. The house would be empty for three days before the Coolidges moved in.

Florence was grateful to arrive at Friendship, and even more so for Evalyn's own. "I can never forget your unfailing friendship . . . when your thoughtfulness in every way has been such a comfort to me," she wrote on the 15th. Ten days later, she added: "Of course I miss you but I am getting on very well, with days full of looking over my papers and repacking some of my things." She was enjoying the upstairs porch as a place to work, but had only walked the peaceful and beautiful grounds once. Visitors were keeping her in touch with the world.[143]

Mrs. Harding would continue reviewing her papers until September 4, boxing the documents in large crates (ten feet by one foot by one foot) for further processing—or burning—in Marion.[144] The destruction began in earnest at Friendship, with "several crates ... marked 'Executive Office of the President'" consumed "in a great bonfire," according to Gary Cohen, among others.[145] This bonfire, Frances Russell noted, included suitcases, bank deposit boxes, and other items. It was fueled, too, by copies of William Estabrook Chancellor's nasty book, seized earlier by the Justice Department, Kenneth Duckett alleges. He writes that this burning was one of "the great stories in American historiography: the censorship, suppression, and destruction of many of the important historical sources material to the Harding Administration."[146] Perhaps so, but it remains unclear how much of significance was destroyed because these boxes comprised only a small part of the Harding opus. Thousands more were left untouched and ended up in the hands of the Harding Memorial Association, and later the Ohio Historical Society and the Library of Congress—enough to consume voluminous rolls of microfilm. Other documents turn up regularly on eBay to this day.

Whatever Florence was doing, she was very busy, as she wrote Esther on August 25: "I can hardly realize, two weeks ago today we laid Mr. Harding away." Her work was a blessing, keeping her mind occupied; nevertheless, she wrote, "my nights are awful." She was strikingly open in this letter to her daughter-in-law. Seeming to echo the popular assessment of her grim fate as a widow, she wrote, "the days are pretty dark to me and I see absolutely nothing for the future." She had the Sawyers and her nurse for company, all the same, and her buoyant spirit would not let her give up entirely either: "Well! I will just have to wait. Time may adjust some things that I cannot see now." Meanwhile, she sent along a little dress for Jean and some other items to be fixed for her, including a "faded" dress with "petal trimming," which could just be thrown away if it was beyond dyeing. "You have much to be thankful for Esther. Three fine children and such a splendid husband," she said gratuitously.[147]

Why did she continue to send her granddaughter these old cast-offs when she had so many beautiful dresses she would never use that might be usefully recycled by Esther? Perhaps she was going to give them to charity, or planning to dye some for bereavement garb. She did send the children's quarterly $100 checks early to help with school, though she got the wrong date. "All days are just alike to me so I am not surprised," said the mourning former first lady.[148]

Mrs. Harding finally left for Marion on September 5, her first priority to attend to her husband's will. Mrs. Coolidge took her to the train, and her friends saw her off, including Postmaster New and his wife. Dressed in mourning black, Florence chatted with them, hugged Grace good-bye, and got into a plush private car lent her by a railroad executive at 4:50 P.M. for the trip to White Oaks with the Sawyers and Baldinger. She had as yet "no plan for returning" to the capital.[149] But others speculated that she would return, like the *Washington Times:* "The capital for years has been a lodestone to former officials and their wives or widows. They cannot forget the lure of officialdom and big affairs." The paper added, "She is a woman of such keen acumen that it does not seem likely she would be willing to settle down very far from the political center of gravity."[150] Indeed, Florence's horizons remained broader than central Ohio, just as they always had.

CHAPTER 8

WIDOWHOOD, AUGUST 1923– NOVEMBER 1924

Her husband's death hit Florence hard, but it did not mean, as correspondent Robert Small put it, that her world was now irreversibly "empty."[1] He had contended, as did others, that her "chief mission was gone," accentuated by Warren's great dependence on her. Although Florence's world had certainly narrowed, it was hardly a void. She had the resources and the gumption to launch a new chapter in her life, and friends to support her in this.

Florence was a rich woman and could live anywhere. The *Washington Star* speculated, however, that she would stay in her small Ohio town, in the bosom of her "little home," with its famed "Front porch"—close to the oomphalos of White Oaks. Still, after the White House, it would be a "world of emptiness."[2] In Marion, she had her friends and support system—and in surrounding towns like Columbus and Westerville too—and her grandchildren. But as the *Star* noted, Washington had the pull of friends, like Evalyn and Catherine New, along with so many others. Moreover, Florence had tasted a bigger life there, and even if she was sixty-three, she hadn't given up on it yet.

As Florence packed to leave the capital, she expressed anew her gratitude to her absent host. The stay had done her much good, she wrote Evalyn: "I am much better, and everyone comments on how well I look considering what I have been through. I owe it all to you and Ned." She hoped she would see them in Cincinnati, where Ned ran the *Enquirer*, and where Evalyn would move the following spring. She was meanwhile leaving the Laszlo picture of herself—her favorite—at Friendship, as she wanted it there "to enjoy" when she returned to the capital. Eventually she would give it to Emily McLean, her goddaughter. "I hope she will know how I prize it and that as she grows to womanhood she may have the same feeling about it," she wrote, somewhat dreamily, adding, "I am always, with much love, affectionately . . . FKH."[3]

Writing back from Palm Beach, Evalyn assured her: "You have been so wonderful through the terrible days that you have the respect and love of the whole world!" She recognized how difficult the homecoming would be for Florence, too: "I . . . dread the thought of what it will be for you to go back to Marion!!" She was struck by how the world had changed for them both: "I think of you so often and of all the wonderful times we all have had together, and it just seems like it can't be true, that they are all over!" The two women did not see each other until after Florence moved back to Washington.[4]

Mrs. New did see her, lunching with her old friend shortly before Florence left for Marion in September. "It was more like old times—pre-campaign times in fact," thought New, "for she seems to have lost the driving and driven expression and was an interesting, normal woman." Others found her still very much focused on her loss. Dolly Gann recalled that "Mrs. Harding received me with her old cordiality, but she was crushed. The entire conversation was of President Harding—his work, aims and ambitions."[5] An optimistic and perceptive Catherine New guessed that Florence was ready to begin life on her own in a stimulating place, however she would not be "settling" in (or for) Marion. She "will come back here and possibly, take a house or apartment, and go to Florida or California during the winter," was Catherine's guess. With "Dockie Sawyer" retained by Coolidge, Florence would have the medical attention she needed. "She will not go far away from him. Faith is a wonderful thing," Catherine commented wryly, well aware of Florence's trust in the old man.[6] She was right. Sawyer had stayed on as head of the Federal Board of Hospitalization and as medical adviser to the president, but he also remained free to attend to the former first lady.[7]

Returning to Marion, Florence settled herself not with Cliff, but at White Oaks Farm, in the Sawyers' quarters. She let her tenant remain at the Mt. Vernon house, suggesting she did not intend to stay in town long. On September 8, she and her husband's executor, Charles Schaffner, along with old friends Daugherty and Baldinger, as well as attorney Hoke Donithen, filed her will. Along with their house, Florence's property included half of the *Star* building (they had sold the paper, but not its home). She had also inherited government bonds and securities, as well as dividends from the Harding Publishing Co. that would bring in some $100,000, sufficient for a tidy income for the rest of her life. In all, Harding's estate was worth about $500,000 (about $6 million in 2008 dollars).[8]

She shared this large sum with his father, George T. Harding Jr., and his three sisters, Charity M. Remsberg, Abigail V. Harding, and Carolyn Votaw. Nephews and nieces got $10,000, along with jewelry, and the DeWolfe children, Harding's stepgrandchildren, received $2,000 each—a rather striking disparity, but one Florence would help make up after her own death. Other recipients included Trinity Baptist and St. Paul's Episcopal Church in Marion, Marion's Park Commission, and a number of friends and colleagues.

Florence had become rich with her father's earlier bequest to her of $100,000. With her new inheritance, she was now among the wealthiest of Americans, at a time when the average unionized worker in her industry, the press, made $1.04 per hour (an excellent wage in those days, all the same). Yet even if a pressman worked 100-hour weeks, as many did, he would still earn less than $5,500 per year. Florence had not just inherited cash, however. She also had Amos Kling's business acumen, and as an impoverished single mother earlier, she had learned the importance of being able to take care of herself. She was not likely to miss a chance to get what she was owed. In early September, she chased down her husband's money still sitting in a Washington bank. She retrieved his paychecks for the time they'd been in Alaska, including the two days of August that he had been president.[9] She did have odd bills left from the White House, among them $800 in food costs, piano shipping, and (alas) men's apparel. Expenses related to the president's death, including $275 in postage, undertaker fees, and railroad expenses, she expected Congress to pay.[10]

Despite her view that such costs related to the presidency were the obligation of the American people, she and her friends in the nascent Harding Memorial Association were convinced that his presidential papers were a private possession to dispose of as they wished. The HMA would manage to keep them closed for forty years after Harding's death, or even longer—Harding's love letters to Carrie Philips are still sealed at the Library of Congress until 2014. Although Florence likely had no wish to recover *those* letters, had she even known about them, she intended to continue her own processing of her husband's papers. As noted in the previous chapter, she had shipped to Marion a half-dozen ten-foot-long crates, and she spent every morning for the next six weeks reading through, censoring, and burning many, professing "we must be loyal to Warren and preserve his memory," according to one historian. George Van Fleet of the *Star*, who witnessed some of this destruction, reckoned that as much as 60 percent of what she brought back was burned.[11] Van Fleet helped dispose of the papers himself in the furnace at the *Star*, and he pointed out that Martha Washington had also destroyed her husband's correspondence. He insisted, however, that Florence incinerated only "unimportant letters," those "from cranks, job seekers, beggars and personal friends." Like Van Fleet, Kathleen Lawler defended her old boss: "Mrs. Harding . . . was scrupulous in separating in her own mind, as well as physically, all public and official papers from those that were personal . . . she destroyed nothing of consequence." Indeed, she burned only "strictly personal" items."[12] There was a serious loss all the same: according to the Ohio Historical Society, when she finished in January 1924, there were only two crates left of her original six.[13]

Florence's "processing" was not initially known to the Library of Congress, which wrote her in October 1923 asking for the president's papers. Charles Moore, acting chief of the manuscript division, told her that his agency could manage and maintain her husband's materials safely even while she "would have complete control" over them. The president's papers would join those of predecessors Theodore Roosevelt, Taft, Lincoln, Jefferson, and Washington—as well as the only recently recovered Arthur Papers. Florence responded that she wanted to take this up with him when she was next in Washington. Because her husband had died so suddenly, she explained, the documents were in "temporary storage until I could reconstruct my life and . . . its orderly process."[14] But sometime in the next year, Moore learned that she had "burned practically all of the letters [Harding] left concerning political and national affairs."[15] Florence said so herself, and she defended her actions by stating that she was only attempting to follow her husband's wishes.[16]

But it was not so dire a picture as she made it; Florence had never had all of her husband's letters. Despite the widespread impression that she had burned the bulk of his archive, an understanding that still persists, she had succeeded in destroying only a fraction of the White House private office material. George Christian had preserved much else—including 100 cubic feet of boxes from the president's official White House papers that were left in the mansion and only discovered by workmen during a 1929 renovation! Another sixteen manuscript boxes of Harding's private materials also survived.[17] Florence, moreover, had no control over letters he'd written to others. All the same, through various means, Harding family members and associates managed to prevent most of the surviving papers from being opened until the mid-1960s, forty years after Harding's death. Shrouded in mystery, the Harding years remained subject to rumor and speculation of the worst kind, chiefly on the basis of the scandals that surfaced after Harding's death. Florence contributed to this poisoned picture in other ways; she refused to endorse any biography or collection of her husband's speeches that she did not direct or edit herself. Her caution came in part from the advice of Mac Jennings, as well as Gus Creager, but she made the ultimate decision.

Jennings was a key support in this period; she called him often, as the White Oaks telephone records show.[18] A good friend, he frequently offered advice on her health and urged her to get out more.[19] He also helped manage her correspondence; she had thousands of letters and telegrams to answer, and she initially requested 16,000 stamps![20] Jennings had in his Columbus office three "young ladies" to help with the typing tasks and acknowledgment of letters. Florence also hired a secretary, Laura Smith, to handle many of her routine correspondence chores.[21]

Jennings thus had much influence, and he urged her to be extremely cautious when people asked for her endorsement, as they did on everything from poems to policy. Thus, when someone sent her a song about Harding that "probably is rubbish," Florence should under no circumstances offer her blessing. If asked whether she would consider running for governor in 1924, or president in 1928, Jennings urged her to say "you would not consider anything of this sort . . . and that you had no personal political ambitions," which he hoped was accurate. He assured her he believed she was perfectly capable of holding such posts; no doubt, he worried about her health. She did not demur.[22]

Jennings also cautioned against lending her support to any set of volumes of the president's speeches, or any memorial tome either, unless Florence herself was involved in the editing work. He emphasized, too, the danger of sanctioning even a single speech by her late husband because doing so might be "looked upon as an attempt to force the hand of the new administration." As a result of this supremely guarded approach, Florence endorsed no speeches![23] Rather than act in any way that could suggest impropriety, she remained neutral about her husband's views.

Florence even attempted to block projects that could have promoted Warren's legacy. Joe Mitchell Chapple, a sympathetic journalist who had been on the Alaska trip, was keen to write a biography; reports were circulating that he was indeed the "named" biographer. But old Harding crony Creager warned Florence, and Jennings, that Chapple was "a monumental grafter and a pest," and claimed that Harding hadn't even wanted him in Alaska.[24] Florence thus discouraged Chapple, like other prospective authors, from proceeding: "I cannot give personal approval or authorization to you or any other writers who are proposing to write biographies." After all, *she* planned to do it. Unfortunately, this would not be soon: "I do not want to enter upon it hastily and will do so only after I have made a careful study and arrangement of the vast amount of material I have long been gathering with that end in view."[25] Creager thought that was just the right approach: "even if you do not enter upon this work at once, it is good that you have forestalled others who might rush in."[26]

But Florence's silence left a vacuum in defense of her husband. Soon highly negative reports mounted in the wake of the Teapot Dome hearings, which intensified that fall. Critical commentary was only exacerbated by the revelations that she had burned his papers. Florence had hindered other voices from speaking, and her husband's positive contributions were now ignored. Chapple's biography, which came out in 1924 despite Florence's wishes, would be one of the few favorable ones! Her claim to an exclusive franchise for the biography only raised questions for those seeking a balanced portrait of the former president, and further hurt "his" cause.[27] It is thus not the case, as one of her obituaries noted, that "there was nothing she could do toward the vindication or the defense of the memory of the man whose name she shared."[28]

Florence did begin to make a start on her own biography of her husband shortly before she became ill the following summer, assisted by Kathleen Lawler and another associate, General William H. Carter. Lawler noted that Mrs. Harding lamented having disposed of campaign material in her earlier bonfire, realizing how useful it would have been. Lawler remembered Florence "sobbing" in 1924 about her assistant's departure after the campaign, robbing them of even more of their history; Kathleen had been a close chronicler of events. "If I had known one-half of what I know now, you would never have left the President's side," Florence railed in remorse at Kathleen, who had left to pursue another job. Mrs. Harding was nevertheless "enthusiastic" about the progress of their biographical project, despite the lack of sources. Sadly, she did not live long enough to finish it. Later, Lawler compiled some of it and her own earlier notes for a manuscript, "The Hardings I Knew," though this work was never published.[29]

Along with planning a biography, Florence also endorsed a memorial for her husband in Marion proposed by the Harding Memorial Association—as yet having no vision of the giant mausoleum that was eventually built.[30] She also made plans to turn their home into a museum. As the site of the famous Front Porch, where 250,000 visited the Harding home before he was elected president, it continued to be a tourist destination, with roughly 10,000 coming each month after he died.[31] She diligently selected pictures and mementos for the home, and refused to lend any items out, afraid they might become fetishized![32] Relic requesters were informed that Harding's remains and effects would stay interred in Marion. Such was her intention to make his hometown the center for remembrance that she resisted other efforts to memorialize him, even those engaged in by her family. When Carolyn Votaw joined the board of a memorial hospital in Harding's name in Pittsburgh, Florence worried this would undermine the national Harding Memorial drive. She was assured by family members it was no threat.[33]

Returning to Marion was bittersweet, Florence wrote an old friend: "the strain . . . with all the old associations it has brought back, has been very great."[34] And she was still "uncertain" about the future; noting, "for the present, I am drifting along from day to day, attending to many details which have to be seen to." She was, at least, glad to be busy. Getting letters from friends like Marion Denby, "thinking of you and radiating silent sympathy," must have been especially heartening. Other friends like Emily Frelinghuysen, Henry Wallace, and John J. Pershing all wrote her that fall. She had not been forgotten—numerous people, mostly unknown to her, also wanted something: money, endorsements, or Laddie Boy's picture![35] Still, the contrast between her present situation and where she would have been if Harding had not died was stark.

In October, the long-simmering allegations about the former secretary of the Department of the Interior, Albert Fall, sprang to life, as the Senate Committee on Public Lands and Surveys opened hearings in the middle of the month to explore Fall's oil leases to Edward Doheny and Harry Sinclair. As the investigation continued over the following months, it became clear that Doheny had provided significant "loans" to the secretary in return for these favors. There were also allegations that Sinclair had provided him bonds (though Sinclair refused to testify). Navy secretary Denby had signed the leases, as the reserves belonged to the navy, and thus had to resign himself in February. Fall, who had resigned much earlier over another matter, was not convicted until 1929. Meanwhile, Attorney General Harry Daugherty's toleration of bribery, kickbacks, and other corrupt practices in his agency's regulation of the liquor trade only compounded the sins of Harding holdovers. Daugherty too resigned under fire in March, although he was never convicted of anything.[36] Members of the Harding administration who testified in these hearings kept in touch with Florence, including Albert Lasker.[37] Had Florence earlier known of these deeds, prompting her to burn her papers, as scholars have suggested?[38] Yet if so, why did she continue to believe in Daugherty, and in Fall too, writing Emma Fall in February 1924, and her husband, Albert, "lovingly," in April, in the midst of the punishing congressional inquiry?[39] Knowing of their actions and what they would mean for her husband's reputation, would she not have cut them off? Instead, it seems that she, like her husband, believed in these men, although she should have known better.[40]

Florence worried about blemishes in her husband's legacy, as her tight management of the biographical enterprise indicated. Fall's demise was just an example of the countless efforts, big and small, so many souls made to get Harding's, and his administration's, consideration for some project or other. Through some sort of distorted lens, perhaps encouraged by her loneliness, Florence thought that scrubbing as many of these letters that she could get her hands on, even if he had mostly turned the appellants down, would remove all stains. If the Teapot Dome scandal did not bring about her documentary mutilations, it was nevertheless a punishing ordeal she had to live with for the rest of her too-short life, and its legacy lives on. To this day, Americans continue to speculate whether Harding was a "crook," or simply someone whose "low standards" led him to befriend crooks.[41] He was neither—just a too-trusting friend.[42]

The hearings upset Florence, not only the allegations that surfaced in them about Cabinet members who were their friends, but also claims about her and her husband—for instance, that they had watched movies of "the Dempsey-Carpentier prizefight, imported into the District of Columbia in spite of the law prohibiting their transportation in interstate commerce," a charge she denied. She also dismissed her connections with many of those named in the hearings, who were only the "merest casual visitors who came with many thousands of other strangers . . . to visit the 'front porch.'"[43]

The day after the Committee on Public Lands began its hearings, Calvin Coolidge wrote that he and Grace looked forward to her return to the capital, and to having "the pleasure of seeing you often." Coolidge was glad, too, that she had "something to occupy" herself. "Dr. Sawyer, who is so faithful in looking after me, keeps me informed as to how you are getting along." She, in turn, thanked the president for sending a wreath for Harding's birthday, "so wonderfully expressive of the deep and sincere friendship" the men had shared.[44] But she would actually see little of the Coolidges.

The developments in Washington might have convinced Florence to stay in Marion, but she felt the pull of returning to the capital that fall. She expressed as much to Alexander Moore, her old friend and the ambassador to Spain, who invited her for a visit to that country and kindly told her to "please look upon me as a big brother." Although she was grateful for the invitation, "I see no possibility of my traveling very much for a long time to come," she said. She was not too ill to do so; rather, she had so many things to "see to" that no one else could do for her, and if she was going anywhere, it was to Washington, she announced: "I am thinking very seriously of going back there to stay for at least part of the year, as all my friends urge me to."[45] She made at least one trip outside Ohio that fall, an enjoyable jaunt to New York City, where John Wanamaker lent her a car. She appreciated this, being "frighten[ed]" by the cabs![46]

Friends were already helping her locate accommodations in the District of Columbia. In September, Bill New had told her she could procure "a good furnished house" for $300. He added, "Everyone hopes and expects that you will come back here to live—you certainly have a place here—which we all want to see you fill."[47] Another old friend, Mrs. H. H. Kohlsaat, who had just stopped in Washington to visit the Coolidges and Hoover, as well as "a number of your friends," gushed that "the spirit of your beloved husband rules Washington." She added, "Mr. Hoover cannot speak of Mr. Harding without choking his emotions. If one man can love another, he does love his great friend." This may have made Florence choke up too—with mirth. Her husband had never been particularly fond of the taciturn commerce secretary.[48]

Going through her husband's papers was taking time, so Florence's move would have to wait until December, she told Sawyer, even though "I work like a dog each day as it is." When old friend Frank Kellogg, just named ambassador to England, remembered Harding's birthday, she responded that "my health is very good, and I hope to see you both in Washington before you sail to Europe."[49]

December would also be the start of the Harding Memorial Association's campaign, to raise money for the imposing mausoleum now being envisioned in Marion; the congressional investigation added new urgency to this project. Of course, many memorials were proposed, and erected, for the late president—and Mrs. Harding was particularly touched by one from the city of San Francisco. She thanked the people of the Bay City for their "wonderful kindness, sympathy, and tact . . . in those sad and trying hours," but in typical fashion, she begged off making any suggestions to the committee.[50] The cautious and solicitous Jennings had urged her to stay out of the discussion: "I am afraid of the San Francisco proposition, and do not think you ought to be involved in the difficulties which will inevitably arise . . . as to the form their memorial should take."[51] San Francisco appropriately developed a golf course to honor the deceased president, Harding Park Golf Club, which opened in 1925, and was recently restored to its former glory as a premier golf destination.

On the other hand, Florence was closely involved with the efforts of the Harding Memorial Association, a group that had been organized shortly after the president's death by close friends including Sawyer, Daugherty, and Donithen. Senator Joseph Frelinghuysen was president; George B. Christian Jr. was secretary, and Andrew Mellon, naturally, was treasurer. President Coolidge served as honorary president. Trustees included most of Harding's Cabinet, as well as Ned McLean, Fred Upham, and John Hays Hammond, among others. The HMA had opened its Washington headquarters in November with much fanfare. Florence stayed in frequent touch with these developments and personally thanked donors.[52]

The association's goal was to raise $3 million to build a mausoleum for the former president, to preserve the Harding home and its collections, and to create a Warren G. Harding Chair of Diplomacy and the Functions of Government, possibly at George Washington University, or even more ambitiously, a Harding Memorial School of Government and Diplomacy.[53] Committees were set up on the state level and locally, including a Women's Committee and a New York City committee, where organizers hoped to net $500,000. Wealthy donors like Judge Elbert H. Gary of the American Iron and Steel Institute assisted with major gifts—he gave $25,000 in December, despite the fact that Harding helped end the twelve-hour day in the steel industry! The Silk Association of America donated nearly $6,000; Charles Evans Hughes gave $500; President Coolidge gave $1,000; and Secretary Week provided $5,000. Smaller amounts came from an Albany Girl Scout troop, which sent $1, and other groups, including South Dakota Indian children, gradeschoolers from Clairton, Pennsylvania, and the Palestine Foundation Fund (for his "expressions of sympathetic interest . . . for the Jewish restoration in Palestine"), also donated small amounts.[54] Less keen were government clerks whose departments fell under the Cabinet men involved in the effort; they claimed they were having their money solicited "under duress."[55]

Such gifts successfully punctuated a kickoff event, Harding Memorial Week, December 9–16, 1923.[56] This week was declared in several states—not only Ohio—and the organizers relied on churches to spread the word on Harding Memorial Sunday, December 9, when all worshippers would be encouraged to "give in such manner to the Memorial as their pastor, priest, rabbi or other spiritual leader may designate." The association's honorary president eulogized his Oval Office predecessor on the radio on December 10, and all stations were forbidden from offering competing programming.[57] A few days later, singer and actress Dorothy Dare offered a new song, "From 'Cross the Borderland," to honor the dead president, broadcast live by the Hotel Commodore's orchestra and inspired by the cross-country trip.[58]

The memorial association was not the only group remembering Harding that fall after his death. His name was under consideration for a Nobel Peace Prize for his work with the Washington conference. Unfortunately, there was no peace prize awarded that year. Nevertheless, international recognition came with the visit of former British prime minister David Lloyd George, his wife, and daughter to pay their respects at Harding's grave on October 23, 1923. With other obligations, the Lloyd Georges hoped Florence could squeeze them in at 7:45 A.M., for a very "quiet" visit.[59]

Although Florence made efforts to accommodate the former prime minister, how much energy did she expend to visit with her grandchildren that fall in Ohio? She sent them their usual holiday money in a December letter, a mailing that suggests she did not see them too often.[60] Another card that month, however, refers to a recent dinner she had with them. She told her daughter-in-law in the rather patronizing tone she often adopted in these letters that "Roscoe is a splendid fellow, and you ought to count yourself a very fortunate woman. Of course, I think he might 'jolly' himself too on having such a nice little wife." If she did not see Esther often, Florence felt close enough to regularly press her advice. "Don't let Jean go about too much alone," this cautious grandmother warned—she, who ran off with a man at nineteen! "If possible, try to be with her." Of course, as this once-wild teenager knew, Jean would not be "crazy" about that.[61]

Florence was not in regular touch with Evalyn that fall either. The McLeans had sent her holiday cards in both Marion *and* Washington, not knowing where she was. Mrs. Harding appreciated her friend's invitation to visit her in Florida: "if everything goes right I may come South later." Meanwhile, Florence was busy with her affairs, her letters, and her financial concerns, and of course planning her move back to Washington, set now for early January. There would be no imminent southern trip, then, for Florence, "although I would feel more at home with you than with almost anyone I know." She looked forward to seeing the McLeans, to "resume our good old talks," but she signed the letter with a formal "yours"—not, as earlier, "lovingly."[62] There was increasingly less love in the McLean household as well; by the end of the decade, Evalyn and Ned would be divorced, their marriage undone by a combination of alcoholism (his), morphine addiction (hers), and the vagaries of a celebrity marriage.

After enjoying a relaxing but socially rich visit for a few weeks at Christmas in Columbus with the Jennings, Florence stopped quickly one last time in Marion to collect her correspondence and then left for Washington to start her new life. Things were looking up for her, even in comparison to life in the White House. A year before, she had been just emerging from her illness, Harding had the grippe, Harry had a stroke, and the Forbes scandal was breaking. Now she was in good health, she had no one else to worry about, and she was "pleasantly located here at the Willard," where "everybody has been wonderful to me."[63]

A NEW LIFE IN WASHINGTON

While Marion carried some bitter associations, including her own unhappy early adulthood and her husband's long affair with Carrie, Florence and Warren had been generally happy, and often even exhilarated, during their Washington years. Florence looked forward to connecting with old friends in the capital too.⁶⁴ She arrived back on January 3, 1924, on the arm of Mrs. Sawyer, who took her to her top floor suite at the Willard. Her return was announced in the paper, indicating that she was still considered a public personality.⁶⁵ She had once thought the hotel "good enough" for the Coolidges; now, it was apparently sufficient for her too! It was not, cheap, however, at $81.62 per week, plus board.

Despite her move, she kept her connections with Marion as director of the Harding Publishing Company, which published the *Marion Star*.⁶⁶ She was named a contributing editor and had plans to write a column, and she looked forward to keeping her connection with the paper "for the remainder of my life," although she actually never did write for it.⁶⁷ A Washington newspaper correspondent, Mrs. Mosby-Coleman, who had met Florence earlier at the White House and heard that she was interested in writing, contacted the former first lady to offer her services as a "free lance" by locating materials at the Library of Congress that were "interesting and worthy of your consideration," and might lend themselves to Florence's own columns. But there are no indications she took up Mrs. Mosby-Coleman on the idea.⁶⁸ Largely, Florence avoided any visible association with her prior profession. She did not attend the annual meeting of the Ohio associated dailies, or that of the Ohio Newspaper Women's Association, for instance. Although she acknowledged her former life, noting, "I am an Ohio newspaper woman, in view of my past work and experience and am always proud of the advancement of my fellow-women," she refrained from an active role.⁶⁹ She promised to join her female colleagues informally if she happened be in Marion when they next met. This was consistent with her overall approach in this period, and her exaggerated concern for the "dignity" of her former post: "I cannot at this time make any public appearances or take an active part in any public movements."⁷⁰

Florence's reticence on so many fronts amounted to a most meticulous mourning observance. Writing to Mary Lee, who had invited her to a June house concert of Florence's favorite singers, the Columbus Republican Glee Club, she declared, "all the proprieties and my own inclinations forbid my taking part in any general or formal affairs except those of a purely Memorial character associated with Mr. Harding and his memory during the present year." There was the issue of precedent, too, she told Mary; others would call on her to attend *their* functions if she attended this one. There was a more poignant reason to turn down the engagement, of course. With this group were too many "memories"—like their performance at the Front Porch after Harding's election—that "frankly I could not venture to stand the strain upon my emotions." For similar reasons, she would not attend the Republican convention that year either.[71]

Nevertheless, old friends found her. Florence had written Boone after her departure for Marion that fall, sorry for having to rush away, and expressing "my real and deep regret that these close associations of the past year had come to an end. . . . I can never forget how you helped me fight my hard battle back to health."[72] She had looked forward to seeing him upon her return to the capital, and he too was happy to see her. He came bearing medicines, at her request. Still, their meeting was not easy to arrange and ended after fifteen minutes. First, Baldinger, still her zealous guardian, had told Boone she was not available. Mandy Sawyer then got the doctor in, but remained for the entire visit, putting a damper on Florence and Boone's conversation! Despite that bit of fuss, he noted, "it was really a joy to see her, sit down, and chat with her." Boone noticed her "good spirits" especially, and came again to see her on February 4.[73]

One of the first people Florence wrote to about her new accommodations was her daughter-in-law. Once again thrilled to be back in the big city and in the midst of its important affairs, she told Esther, "I am very nicely situated here." Once she got a handle on her still-voluminous correspondence with a new secretary who was no "howling success," she was "going to be fairly well satisfied, or, at least, as near as I can [be] anywheres."[74] Sometimes Florence called in Laura Harlan for dinner, to give her ideas with handling her correspondence![75] Along with her letter writing, she had lots of friends visiting, who came to see her much as they had at the White House, although hardly in such numbers. Her rooms were filled with flowers, too, so she was still "going along in the same old way." She was gratified at her friends' attentions. Mandy Sawyer, for instance, came to see her three or four times a day. "Fact is I am never alone," she told Esther.[76]

Florence thus didn't feel she needed to leave her rooms much. Jennings, who continued to assist with her correspondence and to offer advice on her health, worried about this, and urged her to "get out and get some fresh air every day or two." With letters coming from "Heaven knows, where . . . and under what conditions they have been housed and written and transported," she especially needed some outdoor exposure, in case any infectious agents lingered.[77] Friends also brought their various germs—those, at least, who could get past Baldinger, her watchdog.[78] Florence managed to discourage even Grace Coolidge from visiting by attempting to set "a day and hour" for her. The first lady took umbrage at Florence's scheduling propensities. A month after Mrs. Harding's return to Washington, they had only talked on the phone.[79]

Florence stayed put despite offers like Edwin Denby's; remembering her love of the *Mayflower*, he offered her the chance to use the *Sylph*, the navy's yacht, but she never did.[80] Of course, her kidney still troubled her occasionally, but Jennings blamed a cold she had that winter on her indoor lifestyle instead: "I think you should not soften yourself by leading a cloistered life. Cannot you get your machine out and drive some every day? It might be well to trade your big car for a small enclosed one."[81] Jennings's words seem to have had an impact. She wrote Albert Fall that Easter that while she was still in her rooms most of the time, she at least now recognized that "it is not good for me to stay in so close and each day I think, well tomorrow I will go out for some air." She *was* beginning to think about getting her car in order. After all, she used to drive it often, solo. But she acknowledged that in nine years of living in the District of Columbia and knowing its sights, she had not walked much and still "never could find my way around."[82]

A flicker of her former energy sometimes appeared as she looked out the window on the winter scene and missed her days on skates.[83] She also fondly remembered her formerly active life visiting with prominent friends, like Nicholas Murray Butler, president of Columbia University.[84] She was not so insular that she did not notice Congress's work, and lament much of it: "an awful mess. If Warren could only have lived I feel sure some of this would have ceased long ago."[85]

Despite Congress's bunglings, she attended its memorial service for Harding, which was held on February 27. As she entered the Capitol Dome, the marine band played some of Mr. Harding's favorite hymns, including "Lead, Kindly Light," in the lobby. Grace Coolidge had invited Florence to attend the memorial service with "your immediate party of friends," and she got seventeen seats in the gallery.[86] Florence wore a mourning dress with a short veil. With her were old friends and family, but Boone and Captain Andrews had to finagle tickets to the event, much to their dismay. Boone was "incensed at [Mrs. Harding's] improper evidence of gratitude."[87]

Also in attendance at the gathering were Chief Justice Taft and the Supreme Court, and the diplomatic corps, including Florence's favorite, Jules Jusserand. She heard prayers led by old friends like Speaker Gillette, and was no doubt gratified to witness the elocutionary talents of Secretary of State Hughes eulogizing Harding for his work at the Washington conference and other achievements, especially on the economic front. Hughes declared that Harding was a harmonizer who "hated strife[;] his gospel was that of understanding." But alas, he was "broken by strain of duty."[88] Florence was grateful for the speech and thanked Hughes personally.[89]

The investigations of his administration were meanwhile intensifying. With the resignations of Denby—who now could no longer offer her the *Sylph*—and Daugherty, the next month, a Harding eulogy could not have been held with such passion later in the year. Jennings tried to reassure her about the Senate hearings. He was persuaded, for example, that justice had been served by the removal of Daugherty in March 1924.[90] Jennings, who had earlier disliked Harry's leading role in the presidential campaign, all the same felt bad for his fellow Ohioan, who had no evidence of "crookedness" in his record, but could not convincingly deny "his affiliations with people of unsavory transactions and repute—men Warren had to banish from Washington." Feeling bad for him herself, Florence had sent a supportive telegram to Daugherty, vetted carefully beforehand with Harding's brother to be "very good and perfectly safe," implying no criticism of Coolidge.[91] Florence sighed, "Poor Harry my heart aches for him and he is broken in body and spirit. . . . Mack, if he ever needed friends he needs them now. Right or wrong, I could not refrain from sending those few words." She added, "I do not allow myself to worry but I am going to sit tight until the storm blows over." She was a little peeved at the former attorney general all the same: "Guess Harry did not care much for my message—he was in Washington two days, did not call me up, nor have I had a word from him."[92]

The stress had made her kidneys act up: "I don't mind telling you I was quite discouraged for a few days."[93] However, she was much looking forward to a late April visit from Ethel Jennings, and Mack also wrote back with some advice for her in this disheartening time when her old friends were being attacked: "cultivate philosophy, be patient and long suffering, knowing that every president of the US has run the gamut of calumny and been vindicated by time, with the exception of those few who were too weak to leave an impress upon the minds of men or upon the pages of history."[94]

Still, Florence might have suffered less and spoken out more. "Her ultimate decision was to bear these insinuations in silence," in accord with preserving "the dignity which should attach to one who had been known as the first lady of the land." This strategy meant that nothing was said by her "to counteract the efforts made to reflect on her husband's memory." In the end, she avoided being "the center of a public controversy," but her temporary peace left a space for attackers to fill, which they did quite effectively, coloring the debate with calumnies ever since.[95]

She remained largely housebound after the service, and a month later, on March 25, she wrote Esther that she had left her room perhaps seven times since her arrival in January; one of those times was to attend the funeral of Woodrow Wilson.[96] She did not see much of Evalyn, who had just sold her house in town and was planning to live part of the time in Cincinnati. Florence certainly would miss her, but the intensity of their old friendship waned in Florence's new life. Still, she had not been forgotten by her former friends in high places. Harry New contacted her about a man whom she had tried to help in returning to his job in the postal service.[97] And Jenny Davidson Hibben, wife of Princeton president John G. Hibben, wrote her asking for her contribution toward a boat to be used by missionaries to the Indians in Juneau, Alaska. Mrs. Hibben promised to name the boat after President Harding and suggested two dates when she could meet Florence in Washington in April, but it is not clear that Florence ever took her up on this venture.[98]

Florence certainly could afford to give. As Harding's widow, she got monthly dividends from the Harding Publishing Company for a total of over $10,000 per year, as well as additional cash allowances from her own stock holdings of between $3,000 and $6,000 most months, and about $1,100 monthly from her *Star* contract, apparently for her position on its board of directors. There was also the rent she got from the Mt. Vernon Avenue house.[99] She kept up her small donations to animal shelters and humane societies, but not much else.[100]

Her finances eased even further when, on January 26, Coolidge gave Florence mail franking privileges. Of course, it was too late to deal with much of her initial postadministration mail, connected of course nearly entirely with her role as first lady. The government had no policy on former first ladies' support at that time. Congress was considering awarding her a $5,000 pension, although neither of her two predecessors had gotten one. But their husbands had still been living, and in the sexist norms of the time, that would have been considered reason to deny such support. In other words, these wives got no recognition for their work as first ladies, but only support if they were bereaved dependents.[101] On the basis of this logic, Mrs. Harding was entitled to something, although her wealth would have likely been hard to ignore. Congressman Hatton Sumners, a Texas Democrat, was a particularly vocal opponent of a pension for her, yet such an allotment had been made, if quite inequitably and inconsistently, in the past.[102] The *New York Times* called for some uniformity in the policy, arguing how much better it would be to pension not only first ladies, but other former officials who received nothing now, making the compelling point that with such a practice, "none might be tempted to do things which we hold wrong or at least undignified in [an] ex-official."[103]

Had Florence wished to save money given these circumstances, she could have always moved back to Marion; indeed, she told Esther in March that she was still thinking of returning there, when she hoped to see more of the grandchildren, but did not clarify when.[104] She certainly had not seen much of Jean and George when she *was* in Marion, so one wonders what might have changed this practice.

One person who believed it was most salutary for Florence to stay in the capital was Boone, who appreciated the strength she could draw on from so many old friends and the life of the capital, even if she only partook of it from the Willard's confines. She might well have lived longer if she had not gone back to live at the sanitarium in Marion, as she did in July. She seems to have sensed this as well, and she resisted returning even when her illness struck her hard again that summer. Boone was one of those who visited her regularly, including lunch on March 24 at the Willard, where they had "a very nice time together"; she was "most affable and in high spirits." Six weeks later, he recorded another leisurely lunch with Florence, a "delightful" one with his wife and Mrs. Jennings along too. He once again saw how happy she was there, seeing "so many of her friends."[105]

Florence was indeed delighting in her life, despite the ongoing investigations into the expired administration. During Mrs. Jennings's visit, they had taken a "nice ride" with Mandy Sawyer, had Laura Harlan over for a meal, and went to the Christians for dinner. They had also been in touch with the Wallaces. She joshed in a letter to Mack, still helping her with her letters, "If you will work for me, it will give me more time to play." Still, she was too "shy" to entertain the thought of dinner out with the Girl Scouts, or even with Lou Hoover. But she must have been heartened as the honors poured in; the president of Gambier College wanted her to accept an honorary degree on behalf of her late husband, and a Connecticut principal wanted her to lay the cornerstone on a new vocational school that would be named for Harding. Florence also had to deal with old associates who asked for her help, and she complained to Mack that "some of my friends . . . are lying awake nights trying to think up something for me to do." One man, for instance, had just called and "wanted me to intercede" on something. When she put him off, "he got cross and hung [up] the phone on me. Gentlemanly wasn't it."[106]

Her friends in the Harding Memorial Association were also keeping her up. On more than one occasion, conflicts among the men, including Daugherty, old Dr. Harding, George Jr., and the Sawyer father-and-son duo over the planning grew so intense that she decided she would "have to fix things up by my 'little lonesome.'"[107] There were knotty issues, including debates over the land to be acquired, its location and its cost. But at the same time, there was also the pleasant prospect of planning the creation of Harding's portrait for the White House. "I see no need for haste," she said.[108] All the same, Margaret Lindsay Williams, who had already painted Harding for the English-Speaking Union in London, was keen to have Florence's blessing to execute a portrait to hang in the executive mansion.[109]

TO MARION FOR GOOD OR ILL

Florence was thriving in Washington and did not want to leave. It was thus with great sadness and bitterness that she discovered that her body was failing her again in July. Kathleen Lawler, who was with her often that summer, remembered that for some weeks, "her old spirit was still dominant . . . stoutly contending that she could and would soon regain her health." Even so, "on many days, only her will power enabled her to leave her bed." But this strength was not to be underestimated. Florence was, after all, a close student of Coué, and believed she was "equal to the exertion." But by July 19, Lawler and Florence decided they had to contact Dr. Sawyer. He was back in Marion, though still in his national post until the following month. He and Coolidge had by then fallen out, and the Harding Memorial work would provide him a polite reason to depart permanently.

He rushed to the Willard the very next morning to assist Florence, and without hesitation, he announced that "she must go back to Marion, at once, accompanied by a nurse." Florence hated the idea of returning, and moreover adamantly refused a nurse, for what it would suggest. As she declared, "I have not the slightest notion of dying yet, Dr. Sawyer." Sawyer insisted she could not possibly go back on the train without one, so she settled on taking Mandy Sawyer. But Florence was not happy. Not only did she love living in Washington, as Lawler noted, but going back seemed like a defeat. She was content to have caught up on all her old correspondence, and going back threatened chaos in her affairs once again. Moreover, she had a purpose in Washington. She was at last beginning to write Harding's biography, with Lawler's help, "dwelling upon the happiness they had all their lives shared" but also on the shocks of the last year. She told Lawler with wishful stridency, "I cannot be reconciled to going back to Marion. I do not want to go. It is wholly unnecessary. I will be alright. I much prefer to remain here. We are accomplishing so much and we'll have a nice time together. I want to stay here now that we have my work so well in hand."[110]

But her fragile health made this hope a vain one, and on July 21, the day after Sawyer came back, Florence and Mandy dutifully left for Marion. Kathleen lunched with them at Florence's suite and put them in their car to leave for the train. "Though she was suffering intensely," Kathleen reported, she had nevertheless "grown daily more spirituelle" (that is, sprightly) and "looked wonderfully well . . . handsomely outfitted, keen, alert, sparkling and responsive as ever." Kathleen was, as ever, optimistic; Florence's first letter back confirmed that she was "only fair." No doubt returning to Ohio just a year after the Alaska trip and the San Francisco tragedy, and under such circumstances, could have only made everything all the more bitter.[111] Florence would write her husband a heartfelt poem in honor of this anniversary.[112]

Boone got a grateful letter from her after she had returned to Marion, thanking him for remembering the anniversary of her husband's death. She wrote, "The past week, particularly, had been oh! So trying. Each day I have lived over those San Francisco days. The old adage that time softens grief is not true, so far as I am concerned, but I have had to meet it . . . some how, some way." She had been sorry not to see him before she left, but "I was ordered home peremptorily, by Dr. Sawyer, and my last visit in Washington suddenly terminated." Still, she felt she was now "coming out of it and on the whole, am fairly well." She sent her sympathy on the death of young Calvin Coolidge Jr., who had died a month before, at age sixteen, from a foot infection exacerbated by a tennis game.[113]

Despite her strong words, her condition was precarious. When she came home, too, she had much less to occupy herself than she had had in the capital; there were few friends to visit her, and no Lawler there to keep up her focus on writing—had she been strong enough to do it. Her sense of purpose, her interest in life, withered. Her main preoccupation became visiting her husband's tomb, which she did daily.[114] If Sawyer had let her stay in the capital, and better yet, found her good care there, perhaps with Boone, could she have avoided the return to Marion and its necessary dampening of her spirits? What is certain is that Sawyer had effectively made himself indispensable to her. He had been driven out of Washington; now so would she be. Florence was convinced, at any rate, that she could not survive without him. But then, he ultimately let her down in the most final way: dying on her within three months!

The shift in her engagement in life was clear in her first month back in Marion. When Charles Moore, who, along with his work as acting head of the Library of Congress's manuscript division, was also chair of Washington's Fine Arts commission, asked her for money for the Wakefield National Memorial Association, dedicated to the "purchase and preservation of the birthplace of George Washington," she was happy to endorse it in July. She wrote him, "Every project of this nature, every shrine established to perpetuate the memory, and to keep alive the deeds of America's great men ... adds materially to the richness of our country's history." She donated a sum sufficient to purchase "five feet of the venerated ground" to the association. She likely linked Washington's memorial with her husband's own, and was in this case unusually willing to see her name used "for publicity." But a month later, back in Ohio, she changed her tune and made several attempts to tell Moore so by phone. She finally wrote him, "I made a rule that for this year I would not make any contributions of any kind," with exceptions for local Ohio disasters. She had apparently made an exception for Wakefield, too, and now regretted it. He could still use her name as an endorser of the project, but she asked him to "kindly refrain from mentioning my check."[115]

FINAL ILLNESS AND DEATH

Did the atmosphere of White Oaks Sanitarium take away her incentive to engage in life—indeed, to live? Sawyer's own death on September 23, most likely from a heart attack, certainly didn't help. Even having Evalyn relatively close in Cincinnati made little difference; they seem to have gotten together only rarely. Mrs. Harding would last be seen in public on October 16, attending a concert of the U.S. marine band at the tomb, a "funeral dirge" arranged by the local Kiwanis.[116]

That fall had been a difficult one for her, even before her illness turned for the worse.[117] First, she lost General Sawyer. Then Laura Work died in a car crash. And a third death, that of May Wallace, wife of the secretary of the Department of Agriculture, seems to have hit her especially hard. She went to her bed in Rose Cottage upon hearing of it on October 25 and never got up again. Once she landed in bed, she was supported by her old friends, including

George B. Christian, who came back from his new position at the U.S. Shipping Board to assist her with correspondence and other tasks. Her family, too, was now with her "almost constantly." Her niece, Hazel Longshore, canceled a trip to the West Coast with her husband owing to Florence's condition, and joined brother Cliff, Esther, Abigail Harding, and old Dr. George at Florence's bedside. The American people did not hear the full story until October 30, however, when Carl Sawyer announced that Mrs. Harding was not seeing anyone. He was pressed to make this public after Rabbi Joseph S. Kornfeld of Toledo, just returned from his post as U.S. minister to Persia, was prevented from calling on her when he came to town.[118]

Florence meanwhile put the last touches on her new will—an act of finality that could not be missed. Unlike her earlier episode of nephritis in 1922, she was no longer in the White House with her husband in attendance and the prayers of all Americans focused in her direction. Their concern, Warren's "ceaseless devotion," as well as her indomitable will, had all helped keep her alive. Now, just two years later at the White Oaks Sanitarium, she had lost these powerful weapons. She did not have the same will to fight the disease, she did not want outside experts, and she did not even seek publicity to facilitate praying on her behalf. She asked the staff at White Oaks to give out only "the most meager information as to her condition." According to the *Star,* she recalled now the widespread coverage of her earlier attack in the White House as a "siege she did not wish repeated." Yet she had been most appreciative of prayerful intercession in the fall of 1922, as she stated on numerous occasions, affirming that it helped to save her life. More likely, her reticence in Marion owed to her increasingly fragile state of mind rather than resentment of any unwanted "siege" earlier. People sent piles of telegrams and get-well cards all the same.[119]

Although Sawyer's son, Carl, who was attending her, was familiar with her condition, Florence believed in the older doctor's powers in a way she could not anyone else's. To Florence, Sawyer "was not only my faithful physician, but my devoted friend." Of course, he had saved her more than once, most recently in 1922. (Others were less persuaded of his skills. Secretary Work, himself a doctor, told Boone that "Sawyer did not know medicine and was out of touch even with his own school of medicine."[120]) Still, Florence had not yet given up by early November; she still spoke wistfully about returning to Washington before winter, provided her "very slow recovery" and "complications" allowed it. She was then relatively stable. Carl Sawyer said she was "resting easily" and in "no immediate danger." He insisted, despite contrary indications, that she was showing "the fortitude she exhibited during her serious illness in the White House." The *New York Times,* on the other hand, suggested that "the patient's intimate friends fear that she has broken because of sorrow over the death of her husband." Although Florence had not "broken," her spirit had nevertheless been weakened, and she would not resist as she once had.[121]

The election seemed to revive her, especially with the Republicans safely retained in the White House. The country continued to pray for her, regardless of her wishes, and her condition received regular coverage in the national press. However, the grounds for hope proved illusory. She was soon getting worse again, complicated by pain in her upper abdomen, a "menacing mass" that suggested liver cancer, and a worried Carl Sawyer called in a Cleveland specialist, Dr. Woods, on November 8. They discovered that her right ureter was blocked and decided to operate immediately, puncturing it in an "exploratory" procedure under local anesthesia. Any more "radical surgery" was said to be impossible as a result of her weakened condition.[122]

This procedure helped stabilize her over the next few days.[123] Yet though flashes of improvement appeared on the 10th, 11th, and 12th—a little food, some comfortable sleep—she had nevertheless lost her "fighting spirit," Sawyer conceded, and she was "critically ill."[124] Florence was still lucid enough to express her gratitude for a kind note from Mrs. Hoover on November 10. Christian passed on her appreciation to the future first lady, adding in a slight variation on a familiar theme, "While Mrs. Harding's condition is not critical at this writing she is seriously ill and I can offer but little hope."[125]

On the 13th, she had a difficult night, "very restless and painful." The McLeans sent her a telegram the next day, which she had just enough energy left to appreciate.[126] But that night, she entered a "crisis," which became strikingly apparent at 1:45 A.M. on the 15th. She was sleeping badly, she was suffering "air hunger spells" where she breathed with the most punishing struggle, necessitating the opening of all windows and doors to give her air, and she had intermittent minor "heart attacks" as well. Things were now very serious indeed. "Mrs. Harding had a very miserable day and is miserable tonight. She failed considerably during the last 24 hours," came the bulletin from Rose Cottage.[127]

With such dire reports, it is not surprising that "false rumors" kept bubbling up. One was even occasioned by the Emanuel Lutheran church bells, tolling another man's funeral, which led to the *Star* phone lines being tied up in anticipation of the news![128] Yet Florence defied these fears, rallying ever so slightly in the late morning of the 16th, sleeping and eating a little, before growing worse again.[129] That day, she continued to drift in and out of sleep, "weak and exhausted." Ever since late October, Florence had been posed horizontal as if ready for sleep, which Boone thought was a mistake: "she lay in her bed; kept herself relaxed; made no fight to overcome her illness," he concluded. Boone thought her "joy and incentive and desire to live," which had gotten her through her last bout, were gone, and he was right. She was dying.[130] By the 19th, she was only partly conscious, or, as the *Star* described her in the less diplomatic language of that time, "more stupid and dull," and a coma seemed imminent.[131]

November 20 was the beginning of the end. One of her last signs of consciousness was evident just after she heard the good wishes of the Coolidges, who despite the dire news coming from White Oaks boldly declared that they "anxiously await[ed] word of your continued improvement." After hearing their telegram around 3 A.M., she "whispered" her appreciation. By 4:00 that day, she began to fall fast. Her respiration was increasingly labored; her pulse was nearly nonexistent.[132] Her friends and family gathered round her bedside, including Cliff, Esther, Abigail, her niece, Hazel, Mrs. Sawyer, the Carl Sawyers, and Christian.[133] She died on November 21 at 8:55 A.M. Carl Sawyer reported that "chronic nephritis and myocarditis with evidence of hydronephrosis" had killed her. Her obituary appeared on page 3 of the *New York Times*. But it was on the front page of the *Marion Star*, and many old friends came to pay their respects at White Oaks.[134] She would be buried next to her husband the following Monday, November 24. The day after, yet another Harding Cabinet member's wife, the longtime invalid Mrs. Daugherty, also died.

Boone thought it "amusing" that Florence was buried with her glasses on. He was less amused by her will. He read her inheritance documents tersely: "She seemingly unmindful of my services when she made her will, but remembered many others." Yet he noted (inconsistently), "Had not thought of being remembered in will." He also insisted with similar illogic that "I do not believe" Dr. Sawyer (the elder) "could have changed her feeling toward me," although he noted that Sawyer had become "cool and seemed embittered toward me and probably was critical toward me to Mrs. Harding over whom he had great influence."[135] Sawyer, he guessed darkly, had undergone a "cerebral sclerotic change" in his old age. Indeed, the older doctor may have come to resent Boone, especially during Sawyer's brief but unsuccessful tenure into the next administration, when Boone enjoyed an especial intimacy with the Coolidges. His son, Carl, may also have alienated Florence from the navy doctor. The younger Sawyer had made some distasteful remarks to Boone about his "attention to Mrs. Harding," betraying "a suspicious disposition."[136] But Boone decided to let things go. He, after all, had a most enjoyable life at that moment as a White House intimate, a spot where the Hardings had been instrumental in placing him. He could not forget Warren and Florence's "innumerable kindnesses" to his family and himself. Whatever the Sawyers' baneful influence, he felt close to her: "We stood together through trials, sorrows, and anxieties. I felt she was one of the most courageous women that I had known."[137]

Reflecting the importance of her role, the White House flew its flag at half mast and refrained from publishing its winter social calendar for a week. Her obituary in the *New York Times* noted, "Mrs. Florence Kling Harding was extremely popular in Washington . . . those who knew her testified to her charm . . . sympathy and understanding."[138] Such sentiments reflected the real popularity that Florence garnered in the White House, a sentiment that unfortunately did not long outlive her. As Secretary Charles Evans Hughes put it eloquently: "I am inexpressibly saddened by the death of Mrs. Harding. We can never forget the dignity and charm with which she presided as the mistress of the White House or her fortitude when she was suddenly bereft of all that life held dear. She was a woman of extraordinary strength of character and her husband's most faithful counselor." But Hughes, too, made the debatable assertion that Florence had little to live for when Harding died: "When he was taken, she felt that her mission was ended."[139] Some, in fact, thought her illness was actually tied to the increasing scandals affecting the legacy of the Harding administration. One obituary speculated that "To her in solitude must have been borne poignant tidings of the unhappy aftermath of Pres. Harding's career. The[se] attacks . . . must have been doubly hard to bear."[140] There was some truth to this, yet Florence did not let the hearings stop her from enjoying her life in Washington. Moreover, as I have suggested indirectly in this book through an examination of the first lady, her husband's presidency deserved better treatment in these obituaries, and still does today.

Likely more important in amplifying the debilitating nature of her illness was the depressing environment of being confined in Marion at Sawyer's sanitarium, combined with the disappearance of the two most important men in her life: first Harding, then Sawyer. As Jennings noticed: "it was strange about Mrs. Harding. . . . She bore her bereavement wonderfully at first and was her brave, practical, competent self. But month by month I could see that she was feeling her loss more and more and that it was robbing her of her power of resistance and . . . spirit." Sawyer's death was the final blow.[141]

Twelve thousand Americans came to Marion once again at her death, to walk by her bier under a "leaden sky" and even a few snowflakes. Their pleas for an open casket had been heard.[142] Her body lay at the home of Frank and Hazel Longshore on East Church Street, where visitors could see it from 4 to 10 P.M. on Saturday, November 22, and from 8 A.M. to 9 P.M. on Sunday, November 23. Reverend Dr. Jesse Swank led her funeral, at Epworth Methodist Episcopal Church, on Monday afternoon, evoking her strong faith. He offered a short sermon, and the Reverend George W. Landes, clergyman at her late husband's Trinity Baptist church, read Scripture. She was widely remembered in Washington and in Ohio, where the state's newspaper organization hailed her as "among the most popular and successful newspaper workers in the state."[143] Thousands lined the streets, too, as her casket, covered in flowers, passed to the cemetery for the service of "committal." All businesses, of course, were closed. President Coolidge did not attend but sent his naval aide, Captain Adolphus Andrews, who had also served in the Harding White

House.[144] She was buried in the small vault where her husband still lay; a large military presence, including 100 enlisted men and an honor guard, stood by. Pallbearers included Jennings, Carl Sawyer, O. S. Rapp, and George H. Van Fleet, and honorary pallbearers were Secretary Week, Postmaster New, former secretary Denby, Reddy Baldinger, and George Christian.[145] After the benediction, her dear boys from the Columbus Republican Glee Club sang "The End of a Perfect Day," followed by taps. The vault then closed, but only temporarily. The couple would be moved three years later, to be reinterred within a huge classical monument, the massive Greek ionic columned Harding Memorial in Marion.[146]

When Florence's will went to probate on December 3, few were surprised at her excellent money management. The estate was worth $367,179.35, over $3.5 million in today's money.[147] It included stocks and bonds,[148] jewelry,[149] furs,[150] and personal property, including a $36,000 bank account and a $2,000 Locomobile car. Most important was her real estate, including the home on Mt. Vernon Street, which she left to the Harding Memorial Association with all its contents. Other holdings, which would go to her grandchildren, included the *Star* building and another Marion property, as well as a lot in Cocoa Beach, Florida.

She gave to friends and family generous amounts, totaling nearly $60,000. Thus, Mrs. Jennings and Mrs. William Milroy Boyd got $5,000 ($50,000 today), and Carl Sawyer got $10,000. Mrs. Christian got $2,000, as did Barker, and Laura Harlan—who also got some Wrigley shares. Baldinger, Catherine Wynne, Kathleen Lawler, and Ruth Powderly (especially for her "services and kindness") got $1,000 each.

Her nieces, Hazel Longshore and Louise Kling, were particularly well endowed with $12,000 each (including securities). Her brothers, Clifford and Vitalis, each got $10,000—although Tal's was in trust, because Florence, like her father earlier, did not think that her brother could handle such a large infusion at once. He was a drinker, after all.[151] Esther Mezger got $5,000. Three churches, Epworth Methodist Episcopal, Trinity Baptist, and St. Paul's Episcopal, got $2,000 each. But the largest amount, fittingly, was to her grandchildren. Although she often slighted them in life, she was most generous in death. They got the *Star* building and its proceeds and another building at 126–128 Main Street in Marion, to be held for them by a trustee. They would get the rents from these properties directly when they were twenty-one and would inherit them when they turned twenty-eight. Jean was sixteen and George thirteen at the time; they would be rich.[152] The children also got over $100,000 in stocks and bonds to share. After spending their lives eating bread and butter and wearing clothes sewn from scraps of their famous grandmother's cast-off gowns, their lives would change.

If she was parsimonious in life, in death, Florence stretched the will beyond its capacity to pay expenses for cars, repairs, legal fees, taxes, and fur storage. Some $50,000 of her stocks had to be liquidated to cover these items. Hazel Longshore, despite her large allotment, thought she should distribute the jewelry, furs, and clothing, but the executor, Charles Schaffner, and the court disagreed. Instead, the grandchildren got the heirlooms. All told, these items amounted to $18,740, including a $5,000 necklace.

CONCLUSION

Florence had accumulated a large collection of desirable and expensive trinkets, befitting her era's popular culture of consumerism, especially for women. Among her possessions were her emerald and diamond rings, her diamond and pearl elephant, her gold cigarette case, and her Egyptian scarab scarf pin, a sign of good luck. Mrs. Harding had not been so lucky herself, of course. She had been ill much of her adult life, she had lived with her husband's unfaithfulness for years, she had lost him in middle age, and she had forfeited her position as first lady too early. She had, moreover, been disappointed in love as a young woman and lost a son much too young. She had also missed the chance to really enjoy her grandchildren, owing to social conventions she worried excessively about. There was unquestionably much tragedy in her life. Her favorite song, "The End of a Perfect Day," has been described poignantly by one of her contemporaries as "the consoling reality that lighted a life freighted with labor and grief."[153] Nevertheless, Florence did not see the cup as half empty. She was strong and determined, believing, like her mentor, Coué, in her own power despite adversity, and she had used that power to help propel herself back to life and health many times.

She had also used it to push her husband into the highest office in the land, and she had embraced the attributes of her era's celebrity culture to do so, making them both personalities. Accordingly, she had had an unusually high profile in President Harding's political life, as well as his personal one, and as a result, she contributed to a significant transition in the office of first lady in the early twentieth century. Her term in the White House reveals how that office has presented a special challenge to the women occupying it in the modern era, a time when women began to find access to a larger arena for their energies. She promoted a political agenda within a tradition-bound post, pressing for numerous reforms, and did so by skillfully engaging her era's popular media, adapting it to her own purposes and to popularize her office.

Thus, despite the brevity of her span in the White House, less than two and a half years, Florence Kling Harding pioneered a more activist, visible role for the first lady. She fully took on the role of celebrity, borrowing from the techniques of movies and mass marketing. She did this both at her glamorous parties for diplomats and by opening the White House grounds to multitudes, holding countless handshaking marathons and photo ops—an openness to public exposure that was unprecedented for a first lady, and that showed the Hardings' eagerness to connect with the American people. Florence wanted Americans to know what she did; there was no secrecy about her role as first lady. She welcomed the coverage, as women journalists noted with appreciation; she invited them ahead of time to see her table sets and her gowns, even though she hesitated at granting interviews. She kept a crowded wardrobe because the public wanted and expected it—not only because of the celebrity culture that she embraced, but also because of the increasing importance of women in the newly emerging consuming passions of her age. She was pathbreaking as well in her efforts to influence policy, including her work on behalf of veterans, the establishment of a women's prison, and the rights of animals. Certainly other first ladies, like Ellen Wilson, had a progressive agenda and policy goals, but Florence had the opportunity to be far more visible and outspoken about hers. In her inclusion of the public in her own affairs, including her many causes as well as her illness, she was markedly more open and accessible than others in her post, and she paved the way for an enhancement in the prominence and influence of the first lady of the land.

NOTES

INTRODUCTION

1. Doris Kearns Goodwin, *No Ordinary Time: Franklin and Eleanor Roosevelt: The Home Front in World War II* (New York: Simon and Schuster, 1994), 10.

2. See Ira Bennett (*Washington Post* reporter) to FKH, August 24, 1920, FKH Papers, reel 242, frame 51-53. I am grateful to Lewis Gould for this citation. In this book, I use the first lady's first name for simplicity and to avoid confusion with her husband.

3. *Philadelphia Public Ledger*, March 7, 1922.

4. *Philadelphia Public Ledger*, September 9, 1922.

5. "Nominee's Wife Knows the Game," *Chattanooga Times*, October 1920, n.d., reel 244, box 858.

6. Harding has been quoted as saying, "Mrs. Harding wants to be the drum major in every band that passes." See Carol Chandler Waldrup, *Presidents' Wives: The Lives of 44 American Women of Strength* (Jefferson, N.C.: McFarland, 1989), 259, as cited in Ann E. Burnette, "Florence Kling Harding: Bridging Traditional and Modern Rhetorical Roles," in *Inventing a Voice: The Rhetoric of American First Ladies of the Twentieth Century*, ed. Molly Meijer Wertheimer (Lanham, Md.: Rowman & Littlefield, 2004), 135.

7. The poll is the Siena Research Institute First Lady Poll of 2003, http://www.siena.edu/uploadedFiles/Home/Parents_and_Community/Community_Page/SRI/First_Ladies_2003.pdf. On Warren G. Harding's perennially low position in historians' polls, see Robert H. Ferrell, *The Strange Deaths of President Harding* (Columbus: University of Missouri Press, 1996), vii. The earlier poll is the Siena Research Institute First Lady Poll of 1993, cited in Lewis L. Gould, ed., *American First Ladies: Their Lives and Their Legacy* (New York: Garland, 1996), 652-653.

8. Kenneth W. Duckett, "The Harding Papers: How Some Were Burned," *American Heritage* 16 (February 1965): 29-30.

9. Randolph Downes, quoted in *Marion Star*, August 6, 1963.

10. For examples of the harshly critical perspective of the Hardings that reigned by the mid-1930s and that has continued to shape books for the past

eight decades, see Samuel Hopkins Adams, *Revelry* (New York: Boni and Liveright, 1926), William Allen White, *Masks in a Pageant* (New York: Macmillan, 1928); Charles Willis Thompson, *Presidents I've Known and Two Near Presidents* (Freeport, N.Y.: Books for Libraries Press, 1929), chap. 25; and Alice Roosevelt Longworth, *Crowded Hours* (New York: Scribner's, 1933).

11. Gaston B. Means, *The Strange Death of President Harding: From the Diaries of Gaston B. Means, a Department of Justice Investigator* (New York: Guild, 1930), 236, 162.

12. Mark Sullivan, *Our Times: The United States, 1920–1925*, vol. 6, *The Twenties* (New York: Charles Scribner's Sons, 1935), 98; Longworth, *Crowded Hours*, 323. Showing the long-term influences of such portraits, a similar portrait is in Betty Boyd Caroli, *First Ladies*, expanded edition (New York: Oxford University Press, 1995), 155.

13. See, for instance, Carl Sferazza Anthony, *Florence Harding: The First Lady, the Jazz Age, and the Death of America's Most Scandalous President* (New York: Morrow, 1998), 460–462.

14. Francis Russell, "The Shadow of Warren Harding," *Antioch Review* 36 (Winter 1978): 60.

15. See Francis Russell, *The Shadow of Blooming Grove: Warren G. Harding and His Times* (New York: McGraw-Hill, 1968), 5, 91; similar portraits are in Robert K. Murray, *The Harding Era: Warren G. Harding and His Administration* (Minneapolis: University of Minnesota, 1969), 421; and Robert Sobel, *Coolidge: An American Enigma* (Washington: Regnery, 1998), 168.

16. Russell to Charlton Myers, March 20, 1965, Harding file, Marion County Historical Society. I am indebted to Trella Romine for assisting me with these files.

17. "Mrs. Harding on Front Porch Plays an Important Role," *Washington Post*, October 10, 1920, Florence K. Harding Papers, reel 244, box 858, Ohio Historical Society, Columbus, Ohio.

18. "Nebraska and Iowa Citizens Are in Love with Mrs. Harding," no paper indicated, reel 244, box 858, frame 162.

19. Simon Louvish, *Cecil B. DeMille: A Life in Art* (New York: St. Martin's Press, 2007), 154–155, 160.

20. "Mrs. Harding Shops En Suite," *New York Evening Sun*, February 1, 1920.

21. "Nebraska and Iowa Citizens Are in Love with Mrs. Harding," reel 244, box 858, frame 162; "Mrs. Harding Wins Nation as White House Hostess during Year Just Ended," *Washington Post*, March 5, 1922, reel 245, box 866.

22. "Mrs. Harding Wins Nation as White House Hostess during Year Just Ended."

{ *Notes to Pages 5–12* }

23. John A. Morello, *Selling the President, 1920: Albert D. Lasker, Advertising, and the Election of Warren G. Harding* (Westport, Conn.: Praeger, 2001), 7.

24. I am indebted to Catherine Forslund for her observations of Edith Roosevelt.

25. Her sentiments on the women's vote are in Florence Harding to Harriet Taylor Upton, October 31, 1920, Florence Kling Harding Papers, correspondence 1916–1923, roll 242, box 851.

26. "Too Late to Plead for Her Son's Life," *Washington Post*, March 7, 1922.

27. *Anaconda Standard*, June 30, 1923, cited in Anthony, *Florence Harding*, 424.

28. *Marion Newslife*, May 5, 1980, 26.

29. Duckett, "Harding Papers," 29–30.

30. *New York Times*, November 22, 1924.

31. Burnette, "Florence Kling Harding," 142; also see FKH Papers, reel 244, box 858, frame 186.

32. "Mrs. Harding Wins Nation as White House Hostess during Year Just Ended."

33. Margaret Mead quoted in *New York Times*, December 12, 1974, cited in Caroli, *First Ladies*, xvii.

34. See *Nightline* transcript, March 26, 1992, at http://www.pbs.org/wgbh/pages/frontline/shows/clinton/etc/03261992.html.

CHAPTER 1: EARLY LIFE

1. "Mrs. Harding Pictured by One of Her Life Long Friends," February 21, 1921, no source given, FKH Papers, reel 244, box 858.

2. *History of Marion County* (Chicago: Leggett, Conaway, 1883), 600.

3. "Mrs. Harding Pictured by One of Her Life Long Friends."

4. *Kansas City Journal Post*, June 22, 1923.

5. Willis Fletcher Johnson, *The Life of Warren G. Harding: From the Simple Life of the Farm to the Glamour and Power of the White House* (Chicago: John C. Winston, 1923), 123.

6. George Christian Sr., "Biography of Warren G. Harding," George B. Christian Sr. Papers, Outgoing Correspondence, 1918–1923, in Harding Papers, Ohio Historical Society, reel 249, box 892; Ron Cass, "The Duchess of East Center Street," *Marion Newslife*, May 5, 1980.

7. Christian, "Biography of Harding," 34.

8. "When Mrs. Harding Leaves White House She Will Go into a World of Emptiness," *Washington Star*, August 8, 1923.

9. Christian, "Biography of Harding," 36.

10. Susan Burns, "First Ladies: Florence Kling Harding, 1860–1924," proof, July 11, 1975.

11. Divorce document, May 5, 1886, Florence M. DeWolfe against Henry A. DeWolfe, petition filed; granted June 12, 1886; "Cause: gross neglect of duty. Custody of child given to Plaintiff and Defendant given leave to visit child at reasonable vis. 1st Tuesday in each month. Plaintiff restored to maiden name of Florence M. Kling. Deft. Ordered to pay costs and expenses awarded $10 paid." Marion County Courthouse, Marion, Ohio.

12. Mrs. DeWolfe, letter in Ohio Historical Society.

13. FKH diary, undated, First Ladies Library, Canton, Ohio. The diary was found by historian Craig Schermer in 1997. Kathleen Lawler, "The Hardings I Knew," unpublished manuscript, in Ohio Historical Society, Columbus, Ohio, 20:20. FKH asked Lawler to write the story of the campaign in January 1921; Lawler finished it in March 1931.

14. FKH diary, undated; Lawler, "Hardings I Knew," 20:21.

15. Lawler, "Hardings I Knew," 20:21.

16. Jack Warwick, "Growing Up with Warren Harding," in "All in a Lifetime," Harding memorial, 1938, originally published in *Washington Post*, 1920, Marion Public Library, Marion, Ohio.

17. Christian, "Biography of Harding," 40.

18. William Allen White, *Masks in a Pageant* (New York: Macmillan, 1928), 391–392.

19. Christian, "Biography of Harding," 11.

20. Aeolius is the Greek god of the winds.

21. "Harding's Mother Influenced Him to Form High Ideals," *New York World*, August 12, 1923.

22. "No Wedding Ring on Mrs. Harding's Hand; Hates Kitchen, Adores Editor-Husband," newspaper unknown, FKH Papers, reel 244, box 858, frame 166.

23. Florence to Reddy Baldinger, Christmas 1917 (n.d.), copy in author's possession.

24. Carl Sferazza Anthony, *Florence Harding: The First Lady, the Jazz Age, and the Death of America's Most Scandalous President* (New York: Morrow, 1998), 44.

25. "The Editor Gets Married," *Marion Star*, July 9, 1891.

26. Christian, "Biography of Harding," 57.

27. Anthony, *Florence Harding*, 67–68; "President Harding Pens Eulogy to Dog Found Poisoned in Office," reel 244, frame #396.

28. *Marion Star*, March 11, 1913.

29. Trella Romine Collection, Marion County Historical Society.

30. John W. Dean, *Warren G. Harding* (New York: Times Books, 2004), 22; Christian, "Biography of Harding," 33.

31. Joseph De Barthe, *The Answer to "The President's Daughter" and other Defamations of a Great American* (Marion: Ohio: The Answer Publishing), 107–109.

32. White, *Masks in a Pageant*, 392.

33. *Vancouver Daily Providence*, July 25, 1923.

34. Quotes are from draft of Chancellor's notorious manuscript, *Warren Gamaliel Harding: President of the United States*, 22, that is in the Evalyn Walsh McLean Papers, box 96, Library of Congress; page number reflects penciled-in numbers.

35. Edna M. Colman, *White House Gossip: From Andrew Johnson to Calvin Coolidge* (Garden City: N.Y.: Doubleday, Page, 1927), 396.

36. Sherman A. Cuneo, *From Printer to President* (Philadelphia: Dorrance Publishers, 1922), 67.

37. Florence Harding quoted in Carl Sferrazza Anthony, "Florence (Mable) Kling Harding," in *American First Ladies: Their Lives and Their Legacy*, ed. Lewis L. Gould (New York: Garland, 1996), 376.

38. Warren G. Harding (aka "Jerry") to Christians, Christmas Eve, 1907, George C. Christian Sr. Papers, box 892.

39. See, for instance, Florence Harding to Evalyn McLean, July 9, 1921, Carl Sferrazza Anthony Collection, First Ladies Library, Canton, Ohio; undated FKH letter in author's possession. According to Evalyn McLean, the name originated in one of Cyrus Townsend Brady's books, where character Chimmie Fadden was in love with a French lady's maid called the Duchess. See manuscript for *Father Struck It Rich*, 302, Evalyn McLean Papers, box 99, Library of Congress, Washington, D.C. Cecil B. DeMille's movie, *Chimmie Fadden Out West* (1915), popularized the tale.

40. Francis Russell, *The Shadow of Blooming Grove: Warren G. Harding and His Times* (New York: McGraw-Hill, 1968), 91; Robert H. Ferrell, *The Strange Deaths of President Harding* (Columbus: University of Missouri Press, 1996), 46.

41. *Marion Star*, November 21, 1924.

42. Joe Mitchell Chapple, *Warren G. Harding: The Man* (Boston: Chapple Publishing, 1920).

43. Florence Davies, "Our First Lady," July 23, 1923, article sent to FKH, reel 246, box 876.

44. Ellyn R. Kern, *Where the Presidents Lived* (Indianapolis, Ind.: Cottontail Publications, 1982), 57.

45. FKH quoted in Anthony, *Florence Harding*, 55; on companionate marriage, see Steven Mintz and Susan Kellogg, *Domestic Revolutions: A Social History of American Family Life* (New York: Free Press, 1988), 114–116.

46. WGH to Mary Lee, June 22, 1920, responding to a letter that Mary had sent FKH, Mary Lee Papers, Related Harding Correspondence, 1920–1921, box 9/2, Ohio Historical Society.

47. Cass, "Duchess of East Center Street."

48. Anthony, *Florence Harding*, 62; also see Francis Russell, "The Shadow of Warren Harding," *Antioch Review* 36 (Winter 1978): 64.

49. See E. Mont Reilly to Carl Sawyer, May 21, 1931, Sawyer Papers, Ohio Historical Society. Reilly was asking for confirmation from Carl that his father had indeed informed young Carl that Harding had told him that he could have no children and "deplored the fact."

50. Russell, *Blooming Grove,* expurgated notes, 171 (all expurgated passages are taken from Russell's papers at the American Heritage Center at the University of Wyoming, Laramie, box 3); Anthony, *Florence Harding*, 91.

51. Anthony, *Florence Harding,* 79–80; *Marion Star,* November 21, 1924;.

52. FKH diary.

53. Cass, "Duchess of East Center Street."

54. Anthony, *Florence Harding*, 103.

55. Russell found these letters in 1964 at Donald Williamson's house (he was Phillips's legal guardian); Carrie had died in 1960. See letter from Donithen Michel and Davids to Phillips's daughter, Mrs. Isabelle Mathee, May 25, 1964, Marion County Historical Society, which states that "the letters are of considerable value."

56. Russell, *Blooming Grove.* 167, expurgated passages from Russell Papers, box 3.

57. FKH diary.

58. FKH diary.

59. See Stacy A. Cordery, *Alice: Alice Roosevelt Longworth, from White House Princess to Washington Power Broker* (New York: Viking, 2007), 166, 301.

60. Anthony, *Florence Harding,* 83–84.

61. WGH to Mrs. Christian, August 1907 (n.d.), reel 249, box 892.

62. Russell, *Blooming Grove,* 208.

63. See Dale E. Cottrill, *The Conciliator* (Philadelphia: Dorrance Press, 1969), 101; also see Harry P. Harrison (as told to Karl Detzer), *Culture under Canvas* (New York: Hastings House, 1958), 79–80; and FKH diary.

64. WGH to W. S. Luce, September 3, 1918, letter in author's possession. Harding collected about $100 per day for his speeches.

65. Russell, *Blooming Grove*, 218; Anthony, *Florence Harding*, 93.

66. Anthony, *Florence Harding*, 95.

67. See Russell, *Blooming Grove*, 219, 238, and related expurgated passages in Russell Papers, box 3.

68. White, *Masks in a Pageant*, 393.

69. Anthony, *Florence Harding*, 107–109.

70. See Scobey to Harding, June 16, 1914; Harding to Scobey, September 18, 1914, September 28, 1914, box 1, Frank Edgar Scobey Collection, 1914–1928, box 1, in WGH Papers, reel 263.

71. Ferrell, *Strange Deaths*, 158.

72. "Harding's Poetry Shows Love for Marion Mistress," "Biographer: Harding Was Man in Love," in *Marion Star*, November 5, 1981.

73. The opening of Nan Britton's papers in 2000 revealed no letters from Harding except bland ones related to her search for employment, an effort in which Harding helped her. See Glen Abel, "Not the President's Daughter," unpublished manuscript, in Trella Hemmerly Romine Collection, Caledonia, Ohio. Britton's allegations were denied by contemporaries, including a member of Harding's Senate staff who was with him daily. See Ferrell, *Strange Deaths*, 58. Ferrell denied the allegations, but in 2015 DNA evidence shared by Ancestry.com showed the connection. See NPR, "DNA Test Reveals President Warren Harding Had a Love Child," August 13, 2015, www.npr.org/2015/08/13/432122630-dna-test-reveals-president-warren-harding-had-a-love-child.

74. Nan Britton, *The President's Daughter* (NY: Elizabeth Ann Guild, 1927).

75. Samuel Hopkins Adams, *Incredible Era: The Life and Times of Warren Gamaliel Harding* (Boston: Houghton Mifflin, 1939), 101.

76. Harding to Scobey, August 22, 1914, Scobey Papers, box 1.

77. Scobey to George Christian Jr., April 19, 1915; Christian Sr. to Scobey, May 15, 1915; Scobey to Christian, May 20, 1915; Scobey to Harding, November 3, 1914; Harding to Scobey, November 25, 1914, Scobey Papers, box 1.

78. I am indebted to Lew Gould for explaining the pre-1933 (20th Amendment) congressional calendar.

79. Anthony, *Florence Harding*, 91, 112; Lawler, "Hardings I Knew," 20:22.

80. Harding to Scobey, January 15, 1915, March 25, 1915. Harding noted, "Mrs. Harding stood the trip all the way through very finely and is the better for having made it."

81. Harding to Scobey, July 12, 1915, Scobey Papers, box 1.

82. Harding to Scobey, September 6, 1915, Scobey Papers, box 1.

83. Their property manager wondered if Florence rented to Jews: "I didn't think you liked Jews any better than I do," wrote E. E. Bush, Real Estate Insurance, to Mrs. WGH, July 17, 1919, First Ladies Library.

84. *Columbus Saturday Monitor* society page (n.d.), FKH Papers, reel 244, box 858, Clippings.

CHAPTER 2: WASHINGTON LIFE

1. Harding to Scobey, September 6, 1915; Scobey to WGH, January 8, 1916, Scobey Papers (hereafter SP), box 1.

2. See Christian Jr. to Scobey, October 18, 1915, SP, box 1.

3. Harding to Scobey, December 15, 1915, March 9, 1918, SP, box 1. I am indebted to Lewis L. Gould for the salary information.

4. See John C. Knipp and Sons, Decorators, estimate, October 4, 1916; and architectural contract, George N. Ray and Warren G. Harding, May 25, 1916, WGH Papers, collection 345, box 828.

5. See bill from Harry A. Friedman, Home Furnisher, New York, September 11, 1916, WGH Papers, collection 345, box 828.

6. See bill for $1,915 and change from Knipp and Sons for furniture, March 1917, including curtains, brackets, and carpet for stairs.

7. See FKH Papers, reel 244, box 858, #187.

8. In a letter to Senate wife Mrs. Fred Hale, December 14, 1920, Florence wrote, "I shall look to you a great many times for direction, guidance and help in my new life and know I shall not ask in vain. I count you one of my very closest and best friends, and Sen Fred need not take you to task about this, or about asking me to your home. Your intentions were not only right, but very nice and greatly appreciated, and I hope in the near future to be able to avail myself of [them]," and visit.

9. FKH wrote Mrs. Mary Broadfield Meek of Columbus on January 18, 1921, that she was sorry to miss her Bridge Club reunion: "I am going to keep to the thought that I am to see you in my new home in Washington at some time during my stay there, if not all together, then as each can come, all the members of the club." See Anthony Collection, First Ladies Library.

10. Harding to Scobey, February 1, 1916; Scobey to WGH, January 8, 1916, SP, box 1.

11. Harding to Scobey, March 24, 1916, SP, box 1.

12. "Mrs. Harding Shows Slight Improvement," *New York Tribune*, September 10, 1922.

13. *Raleigh News and Observer*, August 8, 1923.

14. Harding to Scobey, February 1, 1916, SP, box 1.

15. Harding to Jennings, April 24, 1916, Jennings to WGH, April 27, 1916, Jennings Collection, box 1, Harding Papers, reel 261.

16. WGH to FKH, October 6, 1916, FKH Papers, roll 242, box 851, 1916–1923.

17. *Kansas City Post,* August 10, 1923.

18. See Harding to Scobey, September 13, 1917, SP, box 1; and John A. Morello, *Selling the President, 1920: Albert D. Lasker, Advertising, and the Election of Warren G. Harding* (Westport, Conn.: Praeger, 2001), 44.

19. Evalyn Walsh McLean with Boyden Sparkes, *Father Struck It Rich* (Boston: Little Brown, 1936), 220.

20. Alice Roosevelt Longworth, *Crowded Hours* (New York: Scribner's, 1933), 322–323.

21. See Florence to Ed McLean, September 6, 1920, thanking him for his editorial in the *Inquirer* on the League of Nations.

22. Longworth, *Crowded Hours,* 202–203.

23. See McLean, manuscript for *Father Struck It Rich,* 302, in McLean Papers, box 99, Library of Congress.

24. Florence to Evalyn, October 17, 1920, Anthony Collection, First Ladies Library.

25. FKH to Evalyn, November 1, 1920, Anthony Collection, First Ladies Library.

26. FKH Papers, Clippings, reel 244, box 858, #48.

27. Esther Neely DeWolfe to Florence K. Harding, April 18, 1917.

28. Miss Margaret O'Flaherty, Dressmaker, Columbus, Ohio, bill, May 30, 1918; Harry A. Friedman, Home Furnisher, New York, September 11, 1916, WGH Papers, collection 345, box 828.

29. See, e.g., Florence Kling Harding to Esther Neely DeWolfe, July 28, 1921, courtesy of Carol Davidson's private collection, Marion, Ohio. Clifford Kling helped Florence manage her money in this period; see his letters to her May 4, 1917, August 17, 1917, September 13, 1917, White House Papers, 1921–1922, First Ladies Library.

30. WGH to Scobey, April 2, 1918, SP, box 1.

31. Harding to Jennings, October 19, 1917, Jennings Papers (hereafter JP), box 1.

32. Harding to Scobey, October 6, 1917, SP, box 1.

33. Harding to Scobey, September 27, 1919: "You are a very great hit with Sen. Elkins, although I think he looks upon you as a very great menace to his supply of alcohol."

34. Harding to Scobey, October 20, 1917, December 6, 1917, SP, box 1.

35. Florence to (Ora) Reddy Baldinger, Christmas 1917, copy in author's possession.

36. January 3, 1918, Harding to Scobey, SP, box 1.

37. They were not meatless, either. In December 1917, for instance, the Hardings were eating plenty of meat, including hamburger, beef cutlet, shank bone, steak, and turkey. See WGH Papers, unmicrofilmed, collection 345, box 829.

38. Harding to Scobey, May 7, 1918, SP, box 1.

39. Francis Russell, *The Shadow of Blooming Grove: Warren G. Harding and His Times* (New York: McGraw-Hill, 1968), 304–305, expurgated portions in Russell Papers, box 3.

40. WGH to Jim, September 4 (n.d.), letter in author's possession.

41. Russell, *Blooming Grove*, 281.

42. "The President We Knew" anniversary issue, *Marion Newslife*, September 2, 1979.

43. Russell, *Blooming Grove*, 307–308, expurgated material is in Russell Papers, box 3.

44. Along with Russell, page 293, see also Samuel Hopkins Adams, *Incredible Era: The Life and Times of Warren Gamaliel Harding* (Boston: Houghton Mifflin, 1939), 101–108; Carl Sferazza Anthony, *Florence Harding: The First Lady, the Jazz Age, and the Death of America's Most Scandalous President* (New York: Morrow, 1998), 90–91, 164–166.

45. See Adams, *Incredible Era*, 105; Russell, *Blooming Grove*, 291.

46. Anthony, *Florence Harding*, 248, 300.

47. See chapter 1, n73.

48. Payments discussed in Britton, *The President's Daughter*, 366, 369, 383, 408.

49. Bob Ferrell to Trella Romine, December 8, 1999, June 28, 2000, letters in author's possession. Also see Steve Neal, "Wrongly Accused," *Chicago Sun Times*, January 14, 1997.

50. De Barthe, *The Answer*, 11–13, 35–37, 155; Edmund W. Starling, *Starling of the White House: The Story of the Man Whose Secret Service Detail Guarded Five Presidents from Woodrow Wilson to Franklin D. Roosevelt*, as told to Thomas Sugrue (New York: Simon and Schuster, 1946), 171. Carl Anthony email to author, August 13, 2015.

51. De Barthe, *The Answer*, 69–71.

52. Harding to Jennings, November 27, 1918, JP, reel 261, box 1; Harding to Scobey, December 4, 1918, SP, box 1.

53. Harding to Scobey, December 14, 1918, SP, box 1.

54. Harding to Scobey, December 30, 1918, SP, box 1.

55. Harding to Scobey, December 4, 1918, SP, box 1; the description of White is Lewis Gould's. See e-mail to author, March 17, 2008.

56. WGH to Scobey, January 14, 1919, SP, box 1.

57. Harding to Scobey, February 19, 1919, March 1, 1919, March 5, 1919, SP, box 2.

58. Scobey to Harding, March 18, 1919, Harding to Scobey, March 29, 1919, SP, box 2.

59. Harding to Jennings, March 4, 1919, JP, box 1.

60. Harding to Jennings, March 22, 1919, JP, box 1.

61. Harding to Scobey, March 29, 1919, SP, box 2.

62. WGH to Florence, n.d., on pictorial stationery of the Hotel Bon Air Winter Resort, Augusta, Georgia. Copy in author's possession.

63. Harding to Scobey, February 7, 1919, SP, box 2.

64. Gary Cohen, "The Lady and the Diamond," *Vanity Fair*, August 1997, 144.

65. See Charles Hard to Cyril Clemson, November 23, 1939, Warren G. Harding Papers, reel 254, #389; Kathleen Lawler, "The Hardings I Knew," unpublished manuscript, in Ohio Historical Society, Columbus, Ohio, 7:2–3.

66. Scobey to Daugherty, December 1, 1919, SP, box 2.

67. Daugherty to Scobey, November 28, 1919; Daugherty to Scobey, December 4, 1919; Harding to Scobey, November 14, 1919, SP, box 2.

68. Mack Jennings complained to Scobey on March 22, 1920, about Harding's acquiescence to Daugherty: "You know and I know that he did not pick H.M.D., but he permitted D. to pick himself and was unwilling to take the trouble to make his own organization or to assert himself in a way which would minimize the hostility to D. . . . it would have been better at the same time to have called in others from the other side," in SP, box 2.

69. See Malcolm Jennings, "A Journey and Its Ending: An Address before the Rotary Club, Columbus, Ohio, Sept 11, 1923," *Rotarian*, November 1923.

70. Joel Boone Memoir Manuscript, 20:180, Boone Papers, box 45, Library of Congress, Washington, D.C.

71. Harding to Scobey, November 29, 1919, December 30, 1919, SP, box 2.

72. Daugherty to Scobey, November 28, 1919, SP, box 2.

73. George Christian Sr., "Biography of Warren G. Harding," George B. Christian Sr. Papers, Outgoing Correspondence, 1918–1923, in Harding Papers, Ohio Historical Society, reel 249, box 892, 85–86.

74. Dolly Madison's "Washington Letter," *Philadelphia Public Ledger*, June 17, 1923.

75. Harding to Jennings, February 4, 1920, JP, box 1.

76. Harding to Jennings, February 14, 1920, JP, box 1.

77. Christian, "Biography of Harding," 81.

78. Lawler, "Hardings I Knew," 8:10–11.

79. Jennings to Scobey, March 22, 1920, SP, box 2.

80. FKH to Evaland and Edwardo, January 1920, handwritten note, n.d., SP, box 2.

81. "Nominee's Wife Knows the Game," *Chattanooga Times*, October 1920, FKH Papers, reel 244, box 858.

82. "Mrs. Harding Shops En Suite," *New York Evening Sun*, February 1, 1920, FKH Papers, reel 244, box 858.

83. See Harry M. Daugherty and Thomas Dixon, *The Inside Story of the Harding Tragedy* (New York: Churchill, 1932), 58, cited in Ann E. Burnette, "Florence Kling Harding: Bridging Traditional and Modern Rhetorical Roles," in *Inventing a Voice: The Rhetoric of American First Ladies of the Twentieth Century*, ed. Molly Meijer Wertheimer (Lanham, Md.: Rowman & Littlefield, 2004), 137.

84. Lawler, "Hardings I Knew," 1:4.

85. Morello, *Selling the President*, 22–23.

86. "Mrs. Harding Has a Part," *Kansas City Star*, October 8, 1920. His voice can still be heard on YouTube, somewhat altered by time. His America First speech is at www.youtube.com/watch?v=lL5aZLlfVy4.

87. Morello, *Selling the President*, 54–56.

88. "Star Gazing Is Latest Fad in National Capital Society," *Denver Post*, August 12, 1920; "No Wedding Ring on Mrs. Harding's Hand," FKH Papers, reel 244, box 858, #166.

89. Lawler, "Hardings I Knew," 17:12–13.

90. *Rochester Democrat and Chronicle*, August 11, 1923, 13.

91. Harry B. Hunt, "Astrologist Who Predicted Nomination of W. G. Harding Also Foretold His Death," in FKH Papers, reel 247, box 880.

92. Lawler, "Hardings I Knew," 17:10.

93. Boone Memoir Manuscript, 27:112.

94. William F. Ogburn, "Why Some Folks Are Superstitious," *Colliers*, May 16, 1925, 43.

95. Lawler, "Hardings I Knew," 17:10, 11.

96. Ibid., 20:18–19.

97. As Edith Wharton adds so aptly, "traditions that have lost their meaning are the hardest of all to destroy." See Wharton, "Autre Temps," in *The Collected Short Stories of Edith Wharton*, ed. R. W. B. Lewis (New York: Scribner's, 1968), 2:279. I am indebted to Carol Singley for bringing this work to my attention.

98. FKH Papers, reel 244, box 858, #48.

99. Simon Louvish, *Cecil B. DeMille: A Life in Art* (New York: St. Martin's Press, 2007), 158.

100. Lawler, "Hardings I Knew," 9:2; Lewis L. Gould, *Grand Old Party: A History of the Republicans* (New York: Random House, 2003), 220–222.

101. Gould, *Grand Old Party*, 221.

102. Lewis L. Gould, *The Most Exclusive Club: A History of the Modern United States Senate* (New York: Basic Books, 2005), 91; Jennings to Scobey, March 22, 1920, SP, box 2.

103. John Milton Cooper Jr., *Breaking the Heart of the World: Woodrow Wilson and the Fight for the League of Nations* (New York: Cambridge University Press, 2001), 389, 390, n25, cited in Gould, *Grand Old Party*, 221.

104. Morello, *Selling the President*, 65.

105. Lawler, "Hardings I Knew," 9:21; Florence Kling Harding, "At the Convention," FKH Papers, reel 244, box 858, #186.

106. Scobey to Howard D. Hannington, Chicago Harding Headquarters, May 20, 1920; Scobey to J. A. Arnold, secretary of Texas Republican Council, March 13, 1920, SP, box 2. Scobey had told an associate that "this negro, William McDonald" was "disgruntled," and defended himself this way: "I use white men on my trucks and for all my warehouse labor I use colored men. They get the same pay as white men, have indemnity insurance—also sick insurance." Regarding McDonald, he declared, "what this negro wants is not political justice but social equality; and you know this can never be." See Scobey to Richard Lynch, October 11, 1920, SP, box 2.

107. *Salt Lake Tribune*, July 31, 1923.

108. Starling, *Starling of the White House*, 167.

109. Morello, *Selling the President*, 52–53.

110. "A little picture of Mrs. Harding at the Notification," 1919, n.d., FKH Papers, roll 242, box 851, Clippings, 1916–1923.

111. Harding to Jennings June 24, 1920, JP, box 1.

112. Lawler, "Hardings I Knew," 21:59.

113. Ibid., 17:9, 20:43.

114. Ibid., 4:1.

115. Joe Mitchell Chapple, *Life and Times of Warren G. Harding, Our After-War President* (Boston: Chapple Publishing, 1924), 129.

116. Lawler, "Hardings I Knew," 4:7–8.

117. FKH to Mrs. Upton, October 31, 1920, FKH Papers, roll 242, box 851.

118. Morello, *Selling the President*, 53.

119. FKH to Sullivan, November 14, 1920, Mark Sullivan Papers, General Correspondence file, box 3, Library of Congress.

120. Stacy A. Cordery, *Alice: Alice Roosevelt Longworth, from White House Princess to Washington Power Broker* (New York: Viking, 2007), 291.

121. Morello, *Selling the President*, 79.

122. Walker Buel, "Peace Reigns at Republican Mecca," August 6, 1920, FKH Papers, reel 244, box 858, #32.

123. Christian, "Biography of Harding," 109, 141.

124. Helen A. Cannon to FKH, February 6, 1920, FKH Papers, roll 242, box 851.

125. Bennett to FKH, August 24, 1920, FKH Papers, roll 242, box 851.

126. Christian, "Biography of Harding," 92–104 passim.

127. *Raleigh News-Observer*, August 8, 1923.

128. "Mrs. Harding Has a Part," *Kansas City Star*, October 8, 1920, FKH Papers, reel 244, box 858.

129. "The President We Knew" anniversary issue, *Marion Newslife*, September 2, 1979; Gould, *Grand Old Party*, 223; also see Morello, *Selling the President*, 54–55.

130. Lawler, "Hardings I Knew," 20:24.

131. FKH to Mrs. Pardee, October 31, 1920, FKH Papers, roll 242, box 851.

132. Hirsch quoted in Anthony, *Florence Harding*, 210.

133. Sherman A. Cuneo, *From Printer to President* (Philadelphia: Dorrance Publishers, 1922), 110.

134. Lawler, "Hardings I Knew," 20:45–49.

135. Ibid., 20:29–30.

136. Ibid., "Hardings I Knew," 4:2.

137. Morello, *Selling the President*, 72.

138. See WGH to Carrie Phillips, 1920 (n.d.), Charlton Myers Collection, Marion County Historical Society, Marion, Ohio; also cited in *Cleveland Plain Dealer*, July 10, 1964; Morello, *Selling the President*, 70, n38. The money may have come from rich donors like Ned McLean and oilman Jake Hamon. Carrie does seem to have bought some expensive jewelry abroad in 1920; see *Marion Newslife*, September 2, 1979. Russell asserts that when she returned, she still hoped for favors and managed to get some token appointments for her relatives; see Russell, *Blooming Grove*, 66.

139. Robert H. Ferrell, *The Strange Deaths of President Harding* (Columbus: University of Missouri Press, 1996), 159.

140. See Richard B. Sherman, *The Republican Party and Black America from McKinley to Hoover, 1896–1933* (Charlottesville: University Press of Virginia, 1973), 138.

141. William Allen White, *Masks in a Pageant* (New York: Macmillan, 1928), 426.

142. Christian, "Biography of Harding," 111.

143. Lawler, "Hardings I Knew," 21:62.

144. Ibid., 21:63ff.

145. See Gould, *Grand Old Party*, 225.

146. Christian, "Biography of Harding," 53; Jennings to Scobey, September 2, 1919, SP, box 2.

147. FKH to Evalyn, October 31, 1920, October 23, 1920, FKH Papers, roll 242, box 851.

148. Lawler, "Hardings I Knew," 20:25ff.

149. Robert Young Thomas letter dated January 9, 1922, in Thomas Papers; MS 167, Western Kentucky University; citation provided by Lewis Gould.

150. See pamphlet from the WGH Memorial Foundation, meeting at First Baptist Church of Greenwich, Connecticut, listing WGH as "1st Negro US President," March 27, 1988, First Ladies Library. The organization was founded by Berenice Norwood Napper.

151. Lawler, "Hardings I Knew," 22:1–4; Abby Gunn Baker, "With the Hardings in the White House," *Christian Herald*, August 27, 1921.

152. Lawler, "Hardings I Knew," 22:5–11.

153. Christian, "Biography of Harding," 109; Malcolm Gladwell, *Blink: The Power of Thinking without Thinking* (New York: Little Brown, 2005), 72–75.

154. "The President We Knew" anniversary issue, *Marion Newslife*, September 2, 1979.

155. Lawler, "Hardings I Knew," 22:13.

156. "A Glimpse of Mrs. Harding," *New York Times*, November 14, 1920.

157. WGH to Jennings, December 14, 1920, JP, box 1.

158. Chapple, *Life and Times*, 154.

159. To quote Harding, "The United Fruit Company is an example of creative business, and I would like to see a hundred such companies engaged in other lines of business." See Chapple, *Life and Times*, 157.

160. See reel 244, box 858, #33, n.d.; Lawler, "Hardings I Knew," 24:6–10; Chapple, *Life and Times*, 152.

161. FKH to Mrs. Hale, December 14, 1920, Mrs. Hale to FKH, December 11, 1920, FKH Papers, roll 242, box 851.

162. FKH to Alexander Moore, December 11, 1920, FKH Papers roll 242, box 851.

163. Lawler, "Hardings I Knew," 24:11–13; Edith Bolling Galt Wilson to FKH, December 6, 1920; FKH to EBGW, December 6, 1920; FKH to EBGW, n.d., 1921 (two letters), Edith Bolling Galt Wilson Papers, box 20, Library of Congress.

164. FKH to Mrs. Marshall, December 9, 1920, FKH Papers, roll 242, box 851.

165. FKH to Grace Coolidge, December 11, 1920, FKH Papers, roll 242, box 851.

166. Robert Ferrell, *Grace Coolidge: The People's Lady in Silent Cal's White House* (Lawrence: University Press of Kansas, 2008), 52–53.

167. Lawler, "Hardings I Knew," 5:5a.

168. Ibid., 24:17–20.

169. "Mrs. Harding Pictured by One of Her Life Long Friends," February 21, 1921, reel 244, box 858.

170. Lawler, "Hardings I Knew," 20:42.

171. Jess Smith to Scobey, January 4, 1921, SP, box 3.

172. FKH to Mrs. Coolidge, January 12, 1921, FKH Papers, reel 242, box 851.

173. FKH to Mrs. Scobey, January 3, 1921, SP, box 3.

174. FKH to Mrs. Scobey, December 10, 1920, SP, box 2.

175. Lawler, "Hardings I Knew," 20:36–37.

176. FKH to Mrs. Hale, December 14, 1920, FKH Papers, reel 242, box 851.

177. FKH to Louise, January 3, 1921, FKH Papers, reel 242, box 851.

178. Clinton Wallace Gilbert, *Behind the Mirrors: The Psychology of Disintegration at Washington* (New York: G. P. Putnam's Sons, 1922), 62.

179. Mrs. Lodge to FKH, November 20, 1920, FKH Papers, box 851, roll 242.

180. Laura Havis to FKH, February 18, 1921, Mrs. R. Reynolds to FKH, February 16, 1921, FKH Papers, reel 242, box 851.

181. Lawler, "Hardings I Knew," 28:1–2.

182. Ibid., 28:27–28.

183. No article identified, reel 244, box 858, frame 48.

184. "Mrs. Harding Shops En Suite," *New York Evening Sun*, February 1, 1920; "Wife of the President Authorizes This Article about Clothes for Wear on the White House: Our Thoughts American, Let Our Dress Be," no paper identified, reel 244, box 858. Worth, a French designer, was one of Mrs. Wilson's favorites. See Ishbel Ross, *Power with Grace: The Life Story of Mrs. Woodrow Wilson* (New York: G.P. Putnam's Sons, 1975), 125.

185. No article identified; FKH Papers, reel 244, box 858, frame 48.

186. Lawler, "Hardings I Knew," 28:35.

187. Robert T. Small, "Warren Harding, Stranger to Hate," *Outlook,* August 15, 1923.

CHAPTER 3: INAUGURAL YEAR

1. "Drab Inaugural? It's Rich in Color, but Quiet in Tone," no paper identified, FKH Papers, reel 244, box 858, #86.

2. See reminiscences in "Mrs. Harding Quits Mansion; Nature Weeps"; "Gloomy Skies, Drizzling Rain, Crowd's Absence, Contrast with that Day in March '21," *Washington Herald,* August 18, 1923.

3. "America's First Ladies Pass Busy Inauguration Day with Plaudits on Every Side," *Washington Herald,* March 5, 1921, FKH Papers, reel 244, box 858.

4. Quoted in Sherman A. Cuneo, *From Printer to President* (Philadelphia: Dorrance Publishers, 1922), 62.

5. "Two Brilliant Balls Add to Gayety of Inaugural," "All Society at Ceremony," "America's New First Ladies Pass Busy Inauguration Day with Plaudits on Every Side," in *Washington Herald,* March 5, 1921. See invitation to ball, Lois Marshall to FKH, January 17, 1921; FKH to Marshall, January 21, 1921.

6. George Christian Sr., "Biography of Warren G. Harding," George B. Christian Sr. Papers, Outgoing Correspondence, 1918–1923, in Harding Papers, Ohio Historical Society, reel 249, box 892, 183; Dolly Madison's "Washington Letter," *Philadelphia Public Ledger,* June 18, 1922.

7. See unnamed article, May 14, 1922, reel 245, box 868.

8. Edmund W. Starling, *Starling of the White House: The Story of the Man Whose Secret Service Detail Guarded Five Presidents from Woodrow Wilson to Franklin D. Roosevelt,* as told to Thomas Sugrue (New York: Simon and Schuster, 1946), 171.

9. *New York Herald,* May 21, 1922.

10. Joel Boone Memoir Manuscript, 27:40, Boone Papers, box 45, Library of Congress, Washington, D.C.

11. Henry Fisher, "Keeping House for Mr. President: The New Mistress of the White House," FKH Papers, reel 244, box 858, #2.

12. I am indebted to Catherine Forslund for this anecdote; e-mail to author, May 22, 2008.

13. "Character," no newspaper recorded, FKH Papers, reel 244, box 858, #85.

14. Carl Sferazza Anthony, *Nellie Taft: The Unconventional First Lady of the Ragtime Era* (New York: Harper Collins, 2006), 274–275.

15. Frances Wright Saunders, *Ellen Axson Wilson: First Lady Between Two Worlds* (Chapel Hill: University of North Carolina Press, 1985), 234.

16. I am indebted to Kristie Miller for these insights on Ellen Wilson.

17. Kristie Miller, e-mail to author, May 24, 2008.

18. The veto of Prohibition in October 1919, for example, while no doubt in accord with the president's sentiments, was utterly useless in the face of Congress's determination, and it seems to have been an initiative undertaken wholly by Joseph Tumulty and Edith Wilson! John Milton Cooper Jr., *Breaking the Heart of the World: Woodrow Wilson and the Fight for the League of Nations* (New York: Cambridge University Press, 2001), 202–208 passim.

19. See Kristie Miller's forthcoming book, *Ellen Axson Wilson and Edith Bolling (Galt) Wilson,* to be published in this series by the University Press of Kansas.

20. "All Society at Ceremony," *Washington Herald,* March 5, 1921.

21. James Williams to editor of *Washington Post,* November 19, 1920, in Evalyn Walsh McLean Papers, box 24; also see commentary in "Mrs. Harding Keeps Promise to Swing Open Iron Gates, Admitting All to White House," Universal Service, March 5, 1921, FKH Papers, reel 244, box 858, #21–22.

22. Kathleen Lawler, "The Hardings I Knew," unpublished manuscript, in Ohio Historical Society, Columbus, Ohio, 29:40.

23. "'First Lady' Declared for 'Open Door' Policy before Election when Policeman Chased Her Away as She Sought to Peep in at Grounds," Universal Service, March 5, 1921, reel 244, box 858.

24. "'First Lady' Enlists to Aid White House Birds and Squirrels," reel 244, box 858, 410.

25. See "Harding Is Forced to Forego Church by Mass of Work," March 6, 1923, *New York Herald,* reel 244, box 858.

26. Chancellor, manuscript for *Warren Gamaliel Harding: President of the United States,* 199, in the Evalyn Walsh McLean Papers, box 96, Library of Congress; page number reflects penciled-in numbers.

27. James Williams to *Washington Post,* November 19, 1920, Francis R. King, Division of Operations of the U.S. Shipping Board Emergency Fleet Corp., to editor McLean at *Post,* November 15, 1920; Julia Summers of the Woman's Made in America League to E. B. McLean, editor of *Washington Post,* November 24, 1920; all in Evalyn Walsh McLean Papers, box 24.

28. Evelyn Hunt, "President and Mrs. Harding Open Season by Reception to Diplomats and Families," FKH Papers, reel 244, box 858, #83.

29. "Keeping House for Mr. President," FKH Papers, roll 244, box 858, #2.

30. The terse vice president was even faster: at an army and navy reception, he once shook 2,096 hands in fifty-five minutes; Harding, by contrast, "was

overly slow and gushy." This according to Irwin "Ike" Hood Hoover, *Forty Two Years in the White House* (Boston: Houghton Mifflin, 1934), 133.

31. Lora Kelley, "Directions for 'Doing the White House,'" FKH Papers, reel 244, box 858, #40.

32. Boone Memoir Manuscript, 27:107.

33. Edna M. Colman, *White House Gossip: From Andrew Johnson to Calvin Coolidge* (Garden City, N.Y.: Doubleday, Page, 1927), 385.

34. WGH to Jennings, March 19, 1921, Jennings Papers (hereafter JP), box 1.

35. See FKH to Mary Lee, June 11, 1921, Mary Lee Papers, Related Harding Correspondence, 1920–1921, box 9/2, Ohio Historical Society, Columbus, Ohio. For details on Florence's appointments schedule, see Laura Harlan, "The End of a Perfect Day: The Life of Florence Kling Harding (1860–1924), The White House Appointment Books," unpublished manuscript, First Ladies Library, Canton, Ohio. This manuscript is divided into four parts addressing "Life in the White House," including part 1, Daily Log, March 4, 1921–December 19, 1921; part 2, Daily Log, December 20, 1921–April 28, 1922; part 3, Daily Log, April 29, 1922–July 12, 1922; and part 4, Daily Log, July 13, 1922–December 31, 1922; referred to below as Daily Log, with dates.

36. Jennings to FKH, March 16, 1921, JP, box 1.

37. See Harlan, Daily Log, March 4, 1921–December 19, 1921.

38. Daisy Fitzhugh Ayres, "President and Mrs. Harding Often Slip Out for Potluck," *Courier Journal*, January 22, 1922.

39. "Mrs. Harding Urges Men Guests to Doff Coats at Luncheon," July 5, 1922, reel 245, box 862, #1200.

40. *Washington Star*, Sunday, March 20, 1921.

41. "The First Lady of the Land Occupies an Exacting Position," no paper identified, FKH Papers, reel 244, box 858, #89.

42. See Harlan, Daily Logs, March 4, 1921–December 19, 1921.

43. FKH to Esther Mezger, November 29, 1921, copy in author's possession.

44. See Harlan, Daily Log, March 4, 1921–December 19, 1921.

45. Kate Marcia Forbes, "Upstairs in the White House," *Washington Post*, January 15, 1922.

46. "Harding Lawn a Vast Omelette When Egg-Rolling Battle Ends," *New York Tribune*, April 18, 1922.

47. Abby Gunn Baker, "With the Hardings in the White House," *Christian Herald*, August 27, 1921; "Mrs. Harding's Secretary," *New York Times*, March 5, 1921; *Time*, July 6, 1925.

48. See her sentiments in Laura Harlan to FKH, July 27, 1922. Harlan's usefulness and graciousness were attested to by Boone, who noted that she "was a delightful lady. I enjoyed immensely working with her." She was as well a great help "in my relationships at the White House." See Boone Memoir Manuscript, 27:111.

49. *Washington Star*, August 26, 1923.

50. Lawler, "Hardings I Knew," 24:15–16.

51. FKH to John W. Weeks, April 15, 1922, reel 242, box 851.

52. "Mrs. Harding Does Her Economy 'Bit,'" *New York Herald*, March 13, 1921, "White House to Save," no paper or date listed, reel 244, box 858, #38.

53. Dolly Madison's, "Washington Letter," Philadelphia Public Ledger, January 22, 1922. Ike Hoover completely misread her when he wrote that "to Mrs. Harding, flowers were just flowers"; Hoover, *Forty Two Years*, 17.

54. "To Make White House a Home Will Be Task of Mrs. Harding," February 24, 1921, reel 244, box 858.

55. See *New York Times*, January 19, 1922; *New York Tribune*, January 19, 1922; *New York World*, January 19, 1922; *Washington Post*, January 21, 1922.

56. Starling, *Starling of the White House*, 168.

57. FKH to Nellie Taft, December 15, 1920; Nellie Taft to FKH, December 17, 1920, FKH Papers, reel 242, box 851.

58. Elizabeth Jaffray, *Secrets of the White House* (New York: Cosmopolitan Book, 1927), 87–89.

59. Ibid., 89, 93.

60. *Chicago Blade*, February 24, 1921, FKH Papers, reel 244, box 858.

61. Kate Forbes, "Home Life in the White House," *Washington Post*, reel 245, box 866, #342.

62. "Sugar Boycott: Mrs. Harding Cutting Back Use of Sugar to Offset 'Sugar Gougers,'" *Washington Herald*, May 6, 1923.

63. Boone Memoir Manuscript, 27:111.

64. FKH to Harvey, June 3, 1922, First Ladies Library.

65. Lawler, "Hardings I Knew," 4:10.

66. Lee to FKH, March 20, 1921, Lee Papers, box 9/2.

67. Edwin Denby to FKH, May 23, 1921, FKH Papers, reel 242, box 851.

68. Butler to FKH, June 20, 1922, FKH Papers, reel 242, box 851.

69. Edward H. Hamilton, "This Woman Shows Politicians, Wins Job through Mrs. Harding," reel 244, frame 303.

70. "Mrs. Harding's Alleged Patronage: No Reason Why a President's Wife Should Be Excluded from Politics," FKH Papers, reel 242, box 858.

71. Lois K. Marshall to FKH, May 29, 1923, FKH Papers, reel 243, box 854.

72. Hoover, *Forty Two Years*, 275.
73. Boone Memoir Manuscript, 27:111–112.
74. "Sway of First Lady's Scepter Is Supreme in White House," *Cincinnati Times Star*, January 30, 1923.
75. Baker, "With the Hardings."
76. The *Mayflower* was built in 1896 for a New York financier, Ogden Goelet; it was 320 feet long, with 315 men and 7 officers serving as the presidential crew. The navy acquired it on the eve of the Spanish-American war, and Teddy Roosevelt used it also to host the negotiations ending the Russo-Japanese war. President Taft especially loved it, and he built a special bathtub on board. Wilson also courted Mrs. Galt there. Despite its electric light and fans, it could get dreadfully hot in summer, especially below decks—the laundry room was "almost unbearable," Boone noted. The Hardings loved it all the same, and the ceremony of its naval auspices appealed to them. As Boone recalled, "our uniforms had to be always immaculate. No tarnished gold braid was tolerated. . . . we were expected to dress well at all times." President Hoover returned the *Mayflower* to the navy in 1929 as an economy measure, and it later saw service in World War II patrolling for U-boats.
77. See Harlan, Daily Log, March 4, 1921–December 19, 1921.
78. Boone diary entries, May 16, 19, 1922, Boone Papers, box 40, Library of Congress; Boone Diary Manuscript, 27:1a.
79. Boone Memoir Manuscript, 27:2–3.
80. Boone diary entry, May 23, 25, 1922; Boone Memoir Manuscript, 27:44.
81. Diners might enjoy at one sitting a meal consisting of, as first course, cream of chicken soup and olive, celery, and sweet pickle relish; as second, mayonnaised fruit salad; and for their main course, roast stuffed young turkey, baked spiced hams, oyster dressing, giblet gravy, cranberry sauce, candied sweet potatoes, peas, mashed potatoes, corn, creamed cauliflower, and fruit, including orange, apple, and banana. For dessert, there would be orange layer cake, ice cream, candied mixed nuts, mince pies, and sweet cider demitasse.
82. *New York Times*, April 26, 1921.
83. FKH to Mrs. Jennings, July 7, 1921, White House Papers, 1921–1922, First Ladies Library; *Union Gazette*, July 1, 1921, FKH Papers, reel 244, box 858, #66.
84. FKH to Mary Lee, July 23, 1921, Lee Papers 9/2.
85. John W. Dean, *Warren G. Harding* (New York: Times Books, 2004), 108.
86. Jennings to WGH, August 11, 1921, Jennings box 1.
87. FKH to William Allen White, August 12, 1921, William Allen White Papers, series C, box 57, Library of Congress. Later, White was not so kind,

describing Harding as having "a weak heart and a thick head" in his *Masks in a Pageant* (New York: Macmillan, 1928), 421.

88. FKH to Mary Lee, July 23, 1921, Lee Papers, 9/2.

89. Starling, *Starling of the White House*, 177.

90. "White House Kept Open by Mrs. Harding's Order," *New York Tribune*, August 9, 1921, FKH Papers, reel 244, frame 408.

91. Unidentified newspaper article, August 4, 1921, FKH Papers, reel 244, box 858, #377.

92. H. F. Alderfer, "The Personality and Politics of Warren G. Harding," Ph.D. diss. (Syracuse, N.Y.: Syracuse University, 1928), 332–337.

93. Boone Memoir Manuscript, 20:140–141.

94. See Harding to Jennings, November 15, 1921, Jennings to Harding, November 17–20, 1921, JP, box 1.

95. On Debs, see WGH to Jennings, April 8, 1921, JP, box 1.

96. See Jennings's musings in a long handwritten letter to WGH, December–January 1922 (n.d.), JP, box 1.

97. "Harding Back at Desk, Bronzed by Holiday," *New York Times*, September 7, 1921.

98. "President to Take Trip Aboard the Mayflower," *Washington Star*, September 4, 1921.

99. "Hotel Floor, Gold Dishes, Orchestra for Harding," *Washington Times*, September 11, 1921, "President Vetoes Gold Dinner Plates and Like Luxuries," September 12, 1921, FKH Papers, reel 244, box 858, #490ff.

100. "Hardings Attend Musical Comedy in New York," no paper identified, reel 244, box 858, #502.

101. "Harding Far Off Golf Form, Plays a Losing Game," September 14, 1921, FKH Papers, reel 244, box 858, #513.

102. "Oh Boy Graduates from Garage to Berth in White House Kennels," *New York World*, August 12, 1921.

103. Harlan, Daily Log, March 4, 1921–December 19, 1921.

104. "Mrs. Harding Again Lessens Social Duties at Capital," *New York Herald*, November 19, 1921; "Mrs. Harding Simplifies Cabinet and House Calls," *Washington Herald*, November 20, 1921.

105. This was Mississippi Senator Pat Harrison, quoted in Richard B. Sherman, *The Republican Party and Black America from McKinley to Hoover, 1896–1933* (Charlottesville: University Press of Virginia, 1973), 150. See Jennings's worries on the Birmingham speech in a long handwritten letter to WGH, December–January 1922 (n.d.), JP, box 1. Harding's progressive views on civil and

political liberties have often been overlooked by historians. As the *Washington Observer* wrote about his address on October 27, 1921, "Probably none of his many utterances since his maiden message to Congress has excited such animated comment pro and con. . . . the president's courage in delivering such a blast in the heart of Dixie's black belt was remarkable and almost unprecedented. Among GOP leaders fears were expressed that the Harding speech may spell trouble for Republic Senators in the Border States." Harding's speech inspired Marcus Garvey to call the president a "sage." On the other hand, white supremacist Julia Evans Cope, speaking at Emory University after Harding's death, also found much to crow about, noting that Harding had defended "the negro's cause for legal equality only" and had "refused to fill the southern post-offices and federal buildings with negro officials, not one is there to be found in the Atlanta federal building today." All the same, Harding certainly appointed more blacks than Wilson had to the federal branch, although it would have been difficult to appoint fewer! See reaction to his Birmingham speech in FKH Papers, reel 244, frames 774-958.

106. Boone Memoir Manuscript, 19:99-100.

107. Lewis L. Gould, *The Most Exclusive Club: A History of the Modern United States Senate* (New York: Basic Books, 2005), 101.

108. "Mrs. Harding Aids in Planting Elms," November 12, 1921, "White House Dinner First Social Event," *New York Times*, November 13, 1921; more in *Washington Star*, November 7, 1921, reel 245, box 862, #1045.

109. FKH to Aunt Nellie November 19, 1921, White House Papers, First Ladies Library.

110. "President and Mrs. Harding Hosts to Arms Visitors," *Washington Star*, November 10, 1921; On Florence's concern for journalists' access, see Constance Drexel, "Mrs. Harding's Simplicity Endears Her to Capital," *Philadelphia Public Ledger*, March 5, 1922, FKH Papers, reel 245, box 866, #411.

111. FKH to Harvey, November 20, 1921, White House Papers, First Ladies Library.

112. Starling, *Starling of the White House*, 181.

113. FKH to Esther Mezger, November 28, 1921, Esther Mezger Collection, First Ladies Library. I am indebted to Craig Schermer for his assistance in locating this collection.

114. Boone Memoir Manuscript, 27:49-50.

115. FKH to Esther Mezger, November 29, 1921, copy in author's possession; also see article in *Washington Star*, December 1, 1921.

116. FKH to Mrs. Scobey, January 26, 1922, SP box 3.

117. "White House to Save," no paper or date listed, FKH Papers, reel 244, box 858, #38.

118. Harlan, Daily Log, March 4, 1921–December 19, 1921.

119. WGH to Mrs. Scobey, February 20, 1922, Scobey Papers, box 3.

120. Christian, "Biography of Harding," 189; Starling, *Starling of the White House*, 182; FKH to Aunt Carrie, January 29, 1923, FKH Papers, roll 242, box 852.

121. Stacy A. Cordery, *Alice: Alice Roosevelt Longworth, from White House Princess to Washington Power Broker* (New York: Viking, 2007), 290.

122. WGH to Scobey, July 19, 1919, Scobey Papers, box 2.

123. Starling, *Starling of the White House*, 169–174 passim.

124. Quoted in *Marion Newslife*, May 5, 1980; Florence ("Mother") to Mr. R. A. Mezger, June 13, 1921, letter provided to author courtesy of Mike Perry.

125. FKH to Esther Mezger, November 29, 1921, copy in author's possession. FKH to Esther Mezger, December 23, 1921, Esther Mezger Collection, First Ladies Library; FKH statement at Marion National Bank, February 24, 1922, First Ladies Library. This amount is approximately $1,000 every quarter in today's dollars.

126. See FKH to Governor Pinkham, December 22, 1921, FKH Papers, reel 242, box 851. France would have reason to complain; in the end, its naval ratio was made the equal of Italy, well behind the United States, Great Britain, and Japan (5:5:3:1.67:1.67).

127. FKH to Mrs. Lee, December 19, 1921, Lee Papers, 9/2.

128. See FKH to Mary Lee, December 12, 1921, Lee Papers, 9/2.

129. FKH to Mary Lee, December 19, 1921, Lee Papers, 9/2.

130. FKH to Mrs. Christian, December 22, 1921, Christian Papers, roll 249, box 892.

131. Forbes, "Upstairs in the White House."

132. FKH to Miss Ford, March 15, 1921, First Ladies Library.

CHAPTER 4: DEFINING THE JOB

1. "Mrs. Harding, in Tacoma Today, Is Example of Highest Ideals in Womanhood; She Has Been Important Factor in Career of Her Distinguished Husband; Whole Nation Admires and Loves Her," *Tacoma News Tribune*, July 5, 1923.

2. Howard Guthery, a Marion native, recalled her kindness to him when "I was just a kid"; see "The President We Knew" anniversary issue, *Marion Newslife*, September 2, 1979.

3. "Mrs. Harding, in Tacoma Today."

4. FKH to Mary Lee, June 16, 1922, Lee Papers, box 9/4; FKH to Christian Sr., June 19, 1922, Christian Papers, reel 249, box 892.

5. "Dolly Madison's "Washington Letter," *Philadelphia Public Ledger,* April 23, 1922.

6. Henry Fisher, "Keeping House for Mr. President: The New Mistress of the White House," FKH Papers, reel 244, box 858, #2.

7. *Washington Star,* January 3, 1922.

8. *Baltimore American,* January 3, 1922; *Washington Post,* January 3, 1922.

9. "Mrs. Harding Nearly Collapses in Greeting 6,500 at White House," *New York Tribune,* January 3, 1922.

10. Joel Boone Memoir Manuscript, 27:107, Boone Papers, box 45, Library of Congress, Washington, D.C.

11. Boone Memoir Manuscript, 19:46.

12. This New Year's tradition was continued by Coolidge, but Herbert Hoover put an end to it in 1932, during the Depression. The Roosevelts revived the tradition of enormous receptions, but more recent administrations, including that of George W. Bush, have kept such gatherings small, although its Christmas reception can have up to 1,000 guests and so does its congressional picnic. Author's e-mails from William Bushong, historian and Webmaster, White House Historical Association, July 30, 2007, and from Bill Allman, White House curator, August 8, 2007.

13. *Washington Star,* January 3, 1922.

14. FKH to Lee, January 5, 1922, Lee Papers, box 9/3.

15. FKH to Mrs. Scobey, January 26, 1922, Scobey Papers, box 3.

16. FKH to Esther Mezger, January 4, 1922, reel 245, box 868.

17. Kathleen Lawler, "The Hardings I Knew," unpublished manuscript, in Ohio Historical Society, Columbus, Ohio, 4:10; FKH to Mary Lee, December 12, 1921, Lee Papers, 9/2.

18. "Washington Gayer than at Any Time in 7 Years; Dinners Set Record"; "Lid Is Off, as Gayety Enters White House," Louisville *Courier Journal,* January 8, 1922, January 15, 1922, reel 245, box 865.

19. Jean Elliot's society column, *Washington Times,* January 26, 1922.

20. WGH to Esther, January 9, 1922, FKH Papers, reel 242, box 852.

21. "Proud of President's Handshake," *Washington Post,* January 29, 1922.

22. "President and Wife to Be Congressional Club Guests," *Washington Herald,* January 15, 1922.

23. See *New York Herald, New York Tribune, Washington Herald, Washington Post* coverage, January 13, 1921.

24. *Washington Post,* January 22, 1922; *New York Times,* January 20, 1922.

25. "Mrs. Harding, in Tacoma Today."

26. Here is a list of "Program of Receptions and Dinners, Season of 1921–22." The receptions began at 9:30 and the dinners at 8 P.M.

    December 15, Thursday, Cabinet Dinner.

    January 2, Monday, New Year's Reception.

    January 12, Thursday, Diplomatic Reception.

    January 19, Thursday, Diplomatic Dinner.

    January 26, Thursday, Judicial Reception.

    January 2, Thursday, Supreme Court Dinner.

    February 9, Thursday, Congressional Reception.

    February 16, Thursday, Speakers' Dinner.

    February 23, Thursday, Army and Navy Reception (postponed).

27. Dolly Madison's "Washington Letter," *Philadelphia Public Ledger,* January 15, 1922.

28. FKH to Charles Kling, October 18, 1921, FKH Papers, reel 242, box 581.

29. FKH Papers, reel 246, box 876.

30. "Many Tickets Sold for Charity Ball," *Washington Star,* January 7, 1922; Jean Elliot society column, *Washington Times,* January 9, 1922.

31. "Hardings Attend Ball for Garfield," *Washington Post,* January 26, 1922. The lyrics to Carrie Jacobs Bond's "The End of a Perfect Day" (1910) are as follows:

> When you come to the end of a perfect day,
> And you sit alone with your thought;
> While the chimes ring out with a carol gay
> For the joy that the day has brought,
> Do you think what the end of a perfect day
> Can mean to a tired heart
> When the sun goes down with a flaming ray
> And the dear friends have to part?
>
> Well this is the end of a perfect day,
> Near the end of a journey, too,
> But it leaves a thought that is big and strong
> With a wish that is kind and true.
> For memory has painted this perfect day
> With colors that never fade,
> And we find at the end of a perfect day
> The soul of a friend we've made.

32. "Expect President at Charity Ball," *Washington Star,* January 9, 1922.

33. See *Washington Star,* January 15, 1922.

34. Dolly Madison, "Washington Letter," *Philadelphia Public Ledger,* January 22, 1922.

35. FKH to Mrs. Scobey, January 26, 1922, Scobey Papers, box 3.

36. FKH to Lee, January 26, 1922; Lee to FKH, February 3, 1922, Lee Papers box 9/3.

37. "Mrs. Harding a Lady of Tact," "Her Vivacity a Foil for Her Husband's Conservatism," *Vancouver Daily Providence,* July 25, 1923.

38. Elizabeth Jaffray, *Secrets of the White House* (New York: Cosmopolitan Book, 1927), 90.

39. Irwin "Ike" Hood Hoover, *Forty Two Years in the White House* (Boston: Houghton Mifflin, 1934), 279.

40. Edmund W. Starling, *Starling of the White House: The Story of the Man Whose Secret Service Detail Guarded Five Presidents from Woodrow Wilson to Franklin D. Roosevelt,* as told to Thomas Sugrue (New York: Simon and Schuster, 1946), 166.

41. "Expert Calls These Most Beautiful Faces He Ever Saw," January 23, 1922, reel 245, box 866, #429.

42. Laszlo to Evalyn, June 21, 1921, Evalyn McLean Papers, box 24.

43. Francis Morris to FKH, August 28, 1921, First Ladies Library.

44. Suffrage had unleashed the energies of many internationalist women. Secretary Hughes twice hosted delegations from the Women's Committee for the Recognition of Russia, who wanted the United States to open diplomatic relations with the Bolsheviks in the early 1920s. See Katherine A. S. Siegel, "The Women's Committee for the Recognition of Russia: Progressives in an Age of 'Normalcy,'" *Peace and Change* 21 (July 1996): 289–317.

45. WGH to Mrs. Scobey, February 20, 1922, Scobey Papers, box 3. The conference's significance is questionable. By the end of the 1920s, new agreements were necessary because of the frequent violations of the tonnage rules set in 1922; however, the 1930 London naval conference's infamous "escalator clause" allowed for even more naval expansion.

46. FKH to Evalyn, February 8, 1922, FKH Papers, reel 242, box 851; "Society," *Washington Post,* March 26, 1922.

47. FKH to Evalyn, February 8, 1922, FKH Papers, reel 242, box 851.

48. *Washington Times,* February 8, 1922.

49. FKH to Esther Mezger, February 25, 1922, Esther Mezger Collection, First Ladies Library; FKH to Evalyn, February 8, 1922, FKH Papers, reel 245, box 842.

50. Daisy Fitzhugh Ayres, "President and Mrs. Harding Often Slip Out for Potluck," *Courier Journal*, January 22, 1922.

51. Kate Scott Brooks, "Diplomatic Reception a Mixed Fete," *Cleveland Plain Dealer*, January 22, 1922.

52. *New York Tribune*, February 28, 1922, reel 245, box 866, #398.

53. WGH to FKH, March 4, 1922, reel 242, box 851.

54. FKH to WGH, March 2, 1922, Lee Papers, box 9/3.

55. FKH to Mary Lee, March 6, 1922; Laura Harlan to Lee, March 24, 1922, Lee Papers, box 9/3; FKH to Mary Lee, July 6, 1921, Lee Papers, box 9/2.

56. "Mrs. Harding's Driving Costume," *Washington Post*, March 12, 1922.

57. "President's Wife Gives Wounded Soldier a 'Lift,'" March 1923, n.d., FKH Papers, reel 244, box 858.

58. FKH to Evalyn, March 20, 1922, Anthony Collection, First Ladies Library.

59. Dolly Madison's "Washington Letter," *Philadelphia Public Ledger*, April 22, 1922.

60. "President and Mrs. Harding Receive Popular Movie Folk," *Washington Star*, March 28, 1922; also see Dolly Madison's "Washington Letter," *Philadelphia Public Ledger*, April 9, 1922.

61. Lillian Gish, *The Movies, Mr. Griffith and Me* (Englewood Cliffs, N.J.: Prentice Hall, 1969), 246.

62. Boone Memoir Manuscript, 16:63–64.

63. Burl Noggle, "The Origins of the Teapot Dome Investigation," *Mississippi Valley Historical Review*, 44, no. 2 (September 1957): 262.

64. "Mrs. Harding Turns Sod for Big Magnolia Tree," *Washington Post*, March 30, 1922.

65. FKH to Lee, April 11, 1922, Lee Papers, box 9/3.

66. *Washington Post*, April 13, 1922.

67. "Hotel Manager and Employees Recall Incidents Connected with Visits of President Harding to Cincinnati," *Cincinnati Tribune*, August 3, 1923.

68. "Letter Saves His Life," no paper identified, May 12, 1922, reel 245, box 868.

69. FKH to Harvey, June 3, 1922, Anthony/Schermer Collection, First Ladies Library.

70. *Washington Times*, May 7, 1922, "Harding Begins Rest Today," Jean Elliot's society page, *Washington Times*, May 12, 1922; "Harding Breaks His Vacation to Talk Politics with Women," May 13, 1922, no paper identified, FKH Papers, reel 245, box 868.

71. FKH to Esther Mezger, May 11, 1922, Esther Mezger Collection, First Ladies Library; FKH to Christian Sr., June 19, 1922, Christian Papers, reel 249, box 892.

72. "Mrs. Harding Gets Ovation from Big Circus Audience," *Washington Herald*, May 16, 1922.

73. *Washington Post*, May 19, 1922.

74. See Robert H. Ferrell, *Grace Coolidge: The People's Lady in Silent Cal's White House* (Lawrence: University Press of Kansas, 2008), 81.

75. Nicholas Murray Butler, *Across the Busy Years: Recollections and Reflections*, 2 vols. (New York: Scribner's, 1939–1940), 1:335–336.

76. Abby Gunn Baker, "With the Hardings in the White House," *Christian Herald*, August 27, 1921.

77. Boone Memoir Manuscript, 27:5–6.

78. Clinton Wallace Gilbert, *Behind the Mirrors: The Psychology of Disintegration at Washington* (New York: G. P. Putnam's Sons, 1922), 183, 185; *New York Times*, June 8, 1922.

79. Dolly Madison's "Washington Letter," *Philadelphia Public Ledger*, June 25, 1922; Sallie V. H. Pickett's column, *Washington Star*, June 25, 1922.

80. *San Francisco Bulletin*, July 30, 1923.

81. "First Lady of the Land Loveable and Gentle," *Portland Oregonian*, July 5, 1922; also see Ann E. Burnette, "Florence Kling Harding: Bridging Traditional and Modern Rhetorical Roles," in *Inventing a Voice: The Rhetoric of American First Ladies of the Twentieth Century*, ed. Molly Meijer Wertheimer (Lanham, Md.: Rowman & Littlefield, 2004), 132–133. One of her letters is cited in "Mrs. Harding Is Grateful," *New York Times*, November 5, 1920. It was a letter to Mrs. Peter Zucker, president of the Women's Harding and Coolidge Club.

82. Kate Marcia Forbes, "The Real Mrs. Harding" series, *Washington Post*, January 22, 1922.

83. "A Glimpse of Mrs. Harding," *New York Times*, November 14, 1920.

84. "Death Comes Peacefully," *Marion Star*, November 21, 1924.

85. "Women of Fashion in Paris Now Sprinkle Hair with Diamond Dust to Make it Shine in Ballrooms," no paper identified, reel 245, box 866, #411.

86. Kate Forbes, "Home Life in the White House," *Washington Post*, January 8, 1922.

87. Jaffray, *Secrets of the White House*, 90.

88. Kate Marcia Forbes, "Mrs. Harding Is Very Fond of Dogs but Has Aversion for Peacock Feathers," *Washington Post*, January 22, 1922.

89. "Mrs. Harding, in Tacoma Today."

90. FKH to Esther Mezger, April 9, 1921, Esther Mezger Collection, First Ladies Library; *Marion Newslife*, May 5, 1980.

91. FKH to Esther Mezger, November 29, 1921, copy in author's possession.

92. FKH to Esther Mezger, May 31, 1922, quoted in *Marion Newslife* May 5, 1980, 27–28.

93. Forbes, "Home Life in the White House."

94. See May dress bills, June 5, 1922, reel 242, box 851.

95. *Washington Star*, March 4, 1923.

96. Fletcher to FKH, July 25, 1922, July 27, 1922, FKH Papers, reel 242, box 852.

97. FKH to Evalyn, February 8, 1922, reel 242, box 851.

98. See, for instance, O. S. Rapp to Hardings, July 18, September 14, 1921, Orlando S. Rapp Papers, Ohio State University, Columbus.

99. See, for instance, "One-Piece Gowns Again in Style; Bright Colors Prevail in First Spring Dresses of Silk and Satin," *Washington Post*, reel 246, box 874.

100. "Marshall Joffre Honored at the White House," *New York Herald*, April 23, 1922.

101. "She Dresses to Win," *New York Times* June 8, 2008, http://www.nytimes.com/2008/06/08/fashion/08michelle.html.

102. "Sway of First Lady's Scepter Is Supreme in White House," *Times Star Cincinnati*, January 30, 1923.

103. Ellery Chandler Hale to FKH, December 26, 1922, FKH Papers, reel 243, box 854.

104. On the Washington conference, see FKH Memo, n.d., FKH Papers, reel 243, box 855, frame 496. Also see her letter about "the relief of suffering in the Near East," FKH to Mrs. Cabot Stevens, March 29, 1921, FKH Papers, reel 244, box 858.

105. Quoted in *New York Times*, November 22, 1924.

106. Harding's veto in September 1922 of this bonus bill was overridden by Congress but sustained in the Senate. It was a highly unpopular move, and in 1924, Congress successfully passed a similar measure over Coolidge's veto, although it was not set to take effect until 1945. During 1932, at the height of the Depression, veterans marched for the bonus in front of the White House.

107. "Society Made Noteworthy by Brilliance and Variety," *Washington Star*, May 14, 1922; Harding to Christian Sr., June 1, 1921, "Christian Biography of Harding," box 892, reel 249, 179.

108. *Washington Times*, May 26, 1922, no article title; "Mrs. Harding to Entertain War Invalids," *Washington Post*, May 28, 1922, reel 245, box 868.

109. Jean Elliot society column, *Washington Times*, May 15, 1922.

110. Teddy Roosevelt Jr. diary in Teddy Roosevelt Jr. Papers, box 1, Library of Congress.

111. See *Washington Herald*, June 11, 1922, reel 245, box 868.

112. FKH to Weeks, March 15, 1921, First Ladies Library.

113. "Petition to Mrs. Harding," reel 243, box 855.

114. Stella Marks to FKH, August 4, 1922; FKH to Stella Marks, August 11, 1922, reel 242, box 852.

115. Mrs. Noblett to FKH, March 27, 1922; Florence to Mrs. Elizabeth Noblett, May 6, 1922, FKH Papers, reel 242, box 851.

116. FKH to Mrs. A. A. Carter, February 8, 1922, reel 242, box 851.

117. "3,500 Vets Ask Harding's Aid," *Chicago Daily* (name obscured), reel 242, box 851, #1217.

118. "Sawyer Told to Aid Veterans or Quit," *New York Times*, April 30, 1922.

119. Boone Memoir Manuscript, 27:44, 50; also see Boone diary entry, July 16, 1922. This was a "rotten business," said Boone; see diary entry, September 29, 1922, Boone Papers, box 40.

120. "Mrs. Harding Has an Unusual Lot of Pluck," no paper identified, reel 244, box 858, #79.

121. See Jennie R. Nichols of American Humane Education Society to FKH, March 4, 1922; FKH to Nichols, March 27, 1922, reel 242, box 851; FKH to Marion Thatcher Rankin, president of the Brockton (Mass.) Humane Society; April 4, 1922; FKH to Mrs. N. W. Baldwin of Sioux City, April 24, 1922; FKH Papers, reel 242, box 852. She also joined the Rockland County Society for the Prevention of Cruelty to Animals; see *Washington Star* August 29, 1922, FKH Papers, reel 242, box 851.

122. FKH to Mrs. Thomas E. Campbell, Phoenix, December 14, 1921, reel 242, box 851.

123. "Laddie Boy Gets Birthday Cake and Photographs from Home," *Washington Star*, July 25, 1922.

124. "Mrs. Harding, in Tacoma Today."

125. President Intercedes for Dog He Thought Court Ordered Shot," *Washington Star*, July 2, 1922; Telegram from Governor Sproul to FKH, June 30, 1922; "President Ready, and Governor, Too, to Save Dick's Life," July 2, 1922, FKH Papers, reel 242, box 852.

126. J. Jaccard to FKH, August 1, 1922, FKH to Dr. G. Myers, August 9, 1922; also see discussion in Carl Sferazza Anthony, *Florence Harding: The First Lady, the Jazz Age, and the Death of America's Most Scandalous President* (New York: Morrow, 1998), 366–367.

127. James W. Henry, Goldstar Kennels, to FKH, July 25, 1922, reel 242, box 852.

128. FKH to Mr. Henry O'Malley, Commission of Fish and Fisheries, Department of Commerce, June 3, 1922, reel 242, box 851.

129. Carolyn Votaw to FKH, FKH Papers, box 858, reel 242, #653.

130. Memorandum, "Project for Federal Prison for Women, Mt. Weather, Va.," reel 243, box 855, #724–730, n.d. Mt. Weather was also being considered as an industrial school for war veterans in 1920. See "School of Handicrafts, Art, Industries, and Civic Service," Mrs. J. H. Boggs to Ned McLean, April 30, 1920, McLean Papers, box 23.

131. "Memorandum in Regard to Project for Federal Prison for Women at Mt. Weather, Va.," FKH Papers, reel 242, box 858, #724. For further evidence of FKH's interest in this topic, see FKH Papers, box 858, reel 242, #800.

132. See reel 246, box 873, #650.

133. FKH to Mrs. Mary Tillinghast, November 21, 1921, reel 242, box 851, #324.

134. FKH to Mrs. Lorimer, April 10, 1922, FKH Papers, reel 242, box 851; much of this was expressed in an unsent letter.

135. *New York Tribune,* January 8, 1922.

136. FKH to Mrs. Arthur L. Livermore, President of Women's National Republican Club, January 13, 1922, FKH Papers, reel 242, box 851.

137. *Washington Herald,* January 13, 1922.

138. FKH telegram to Mrs. Medill McCormick, reel 242, box 851.

139. "Mrs. Harding Urges Loyalty to Party," *New York Herald,* January 15, 1922; "Forceful Letter Favoring GOP Read to National Republican Women," *New York Tribune,* January 15, 1922, FKH Papers, roll 244, box 863.

140. "Sane partisanship," the *Washington Post* favorably termed it; see paper of January 15, 1922; also see FKH to Mrs. Arthur L. Livermore, president of the Women's National Republican Club, January 13, 1922.

141. *Washington Post,* January 15, 1922.

142. "Women Divided on Party Loyalty," *Philadelphia Public Ledger,* January 18, 1922.

143. "Mrs. Harding to Greet Women Voters' League," *Philadelphia Public Ledger,* March 26, 1922.

144. FKH to Mrs. Chas. E. Broomfield, January 30, 1922, Mrs. Broomfield to FKH, January 18, 1922, FKH Papers, reel 244, box 865.

145. FKH to Mrs. Todd, January 25, 1923, First Ladies Library.

146. See Jennings to WGH, long letter, December–January 1922 (n.d.), Jennings Papers, box 1.

147. Mrs. George H. Lorimer to FKH, April 6, 1922, FKH Papers, reel 242, box 851.

{ *Notes to Pages 130–135* }

148. "Women Voters Visit Mrs. Harding," *Philadelphia Public Ledger,* March 24, 1922.

149. H. H. Kohlsaat to Florence, March 17, 1922, FKH to Kohlsaat, March 20, 1922, Thelma (no last name) to FKH, March 24, 1922, Mrs. George H. Lorimer to FKH, April 6, 1922, all in FKH Papers, reel 242, box 851.

150. FKH to Mrs. Kirby, February 7, 1922, reel 242, box 851.

151. Forbes, "Home Life in the White House."

152. *Daily Leader,* Pontiac, Ill., n.d., 1923, FKH Papers, reel 246, box 872.

153. FKH to Winnie Galloway Kirby, February 7, 1922, reel 242, box 851.

154. Harlan to Allen F. Moore, June 21, 1922, reel 242, box 851.

155. FKH Letter, n.d., reel 243, box 855, #855–856.

156. Harlan to Mr. ? (unreadable), August 19, 1922, reel 242, box 852.

157. FKH to Lee, May 3, 1921, May 30, 1921, Lee Papers, box 9/2.

158. WGH to Lee, March 25, 1922, Lee Papers, box 9/3.

159. Federal Prohibition director J. E. Russell to FKH, n.d., reel 242, box 852, #627.

160. Mary Wiggin to FKH, March 9, 1921; FKH to Mary Wiggin, March 29, 1921, First Ladies Library.

161. Nicholas Murray Butler to FKH, June 20, 1922, reel 242, box 851.

162. Hilles to FKH, July 15, 1922, FKH Papers, reel 242, box 852.

163. Office of the Postmaster, Philadelphia, Pennsylvania, to Miss C. Mattern, Secretary, White House, March 19, 1921, First Ladies Library.

164. "First Lady Aids Mother to Regain Her Truant Son," *Chicago Daily,* January 16? (date not clear), 1922, reel 244, box 862, #1217.

165. FKH to Georgia governor (late 1921–early 1922), n.d., FKH Harding Papers, roll 242 box 851, #1217ff.

166. Harry Dougherty to FKH, July 13, 1922, FKH Papers, reel 244, box 858.

167. "Mrs. Harding Intervenes for Boy Prisoners," *Washington Star,* March 27, 1922.

168. Nathan C. Miller, New York governor, to FKH, June 4, 1921 "acknowledg[ing] the receipt of your very courteous letter of the 25th of May," FKH Papers, reel 242, box 851.

169. Lee to FKH, July 19, 1921, Lee Papers box 9/2; FKH to Lee, January 26, 1922, June 16, 1922, Lee Papers box 9/3, 9/4.

170. FKH to Jim Prendergast, December 28, 1921, reel 242, box 851.

171. FKH to Mrs. Brink, June 24, 1922, reel 242, box 851.

172. "Redrafting Report on Pardon of Debs," reel 244, box 862, 244, #1006.

173. *Washington Herald,* January 16, 1922.

174. FKH to Mrs. Cabot Stevens, March 29, 1921, FKH Papers, reel 244, box 858.

175. Assistant Secretary to Mrs. W. W. Carrhuth, January 20, 1922, reel 242, box 851.

176. Rumpf to FKH, September 22, 1921, Mattern to Miss Rumpf, January 5, 1922, FKH Papers, reel 242, box 851.

177. "Harding Hospitality Undampened by Double Strike Emergency," *Washington Star,* July 16, 1922.

178. FKH to Lee, August 22, 1922, box 9/4.

179. Birch Helms to FKH, August 5, 1922, Dewey Hilles to FKH, August 1, 1922, reel 242, box 852.

180. See Fitzgerald to McLean (in Bar Harbor), July 17, 1922, McLean Papers, box 24; FKH to Moore, August 17, 1922, reel 242, box 852.

181. Jennings to WGH, July 11, 1922, Jennings Papers, box 1.

182. FKH to Harvey, June 3, 1922, First Ladies Library.

183. FKH to Esther Mezger, July 31, 1922, First Ladies Library.

184. FKH to Evalyn, June 24, 1922, First Ladies Library.

185. FKH to Lee, June 16, 1922, Lee Papers, box 9/4.

186. Lawler, "Hardings I Knew," 4:9.

187. Starling, *Starling of the White House,* 185.

188. *Washington Star,* July 6, 1922.

189. "The Joy of President and Mrs. Harding in Renewing Friendships at Marion Is Shared by the Nation," *Washington Star,* July 4, 1922.

190. FKH to Evalyn, July 30, 1922, postmarked July 31, 1922. Copy in author's possession.

191. FKH to Esther Mezger, June 4, 1922, First Ladies Library.

192. *Washington Times,* July 29, 1922.

193. Llewellys F. Barker to Evalyn Walsh McLean, July 31, 1922, McLean Papers, box 24.

194. Evalyn to FKH (July 1922), n.d., reel 243, box 855; FKH to Evalyn Walsh McLean, July 28, 1922, reel 242, box 852.

195. FKH to Harlan, July 31, 1922, reel 242, box 852.

196. FKH to Emmie, July 17, 1922, reel 245, box 868.

197. Forbes, "Real Mrs. Harding" series.

198. Harlan, Daily Log, April 29, 1922–July 12, 1922; FKH to Esther Mezger, June 4, 1922, July 30, 1922, Esther Mezger Collection, First Ladies Library.

199. FKH to Esther Mezger, July 31, 1922, First Ladies Library.

200. FKH to Esther Mezger, July 30, 1922, Esther Mezger Collection, First Ladies Library.

201. "As Dolly Madison Sees It: Washington as a Summer Resort," *Philadelphia Public Ledger,* July 16, 1922.

202. Dolly Madison, "Political Affairs Engage the Capital," *Philadelphia Public Ledger,* August 27, 1922.

203. FKH to Esther Mezger, August 26, 1922, First Ladies Library.

204. FKH to Esther Mezger, August 24, 1922; FKH to Esther Mezger, August 19, 1922, letters in author's possession.

205. Teddy Roosevelt Jr. diary in Teddy Roosevelt Jr. Papers, box 1.

206. Boone Memoir Manuscript, 27:51–52; Boone diary entry, August 26, 1922.

207. "Mrs. Harding Is Critically Ill, Recovery Held 'Not Assured,' Noted Specialists Summoned," *New York Tribune,* September 9, 1922.

CHAPTER 5: CRISIS AND CONVALESCENCE

1. See, e.g., *Washington Times,* September 1, 1922.

2. FKH to Evalyn, September 6, 1922, First Ladies Library, Canton, Ohio.

3. Joel Boone Memoir Manuscript, 27:51, 54, Boone Papers, box 45, Library of Congress, Washington, D.C.; Boone diary entry, September 7, 1922, Boone Papers, box 40, Library of Congress.

4. See "Mrs. Harding's Condition Regarded as Desperate," *Washington Star,* September 9, 1922; "Turn for Worse Follows Fairly Restful Night"; "The Decision to Operate Awaits Arrival of Dr. Mayo."

5. Boone Memoir Manuscript, 20:96.

6. Kathleen Lawler, "The Hardings I Knew," unpublished manuscript, in Ohio Historical Society, Columbus, Ohio, foreword.

7. As Miss Harlan described it in the appointment book, this day began a "crisis" in the White House. Even so, the president received Dr. Rikitare Fujisawa, a lecturer in math and political economy at Japan's imperial academy, at the White House on the 8th. See Laura Harlan, "Life in the White House," Daily Log, July 13, 1922–December 31, 1922 in "The End of a Perfect Day: The Life of Florence Kling Harding (1860–1924), The White House Appointment Books," unpublished manuscript, First Ladies Library.

8. Boone diary entry, September 11, 1922.

9. Boone Memoir Manuscript, 27:56; Boone diary entry, September 8, 1922.

10. Harry New replaced Bill Hays as postmaster in March 1922, when Hayes became head of the National Association of Motion Picture Producers and Distributors of America. "Mrs. Harding Gravely Ill; Specialists Are Called," *Washington Post,* September 9, 1922; "Mrs. Harding Critically Ill after Relapse," *Washington Herald,* September 9, 1922.

11. *New York Times*, September 12, 1922.

12. Boone Memoir Manuscript, 27:57.

13. Ibid., 27:58.

14. "Mrs. Harding's Condition More Encouraging, but Still Declared Critical," *Washington Herald*, September 10, 1922; Boone diary entry, September 9, 1922.

15. Boone Memoir Manuscript, 27:92.

16. "Mrs. Harding's Fever Down; Still in Crisis," *New York Tribune*, September 11, 1922; "Mrs. Harding Still Holding Her Own in Fight for Life," *Washington Star*, September 10, 1922; Boone Memoir Manuscript, 27:59.

17. "Mrs. Harding Shows Slight Improvement," *New York Tribune*, September 10, 1922.

18. Lawler, "Hardings I Knew," 4:7.

19. Joe Mitchell Chapple, "The Will to Live that Won," *National Magazine*, 1923 (n.d.), reel 246, box 673.

20. See *New York Times*, January 18, 1923.

21. Boone Memoir Manuscript, 27:63a.

22. "Mrs. Harding Still in Critical State; Shows Slight Gain," *New York Times*, September 10, 1922.

23. "Mrs. Harding's Condition More Encouraging."

24. *New York World*, September 11, 1922.

25. "Mrs. Harding Shows Much Improvement," *Washington Post*, September 12, 1922.

26. "Mrs. Harding Grows Worse as Fever Sets In; Wilson Calls," *New York World*, September 10, 1922.

27. "Mrs. Harding Still Holding Her Own."

28. *New York Times*, September 12, 1922.

29. Boone Memoir Manuscript, 27:60.

30. Lawler, "Hardings I Knew," 5:5.

31. Boone Memoir Manuscript, 27:62.

32. Kathleen Lawler, Florence's assistant, gave Sawyer full credit as the only doctor who opposed an operation as well as saving Florence's life. See Lawler, "Hardings I Knew," 5:4. On her volatile condition, see other articles, including "Mrs. Harding Still Holding Her Own"; "Mrs. Harding Is Still in Critical Condition," *Washington Post*, September 10, 1922; "Mrs. Harding's Fever Down"; "Mrs. Harding Still in Critical State, Her Physicians Say," *New York Tribune*, September 10, 1922; and "President's Wife Steadily Gaining against Illness," *Philadelphia Public Ledger*, September 12, 1922.

33. "Mrs. Harding Keeps Improving Steadily," *New York Herald*, September 12, 1922.

34. "Fever Drops," *Washington Herald*, September 12, 1922.

35. "Defer Operation as Mrs. Harding Regains Strength," *Washington Star*, September 11, 1922.

36. WGH to Chapple, September 14, 1922, quoted in Joe Mitchell Chapple, *Life and Times of Warren G. Harding, Our After-War President* (Boston: Chapple Publishing, 1924), 144.

37. See "Church People in Home Town Pray for Mrs. Harding to Live," *New York Tribune*, September 11, 1922; "All Marion Hopes for Mrs. Harding" *Washington Post*, September 11, 1922.

38. See, e.g., "Mrs. Harding's Condition Regarded as Desperate," *Washington Star*, September 9, 1922; "Mrs. Harding Critically Ill after Relapse."

39. *Philadelphia Public Ledger*, September 12, 1922, quoted in Carl Sferazza Anthony, *Florence Harding: The First Lady, the Jazz Age, and the Death of America's Most Scandalous President* (New York: Morrow, 1998), 377.

40. "Mrs. Taft Taken Ill," *Washington Post*, May 18, 1909; "Mrs. Taft's Health Better," *Washington Post*, July 9, 1909; I am indebted to Lewis Gould for these citations.

41. "Mrs. Harding Is Critically Ill, Recovery Held 'Not Assured,' Noted Specialists Summoned," *New York Tribune*, September 9, 1922.

42. See May Warner, "Prayer of All the People of the United States for the Wife of Their Chief Magistrate," reel 242, box 855.

43. "Mrs. Harding Shows Solicitude from Comfort of Her Physicians," *Washington Post*, September 10, 1922.

44. "Mrs. Harding Still in Critical State; Shows Slight Gain"; "Mrs. Harding Shows Slight Improvement."

45. "Mrs. Harding's Condition More Encouraging"; "Mrs. Harding Grows Worse as Fever Sets In; Wilson Calls."

46. "Science Rushes to Help President Save Wife's Life," *Washington Post*, September 11, 1922.

47. *Washington News*, September 9, 1922.

48. *Philadelphia Public Ledger*, September 12, 1922.

49. *Philadelphia Public Ledger*, September 9, 1922; *Washington News*, September 9, 1922.

50. "Mrs. Harding Shows Slight Improvement"; "Mrs. Harding Still in Critical State, Her Physicians Say," *Philadelphia Public Ledger*, September 10, 1922; "Mrs. Harding Fights against Great Odds; Operation Possible," *New York Herald*, September 10, 1922.

51. *Washington Post*, September 11, 1922.

52. "Mrs. Harding Keeps Improving Steadily."

53. "Mrs. Harding Shows Much Improvement."

54. "Mrs. Harding Keeps Improving Steadily."

55. *New York Times*, September 12, 1922.

56. WGH to Christian Sr., January 29, 1923, Christian Papers, box 892.

57. Boone Memoir Manuscript, 27:72, 73.

58. Boone diary entry, September 26, 1922.

59. Laura Harlan to Mrs. Woods, September 30, 1922, James Woods Papers, MS 88, box 1, Ohio Historical Society.

60. Boone Memoir Manuscript, 27:76, 78.

61. "To the Delight of Tourists, Mrs. Harding from Her Sick Bed Orders Lower Floor of White House Thrown Open to Them," *Washington Star*, October 1, 1922.

62. *Washington Post*, October 4, 1922.

63. FKH to Evalyn Walsh McLean, October 25, 1922, McLean Papers, Library of Congress, box 24.

64. Boone Memoir Manuscript, 21:82–83.

65. Boone Memoir Manuscript, 27:84–90 passim; Boone diary entry, November 13, 1922.

66. WGH to Lee, November 9, 1922, Lee Papers, box 9/4.

67. See Boone Memoir Manuscript, 27:88, Evalyn to FKH, November 22, 1922, reel 242, box 851.

68. Boone Memoir Manuscript, 27:89.

69. George Christian Sr., "Biography of Warren G. Harding," George B. Christian Sr. Papers, Outgoing Correspondence, 1918–1923, in Harding Papers, Ohio Historical Society, reel 249, box 892, p. 193B.

70. Laura Harlan to Mark Sullivan, December 6, 1922, Mark Sullivan Papers, box 3, Library of Congress.

71. Boone Memoir Manuscript, 27:91–94; Boone diary entry, December 7 and 8, 1922.

72. FKH to Esther Mezger, postmarked December 19, 1922, copy in author's possession; Boone Memoir Manuscript, 27:95.

73. Mary Hutchins Drake to FKH, n.d., reel 243, box 855, #398–401; FKH to Esther Mezger, January 4, 1923.

74. Boone Memoir Manuscript, 27:108.

75. WGH to Evalyn, January 1, 1923, First Ladies Library.

76. FKH to Evalyn, January 13, 1923, Anthony Collection, First Ladies Library.

77. FKH to Esther Mezger, January 17, 1923, Esther Mezger Collection, First Ladies Library.

78. Harlan to Lawler, January 20, 1923; Lawler to Harlan, January 23, 1923; Harlan to Lawler, January 30, 1923, First Ladies Library.

79. FKH to Ada Denman (Mrs. J. H. Denman), January 17, 1923, First Ladies Library.

80. Edmund W. Starling, *Starling of the White House: The Story of the Man Whose Secret Service Detail Guarded Five Presidents from Woodrow Wilson to Franklin D. Roosevelt*, as told to Thomas Sugrue (New York: Simon and Schuster, 1946), 189.

81. FKH notes in bond book, WGH Papers, box 385, Ohio Historical Society.

82. FKH notes in bond book, WGH Papers, box 385.

83. Boone Memoir Manuscript, 27:113–114; Boone diary entry, January 18, 1923.

84. Boone Memoir Manuscript, 27:115.

85. Edythe Tate Thompson to FKH, December 29, 1922, reel 242, box 852.

86. "Plundering the Wounded Men: The Sordid Story of the Veterans' Bureau, which Forbes Was Chosen to Manage as a Sacred Trust," *World's Work*, June 1924, from Anthony Collection, First Ladies Library.

87. *Philadelphia Record*, January 28, 1923.

88. Boone Memoir Manuscript, 27:116.

89. Earlier, Forbes had deserted from the Signal Corps, and he may not have been entirely stable. The bureau staffer told Laura Harlan the White House should effect "the immediate hospitalization of Col. Forbes. He is certainly a sick man and this Bureau is not the place for him at this time." See Office of the Director, United States Veterans Bureau, to Miss Laura Harlan, January 15, 1923, reel 242, box 853.

90. Boone Memoir Manuscript, 27:117–120.

91. Ibid., 27:120–121.

92. FKH to Evalyn, January 22, 1923, reel 243, box 854.

93. FKH to Evalyn, February 5, 1923, FKH to Mrs. Todd, January 25, 1923, FKH Papers, reel 243, box 855.

94. *Philadelphia Public Ledger*, December 21, 1922.

95. FKH to Evalyn, February 5, 1923, reel 243, box 855.

96. Evalyn to FKH, February 25, 1923, Anthony Collection, First Ladies Library. Also see Evalyn to FKH, January 17, 1923, reel 243, box 854.

97. Evalyn hadn't been well herself. See telegram from Cissy (McCormick) to Evalyn, February 16, 1923. On February 23, 1923, Evalyn wrote Cammilla Lippincott, "I am beginning to feel a little better." Evalyn McLean Papers, box 24.

98. Catherine to Evelyn, February 23, 1923, Anthony Collection, First Ladies Library.

99. Boone diary entry, February 20, 1923.

100. "Mrs. Harding, Though Ill, Always Potent Influence Aiding President's Work," *Philadelphia Public Ledger*, August 3, 1923.

101. Boone Memoir Manuscript, 27:124.

102. Warren G. Harding, "Obituary notices, editorial comment, etc., clippings chiefly from Ohio newspapers," vol. 1, 1923, Ohio Historical Society.

103. WGH to Mary E. Lee, February 20, 1923, Lee Papers, box 9/5.

104. FKH to Aunt Nellie, February 13, 1923.

105. Jean Elliot, "Congress Off, Capital Faces Quiet Summer," *Washington Times*, February 11, 1923.

106. FKH to Evelyn, February 17, 1923.

107. Letter to Mrs. Jennings, February 21, 1923; *Philadelphia Public Ledger*, "Mrs. Harding Out after Five Months," February 13, 1923.

108. "Sway of First Lady's Scepter Is Supreme in White House," *Times Star Cincinnati*, January 30, 1923.

109. See *Christian Union Herald*, May 1, 1923. The paper reported, "She has told her intimate friends that while she was lying near the border line, the thought that so many thousands of so many creeds—the rich and the poor, the educated and the unlettered—were offering up their prayers was an inspiration for her to make the supreme effort."

110. Joe Mitchell Chapple, "The Will to Live that Won," *National Magazine*, [1923] (n.d.), reel 246, box 673.

111. See Edna M. Colman, *White House Gossip: From Andrew Johnson to Calvin Coolidge* (Garden City, N.Y.: Doubleday, Page, 1927), 387-388. Jean Elliot, "Mrs. Harding Gives Tea for Press Women," *Washington Times*, n.d., reel 246, box 872, #689; "Women Writers Glimpse White House Sanctums," *New York Herald*, March 4, 1923; "President's Wife Demonstrates Recovery by Re-entry in Public Affairs and Reception at WH," *New York Evening World*, February 26, 1923.

112. In 1921, Congress was in session through the summer at Harding's behest, with a break only from August 24 to September 21. There was then an extra session until November 23, and then a second session for the new Congress, which ran December 5 to September 22, 1922. A final, third session was called on November 20, which lasted until March 1923.

113. See *Washington Post*, March 18, 1923.

114. *Marion Star*, March 6, 1923.

115. FKH to Esther Mezger, February 28, 1923, Esther Mezger Collection, First Ladies Library.

116. Evalyn to FKH, February 1923, n.d., reel 243, box 854.

117. Boone Memoir Manuscript, 28:5, 8.

118. Boone Memoir Manuscript, 28:10–12.

119. Jean Downey to Mrs. Harding, March 12, 1923; Mrs. Harriet M. Christian to FKH, March 10, 1923, reel 242, box 853.

120. *Washington Post*, March 9 and 11, 1923.

121. Boyden Sparks interview, oral history of Mrs. McLean, BLS 511, First Ladies Library.

122. Evalyn Walsh McLean with Boyden Sparkes, *Father Struck It Rich* (Boston: Little Brown, 1936), 380–383; see also Boyden Sparkes interview, oral history of Mrs. McLean, BLS 511, First Ladies Library.

123. Christian, "Biography of Harding," 185. Rumors have persisted that Harding carried on in a "little White House" on I Street with Harry Daugherty and Jess Smith, dealing in poker, women, and booze, but they are just that—rumors. No compelling evidence has been produced to confirm Harding's carousing at this address.

124. Evalyn to FKH, February 1923, n.d., reel 243, box 854.

125. Evalyn to FKH, January/February 1923 (n.d.), reel 243, box 855. When Florence was sick, Evalyn wrote, "I'm so glad you are feeling better this week. I don't think you realize, dear Mrs. H, how much I miss you." See her letter, reel 243, box 854, #695–698.

126. George Lorimer to Boyden Sparkes, June 17, 1935; Sparkes to Lorimer, June 10, 1935, Scaife to Evalyn, June 7, 1935, Evalyn to Lorimer, June 11, 1935, Charles Baker to Scaife, June 15, 1935, Baker and Graeme Lorimer conversation, June 10, 1935, all in Hope Ridings Miller Papers, box 2, Library of Congress.

127. Boone Memoir Manuscript, 28:11–12.

128. Ibid., 28:13.

129. Ibid., 28:21.

130. *New York Times*, March 14, 1923.

131. *Washington Post*, March 18, 1923. "Mrs. Harding Is Ordered to Take Rest," *Washington Times*, March 21, 1923.

132. *Washington Star*, March 26, 1923.

133. *Florida Times Union*, March 31, 1923.

134. Edith C. Dunton interview, March 12, 1923, in FKH Papers, reel 242, box 853.

135. FKH to Esther Mezger, February 28 and March 27, 1923, Esther Mezger Collection, First Ladies Library.

136. "Field Now Cleared for Harding in 1924; Johnson Not to Run," *New York Times,* February 11, 1923.

137. Boone Memoir Manuscript, 28:30.

138. Boone Memoir Manuscript, 28:39–40; WGH to Jennings, April 16, 1923, Jennings Papers, box 1.

139. See, e.g., *Miami Herald,* April 1, 1923. WGH gave this old house to his nephews—sons of George T. Harding Jr.

140. Daugherty to Florence, April 11, 1923, FKH Papers, reel 243, box 853.

141. *Washington Times,* March 23, 1923; *Washington Star,* May 2, 1923.

142. WGH to Jennings, April 16, 1923, Jennings Papers, box 1.

143. FKH to Mrs. Jennings, April 11, 1923, reel 243, box 853.

144. FKH to Mrs. Knox, April 18, 1923, reel 243, box 853.

145. FKH to Esther Mezger, April 1923 (n.d.), letter in author's possession.

146. FKH to Esther, May 25, 1923, letter in author's possession.

147. "Mrs. Harding's 'First' Day Is Busy," *Cosmopolitan News Service,* reel 246, box 873, #651.

148. FKH Papers, Clippings, April 1923, n.d., reel 246, box 873, #650; Lawler, "Hardings I Knew," 1:4.

149. *Washington Herald,* May 3, 1923.

150. FKH to Wrigley, April 26, 1923, Wrigley to FKH, April 20, 1923, and undated April letter, all in reel 243, box 853. Wrigley had hoped to see them at Catalina Island on their West Coast trip.

151. Boone diary entry, May 11, 1923.

152. Reel 243, box 853, #642.

153. *Washington Post,* May 6, 1923.

154. *Philadelphia Record,* n.d., reel 246, box 876, #1165ff.

155. *Washington Star,* May 3, 1923.

156. Boone Memoir Manuscript, 28:52a–54.

157. Ibid., 20:162.

158. Mrs. Todd to FKH, May 12 and 16, 1923, reel 243, box 853.

159. FKH to Esther Mezger, May 27, 1923, Esther Mezger Collection, First Ladies Library. See also Dolly Madison's "Washington Letter," *Philadelphia Public Ledger,* June 17, 1923.

160. Boone Memoir Manuscript, 28:69–72.

161. Daugherty was never found guilty of any crime, but his management of the Justice Department came under sharp scrutiny in the early Coolidge

administration, when the president asked him to resign. He did, with "a heavy heart and a feeling of disappointment." See David Lawrence, "Resignation Seen as Aid to Party; Elimination of Daugherty Is Termed Ending of 'Intolerable Situation,'" March 28, 1924, in Boone Memoir Manuscript, 21:143–144.

162. See *Washington Star* and *Washington Times*, June 1, 1923.

163. In the summer of 1919, an army convoy had taken two months to travel from Washington to San Francisco; its members determined that "weak" bridges and wet dirt roads made travel impossible; sand in the desert also was treacherous. Moreover, "economic development, as well as the national security, required the construction of a comprehensive system of national highways," the army declared. So in June 1920, Congress created a Zero Milestone to begin the process. The milestone, located south of the Ellipse, was unveiled on June 4, 1923, as the "point for the measurement of distances from Washington on Highways of the United States." See *Washington Herald*, June 5, 1923.

164. *Washington Herald, Washington Post*, June 6, 1923; *Philadelphia Public Ledger*, June 10, 1923.

165. See "Mrs. Harding Salutes Each Flag in Parade," *Washington Post*, June 7, 1923.

166. "White House Party for Ohio Shriners," *Washington Post*, June 7, 1923; *Philadelphia Public Ledger*, June 10, 1923.

167. *Wilmington Evening Journal*, June 11, 1923.

168. "Presidential Party Reaches Capital," *Washington Star*, June 11, 1923.

169. "Mrs. Harding Tests Strength by Staying up til 2 in the Morning," *Washington Post*, June 12, 1923.

170. See FKH to Esther Mezger, June 13, 1923, Esther Mezger Collection, First Ladies Library.

CHAPTER 6: CROSSING THE COUNTRY

1. *Kansas City Journal*, June 22, 1923.

2. FKH to Evalyn, June 19, 1923, Anthony Collection, First Ladies Library.

3. William Allen White, "A Common Man on an Uncommon Job," *New York Tribune*, March 1, 1923. The paper was sold to Louis H. Brush and Roy D. Moore on June 20, 1923.

4. FKH to Louis Brush, January 1, 1924, reel 243, box 854.

5. Gaston B. Means, *The Strange Death of President Harding: From the Diaries of Gaston B. Means, a Department of Justice Investigator* (New York: Guild, 1930), 249–253.

6. Edmund W. Starling, *Starling of the White House: The Story of the Man Whose Secret Service Detail Guarded Five Presidents from Woodrow Wilson to Franklin D. Roosevelt*, as told to Thomas Sugrue (New York: Simon and Schuster, 1946), 195–196.

7. Stacy A. Cordery, *Alice: Alice Roosevelt Longworth, from White House Princess to Washington Power Broker* (New York: Viking, 2007), 300.

8. Herbert Hoover, *The Memoirs of Herbert Hoover: The Cabinet and the Presidency* (New York: Macmillan, 1952), 49.

9. Plans were made to speak and or stop in the following cities before embarking for Alaska:

    St. Louis, June 21

    Kansas City, June 22

    Hutchinson, Kansas, June 23

    Denver, June 25

    Cheyenne, Wyoming, June 25

    Ogden and Salt Lake, June 26

    Cedar City and Zion Park, Utah, June 27

    Pocatello and Idaho Falls, June 28

    Butte and Helena, Montana, June 29

    Yellowstone National Park and Spokane, July 2

    Meacham, trail anniversary celebration, and Pendleton, Oregon, July 3

    Portland, July 4

    Tacoma, July 5

In Alaska, the party would visit Juneau, Skagway, Anchorage, Seward, and Fairbanks, as well as many other spots, leaving from Sitka, July 22

    He would then visit Vancouver, July 26

    Seattle, July 27

    San Francisco, July 30

    Los Angeles, August 1

    San Diego, August 4

Speeches included "Service Is the One Great Ideal," to the St. Louis Rotary International Convention, June 21, 1923; "Fraternity among Nations," on the back of a train platform in Colorado Springs at 6:55 A.M., June 24, 1923; and "Social Justice, Women and Labor," June 29, 1923, at the Shriner's Hall in Helena.

10. Starling, *Starling of the White House*, 195–196.

11. *Marion Star*, July 6, 1923; also see "President Faces Alaskan Storm," *New York World*, May 12, 1923.

12. "Harding Cuts Cross-Country Speaking Tour," *New York Tribune*, May 11, 1923.

13. Boone diary entries, program for August 6–August 28, 1923, Boone Papers, box 40, Library of Congress.

14. Kathleen Lawler, "The Hardings I Knew," unpublished manuscript, in Ohio Historical Society, Columbus, Ohio, 30:3.

15. *Denver News,* June 25, 1923.

16. "Harding and First Lady Are Idolized by Pullman Attendants," *Denver Post,* June 25, 1923.

17. "President Has Friendly Word for Everyone," *Pocatello Tribune,* June 28, 1923.

18. The following support staff joined them: Mr. Richard Jervis, head of the Secret Service, and nine other Secret Service men; eight trainmen, including communications men; nurse Ruth Powderly, maid Catherine Wynne, and valet Arthur Brooks; a number of secretaries for the Cabinet, including Mr. Bain, secretary to Secretary Wallace; Mr. Donald, for Secretary Work; and Mr. Mullendore, for Secretary Hoover. Newspapers represented included *New York Times, New York World, New York Tribune, New York Post, Chicago Tribune, Boston Post, St. Louis Post-Dispatch, Los Angeles Times, Detroit News, Denver Post, Spokane Chronicle,* and *Seattle Times.* Joe Mitchell Chapple from *National Magazine,* a friend of the Hardings, also came along. There were a total of twenty-nine journalists on the trip, including seven photographers; more information is in Boone Papers, box 29.

19. *Anaconda Standard,* June 30, 1923.

20. *Kansas City Journal Post,* June 22, 1923; Joel Boone Memoir Manuscript, 19:40e, Boone Papers, box 45, Library of Congress, Washington, D.C. The *Idaho Falls Post* noted that "Mrs. Harding feels safer with scouts," June 28, 1923.

21. *Kansas City Journal Post,* June 22, 1923.

22. Boone Memoir Manuscript, 19:10; also see Emma Fall letter, June 20, 1931, in Christian Papers, reel 249, box 894.

23. "K.C. Accepts 'First Lady' as 'All Right,' " *KC Journal Post,* June 22, 1923.

24. "Wheat Growing—Executive Learns Why Many of Them Are Discontented," *Denver Post,* June 24, 1923.

25. "President Deplores Digging for Dollars as Sordid Tendency," *Denver News,* June 25, 1923.

26. "President Spends Sunday Obtaining Much Needed Rest," *Denver Post,* June 25, 1923.

27. Frances Wayne, "Father Time Stands Still for Mrs. Warren G. Harding When It Comes to Looks," *Denver Post*, June 25, 1923.

28. See Boone Memoir Manuscript, 19:40d/e.

29. *Anaconda Standard,* June 30, 1923.

30. Wayne, "Father Time Stands Still."

31. Boone Memoir Manuscript, 19:14. Despite the timing, there was no evidence that the journalists' deaths were caused by drinking.

32. *New York Times,* June 29, 1923. Although he had always supported the Volstead Act as a law-abiding senator and president, "To his very close and intimate friends, however, he gave vent to his pessimistic doubts and fears for the future of the cause of absolute Prohibition," but then before Alaska, he became committed to it. See George Christian Sr., "Biography of Warren G. Harding," 189, George B. Christian Sr. Papers, Outgoing Correspondence, 1918–1923, in Harding Papers, Ohio Historical Society, reel 249, box 892.

33. Elizabeth Jaffray, *Secrets of the White House* (New York: Cosmopolitan Book, 1927), 84.

34. Alice Roosevelt Longworth, *Crowded Hours* (New York: Scribner's, 1933), 314.

35. *Iron City Record,* Cedar City, Utah, June 29, 1923.

36. Boone Memoir Manuscript, 19:24–26.

37. FKH, June 25, 1923.

38. Boone Memoir Manuscript, 19:27.

39. *Daily Post,* June 29, 1923.

40. Florence Davies, "Our First Lady," manuscript written around July 23, 1923, and sent to Florence. FKH Papers, reel 246, box 876.

41. Boone Memoir Manuscript, 19:30.

42. *Spokane Press,* July 2, 1923.

43. "Hundreds Shake Harding's Hand," *Spokane Spokesman-Review,* July 3, 1923; "President and Wife Gracious," *Tacoma Times,* July 5, 1923.

44. "First Lady of the Land Loveable and Gentle," *Portland Oregonian,* July 5, 1923.

45. "Welcome Given to President by City," *Portland Oregonian,* July 5, 1923.

46. *Portland Oregonian,* July 5, 1923.

47. "Secret Service Men Keep Eye on Woman Fanatic," *Portland Journal,* July 4, 1923.

48. Boone Memoir Manuscript, 19:40c.

49. "First Lady of the Land Loveable and Gentle." According to T. J. Ritter's *Mother's Remedies: Over One Thousand Tried and Tested Remedies from*

Mothers of the United States and Canada (http://www.oldtimeremedies.co.uk/2008/03/croup-coal-oil-turpentine-and-snuff.html), "A little coal oil and a few drops of turpentine soaked up by snuff, and used as plaster [m]akes the child sneeze after a few minutes. The poultice loosens the phlegm and the sneezing throws it off."

50. "Welcome Given to President by City," *Portland Oregonian*, July 5, 1923.

51. *Portland Journal*, July 4, 1923.

52. Boone Memoir Manuscript, 19:40a.

53. Malcolm Jennings, "A Journey and Its Ending: An Address before the Rotary Club, Columbus, Ohio," September 11, 1923, in *Rotarian*, November 1923.

54. *Tacoma Tribune*, July 5, 1923.

55. Boone Memoir Manuscript, 19:38–39.

56. Ibid., 19:50.

57. *Vancouver Daily Providence*, July 25, 1923.

58. *Anchorage Times*, July 14, 1922.

59. Jas. G. Steese to FKH, January 9, 1924, reel 243, box 854.

60. Boone Memoir Manuscript, 19:71a.

61. *New York Times*, November 22, 1924; Boone Memoir Manuscript, 19:72–75.

62. Boone Memoir Manuscript, 20:163–164.

63. Joe Mitchell Chapple, *Life and Times of Warren G. Harding, Our After-War President* (Boston: Chapple Publishing, 1924), esp. chap. 29, "The Last Transcontinental Journey"; also *New York Times*, November 22, 1924.

64. Boone Memoir Manuscript, 19:75.

65. Ibid., 19:113–114.

66. *Vancouver Daily World*, July 26, 28, 1923.

67. Boone Memoir Manuscript, 19:106–107.

68. Ibid., 19:113–114.

69. WGH to Scobey; January 4, 1921, Scobey Papers, box 3.

70. See Emma Fall letter, June 20, 1931, in Christian Papers, reel 249, box 894.

71. Starling, *Starling of the White House*, 178.

72. Boone Memoir Manuscript, 20:3.

73. *Seattle Daily Times*, July 27, 1923.

74. "The President Gains," *Evening Record* (no city identified; Boston?), August 2, 1923.

75. Lawler, "Hardings I Knew," 30:3a.

76. Boone Memoir Manuscript, 20:165.

77. "Work Praises President for Cheerfulness," *San Francisco Chronicle*, July 31, 1923.

78. "Harding Fete Plans Stand," *San Francisco Chronicle*, January 29, 1923.
79. Boone Memoir Manuscript, 20:26.
80. Ibid., 21:70, 71.
81. Ibid., 20:35.
82. "Work Praises President for Cheerfulness."
83. "Oxygen Tanks Reported Taken to Sick Room for Emergency Case," *San Francisco Chronicle*, July 31, 1923.
84. *Riverside Press*, July 31, 1923.
85. "President Cheered by Mrs. Harding," *Portland Oregonian*, July 31, 1923.
86. "President Regular Fellow; He Never Gets Peeved Says Waiter Who Serves," *Riverside Daily Press*, August 2, 1923.
87. "President Cheered by Mrs. Harding," *Portland Oregonian*, July 31, 1923; "First Lady of Land Denies Self to San Francisco Admirers as She Nurses Famed Husband," *San Francisco Chronicle*, July 30, 1923.
88. "First Lady of Land Receives Group in Hall," *San Francisco Chronicle*, July 31, 1923.
89. Ibid.
90. "Sister Says President Cheerful," *Santa Ana Register*, August 2, 1923.
91. *Riverside Daily Press*, August 2 and 3, 1923.
92. See, e.g., *Oakland Tribune*, August 2, 1923; *Salt Lake Tribune*, August 2, 1923; *San Bernardino County Sun*, August 2, 1923.
93. *Oakland Tribune*, August 2, 1923.
94. "President Continues to Gain Slowly," *San Francisco Examiner*, August 2, 1923; Boone Memoir Manuscript, 20:47.

CHAPTER 7: HARDING'S DEATH AND ITS AFTERMATH

1. *Salt Lake Tribune*, August 3, 1923.
2. "Harding Slowly Fighting Way to Strength," *Glendale Press*, August 2, 1923; "President Continues to Gain Slowly," *San Francisco Examiner*, August 2, 1923. Harding thought he was leaving even sooner; his wife kept the real story from him.
3. Kathleen Lawler, "The Hardings I Knew," unpublished manuscript, in Ohio Historical Society, Columbus, Ohio, 30:4.
4. See Jennings Collection, reel 261, box 1.
5. Joel Boone Memoir Manuscript, 20:51, Boone Papers, box 45, Library of Congress, Washington, D.C.
6. This is nearly always cited as Harding's reading material, but Boone suggests it was instead a piece about Henry Ford in the *Dearborn Independent*.
7. Boone Memoir Manuscript, 20:52.

8. Ibid., 20:53, 54; see also *New York Times*, August 5, 1923.

9. Boone Memoir Manuscript, 20:55.

10. "Mrs. Harding Is Facing Greatest Ordeal in Calm: Former First Lady Takes Personal Charge of Train Journey," *Deseret News*, August 3, 1923; also see *Fresno Bee*, August 3, 1923.

11. *Salt Lake Tribune*, August 3, 1923.

12. Quoted in *Marion Star*, August 3, 1923; also see *San Francisco Bulletin*, August 3, 1923, and *San Francisco Chronicle*, August 3, 1923.

13. See *Weekly Democratic Gazette* (McKinney, Texas), August 1923, n.d., reel 247, box 881.

14. Zanesville (Ohio) *Times*, August 4, 1923.

15. "Takes Charge of Funeral Details," *Anaheim Press Democrat*, August 3, 1923.

16. Boone Memoir Manuscript, 20:55, 57.

17. Sue Dauser to Boone, no date, Boone Papers, box 29.

18. "End Comes as Sunset Glow Fades," *Pomona Progress*, August 3, 1923.

19. *New York Times*, August 5, 1923.

20. *Salt Lake Tribune*, August 3, 1923.

21. Edmund W. Starling, *Starling of the White House: The Story of the Man Whose Secret Service Detail Guarded Five Presidents from Woodrow Wilson to Franklin D. Roosevelt*, as told to Thomas Sugrue (New York: Simon and Schuster, 1946), 201.

22. "All Physicians Agree on Cause," *Salt Lake Tribune*, August 3, 1923; Warren G. Harding, "Obituary notices, editorial comment, etc., clippings chiefly from Ohio newspapers," vol. 1, 1923, Ohio Historical Society.

23. Ray L. Wilbur and Charles M. Cooper noted on August 3 that "the heart was enlarged and probably the blood vessels which carry to it its nutriment thickened, for his history shows that previously he had had anginal manifestations, and that during sleep the respiratory center was insufficiently fed." See their "Statement by Consulting Physicians," August 3, 1923.

24. See Carl Sferazza Anthony, *Florence Harding: The First Lady, the Jazz Age, and the Death of America's Most Scandalous President* (New York: Morrow, 1998), 464; also see Phillip G. Payne, *Dead Last: The Public Memory of Warren G. Harding's Scandalous Legacy* (Athens: Ohio University Press, 2009), 55.

25. A cogent discussion of the president's death from heart disease resulting from his medical history and a propensity to overexert himself, along with an effective refutation of Gaston Means's allegations that Florence Harding poisoned her husband, is in Robert H. Ferrell, *The Strange Deaths of President*

Harding (Columbus: University of Missouri Press, 1996), chaps. 1–2. Dr. Boone, when writing his memoirs in the 1960s, was irked that some were suggesting myocardial infarction; see Boone Memoir Manuscript, 20:200ff. Despite Ferrell's careful research, a brand-new book asserts, once again, that Harding died of a stroke! See Laton McCartney, *The Teapot Dome Scandal: How Big Oil Bought the Harding White House and Tried to Steal the Country* (New York: Random House, 2008), 151.

26. *City Democrat,* August 8, 1923.

27. "Harding's Death Revives Plans for Easing Burdens," *New York Times,* August 5, 1923.

28. "Is the Burden Too Great?" *San Bernardino Evening Telegram,* July 31, 1923.

29. Carl W. Ackerman, "How the President Keeps Well," interview with Brigadier General Charles Sawyer, reel 246, box 873.

30. *San Francisco Call,* August 4, 1923, reel 247, box 878.

31. Boone Memoir Manuscript, 20:203–205.

32. See Means, *Strange Death of President Harding,* 260–65.

33. He died in the Atlanta penitentiary, where he was jailed for the kidnapping caper.

34. See, e.g., "American President: An Online Reference Resource" (http://millercenter.org/academic/americanpresident/harding/essays/biography/print), which states: "Word quickly spread that Mrs. Harding, the last person to be with him that evening, had poisoned him to prevent him from being brought up on charges of corruption that soon engulfed his administration. A sensationalist book published in 1930 detailed the allegations against her. Her refusal to allow an autopsy of the President only fed the rumors. Harding left the bulk of his estate, valued at $850,000, to his wife." Accessed January 29, 2009.

35. See discussion of Florence's "complicitious" role in Anthony, *Florence Harding,* 460–462, 467.

36. Heart disease overall remains the leading cause of death in the United States. See "What are the Leading Causes of Death in the U.S.?" *Medical News Today,* March 11, 2024 (https://www.medicalnewstoday.com/articles/282929#heart-disease).

37. "End Comes as Sunset Glow Fades."

38. Madame Marcia, "What the Stars Told Mrs. Harding," *Colliers,* May 16, 1925, 42.

39. Harry B. Hunt, "Astrologist Who Predicted Nomination of W. G. Harding Also Foretold His Death," in FKH Papers, reel 247, box 880.

40. Ibid.; *Rochester Democrat and Chronicle*, August 11, 1923.

41. *San Francisco Bulletin*, August 10, 1923.

42. "City in Gloom at Death of President," *Santa Ana Register*, August 3, 1923.

43. *East Palestine* (Ohio) *Leader*, August 6, 1923.

44. *Dallas Journal*, August 3, 1923, emphasis added.

45. "Harding—The Man," (Montana) *Park County News*, August 10, 1923.

46. "When Mrs. Harding Leaves White House She Will Go into a World of Emptiness," *Washington Star*, August 5, 1923.

47. "Long, Dreary Days Ahead of Mrs. Harding, Who Does Not Feel Her Loss as Yet," *Los Angeles Times*, August 4, 1923.

48. *Anaheim Press Democrat*, August 3, 1923.

49. See Samuel R. Lehrman, "Reactions to Untimely Death," in *Death and Mourning*, ed. Hendrik M. Ruitenbeek (London: Jason Aronson Publishers, 1995), 234; Dana G. Cable, "Grief in the American Culture," in *Living with Grief: How We Are, How We Grieve*, ed. Kenneth J. Doka and Joyce D. Davdison (Washington: Hospice Foundation of America, 1998), 62.

50. *Anaheim Press Democrat*, August 3, 1923.

51. See "Mrs. Harding Brave under Bitter Blow," *St. Louis Telegram*, August 3, 1923. This speech, an "eloquent plea for Christianity," was received in "tumultuous" fashion, as Christian called the sickroom to report, which greatly cheered the president. The Los Angeles trip, never made, was to be another extravaganza. Upon his August 2 arrival, there would of course be a parade, a well as a pageant devoted to California history, including "the largest gathering of children ever assembled to greet the ruler of any nation," followed by an address to 80,000 children in the coliseum, a visit to a veterans' home, a tree planting, Knights Templar ceremonies, and "a monster public reception at Exposition Park" in the evening. The next day there would have been a tour of film studios, a suburban trip, a lunch in Pasadena, and then the departure for Catalina with the Wrigleys. His final California event would be in San Diego, including another address at their bowl for 50,000—and a visit with his aunt, Mrs. Frances Wyant. But all was called off on July 30.

52. *New York Times*, November 22, 1924.

53. "Spirit of Harding to Advise President Coolidge . . . Declared Sir A. Conan Doyle," *Chicago Tribune Leased Wire*, August 4, 1923.

54. *Washington Star*, August 10, 1923, emphasis added.

55. Francis W. Schruben, "An Even Stranger Death of President Harding," *Southern California Quarterly* 47 (March 1966): 75.

56. See *Coshocton Tribune*, August 4, 1923.

57. Joseph De Barthe, *The Answer to "The President's Daughter" and Other Defamations of a Great American* (Marion: Ohio: The Answer Publishing), 223–224, emphasis in original.

58. "Ship Captain Voices Sorrow," *Salt Lake Tribune,* August 3, 1923; Filmer cited in same paper, August 4, 1923.

59. "Mrs. Harding Is Calm While Prayers Read," *San Bernardino County Sun,* August 4, 1923.

60. "Body Starts Long Trip Back to Washington as Thousands Pay Homage," *Arizona Star,* August 4, 1923.

61. *Kansas City Post,* August 4, 1923, *Denver Post,* August 4, 1923, *Sacramento Star,* August 3, 1923, all in FKH Papers, reel 247, box 878.

62. "When Mrs. Harding Leaves White House."

63. "Long, Dreary Days Ahead of Mrs. Harding."

64. Boone Memoir Manuscript, 20:115.

65. "Mrs. Harding Slows Train for Throngs," *New York Tribune,* August 8, 1923.

66. Words from *The Funeral Train* (Cincinnati: Miami Press, 1924):

> A woman kneels and holds in check/tears she's shed for her mate/the sun is down the chief has gone/west through the Golden Gate.
>
> From days of weeping, eyes are red/aboard the funeral train/ . . . from grief at loss of him we loved; hearts . . . weighted down with pain.
>
> The shrouds are flapping in the wind/the sable shrouds of doom/ . . . the train flies o'er a trestle high/with the dead to his tomb . . .
>
> It rocks and swerves around the curves, each rock and swerve a moan; on over joints and clicking on in awful monotone.
>
> The shrouds are flapping hard outside, as on and on we fly. Along the dim lit aisles is heard The breathing of a sigh—tis sigh of breath in hour of death at thought that all must die.

67. Schruben, "An Even Stranger Death," 83, n71.

68. *Lead Kindly Light* (1833) was also played at Calvin Coolidge's funeral a decade later:

> Lead kindly Light, amid the encircling gloom, Lead thou me on!
> The night is dark, and I am far from home;
> Lead thou me on!
> Keep thou my feet; I do not ask to see
> The distant scene; one step enough for me.
>
> I was not ever thus, nor prayed that thou
> Shouldst lead me on;

I loved to choose and see my path; but now
Lead thou me on.
I loved the garish day, and, spite of fears;
Pride ruled my will. Remember not past years!

So long thy power hath blest me, sure it still
Will lead me on,
O'er moat and fen, o'er crag and torrent, till
The night is gone;
And with the morn those angel faces smile,
Which I have loved long since, and lost awhile!

Meantime, along the narrow rugged path,
Thyself hast trod
Lead, Savior, lead me home in childlike faith,
Home to my God.
To rest forever after earthly strife
In the calm light of everlasting life.

69. "Solemn Dignity and Sorrow Attend Departure of Train," *Salt Lake Tribune*, August 4, 1923.

70. "Body Starts Long Trip Back to Washington."

71. "Mrs. Harding Shows Her Brave Spirit in Ordeal While All Nation Weeps," *Fresno Bee*, August 4, 1923.

72. See *Kansas City Journal-Post*, August 4, 1923; also, "Rail Special Speeds East with Body," *Deseret News*, August 4, 1923.

73. Starling, *Starling of the White House*, 201.

74. Current grief counselors would applaud her. As they point out, "viewing the body can facilitate adjustment to the death," allowing for a "confrontation" that lets grieving begin. See Dana G. Cable, "Grief in the American Culture," in *Living with Grief: Who We Are, How We Grieve*, ed. Kenneth J. Doka and Joyce D. Davidson (Washington: Hospice Foundation of America, 1998), 65.

75. "Harding, Man and President," in *American Review of Reviews* article found in Boone Papers, box 29, 259.

76. "Desert Towns Turn Out"; "Pioneers Cast Flowers before Funeral Train," *Los Angeles Times*, August 5, 1923; in Harding Papers, box 879, reel 247.

77. "Rail Special Speeds East with Body."

78. Boone Memoir Manuscript, 20:120.

79. *New York Times*, August 8, 1923, cited in Boone Memoir Manuscript, chap. 20.

80. Boone Memoir Manuscript, 20:121.

81. "Train Bearing Body of Harding Hurries across Open Spaces," *Salt Lake Tribune*, August 5, 1923.

82. "Iowans Bow to Funeral Train," *Kansas City Post*, August 6, 1923.

83. See *Philadelphia Public Ledger*, August 7, 1923.

84. "A Path of Sorrow," *Cleveland Plain Dealer*, August 8, 1923.

85. Boone Memoir Manuscript, 20:120; also see *Washington Evening Star*, August 7, 1923; *New York Times*, August 7, 1923.

86. "Middlewest Ready to Accord Homage to Funeral Train," *Salt Lake Tribune*, August 5, 1923.

87. *Philadelphia Public Ledger*, August 8, 1923.

88. Over and over, as the *Ledger* noted on August 7, there were "the same line of bowed figures, with their hats on their breasts; the same ranks of servicemen at 'attention,' the same lines of fraternal organizations in all their regalia"; there were "weeping women" and "awestruck children."

89. Boone Memoir Manuscript, 20:123.

90. *New York World*, August 7, 1923.

91. *Philadelphia Public Ledger*, August 9, 1923; *New York Times*, August 8, 1923.

92. Boone Memoir Manuscript, 20:125.

93. "Route of Two Funeral Corteges Are Determined," *Washington Post*, August 5, 1923.

94. "East Room, Where Harding Lies, Looks Out on Brilliant Blooms," *New York Tribune*, August 5, 1923.

95. Quoted in Gary Cohen, "The Lady and the Diamond," *Vanity Fair*, August 1997, 146.

96. "East Room, Where Harding Lies."

97. *Philadelphia Public Ledger*, August 9, 1923.

98. See full coverage in *New York World*, August 9, 1923; *New York Herald*, August 9, 1923; *New York Times*, August 9, 1923.

99. "Nation Bows in Capitol Rites; Hymns Harding Loved Are Sung," *New York Times*, August 9, 1923.

100. Ibid.

101. *Washington Herald*, August 9, 1923.

102. *Kansas City Post*, August 9, 1923; *Washington Post*, August 9, 1923.

103. See *Philadelphia Public Ledger*, August 9, 1923; "Nation Bows in Capitol Rites."

104. "The Nation's Tribute to Its Martyr," *National Republic*, August 18, 1920.

105. "Mrs. Harding, on Train, Entirely Self Possessed," *Washington Post*, August 9, 1923; "On Board Harding Funeral Train en Route to Marion, [dateline] Harrisburg, Pa., Aug. 8," *Washington Herald*, August 9, 1923; also *Kansas City Post*, August 9, 1923.

106. "Father Bears Burden of Grief," *Washington Times*, August 10, 1923.

107. "Until Death Do Us Part," *Washington Star*, August 6, 1923.

108. See *Kansas City Post*, August 4, 1923.

109. "Cortege to Traverse Street along which President, as Youth, Sought Work," *New York Tribune*, August 7, 1923.

110. See *New York Tribune*, August 8, 1923.

111. Marion's funeral was organized by a "civic committee" including old Harding friends Hoke Donithen and Orlando S. Rapp. "We have all the committees organized," Rapp wrote Christian, August 6, 1923, in Orlando S. Rapp Papers, Ohio State University Library.

112. "The People Honor Their Dead Leader," *Outlook*, August 22, 1923.

113. See *Washington Herald*, August 10, 1923; "Mrs. Harding Still Keeps Up Courage," *Washington Star*, August 10, 1923; "Crowds to the End See Funeral Train," *New York Times*, August 9, 1923.

114. "People Honor Their Dead Leader."

115. "Father Bears Burden of Grief."

116. "Crowds to the End See Funeral Train."

117. *Philadelphia Public Ledger*, August 16, 1923; *Washington Herald*, August 11, 1923.

118. "Floral Offerings Fill Four Big Army Trucks—KKK Sends Red Tiger Lily Emblem," *Washington Herald*, August 11, 1923; "Rites in Marion to Be for Plain W. G. Harding," *New York Tribune*, August 8, 1923.

119. Boone Memoir Manuscript, 20:150.

120. *Philadelphia Public Ledger*, August 11, 1923; Starling, *Starling of the White House*, 203.

121. "Whole City Hushed at Hour of Burial: Courts, Business, Theatres and Sports Give Up Day to Honor Dead President," *New York Times*, August 11, 1923.

122. "Mr. Harding's Administration," *Birmingham Age-Herald*, n.d., noted Harding's passion for "the permanent establishment of an American merchant marine and the saving to the nation of our war-built fleet of merchant ships."

123. "Whole City Hushed at Hour of Burial."

124. *Philadelphia Public Ledger*, August 11, 1923.

125. Warren G. Harding, "Obituary notices, editorial comment, etc. Clippings chiefly from Ohio newspapers," vol. 1, 1923.

126. *Washington Star*, August 10, 1923.

127. Boone Memoir Manuscript, 21:59–64, 127.

128. Lawler, "Hardings I Knew," 32:1.

129. "Coolidge Voids Sherrill's Order; Keeps Baldinger," *Washington Herald*, August 11, 1923. Apparently, when Baldinger returned to Washington with the funeral train, he "learned for the first time that he had been separated from the White House." Sherrill had written him, "saying that the officer would be relieved temporarily so he could be at the personal convenience of Mrs. Harding." Although Coolidge restored him to his position, Baldinger returned to Marion with Florence that fall.

130. "Mrs. Harding at White House, Spends Two Hours Going over Papers in the Late President's Desk," *New York World*, August 12, 1923; "Mrs. Harding Back at White House," *Washington Star*, August 11, 1923.

131. "Mrs. Harding to Quit the White House Soon," *Washington Post*, August 11, 1923.

132. Jackie stayed on for fourteen days, from November 22 to December 6, 1963, but she went back to Hyannisport for at least four days at Thanksgiving, so the two widows actually spent just about the same number of nights in the executive mansion. I am grateful to Bill Allman for this information; see e-mail to author, July 1, 2008.

133. "Doctors Worry as Mrs. Harding Goes to Capital"; "Widow Facing Supreme Ordeal in Final Separation from Dead, Though Brave and Contained to Last," *New York Herald*, August 11, 1923.

134. Surviving were 800 manuscript boxes, amounting to 350,000 pages. See Donald E. Pitzer, "An Introduction to the Harding Papers," *Ohio History*, 75 (1998): 77.

135. Harvey Firestone to FKH, August 13, 1923.

136. "Mrs. Harding Rests Most of Day Alone in Room at White House," *New York Tribune*, August 13, 1923.

137. Boone Memoir Manuscript, 20:160.

138. "Mrs. Harding Busy with Final Packing," *Washington Star*, August 14, 1923.

139. "Mrs. Harding Bids White House Goodbye and Departs Today," *Washington Star*, August 17, 1923.

140. *Marion Newslife*, May 5, 1980, 28.

141. "Mrs. Harding Calm in Her Farewell at White House Door," *New York Tribune*, August 18, 1923.

142. "Mrs. Harding Quits Mansion; Nature Weeps," *Washington Herald*, August 18, 1923.

{ *Notes to Pages 233–239* }

143. FKH to Evalyn, August 15, 1923, August 25, 1923, Anthony Collection, FLL.

144. See discussion in Kenneth W. Duckett and Francis Russell, "The Harding Papers: How Some Were Burned . . . and Some Were Saved" (Duckett covered "burned" and Russell, "saved"), *American Heritage* 16, February 1965, 25–31, 102–110.

145. Cohen, "The Lady and the Diamond," 146.

146. Duckett, "How Some Were Burned," 26–28.

147. Letter quoted in *Marion Newslife*, May 5, 1980, 28.

148. Quoted in *Marion Newslife*, May 5, 1980, 28.

149. "Mrs. Harding Leaves for Marion to Probate Late Husband's Will," *Washington Star*, September 5, 1923.

150. "Mrs. Harding Is Back at Home in Marion," *Washington Times*, September 6, 1923.

CHAPTER 8: WIDOWHOOD

1. See Small's article, August 4, 1923, in FKH Papers, reel 247, box 878.

2. "When Mrs. Harding Leaves White House She Will Go into a World of Emptiness," *Washington Star*, August 5, 1923.

3. FKH to Evalyn, September 25, 1923, First Ladies Library.

4. Evalyn to FKH, FKH Papers, reel 243, box 854, frames 10–13, 14–16, 18–21, 84–87.

5. Gann quoted in Joel Boone Memoir Manuscript, 20:194, Boone Papers, box 45, Library of Congress, Washington, D.C.

6. Catherine New to Evalyn, August 31, 1923, Evalyn McLean Papers, box 24.

7. "Coolidge Reappoints Sawyer to Post," *New York Times*, August 25, 1923.

8. "Harding's Will Filed; $100,000 Given to Widow," *Washington Tribune*, September 8, 1923; "Bulk of Harding's Estate for Widow," *Washington Herald*, September 8, 1923; "Family Gets Bulk of Harding Estate," *New York Times*, September 8, 1923.

9. Department of Commerce, *Statistical Abstract of the United States* (Washington, D.C.: Government Printing Office, 1925), 320; Charles E. Hard to FKH, September 7, 1923, FKH Papers, reel 243, box 853.

10. Schaffner to FKH, October 6, 1923, N. Webster to FKH, October 4, 1923, FKH Papers, roll 243, box 853.

11. Kenneth W. Duckett and Francis Russell, "The Harding Papers: How Some Were Burned . . . and Some Were Saved" (Duckett covered "burned" and Russell, "saved"), *American Heritage* 16 (February 1965): 29–30.

12. Kathleen Lawler, "The Hardings I Knew," unpublished manuscript, in Ohio Historical Society, Columbus, Ohio, 32:4–9 passim.

13. Andrea Lentz, *The Warren G. Harding Papers: An Inventory to the Microfilm Edition* (Columbus: Ohio Historical Society, 1970), 3.

14. Moore to FKH, October 12, 1923, reel 242, box 853.

15. "Harding Papers Burned by Widow," *New York Times*, December 25, 1925, 1.

16. Duckett, "Some Were Burned," 29–30.

17. Donald E. Pitzer, "An Introduction to the Harding Papers," *Ohio History*, 75 (1998): 78, 82.

18. Sawyer Sanatorium records, November 22, 1923, Sawyer File, Marion County Historical Society.

19. Malcolm Jennings to FKH, October 14, 1924, Anthony Collection, First Ladies Library.

20. Jennings to FKH, December 13, 1923, Anthony Collection, First Ladies Library.

21. Jennings to FKH, September 19, 1923, Anthony Collection, First Ladies Library.

22. Jennings to FKH, April 9, 1924, Anthony Collection, First Ladies Library.

23. Daugherty's office oversaw the publication of a book of all his Alaska speeches, including the impromptu rear platform ones, that was published in December 1923, and Florence approved of this, sending it out to friends. See Elmer Landes to FKH, March 27, 1924, reel 243, box 854.

24. R. B. Creager to Jennings, November 9, 1923, Anthony Collection, First Ladies Library.

25. *Washington Star*, September 7, 1923.

26. Creager to FKH, August 27, 1923, Anthony Collection, First Ladies Library.

27. For a multifaceted portrayal of the dangers of writing biographies and the ways in which perceived partisanship can poison a book's reception, see Janet Malcolm, *The Silent Woman* (New York: Vantage, 1993). Malcolm looks at biographers of Sylvia Plath and Ted Hughes.

28. See *Outlook*, December 3, 1924.

29. Lawler, "Hardings I Knew," 32:3–5.

30. "Widow Backs Harding Home Town Memorial," *Washington Star*, September 7, 1923.

31. "Campaign for Harding Shrine to Open Dec. 9," *Springfield* (Mass.) *News*, November 9, 1923.

32. Dean Hamilton to FKH, October 29, 1923, reel 242, box 853.

33. George Harding Jr. to FKH, November 9, 1923.

34. FKH to Mrs. Poindexter, October 3, 1923, reel 243, box 853.

35. See Laura Harlan to FKH, October 23, 1923, reel 242, box 853.

36. In a March 28, 1924, article, journalist David Lawrence wrote, "Mr. Daugherty furnished himself the ground on which the resignation was requested by refusing to disclose the files of his correspondence and bureaus, which the Senate investigation committee demanded." See "Resignation Seen as Aid to Party; Elimination of Daugherty Is Termed Ending of 'intolerable situation,'" quoted in Boone Memoir Manuscript, 21:142. Boone noted that Daugherty accepted the demand he resign, "but with a heavy heart and a feeling of disappointment." The Coolidges also felt bad about it, but the scandal was proving a damaging distraction. Christian, meanwhile, defended the attorney general for his hard work in prosecuting Prohibition cases (over 115,000 in the court system; 92,000 convictions; $16 million in fines). Daugherty's investing went on until 1927, when he was acquitted "on charges of conspiracy to defraud the Government of the United States," but his secretive, obstructionist behavior had not helped him. Despite his acquittal, Daugherty blamed "eight Jews" on the jury who didn't "understand" him. Coolidge didn't doubt Daugherty, he told Boone, but "he needed now more than ever an Attorney General free from attack." It was an election year, after all. The whole affair "made me sick," said Boone. Joel Boone Memoir Manuscript, 21:181–182, Boone Papers, box 45, Library of Congress, Washington, D.C.; Daugherty to Coolidge, April 5, 1927, Boone Papers, box 29.

37. See A. D. Lasker to FKH, March 20, 1924, reel 243, box 854.

38. Duckett, "Some Were Burned," 29–30.

39. FKH to Fall, April (n.d.), 1924, Anthony Collection, First Ladies Library.

40. Harding wrote Scobey, January 31, 1920: "I am very much interested in what you said about Sens. Fall and Smith. I think Fall is a star of a fellow." See Scobey Papers, box 2. However, in a new book, Laton McCartney maintains that Harding knew all about it, although he introduces no evidence for this claim, only assertions (e.g., referring to Harding's words to Fall as "hardly the sentiments of a man betrayed"). See *The Teapot Dome Scandal: How Big Oil Bought the Harding White House and Tried to Steal the Country* (New York: Random House, 2008), 148.

41. Alice Roosevelt Longworth, *Crowded Hours* (New York: Scribner's, 1933), 202–203; Boyden Sparkes interviews with Evalyn Walsh McLean, sixth sitting, March 30, 1935, Hope Ridings Miller Papers, box 2, Library of Congress.

42. As the *Uniontown* (Pa.) *Herald* noted on August 4, 1923: "He was a good listener, a good talker, a 'real fellow.' . . . He had a peculiar capacity for making friends, for attracting new friends and holding old ones," and of

course his appeal was also evident in his "broadmindedness, his bigness of heart... his desire to give his fellowman the benefit of any doubt."

43. *New York Times,* November 22, 1924 (obituary).

44. Calvin Coolidge to FKH, October 16, 1923, FKH to Calvin Coolidge, November 9, 1923, Calvin Coolidge to FKH, November 10, 1923, reel 242, box 853.

45. FKH to Moore, October 5, 1923, reel 242, box 853.

46. FKH to Wanamaker and Mr. Keller, n.d., reel 243, box 854, frames 23–25.

47. Bill New to Florence, September 21, 1923, FKH Papers, reel 242, box 853.

48. Kohlsaat to FKH, September 23, 1923, FKH Papers, reel 242, box 853. Harding once told Jennings that although Hoover "will say things which are very worth while . . . he is less attractive than many others in presenting his thoughts." Harding to Jennings, March 30, 1922.

49. FKH to Kellogg, November 2, 1923, FKH Papers, reel 242, box 853.

50. FKH to E. A. Crothers of the *San Francisco Bulletin,* September 13, 1923, FKH Papers, reel 242, box 853.

51. Jennings to FKH, September 11, 1923, Anthony Collection, box 7, First Ladies Library.

52. "Women Thanked by Mrs. Harding," January 18, 1924, Charles E. and Carl W. Sawyer Papers, reel 248, box 889.

53. See letter of Charles E. Sawyer, Chairman, Executive Committee, Harding Memorial Association, September 5, 1924, Sawyer Papers, box 889.

54. See, for instance, Harding Memorial Association release, December 24, 1923, regarding donation of Morris Rothenberg, Chairman, Board of Directors, Palestine Foundation Fund, box 889, reel 248.

55. "Levy Tributes on Wages of Government Clerks," *Washington Record,* January 12, 1924.

56. Press release, Office of the Governor, State of Ohio, Proclamation of Harding Memorial Week (December 9–16, 1923), from Harding Memorial Organizing Committee Plan for the Nation Wide Organization, Papers of the Harding Memorial Association, Correspondence, box 889, Ohio Historical Society.

57. *Newark News,* December 10, 1923.

58. "New Song in Harding Memorial Will Be Broadcast Tonight," *New York Tribune,* December 16, 1923.

59. S. Cope to FKH, October 4, 1923, reel 242, box 853.

60. FKH to Esther, December 19, 1923, copy in author's possession.

61. FKH to Esther Mezger, December 2, 1923, Mezger Papers, First Ladies Library.

62. FKH to Evalyn and Ned, January 26, 1924.

63. Ibid.

64. FKH to Mrs. George Harvey, January 1924 (n.d), reel 243, box 854.

65. "Mrs. Harding Back in Washington," *New York Times*, January 4, 1924.

66. Jennings to FKH, January 24, 1924, Anthony Collection, First Ladies Library; *New York Times*, January 24, 1924.

67. FKH to Louis H. Brush, President, Harding Publishing Company, January 1, 1924, reel 243, box 854.

68. Mrs. S. Mosby Coleman to FKH, January 27, 1924, reel 243, box 854.

69. See FKH Harding Papers, roll 242, box 851.

70. FKH letter, December 1923 (n.d.), FKH Papers, reel 242, box 853.

71. Lee to FKH, June 3, 1924; FKH to Lee, June 9, 1924, Lee Papers, box 9/5.

72. FKH to Boone, September 6, 1923, Boone Papers, box 29.

73. Boone Memoir Manuscript, 21:65, 74; also see Boone diary entry, January 16, 1924, Boone Papers, box 40, Library of Congress.

74. FKH to Esther, January 11, 1924, Mezger Papers, First Ladies Library.

75. FKH to Harlan, undated letter in Anthony Collection, box 7, First Ladies Library.

76. FKH to Esther, March 25, 1923, in *Marion Newslife*, May 5, 1980.

77. Jennings to FKH, January 12, 1924; Anthony Collection, box 7.

78. Boone diary entry, January 24, 1924.

79. Boone Memoir Manuscript 21:74; Boone diary entry, February 7, 1924.

80. Edwin Denby to FKH, October 9, 1923, reel 242, box 853.

81. Jennings to FKH March 11, 1924, Anthony Collection, box 7, First Ladies Library.

82. FKH to Fall, April (n.d.) 1924, Anthony Collection, box 7.

83. FKH to Esther Mezger, January 11, 1924, Mezger Papers, First Ladies Library.

84. FKH wrote Butler, "I recall those memories of the pleasant little dinners Mr. Harding and I used to have with you." Letter dated February 25, 1924, in author's possession.

85. FKH to Jennings, n.d., Anthony Collection, box 7.

86. Grace Coolidge to FKH, February 22, 1924, reel 243, box 854.

87. Boone diary entry, February 27, 1924.

88. *New York Times*, February 28, 1924.

89. See Charles Evans Hughes to FKH, February 28, 1924, reel 243, box 854.

90. Jennings to FKH, April 9, 1924, Anthony Collection.

91. Jennings to FKH, April 25, 1924; FKH to Jennings, March 29, 1924, Anthony Collection, First Ladies Library.

92. FKH to Jennings, n.d., in Anthony Collection, box 7.

93. Ibid.

94. Jennings to FKH, March 29, 1924, Anthony Collection, box 7, First Ladies Library.

95. *New York Times*, November 22, 1924.

96. FKH to Esther, March 25, 1924; also see Edith Wilson to FKH, February 8, 1924, thanking her for her sympathy after death of Wilson, FKH Papers, roll 243, box 854.

97. New to FKH, May 15, 1924, FKH Papers, roll 243, box 854.

98. Jenny Hibben to FKH, roll 243, box 854. Florence was likely warmed by the offer, but then again, because she was also unsure that "one of the Tennessee National Forests" was of sufficient "importance" to bear her husband's name, possibly a missionary boat might not be either! See Henry Wallace to FKH, February 25, 1924, reel 243, box 854.

99. See figures in WGH Papers, collection 345, box 826.

100. See WGH Papers, collection 345, box 856.

101. "Opposes Pension for Mrs. Harding," *New York Times*, February 9, 1924.

102. Mrs. Washington got franking privileges, as did Mrs. Taylor; Dolley Madison got franking plus $30,000 for her husband's manuscripts; Louisa Adams was granted franking plus $25,000 in cash; the widows of Tyler and Polk got $5,000 a year; Mrs. Lincoln received franking and $5,000; Mrs. Garfield, the wife of an assassinated president, got franking, one payment of $50,000, and annual payments of $5,000; and most recently, Mrs. McKinley and Mrs. Roosevelt had gotten $5,000 each.

103. *New York Times* editorial, February 11, 1924.

104. FKH to Esther, March 25, 1924, cited in *Marion Newslife*, May 5, 1980.

105. Boone Memoir Manuscript, 21:126, 161; Boone diary entry, March 24, 1924, May 6, 1924.

106. FKH to Mac Jennings, undated letter from Anthony Collection, box 7.

107. Ibid.; see also Malcolm Jennings to R. B. Creager, February 18, 1924, where Jennings mentions visiting Florence to discuss the project.

108. FKH to Jennings, undated letter from Anthony Collection, box 7.

109. Williams to FKH, February 5, 1924, reel 243, box 854.

110. Lawler, "Hardings I Knew," 32:2–3.

111. Ibid., 32:9.

112. It went like this:

> In the graveyard softly sleeping,
> Where the flowers gently wave,

> Lies the one I loved so dearly,
> And tried so hard to save.
> Husband how hard I tried to keep you,
> Prayers and tears were all in vain.
> Happy Angels, came and took you
> From this world of sorrow and pain.
> I would love to see your smiling face
> And kiss your fevered brow.
> I would love to clasp you in my arms
> And have my husband now.
> In my heart your memory lingers,
> Tenderly fond and true.
> There is not a day, dear husband,
> That I do not think of you.
> Your loving wife, Florence K. Harding.

113. Boone Memoir Manuscript, 21:239, citing letter, FKH to Boone, August 9, 1924.

114. On Defense Day, September 13, 1924, twenty-one soldiers doing duty at the Harding tomb saluted her. See "Tomb Guard Salutes Mrs. Harding," *New York Times*, September 14, 1924.

115. FKH to Charles Moore, July 10, 1924 (from Washington); Ella Loraine Dorsey to Administrator, WGH Estate (n.d.), FKH to Moore, August 12, 1924 (at White Oaks Farm), all in FKH Papers, reel 243, box 854.

116. "Death Comes Peacefully," *Marion Star*, November 21, 1924.

117. *New York Times*, November 22, 1924.

118. "Death Comes Peacefully." Rabbi Kornfeld had been sent to Persia on a beefed-up mission in part related to Standard Oil's "valuable concessions" there. See *New York Times*, January 27, 1922.

119. "Death Comes Peacefully," "Mrs. Harding Dies after Long Fight: She Succumbs to Old Ailment in Sawyer Home at Marion, Ohio," *New York Times*, November 22, 1924.

120. Boone diary entry, June 14, 1924.

121. "Harding's Widow Is Seriously Ill," *New York Times*, November 4, 1924.

122. "Death Comes Peacefully," *New York Times*, November 5, 7, and 9, 1924.

123. "Mrs. Harding Unchanged," *New York Times*, November 10, 1924.

124. *New York Times*, November 11 and 13, 1924.

125. George Christian to Lou Hoover, November 10, 1924.

126. George Christian to Ned, November 14, 1924, box 25, Marion County Historical Society.

127. "Mrs. Harding Suffers Air-Hunger Attack," *Marion Star*, November 14, 1924; *New York Times*, November 14, 1924; "Mrs. Harding at Crisis," *New York Times*, November 15, 1924.

128. "False Rumors of Death Current Last Few Days," *Marion Star*, November 21, 1924.

129. "Mrs. Harding Weaker as Night Wears On," *New York Times*, November 16, 1924.

130. Boone Memoir Manuscript, 20:217; also see *New York Times*, November 17, 1924, November 18, 1924, November 19, 1924.

131. "Mrs. Harding Worse, Nears Coma State," *Marion Star*, November 19, 1924.

132. "Mrs. Harding Now Failing Rapidly," *New York Times*, November 21, 1924.

133. "Death Comes Peacefully."

134. "Mrs. Harding Dies after Long Fight"; "Mrs. Harding's Funeral Rites Monday," *Marion Star*, November 21, 1924.

135. Boone Memoir Manuscript, 21:274.

136. Boone diary entry, September 11, 1922.

137. Boone Memoir Manuscript, 21:272. These sentiments were echoed as well by her friend Frances Parkinson Keyes, who noted Florence to be a "living example of the beauty of bravery" in her transcending not only a crippling illness, but also the vindictive opposition of her father to her husband, not to mention her role in propping up the *Star* when a sick Warren could not, and supporting him through his disappointing race for governor and the more successful one for Senate and president. See Keyes, "Mrs. Harding," *Good Housekeeping*, February 1925, draft in Marion Public Library, Marion, Ohio.

138. "Mrs. Harding Dies after Long Fight."

139. *New York Times*, November 22, 1924.

140. *Outlook*, December 3, 1924.

141. Jennings to R. B. Creager, December 30, 1924, Anthony Collection, box 7.

142. "Thousands Pass Mrs. Harding's Bier," *New York Times*, November 24, 1924; "Thousands See Noted Woman's Body in Casket," *Marion Star*, November 23, 1924.

143. "Associated Publishers to Attend Funeral Monday," *Marion Star*, November 21, 1924.

144. "Funeral at Epworth M. E. Church 2 P.M.," *Marion Star*, November 24, 1924.

145. "Mrs. Harding Laid Beside Her Husband: Taps Are Sounded as Last Tribute Is Paid at Tomb in Marion," *New York Times*, November, 25, 1924.

146. For this, the association had raised $876,709.36, almost $100,000 more than the structure cost to build, and enough to create an endowment. Ground was broken and the cornerstone laid in May 1926, three months after the first floor of the Harding home was opened for visitors, and the bodies were reburied in December 1927. The memorial would not be dedicated until President Hoover and former President Coolidge came to Marion on June 16, 1931; Calvin Coolidge could not bring himself to do it as president, in the midst of the investigations of Fall and Daugherty in 1926.

147. Other sources say $348,876.50. Deducted before taxes was $98,747.24 to cover her funeral ($3,268), executor commission ($7,000), attorneys' fees ($2,000), and her debts ($3,535), as well as her charitable gifts ($6,000), leaving her taxable estate worth $249,929.25. Her debts included medical treatment by Dr. Wood, $600; her car storage at Buick Garage; salaries for her chauffeur and the nurses at White Oaks; safety deposit box rent; and miscellaneous items including bills for dry cleaning, flowers, beauty parlor, auto insurance, fur storage, taxes, and work at her residence. The figures on her will come from the probate court of Marion County, Ohio, Inventory and Appraisement Estate of Florence Kling Harding, dec'd.; also see letter of Charles D. Schaffner, Executor and Trustee of the Last Will and Testament of FKH, January 16, 1926, both in FKH Estate: Correspondence, legal documents, receipts and accounts of the estate 1924–1926, reel 243, box 857, #999ff; also see, "Mrs. Harding Left Estate of $500,000," *New York Times*, November 24, 1924.

148. These included:

300 shares in Columbus Railway Power and Light Co. (worth $24,000).

711 shares in Wm. Wrigley Jr. Co. (worth $28,440).

30 shares in Harding Publishing Co. ($3,000).

Also included were numerous bonds for the cities of Columbus, Toledo, and Youngstown, among others, and extensive Liberty Loan bonds (around $50,000).

149. Jewelry included her pearls, wristwatch, gold mesh bag, two hatpins, enamel vanity box, gold cigarette case, old gold bracelet, clock, pins and small diamond necklace, black and diamond bracelet, diamond bar pin, string ivory beads, jade neckpiece, gold nuggets, two diamond neckpieces, diamond and pearl elephant, Egyptian scarab scarf pin, six unset turquoise, ivory ornament for chain, four scarf pins, gold chain and locket, diamond and platinum neckpiece, gold cuff links, twelve crystals, two pearl hairpins, black bracelet, garnet

cross, cameo collar, pearl comb, gold chain, emerald and diamond rings, cameo brooch, three gold pins, three pearl pins, three odd pins, diamond and sapphire pins, shrine pin, and four diamond cluster rings. These baubles were worth $13,743.

150. She had furs in the amount of $5,000, including a green and gold wrap with sable trimming, baby lamb coat with chinchilla collar, a black silk wrap trimmed with squirrel, silver fox scarf with a silver emblem attached, a brocaded red plush finish wrap lined with white fur and with a Persian lamb collar, a civet cat robe, and a bearskin rug.

151. Florence, of course, was much closer to Cliff, who served as an adviser to her on financial matters, than she ever was to Tal. Cliff and Tal were not close either; Tal was ill for some time before he died in 1938, and Cliff died the year before. "Neither Cliff nor Tal ever amounted to much—ever did anything or achieved anything independent of their father," says Glen Chasson, a neighbor, only underlining further Florence's unusual role in her family. See Glen Chasson to Carl Anthony, July 4 (no year listed), Anthony Collection, First Ladies Library.

152. A list of some of the heirs' and friends' gifts:

Harding Memorial Assoc., $22,535.

Hazel Longshore, $12,000.

Louise Kling, $12,000.

Carl W. Sawyer received $10,000 "in recognition of my gratitude for the uniform faithful service and kindness to me at all times, and in further recognition of the long, faithful and devoted professional services of his father" (quotation from reel 243, box 857, #888).

Mrs. Wm. Milroy Boyd, $5000.

Mrs. Malcolm Jennings, $5000.

Mrs. Roscoe Mezger, $5000.

Mrs. Geo. H. Van Fleet, $2000.

Miss Jane Wallace, $2000.

Mrs. Christian, $2000.

Harry Barker, $2000.

Major Baldinger, $1000.

Ruth Powderly, $1000.

Laura Harlan, $2440.00 (including the Wrigley shares).

Catherine Wynne, $1000, for "devotion and kindness."

Kathleen Lawler, $500.

Vitalis Kling, $10,000—but through a trustee who would manage the proceeds for him.

Clifford Kling, $10,000.

Churches including Epworth, Trinity Baptist, St. Paul's, $2000 each.

Hoke Donithen, $1000.

153. Joseph De Barthe, *The Answer to "The President's Daughter" and Other Defamations of a Great American* (Marion: Ohio: The Answer Publishing), 115.

BIBLIOGRAPHIC ESSAY

Florence Harding's fiery destruction of her husband's archive has appeared to many as a brazen attempt to remove all trace of his role in the scandals that erupted soon after his death. Yet just as the Hardings' connections with Teapot Dome and other scandals were more limited than is popularly understood, a result of unwonted trust in their friends rather than criminal activity, so too was Florence's ash heap: it was a controlled burn, not a mass immolation. Thus, though it is widely thought that she undertook an archival bonfire at Friendship in the summer of 1923, and another, even greater conflagration in the offices of the *Star* afterward, what remained untouched by fire is still voluminous. Her "processing" was sensationalized by Kenneth W. Duckett and Francis Russell in their joint article, "The Harding Papers: How Some Were Burned . . . and Some Were Saved," in *American Heritage* (February 1965): 25–31, 102–110, but its more defined dimensions are persuasively discussed in Donald E. Pitzer's "An Introduction to the Harding Papers," in *Ohio History* 75 (1998): 76–84.

The surviving records in the Ohio Historical Society's Warren G. Harding Collection in Columbus, Ohio, where any work on the Hardings must begin, are indeed extensive, consisting of twenty series of documents in 907 boxes, microfilmed on 263 reels. Most of the collection, including its first thirteen series, remained not only untouched by Florence, but out of reach of nearly everyone until 1964, when the small group of men in charge of the Harding Memorial Association at last decided that the Harding reputation might actually improve, rather than worsen, with the release of long-secreted boxes. The Library of Congress's manuscript division had first attempted to get the files nearly forty years earlier, in 1925, but had been consistently rebuffed, at first by Florence herself. In addition to accessing the thirteen series, the Ohio Historical Society separately collected an additional eight series of records from Harding associates, including the collections of such intimates as Frank Scobey, Malcolm Jennings, and Charles and Carl Sawyer.

{ *Bibliographic Essay* }

The most important source for this book was of course the Florence Kling Harding Papers, series 8 in the collection, consisting of thirty-seven manuscript boxes or six microfilm reels available on loan from the society and also located at the Library of Congress in Washington, D.C. These papers contain hundreds of newspaper clippings from the couple's short tenure in the White House, covering every aspect of the public life of members of this administration and a full view of its activities, from social gatherings to the Alaska trip. Florence was particularly attentive to the way in which the press covered Warren and herself, which will not surprise readers of this book. She was eager to please, providing journalists access to her life, from fancy balls to her experience of a near-fatal illness, in ways that few previous first ladies had done. Most prominent in her collection are New York and Washington papers (with five thriving papers in each city), but represented too are many more from other cities and small towns the couple traversed on their transcontinental journey in 1923, from the *Anchorage Times* to the San Bernardino County *Sun,* for a total of more than eighty publications.

Her papers also contain much on her personal life in the White House (if a good deal less from the earlier years), including letters to close friends like Evalyn Walsh McLean, Beatrice Fletcher, Catherine New, Mary Chandler Hale, George Harvey, and many others. The letters to her girlfriends, especially to Evalyn, are of particular interest, as they show in detail how important these friendships were to her. When she could, she loved spending time with these women friends, and sharing gossip and advice with them. Her papers also illustrate other aspects of her public life, with a large quantity of correspondence to Cabinet officials, newspapermen, and others involved in causes she cared about, from humane societies to women's political organizations. The imprint of Laura Harlan is unmistakable here as well, because Harlan wrote many letters on Florence's behalf.

Other key collections in the larger Warren G. Harding Collection that provide insight on Florence, Warren, and their public and private partnership are the collections of close friends Malcolm Jennings (series 18, with much on the presidential campaign), Frank Scobey (series 20, particularly important for its coverage of the Hardings' Senate years), and George Christian Sr. (series 11 and 12, which contains his "biography" of the president). Jennings's and Scobey's papers are particularly rich and personal in nature. A very helpful source for the presidential campaign, as well as the period of Florence's illness in the White House, is personal assistant Kathleen Lawler's unpublished manuscript, "The Hardings I Knew," held in series 13. Lawler is largely laudatory in her coverage, but her close observations of the Hardings and the stresses and joys they experienced during the campaign are nevertheless illuminating. The last, postpresidential year of Florence's life is covered in the collections of the Harding Memorial Association, series 10, which detail the attempt to adequately commemorate the late president and Florence's role in that effort.

A full discussion of the entire collection's scope is in Andrea Lentz, ed., *The Warren G. Harding Papers: An Inventory to the Microfilm Edition* (Columbus: Ohio Historical Society, 1970). Yet not all the relevant material is on microfilm, and those wishing a full picture of the Harding legacy need to visit the society's airy research room in Columbus, where the helpful staff can provide such materials as collection 345, a miscellaneous batch of Florence's bills, itemized purchases for two Senate-era Washington houses, and even notes on astrology scrawled on the back of bank account books. A separate collection at the OHS, the papers of Mary Lee, a close Ohio friend of Florence, are also invaluable for showing Florence's continuing interest in local politics, as well as the way in which her new life in Washington affected her.

Florence's life is further detailed in materials at another Ohio archive, the First Ladies Library, situated in a beautifully restored bank next to the equally well-cared-for home of former first lady Mrs. Ida McKinley in downtown Canton, Ohio. Carl Sferazza Anthony, author of many biographies of first ladies as well as the library's bibliographer, and Craig Schermer, an Ohio historian and collector, have both donated materials here of considerable interest to scholars of Florence Harding. Anthony's materials consist of documents he gathered for his book, *Florence Harding: The First Lady, the Jazz Age, and the Death of America's Most Scandalous President* (New York: Morrow, 1998), and include numerous letters, most revealing being those between Florence and her close friends Evalyn McLean and Malcolm Jennings. Schermer's collection also has a good number of notes between Florence and her daughter-in-law, Esther Neely DeWolfe Mezger, which are similarly illuminating about this conflicted relationship. Many of these were also published in an article by Ron Cass, "The Duchess of East Center Street," *Marion Newslife* (May 5, 1980). Schermer also located Florence's diary in an Ohio barn in 1997, an enlightening source—if one which must be used carefully, because it lacks dates. Finally, the First Ladies Library has a daily appointment book for Florence lasting through the end of 1922 which *does* have dates, Laura Harlan's unpublished manuscript, "The End of a Perfect Day: The Life of Florence Kling Harding (1860–1924), The White House Appointment Books," in four chronological parts.

Florence's hometown of Marion is also a vital stop for any researcher seeking a fuller picture of her life, augmented by the presence there of many Harding enthusiasts. Although Florence's birthplace was razed long ago, the Front Porch is preserved at the Harding Home State Memorial, and well tended by its expert manager, Melinda Gilpin, and her staff. A visit to the home at 380 Mt. Vernon Avenue offers a striking aura of Florence and Warren's life in Marion, both before and during the campaign. At the Marion County Historical Society nearby, there are materials on Charles Sawyer, whose local sanitarium figured so prominently in Florence's life, as well as the papers of Charlton Myers, a former judge and founder of the society who shared a revealing correspondence with several Harding biographers, including Frances Russell. The Marion Public Library has also an excellent local history section, with the *Marion Star* available on microfilm. And no visit to Marion would be complete without a moment of silent appreciation at the imposing mausoleum where the souls of Florence and Warren have rested since 1927. A fifty-foot-tall structure of Georgia marble pillars, 250 feet in circumference, it is surrounded by tall trees and other greenery and provides a peaceful spot for meditation on their lives.

Of course, the Hardings were hardly just a local couple, as their presence in the holdings of the Library of Congress in Washington, D.C., confirms. By far the most significant source for this book at the library were the Joel T. Boone papers, including Dr. Boone's diary entries, particularly those for the period of April 1922–August 1923, and continuing until Florence's death, and his invaluable memoir manuscript, which he began in the 1960s and continued until he became too ill to complete it. Boone, who always thought his close access to the Hardings was a "privilege," left an incomparable trove of material on Florence's illness, the 1923 Florida and Alaska trips, and the personalities of both Hardings, as well as their marital relationship. His diary is also helpful for pinpointing chronology, especially during Florence's crisis of the fall of 1922.

Other materials at the Library of Congress important to this study include the papers of Evalyn Walsh McLean, which feature correspondence with many of Florence's friends, providing a fuller picture of her social circle. Transcripts from Boyden Sparkes's interviews with Evalyn for her later biography, *Father Struck It Rich* (New York: Scribners, 1936), contain much about Florence, not all of it trustworthy, and are located in the library's Hope Ridings Miller papers. Florence's relationship with Evalyn is not only detailed in *Father Struck It Rich*, but also in Gary Cohen, "The Lady and the Diamond," *Vanity Fair* (August 1997): 134-148. Other collections in the Manuscript Reading Room that provide insights about Florence—though in smaller amounts—are the Mark Sullivan Papers, the William Allen White Papers, the Edith Bolling Galt Wilson Papers, and the Teddy Roosevelt Jr. Papers.

Historian Francis Russell left his papers at the American Heritage Center in Laramie, Wyoming, and it is here that the letters which Harding wrote his paramour, Carrie Phillips, may be found. Still sealed by agreement at the Library of Congress until 2014, they are open in the Russell Papers, which were subject to no such agreement, and are an important source of the nature of this affair and the ways it affected Florence and her personal happiness.

For an understanding of Florence's professional life, and how she fits into the pantheon of presidential wives, readers should begin with some of the standard works on first ladies. These include Carl Sferazza Anthony, *First Ladies: The Saga of the Presidents' Wives and Their Power, 1789-1961* (New York: William Morrow, 1990); Betty Boyd Caroli, *First Ladies: Expanded Edition* (New York: Oxford University Press, 1995); and Lewis L. Gould, ed., *American First Ladies: Their Lives and Their Legacy* (New York: Garland Publishing, 1996).

Gould is also the author of two other books helpful in illuminating the political milieu in which the Hardings came to power, including *Grand Old Party: A History of the Republicans* (New York: Random House, 2003), and *The Most Exclusive Club: A History of the U.S. Senate* (New York: Basic Books, 2005). Similarly, John Milton Cooper Jr., *Breaking the Heart of the World: Woodrow Wilson and the Fight for the League of Nations* (New York: Cambridge University Press, 2001), helps explain as well the political environment that made Harding's candidacy so popular, as well as the ways in which Edith Bolling Galt Wilson presents a striking contrast to her successor.

Despite the popularity, the Hardings' story has been told with a rather pronounced tilt since the 1920s, as this book's introduction has suggested. The year 1922 saw William Estabrook Chancellor's error-filled and scurrilous *Warren Gamaliel Harding, President of the United States: A Review of Facts Collected from Anthropological, Historical, and Political Researches* (Dayton: Sentinal Press, 1922), and Clinton Wallace Gilbert's similarly negative *Behind the Mirrors: The Psychology of Disintegration at Washington* (New York: G. P. Putnam's Sons, 1922). After Harding's death, things got to a particularly low level, with Nan Britton's notorious *The President's Daughter* (New York: Elizabeth Ann Guild, 1927), which purports to tell the story of Nan and Warren's affair (from the Senate into the White House) and details what Britton claims were the president's unflattering views of his wife. Other critical writings include H. F. Alderfer's Syracuse University dissertation, "The Personality and Politics of Warren G. Harding" (1928), and the markedly mendacious Gaston B. Means's *The Strange Death of President Harding: From the Diaries of Gaston B. Means, a Department of Justice Investigator* (New York: Guild Publishing, 1930), where Florence's role as "poisoner" is fully proclaimed. Of course, it had been proclaimed earlier in Samuel Hopkins Adams's novel, *Revelry* (1926), not so loosely based on the Hardings. Particularly influential because of its author's effective style is Alice Roosevelt Longworth's *Crowded Hours* (New York: Scribner's, 1933), which likely retains the most indelible caricature of Florence to this very day: the dour, drinks-toting barmaid at her husband's raucous card parties. Rounding out the early attacks was Samuel Hopkins Adams's venture into nonfiction, *Incredible Era: The Life and Times of Warren Gamaliel Harding* (Boston: Houghton Mifflin, 1939), which continued to parrot the theories of black blood and love child, citing Means as a source (even as Adams inconsistently charged Means was neither "authentic and reliable") as well as accusing Florence of "continuous nagging."[1] Such works had influence for decades. In 1963, a *CBS News* portrait of first ladies used both Adams and Longworth as sources![2] Although published too late to be fully used in this study, Philip Payne's *Dead Last: The Public Memory of Warren G. Harding's Scandalous Legacy* (Athens: Ohio University Press, 2009), promises a fresh look at the long history of attacks on this administration.

Although fewer and less influential, there were more positive contemporary portrayals, including Joe Mitchell Chapple's two self-published works: *Warren G. Harding: The Man,* and *Life and Times of Warren G. Harding, Our After-War President* (Boston: Chapple Publishing, 1920 and 1924). In addition, several "insider" books, if not always sympathetic, at least provide a more balanced approach, including usher Irwin "Ike" Hood Hoover, *Forty Two Years in the White House* (Boston: Houghton Mifflin, 1934), housekeeper Elizabeth Jaffray, *Secrets of the White House* (New York: Cosmopolitan Book Corporation, 1927), and Secret Service agent Edmund Starling (with Thomas Sugrue), *Starling of the White House* (New York: Simon and Schuster, 1946). These memoirs provide a selection of useful nuggets on Florence's role as first lady and her marriage.

But the more critical earlier books have left by far the strongest legacy in scholarship. Probably still the most influential study of Harding despite the passage of forty years, Francis Russell's *The Shadow of Blooming Grove: Warren G. Harding and His Times* (New York: McGraw-Hill, 1968) offers a dark portrait of the president and portrays his wife in such scathingly negative terms as to strain credulity. Despite the author's corrosive bias, and the even more assiduous mudslinging of his later article, "The Shadow of Warren Harding," *Antioch Review* (Winter 1978): 57–76, Russell still dominates the popular landscape: Harding's Wikipedia entry, accessed in July 2008, listed Russell's book twice in its notes, more than any other book cited. Other books, less immediately harsh, include Robert K. Murray, *The Harding Era: Warren G. Harding and His Administration* (Minneapolis: University of Minnesota, 1969), which nonetheless resorts to misogynistic and sexist language when referring to Florence. Attempting to provide a fuller perspective of this popular first lady is Carl Sferazza Anthony, *Florence Harding: The First Lady, the Jazz Age, and the Death of America's Most Scandalous President,* mentioned above. Anthony's book portrays Florence as a woman of strength and drive, and a full partner with her husband; his portrait draws in part on the Boone papers. Nevertheless, Mrs. Harding slips too often into the background here, as the work puts great emphasis on Warren's peccadilloes, offering detailed and gossipy descriptions, if less evidence, of his involvement in numerous extramarital affairs. When Florence comes to the fore, she is a contributor to her husband's death, conspiring with his doctors to keep their "negligence" under wraps. Books on the Harding administration as a whole have continued a relentlessly negative focus down to the present day.

Most recent is Laton McCartney, *The Teapot Dome Scandal: How Big Oil Bought the Harding White House and Tried to Steal the Country* (New York: Random House, 2008), which declares the president knew of Secretary Fall's corrupt practices, although the author produces no evidence to support this assertion.

The existing histories do contain some more balanced works, although none that focus on Florence herself. High on the list is Robert H. Ferrell, *The Strange Deaths of President Harding* (Columbia: University of Missouri Press, 1996), which provides a well-researched and revisionist portrayal. Ferrell persuasively argues that Harding had only one affair, with Carrie, effectively debunking the Britton tale, and further asserts that Harding died of a heart attack, not incompetence, or poison. His book also offers a nuanced portrayal of Florence. John Dean, *Warren G. Harding* (New York: Times Books, 2004), is also generally sympathetic, showing Florence's beneficial role in the Harding marriage and finding Britton's tale a fabrication.

In an attempt to provide a more multidimensional and compelling portrait of the Hardings in their time, and of Florence in particular, while writing this book, I benefited from a number of specialized studies. Although Simon Louvish's *Cecil B. DeMille: A Life in Art* (New York: St. Martin's Press, 2007) is not about Florence, it provides excellent background for understanding her era and her position as a public figure who fully embraced the celebrity culture of the 1920s. John A. Morello, *Selling the President, 1920: Albert D. Lasker, Advertising, and the Election of Warren G. Harding* (Westport, Conn.: Praeger, 2001), is a key text for illuminating the pioneering way in which the Hardings ran their campaign, using advertising, recordings, and other modern gimmicks to generate interest. Ann E. Burnette, meanwhile, offers a compelling discussion of Florence's transitional rhetorical style in "Florence Kling Harding: Bridging Traditional and Modern Rhetorical Roles," in *Inventing a Voice: The Rhetoric of American First Ladies of the Twentieth Century*, ed. Molly Meijer Wertheimer (Lanham, Md.: Rowman & Littlefield, 2004), 125–144. Such works, by providing needed background on Florence as a celebrity, advocate, and political figure, offer a fuller picture of her contributions and have served as a foundation for this study of her role as a transitional first lady.

INDEX

The abbreviations FKH and WGH refer to
Florence Kling Harding and Warren G. Harding respectively.

Adams, Abigail, 100
Adams, Mrs. John T., 129
Adams, Samuel Hopkins, 30, 39
Advertising, 4–5, 46
African Americans
   federal appointments, 288–289n105
   Front Porch visits, 55–56
   lynchings, 54, 88
   participation in 1920 campaign, 58
   Republican convention delegates, 50
   rumors of Harding family's African descent, 17, 58–60
   servants, 109
   views of WGH, 92
   Washington, D.C., residents, 74
   See also Race relations
Alaska trip
   cross-country journey, 182–190, 310n9
   FKH's activities, 183, 184, 186–187, 188
   FKH's fatigue, 191–192, 194, 202
   food, 199
   goals, 181
   greeting public, 183, 186, 187, 188, 192–193, 195–196
   hectic schedule, 180, 187, 188–190, 208, 209
   on *Henderson*, 173–174, 181, 189–190, 191(photo), 192, 194–195, 213–214
   journalists on, 182–183, 184, 185, 200, 241, 311n18
   participants, 182–183, 193(photo), 230
   plans, 168–169, 173–174, 175, 178, 180, 181–182, 183
   speeches, 185, 188, 189, 189(photo), 196, 200, 310n9, 324n23
   staff accompanying Hardings, 182, 311n18
   stops in Alaska, 190–193, 193(photo)
   WGH's fatigue, 188–190
   WGH's illness, 194–202
Alderson Federal Prison Camp, 126
American Legion, 123, 137, 222
American Women's Legion, 173
Anaconda Copper Company, 186
Anderson, Mary, 132
Andrews, Adolphus, 252, 263–264
Animal Rescue League, 124, 177
Animals
   FKH's interest in, 6, 8, 113, 117, 124–125, 177
   mistreatment, 125
   seals killed by fisherman, 125
   WGH's sympathy, 125
   See also Dogs; Horses
Anthony, Carl Sferrazza, 22, 30, 39–40, 208–209
Arlington Cemetery, Tomb of the Unknowns, 92, 153, 224
Astor, Lord and Lady, 113
Astrology
   FKH's interest in, 24, 46–47
   psychic readings, 46–47, 180, 209–210
   skeptics and, 47–48
   WGH's horoscope, 47, 157–158

{ *Index* }

Atlantic City, New Jersey, 90–91, 195
Ayres, Daisy, 78, 109

Baker, Charles, 167
Baldinger, Ora "Reddy," 174(photo)
   on Alaska trip, 182
   bequest from FKH, 264
   help to FKH in widowhood, 232, 233, 250, 251
   as newsboy, 20
   as pallbearer for FKH, 264
   relationship with FKH, 238
   WGH's funeral and, 221
   White House job, 72–73, 82, 231, 322n129
Baldwin, James Fairchild, 22
Barker, Harry, 73, 81, 146, 153, 221, 233, 264
Barrymore, Ethel, 54–55
Baseball, 112, 114
Bennett, Ira E., 54
Bicyclists Association, 56
Big Brothers and Big Sisters, 173
Bond, Carrie Jacobs
   "The End of a Perfect Day," 104, 264, 265, 292n31
   White House visit, 113
Bone, Scott C., 190
Bonus bill, 88, 121, 124, 151, 296n106
Boone, Joel, 148(photo)
   on Alaska trip, 181, 182, 183, 184, 187, 188, 189, 192, 194, 195
   Alaska trip planning, 173–174
   background, 111
   on Barker, 73
   care of FKH, 144–147, 148, 151, 153, 154, 155, 192, 217
   care of WGH, 157, 158, 192, 194, 196, 197–202, 203, 204–205
   in Coolidge administration, 230, 262
   Daugherty and, 44, 159–160, 325n36
   on Evalyn McLean, 87
   on FKH, 47, 84–85, 86, 161, 261, 262

Florida trip, 164, 165, 167, 169–170
   on funeral train, 218
   as Hardings' personal physician, 82
   on Harlan, 286n48
   as *Mayflower* medical officer, 87, 111, 141–142, 152, 153, 287n76
   at McLeans' ball, 155
   on New Year's reception, 100–101
   relationship with FKH, 87, 173, 230, 250, 252, 254–255, 257, 262
   Sawyer and, 94, 111, 124, 196, 262
   on Washington Disarmament Conference, 92
   on WGH, 185, 208
   on WGH's death, 206, 209
   WGH's funerals and, 229
   White House stays, 145, 151, 152, 158
Boone, Suzanne, 111, 151, 170, 255
Borah, William, 93
Boyd, Mrs. William Milroy, 41, 42, 141, 264
Boy Scouts, 104, 195–196
Briand, Aristide, 93
Bribery. *See* Corruption; Teapot Dome scandal
Briggs, Helen, 176
Britton, Nan
   alleged affair with WGH, 29–30, 39–41, 43, 273n73
   blackmailing of Daisy Harding, 40
   child, 29
   WGH's help with job, 40
Brooks, Arthur, 120, 157, 182, 194, 197
Broomfield, Mrs. Charles E., 129
Brown, Walter, 180, 190, 208
Buchanan, Allen, 213–214
Burns, William J., 158
Butler, Nicholas Murray, 85, 114, 132–133
Butte, Montana, 186–187

Campfire Girls, 127
Canada, visit to Vancouver, 193–194
Cantacuzene, Princess, 93, 106

{ Index }

Cars
  driven by FKH, 94, 111, 138
  Firestone tires, 232
  of FKH, 232, 251, 264
Carter, Mrs. A. A., 123
Carter, William H., 242
Celebrities, Hardings as, 46, 55, 75, 91, 93, 117, 120, 177–178, 265–266
  See also Movie stars
Champrey, Marcia (Madame Marcia), 46–47, 180, 209–210
Chancellor, William Estabrook, 19, 58–60, 76, 234
Chapple, Joe Mitchell, 241, 242
Chautauqua circuit, 26, 31, 39
Chicago
  passage of funeral train, 218–219
  Republican convention (1920), 49–51
Christian, George B., Jr.
  campaign trips for WGH, 55
  Front Porch campaign and, 53
  Harding Memorial Administration and, 246
  at Hardings' wedding, 18
  speech given for WGH, 211, 212, 317n51
  as WGH's secretary, 72, 79
  White House visits, 154
Christian, George B., Sr.
  on Alaska trip, 182, 183, 195
  Front Porch campaign and, 53
  on funeral train, 215, 217, 225
  Harding papers held by, 240
  on Marion society, 17
  Mayflower cruises, 141
  as pallbearer for FKH, 264
  on presidential campaign, 45
  relationship with FKH, 231, 233, 255, 259, 261
  relationship with WGH, 90
  travels with Hardings, 89, 113, 164, 165
  on WGH, 19, 30, 95, 166
  WGH's funerals and, 223, 224, 227
  White House visits, 79, 80, 145, 152, 154, 155, 162
Christian, Mrs. George B., Sr.
  after WGH's death, 214
  on Alaska trip, 182
  bequest from FKH, 264
  on funeral train, 217
  relationship with FKH, 255
  travels with Hardings, 164
  WGH's letters to, 97
  White House visits, 141, 152, 155
Cincinnati Conservatory of Music, 12
Cincinnati Enquirer, 36, 237
Cincinnati Tuberculosis Sanitarium, 121
Civil War veterans, 54, 104, 122, 123
Clemenceau, Georges, 154
Clinton, Hillary Rodham, 7
Clothing of FKH
  accessories and shoes, 117–118, 184
  on Alaska trip, 184, 188, 200
  American-made, 68
  colors, 5
  conservative, 68
  descriptions in press, 102, 104, 117, 119, 120, 172, 188, 200
  expenditures, 37, 118–119
  as First Lady, 68, 117–120, 161, 162, 172, 232, 234, 266
  on Florida trip, 165
  for funerals, 233
  "Harding blue," 5, 71, 117, 119
  at inauguration, 68, 71
  interest in fashion, 34
  seal coat gift, 91
  as Senate wife, 37
  shopping for, 68, 119, 162
  stylish, 117, 118–119
  for White House events, 93, 100, 102, 104, 117, 119, 162
Clothing of WGH, 36, 120, 197
Cohen, Gary, 234
Coleman, Edna, 77

Collins, Harry, 162
Columbus, Ohio
  bridge club, 33, 68, 274n9
  Hardings in, 21, 248
  Republican Glee Club, 50, 61, 137, 138, 249–250, 264
Commerce Department, Hoover as secretary, 62, 73, 78, 79, 141
Concerts, 113–114
Confederate veterans, 104, 122
Congress
  female members, 129, 130
  memorial service for WGH, 251–252
  midterm elections (1922), 152
  party politics, 130
  See also Senate
Congressional Club, 104–105, 109
Coolidge, Calvin
  cabinet members, 219, 230, 308–309n161, 325n36
  election (1924), 260
  eulogy for WGH, 247
  hands shaken, 284–285n30
  Harding Memorial Administration and, 246
  Harding museum dedication, 331n146
  at inaugural ball, 71
  as president, 124, 212, 219, 296n106
  relationship with FKH, 244–245, 254
  relationship with WGH, 114
  as vice president, 64, 114, 121, 155
  vice presidential nomination, 50
  WGH's funerals and, 219, 221, 222, 224, 225–226, 227, 229
Coolidge, Calvin, Jr., 257
Coolidge, Grace
  as first lady, 84, 114, 227, 231, 233, 251, 252
  Harding inauguration and, 66, 71
  Mayflower cruises, 138
  quarters at Willard Hotel, 64, 114
  relationship with FKH, 64, 114, 231, 235, 251, 261
  at Republican women's events, 128
  social life, 64, 155
  at Washington Disarmament Conference, 93, 106
  WGH's funerals and, 219, 224, 229
  White House events for, 121
Cooper, Charles Minor, 198–199, 202, 206, 207, 315n23
Cooper, John Milton, Jr., 75
Corruption, in Justice Department, 2, 243, 252–253
  See also Teapot Dome scandal
Coué, Emile, 146, 168, 256, 265
Cox, James, 48–49, 51, 53, 61
Creager, R. B., 38, 62, 78, 240, 241
Creel, George, 38
Crissinger, D. R., 145, 152
Cuba, trip to, 25
Curie, Marie, 87, 131
Curtis, Mrs. Cyrus H. K., 168

Dare, Dorothy, 247
Daugherty, Harry
  as attorney general, 2, 44, 73, 133, 243, 325n36
  as campaign manager, 44, 65
  cerebral hemorrhage, 159–160
  corruption in Justice Department, 2, 243, 252–253
  Florida trip, 164, 167, 169–170
  on funeral train, 217
  Harding Memorial Administration and, 246, 255
  inaugural ball and, 66
  Mayflower cruises, 141
  as pallbearer for WGH, 215
  relationship with FKH, 238, 244
  relationship with WGH, 21, 44, 307n123
  resignation, 243, 252, 308–309n161, 325n36
  Smith and, 89, 175
  strengths and weaknesses, 44
  travels with Hardings, 89, 113, 164

Index

WGH's funerals and, 226, 229
WGH's political career and, 28, 44
White House visits, 78, 145, 152, 153, 154, 155
Daugherty, Lucie, 89, 261
Daugherty Injunction, 136
Daughters of the American Revolution, 86, 110, 112, 152, 222
Dauser, Sue, 206
Davis, Norman, 80, 135, 145, 164
Dayton, Ruth, 172
De Aryan, Harold Alexander Leon, "The Funeral Train," 215, 318n66
De Barthe, Joseph, 19, 40, 41, 213
Debs, Eugene, 28, 90
Delaware, trip to, 177–178
DeMille, Cecil B., *Old Wives for New*, 48
Democratic Party, Cox's presidential campaign (1920), 48–49, 51, 53, 61
Denby, Edwin
   as pallbearer for FKH, 264
   resignation, 252
   as secretary of navy, 62, 85, 243, 251
   Teapot Dome scandal and, 243
   WGH's funerals and, 226
   White House visits, 145
Denby, Mrs. Edwin, 93, 106
Denman, Ada, 157
Denver, Colorado, 184–185
DeVeyra, Mrs. Jaime C., 115
DeWolfe, Esther Neely
   children, 28, 37, 96
   FKH's control of inheritance, 37
   FKH's letters to, 94
   marriage, 22
   relationship with FKH, 36–37
   remarriage, 96
   as widow, 36–37
   See also Mezger, Esther
DeWolfe, Eugenia (Jean), 28, 96, 156, 238, 248, 254
   See also Grandchildren of FKH

DeWolfe, George Warren, 28, 96, 140, 156, 175, 238, 254
   See also Grandchildren of FKH
DeWolfe, Henry "Pete," 13–14, 18
DeWolfe, Marshall Eugene
   birth, 13
   burial, 32
   childhood, 14, 16(photo), 18–19
   children, 28
   death, 30
   drinking, 22
   marriage, 22
   relationship with WGH, 18–19
   tuberculosis, 22, 28, 30, 121
Disarmament treaties. *See* Washington Disarmament Conference
Divorces
   of FKH, 14–15, 48
   societal view of, 48–49
Dixon, Hattie, 134
Dogs
   FKH's reluctance to have one in city, 38
   Hardings' pets, 8, 18–19, 80, 91, 124, 139
   Hardings' sympathy for, 125
   See also Laddie Boy
Doheny, Edward, 111, 243
Donithen, Hoke, 238, 246, 321n111
Doyle, Arthur Conan, 212
Drake, Mary Hutchins, 155
Drexel, Constance, 7
Duckett, Kenneth, 234
Dunton, Edith C., 168–169
Dupont, Emile, 164

Easter Egg Rolls, 80, 81(photo), 112, 170
Edison, Thomas A., 88–89, 228, 232
Einstein, Albert, 75, 87
Elections. *See* Presidential campaign; Women's suffrage
Eliot, George, 131
Eliot, Jean, 102, 170

"The End of a Perfect Day" (Bond), 104, 264, 265, 292n31
Epworth Methodist Episcopal Church (Marion), 21, 263, 264
European travels, 25, 27

Fairbanks, Alaska, 190, 192
Fall, Albert, 2
   conviction, 243
   investigations of, 111, 194, 243
   Mayflower cruises, 141
   relationship with FKH, 244, 251
   resignation, 111, 171, 194
   as secretary of interior, 62
   as senator, 43
   travels with Hardings, 62
   See also Teapot Dome scandal
Fall, Emma, 183, 194, 244
Farmers, 105
Federal Board of Hospitalization, 123–124, 237
Feminism, 18, 126–127, 130–131
Ferrell, Robert, 20, 207
Filmer, George, 214
Film stars. *See* Movie stars
Finney, John M. T., 145
Firestone, Harvey, 88–89, 94, 168, 228, 232
Firestone, Isabella, 89, 168
First ladies
   challenges of modern, 7
   clothing, 119
   financial support for widows, 254, 328n102
   roles of FKH's predecessors, 73–75
   social secretaries, 73
First Lady, FKH as
   adjustment, 97
   advocacy and causes, 5–6, 75, 120–135, 163, 173, 266
   car driven by, 94, 111, 138
   celebrity status, 4, 265–266
   criticism of, 83
   daily schedule, 78–79
   delegations received, 81, 86, 110, 112, 115, 116(photo), 120–121, 129
   differences from predecessors, 73–75
   enjoyment of position, 99, 102, 115, 201
   event endorsements, 173
   floral decorations, 82–83, 103, 173, 221
   gifts from public, 91
   golfing, 94
   guests, 5, 78, 79–80, 102, 109, 110, 141
   hands shaken, 5, 77, 88, 100–101, 102–103, 108, 165, 187, 266
   health crisis of 1922–23, 143–149, 169
   historians' views, 2–4
   housekeeping, 82–84
   at inauguration, 72(photo)
   informality, 71–72
   legacy, 7
   openness, 75–76, 149, 150–151, 162, 266
   personnel decisions and, 85, 132–133, 159
   political role, 1, 73, 84–86, 125–126, 128, 266
   portrait, 106, 107(illus.), 163, 237
   private quarters, 163
   public admiration, 4, 7, 72, 76, 151, 176
   reading, 97
   relations with public, 4, 75–77, 266
   requests for assistance from public, 67
   secretaries, 66–67, 80–81
   Secret Service protection, 5, 57, 73, 81
   social demands and resulting fatigue, 99, 101–102, 105, 108, 128, 171
   social life with friends, 68, 71–72, 79, 95–96, 109
   social responsibilities, 2, 80, 98–115
   speeches, 6, 173

staff, 80–82, 86, 153
traditional role, 2, 80
as transitional figure, 3, 4, 7, 73, 84–85, 129, 266
visibility, 5, 120, 266
at Washington Disarmament Conference, 93, 96, 106–108, 120
See also Social events at White House; Travels
Fletcher, Beatrice, 79, 86, 119
Florida, trips to, 25, 26(photo), 42–43, 68–69, 110, 161, 163–170, 171
Flowers
from Alaska, 192
FKH's love of, 221
on funeral train, 217
at WGH's funeral, 227–228
in White House, 82–83, 103, 173, 221
See also Gardens
Foraker, Joseph, 29
Forbes, Charles R.
meeting Hardings, 31
mental health, 305n89
resignation, 180
thefts, 124, 158–159
as Veterans Bureau head, 62, 123, 124, 158–159
Forbes, Marcia, 116, 138
Ford, Henry, 88–89, 228, 232
Forster, Rudolph, 79, 231
France, Joseph, 59
Frelinghuysen, Emily, 79, 164, 165, 243
Frelinghuysen, Joseph
Front Porch campaign, 51
Harding Memorial Administration and, 246
New Jersey estate, 88, 115
as senator, 130
travels with Hardings, 39, 42, 89, 113, 164, 165
White House visits, 79
Freud, Sigmund, 211
Friendship estate, 36, 139, 231, 233–234, 236–237

Friends of FKH
bequests to, 264, 332–333n152
Columbus bridge club, 33, 68, 274n9
letters from FKH, 66–67
from Marion, 33, 79–80, 171, 258–259
from Ohio, 105, 109–110, 141, 161
during presidency, 68, 71–72, 79, 95–96, 109
Scobeys, 31, 38
Senate wives, 32, 33, 46, 64, 71, 104–105, 109, 113
White House visits, 68, 78, 79, 109
in widowhood, 243, 245, 250, 253, 255
See also McLean, Evalyn Walsh; Social life; Travels
Front Porch campaign, 51–57, 53(photo), 55(photo), 242
"The Funeral Train" (De Aryan), 215, 318n66

Gambier College, 255
Gann, Dolly, 237
Gardens
in Marion, 21–22
White House, 76, 111, 139, 170–171, 221
See also Flowers
Garfield, Harry A., 110
Garfield Hospital Nurses Home Fund, 104
Garvey, Marcus, 288–289n105
Gary, Elbert H., 246
Gilbert, Clinton Wallace, 67
Gillett, Frederick H., 108, 182, 252
Gillett, Mrs. Frederick, 93, 106
Girl Scouts, 104, 127, 173
Gish, Dorothy, 5, 75, 110, 173
Gish, Lillian, 5, 54–55, 75, 110
Gladwell, Malcolm, 60–61
Gleason, Lafayette B., 132–133
Goldstein, Isadore, 190

Grandchildren of FKH
  bequests from FKH, 264–265
  bequests from WGH, 238
  births, 28
  gifts from FKH, 156
  kept at distance, 28–29, 48, 96, 108–109, 137–138, 140–141, 254
  money sent to, 96, 108–109, 118, 155, 156, 169, 234, 247
  relationship, 15, 247–248, 254
  See also Mezger, Esther
Grant, Julia (Princess Cantacuzene), 93, 106
Grant, Ulysses S., 93, 112
Grayson, Cary T., 75
Green, H. R., 50
Griffith, D. W., 5, 75, 106, 110

Hagner, Isabella "Belle," 73
Hairstylist, 105–106
Hale, Frederick, 89, 151, 164
Hale, Mrs. Frederick, 62, 67, 79, 89, 274n8
Haley, Jim, 233
Hammond, John Hays, 246
Handshaking sessions
  on Alaska trip, 187, 188
  on election night, 61
  in Florida, 165
  health risks, 102–103
  at Republican convention (1920), 50
  at White House, 77, 88, 100–101, 102–103, 108, 266
Hard, Charles E., 43–44
Harding, Abigail V., 238, 259, 261
Harding, Carolyn, 31
  See also Votaw, Carolyn
Harding, Charity, 17
  See also Remsberg, Charity M.
Harding, Daisy, 29, 34–35, 40, 141
Harding, Florence Kling
  astrological interest, 24, 46–47
  birth, 8
  childhood, 8, 9(photo), 11, 12

  death, 7, 261
  diary, 24–25
  divorce, 14–15, 48
  education, 12
  family, 8–12
  femininity, 3–4
  feminist views, 18, 126–127, 130–131
  first marriage, 13–14, 15, 28–29, 48–49, 115, 138
  on Front Porch, 53(photo)
  funeral, 263–264
  on funeral train, 215–219
  homes in childhood, 12, 13(photo), 14(photo)
  interest in flowers, 111–112
  interest in music, 113–114
  interest in occult, 24, 46–48
  obituaries, 7, 261, 262, 263
  organizational skills, 57
  personality, 84, 265, 330n137
  as pianist and piano teacher, 12, 13, 14, 17, 100, 172
  political interest and skills, 1, 85, 131
  role in WGH's political career, 1–2, 28, 29, 35, 43–44, 45, 52, 128, 266
  as Senate wife, 31, 32–49
  son's birth, 13
  tomb, 261, 264
  voting, 6, 60, 61(photo)
  wealth, 119, 236, 238, 253–254, 264–265
  will and estate, 238, 259, 262, 264–265, 331n147, 332–333n152
  as young woman, 12–17, 15(photo)
  See also First Lady, FKH as; Grandchildren; Harding marriage; Travels
Harding, Florence Kling, illnesses
  on Alaska trip, 192
  debate on surgery, 147–148
  first bout of kidney disease (1905), 22–23
  food poisoning, 89

information provided to public, 6, 149, 150–151, 162
kidney disease, 28, 32, 36, 40, 42–43
kidney disease while First Lady, 68, 143–149, 169
kidney surgery, 22–23, 148
mental control, 146–147, 265
public concern and prayers, 149, 150–151, 162, 169, 259
recovery (1923), 151–157, 160–163, 169, 171, 172–173
strength and endurance, 146–147, 256
sympathy for disabled veterans related to, 121
treatments, 145, 148, 151, 192
in widowhood, 251, 253, 256, 257, 258–261
Harding, Florence Kling, physical appearance
beauty, 67, 68, 106, 161
change after presidential election, 67
as child, 8
descriptions in press, 104, 172, 184, 187, 188, 200–201
dissatisfaction with photographs, 5, 45–46
effects of illness, 36, 104
friends' descriptions, 36, 68, 106, 161
hairstylist and face artist, 105–106
hands, 172
during recovery (1923), 161, 162–163, 173
See also Clothing; Jewelry
Harding, Florence Kling, widowhood
advisers, 240–241, 246, 250–251, 252, 253
biographies of WGH, 240, 241, 242, 256
congressional memorial service, 251–252
correspondence, 240, 250–251

departure from White House, 230–235
first anniversary of WGH's death, 257
friends, 243, 245, 250, 253, 255
at Friendship estate, 233–234, 236–237
grieving, 217, 237, 257, 263
illnesses, 251, 253, 256, 257, 258–261
mail franking privileges, 254
in Marion, 238, 243–247, 256–258
mourning observance, 249–250, 258
optimism, 236
papers burned, 2, 233–234, 239, 240, 242, 243
pessimism, 234
plan to stay in Marion, 227, 231, 235, 236, 237
poem, 257, 328–329n112
requests for endorsements, 240–241, 243, 258
response to WGH's death, 205–206, 208–209
secretary, 240, 250
self-control, 210–211, 213–214, 223, 229, 256
settlement of WGH's estate, 238
strength shown, 6–7, 214, 256
in Washington, 245, 248–256
wealth, 236, 238, 253–254, 264–265
at White Oaks Farm, 238
Harding, George T., II (brother of WGH), 40, 70, 147, 255
Harding, George Tryon (father of WGH)
care of FKH, 41
dream of WGH's death, 210
family history, 59
FKH and, 34–35
Harding Memorial Administration and, 255
as homeopath, 17, 18
at inauguration, 70

Harding, George Tryon *(continued)*
  relationship with FKH, 259
  on WGH's appearance, 60
  WGH's bequest to, 238
  at WGH's funeral, 229, 230
  White House visits, 78, 154
Harding, Phoebe, 17, 18
Harding, Warren G.
  biographies, 240, 241, 242, 256
  birth and childhood, 17
  birthplace, 170
  "black blood" issue, 17, 58–60
  Carrie Phillips affair, 23–26, 27–28, 29, 30, 39
  on Chautauqua circuit, 26, 31, 39
  clothing, 36, 120, 197
  death, 6, 203–205, 206–209, 210, 238
  drinking habits, 95, 166, 185
  early career, 17–18
  education, 17
  family, 17
  friends, 38, 39, 42, 90, 95–96, 185
  on Front Porch, 53(photo)
  funerals, 209, 212, 214, 220–229, 223(photo), 225(photo), 228(photo)
  funeral train, 209, 212, 213, 213(photo), 215–219
  golfing, 37–38, 42, 88, 89, 90, 91, 94–95, 110, 113, 137–138, 151, 163–164, 165, 168, 170, 207
  income, 33, 119
  as Mason, 177
  memorials, 255
  moderate drinking, 30
  personality, 18
  physical appearance, 36, 60–61, 71
  portrait, 255–256
  public mourning for, 215–219, 221–222, 225–226, 225(photo), 229–230
  on race relations, 6, 50, 55–56, 58, 92, 288–289n105
  sale of *Star*, 179–180, 210
  tobacco chewing, 135
  tomb, 227–229, 257, 258, 261, 264, 329n114
  wealth, 179–180, 238
  will, 238
  See also Harding marriage; Travels
Harding, Warren G., health
  decline, 163–164, 175
  final illness, 194–202
  food poisoning in Alaska, 192, 199
  grippe attack, 157, 158, 160, 162, 164, 169
  heart problems, 207, 315n23
  hemorrhoids, 186, 199
  infection on Alaska trip, 192
  information released to public, 199–200, 201–202
  nervous breakdowns, 19
Harding, Warren G., political career
  FKH's role, 1–2, 28, 29, 35, 43–44, 52, 128, 266
  gubernatorial candidacy, 27, 28
  as lieutenant governor, 21
  national recognition, 28
  progressive positions, 54, 92
  relations with press, 53
  Republican convention (1912), 28
  Republican convention (1916), 34
  Senate race (1914), 28, 29, 30
  as senator, 31, 34, 43, 64
  speeches written or edited by FKH, 29, 51, 70–71, 188
  as state senator, 21
  support of Prohibition, 27, 95, 185, 312n32
  support of Republican candidates, 28, 34
  support of women's suffrage, 35, 54, 56, 113
  talk of presidential candidacy, 34, 41–42, 43
  See also Harding presidency; Presidential campaign
"Harding blue," 5, 71, 117, 119

Harding-Coolidge Theatrical League, 54–55
Harding error, 60–61
Harding marriage
  age difference, 18
  alleged affairs, 22, 29–30, 307n123
  alleged plan of FKH to kill WGH, 6, 180, 208–209
  Carrie Phillips affair and, 23–26, 27–28, 29, 30, 39
  childlessness, 22, 40
  closeness, 150, 208
  "Duchess" nickname, 20
  egalitarianism, 21
  emotional support, 43, 150
  happiness, 21, 43
  meeting, 17
  relationship during presidential campaign, 52
  relationship with Marshall, 18–19
  wedding, 18
  WGH's final illness and, 197–202, 203, 204–205
  WGH's presence during FKH's illness, 144, 145, 146, 147, 148–150, 153, 155, 160, 163
  WGH's visits to women on Florida trip, 165, 166
Harding Memorial Administration (HMA)
  control of WGH's papers, 2, 23, 234, 239–240
  fundraising, 245–247, 331n146
  mausoleum, 230, 242, 245–247, 255, 264, 331n146
  museum, 242, 246, 264, 331n146
  officers and trustees, 246, 255, 256
  Washington headquarters, 246
Harding Memorial Week, 247
Harding Park Golf Club (San Francisco), 246
Harding presidency
  bonus bill veto, 88, 121, 124, 151, 296n106
  cabinet members, 62, 73, 79, 219, 226, 230
  celebrity culture and, 4–5, 55, 75, 265–266
  daily schedule, 79
  historians' views, 2, 111, 244
  historical context, 4
  inauguration, 66, 70–71, 72(photo)
  issues, 88
  League of Women Voters building, 129
  meetings with public, 77, 284–285n30
  papers, 2, 232, 233–234, 239–240, 242, 243, 322n134
  pardons, 133–134
  peace treaty with Germany, 88
  physical demands of job, 163–164, 207–208
  public support, 77, 176, 210, 266
  railroad strike, 136, 138, 140, 141
  re-election bid discussed, 169–170
  relations with press, 120, 149
  reputation, 2, 111, 241–242, 244
  scandals, 2, 124, 158–159, 252–253
  speeches, 92, 153–154, 162, 177, 178, 185, 212, 288–289n105, 317n51
  staff, 79
  valet, 120, 157, 182, 194, 197
  Washington Disarmament Conference, 88, 92–94, 96, 106–108, 120, 169, 247, 293n45
  See also Alaska trip; Presidential campaign; Teapot Dome scandal
Harding Publishing Company, 238, 249, 253–254
Harlan, John Marshall, 80
Harlan, Laura, 174(photo)
  background, 80
  bequest from FKH, 264
  Boone on, 286n48
  on FKH's recovery, 152, 153
  at handshaking sessions, 77
  help to FKH in widowhood, 232, 233, 250, 255

Harlan, Laura *(continued)*
  letters by, 154
  Mayflower cruises, 138
  at White House events, 162
  White House position, 67, 78, 80–81, 86, 105, 132, 157
Harmon, Judson, 27
Harvey, George B. M., 49, 85, 94, 113, 156
Havis, Laura, 67
Hawaii, travels to, 31, 159
Hays, Will, 46, 49, 50, 57, 148–149, 173, 301n10
Haywood, Bill, 166
Haywood, Maizie, 166
Hearst, William Randolph, 164
Henderson
  captain, 213–214
  description, 190
  Hardings aboard, 191(photo)
  use on Alaska trip, 173–174, 181, 189–190, 192, 194–195
Henderson, John B., 114
Hibben, Jenny Davidson, 253
High, Ephram, 133
Highways, 176, 309n163
Hilles, Charles Dewey, 133
Hirsch, Arthur, 56
Hitchcock, Gilbert, 42
HMA. *See* Harding Memorial Administration
Hodder, Susan P. M., 22
Hogan, Timothy, 30
Hollywood stars. *See* Movie stars
Hood, Marjorie, 173
Hoover, Herbert
  on Alaska trip, 180–181, 198
  as commerce secretary, 62, 73, 78, 79, 141
  as president, 287n76, 331n146
  relationship with WGH, 181, 245, 326n48
  travels with Hardings, 91
  WGH's death and, 205, 206, 226

Hoover, Irwin "Ike," 82, 85, 106, 153
Hoover, Lou Henry, 78, 118, 121, 205, 260
Horoscopes. *See* Astrology
Horses
  gifts to Hardings, 94, 232
  of Hardings, 124
  ridden by FKH, 8, 100, 172
  riding in Zion National Park, 186
  riding prevented by health problems, 94
Horse shows, 113
House of Representatives. *See* Congress
Hughes, Antoinette, 91
Hughes, Catherine, 135
Hughes, Charles Evans
  daughter, 135
  eulogy for WGH, 252
  on FKH's death, 262–263
  Front Porch visits, 55
  Harding Memorial Administration and, 246
  presidential candidacy (1916), 34, 35
  as secretary of state, 62, 73, 79, 155, 220, 293n44
  WGH's funerals and, 220, 226, 227
Hunt, Evelyn, 76–77

Immigration
  Harding speech on, 188
  quotas, 134
Inauguration, 66, 70–71, 72(photo)
Indians, 188, 190
Industrial Workers of the World (IWW), 187, 188
Interior Department, 62
  See also Teapot Dome scandal
IWW. *See* Industrial Workers of the World

Jackson, Wilson X., 139, 221
Jaffray, Elizabeth, 83–84, 86, 105–106, 117, 185

Index

Jennings, Ethel, 88, 138, 182, 253, 255, 264
Jennings, Malcolm (Mack), 34, 42, 136
   as adviser to FKH, 240–241, 246, 250–251, 252, 253
   on Alaska trip, 182
   on Daugherty, 252
   on FKH, 263
   in Ohio, 138
   as pallbearer for FKH, 264
   physical appearance, 90
   on politics, 130
   at Republican convention (1920), 49–51
   WGH and, 44, 88, 90, 203
   WGH's letters to, 45, 62
   White House visits, 78
Jewelry of FKH
   in estate, 264, 265, 331–332n149
   at inauguration, 71
   neckband, 5, 71, 93, 104, 172
   worn for White House events, 117
Jews, 134
Johnson, Hiram, 49
Johnson, S. M., 176
Jolson, Al, 5, 54–55, 55(photo), 171
Jones, Mrs. E. Clarence, 166
Journalists
   on Alaska trip, 182–183, 184, 185, 200, 241, 311n18
   WGH's death and, 209, 211, 214
   See also Press; Women journalists
Judges, 105
   See also Supreme Court justices
Jules (hairstylist), 105–106
Juneau, Alaska, 190
Jusserand, Jules, 93, 146, 154, 252
Justice Department
   corruption, 2, 243
   presidential pardons, 133–134
   Prohibition enforcement, 89, 132, 243, 325n36
   See also Daugherty, Harry

Kansas City, Missouri, 183–184
Kellogg, Frank B., 42, 141, 151, 152, 153, 245
Kellogg, Mrs. Frank B., 93, 106, 141
Kellogg sanitarium, 19, 23
Kennedy, Jacqueline, 231, 322n132
Keyes, Frances Parkinson, 330n137
King, Alfred A., 132
King, George, 227
Kling, Amos, 10(photo)
   background, 10
   businesses, 238
   death, 28
   Florida home, 25
   marriages, 10–11, 25
   opposition to FKH's marriages, 14, 17, 18
   relationship with FKH, 8, 12
   relationship with WGH, 19
Kling, Caroline Denman, 25
Kling, Clifford
   bequest from FKH, 264
   as child, 8, 9(photo)
   death, 332n151
   FKH's final illness and death, 259, 261
   Florida home, 165
   hotel, 226
   Marion home, 227, 233
   relationship with FKH, 20, 275n29, 332n151
   White House visits, 147
Kling, Louisa M. Bouton, 8, 10–11, 11(photo), 18
Kling, Louise, 264
Kling, Vitalis ("Tal"), 8, 264, 332n151
Klunk, Charles A., 40
Knickerbocker theater, 106
Kohlsaat, Mrs. H. H., 245
Kohn family, 134
Kornfeld, Joseph S., 259, 329n118
Ku Klux Klan (KKK), 227–228

Labor
  eight-hour workday, 189
  miners, 134–135, 136, 186
  railroad strike, 136, 138, 140, 141
  wages of pressmen, 238
Laddie Boy (dog), 8, 91
  after WGH's death, 214, 221
  at benefit events, 124
  birthday, 139, 140(photo)
  at Easter Egg Rolls, 80
  feeding from table, 161
  during FKH's illness, 145
  pedigree, 124
  photographs of, 5, 177, 243
LaFollette, Robert, 111
Landes, George W., 263
Lasker, Albert D.
  advertising firm, 46
  Mayflower cruises, 141
  payments to Phillips, 58
  presidential campaign role, 46, 50
  Teapot Dome investigation and, 243
  travels with Hardings, 164
  White House visits, 149, 152
Laszlo de Lombos, Philip Alexius, portrait of FKH, 106, 107(illus.), 163, 237
Lawler, Kathleen
  bequest from FKH, 264
  as campaign assistant, 45, 50, 51–54, 56–57, 59, 60
  on FKH, 15–17, 47, 48, 57, 68, 85, 101–102, 172, 257
  on FKH leaving White House, 230, 239
  as FKH's assistant, 64, 242, 256
  on FKH's illnesses, 144, 256
  "The Hardings I Knew," 242
  move to Washington, 64–65
  on rumors about FKH, 157
League of American Pen Women, 86, 112, 173
League of Nations, 75, 88, 92, 120

League of Women Voters, 86, 126, 129, 222
Lee, Mary
  FKH's letters to, 78, 96–97, 101, 105, 109, 111, 136, 137, 249–250
  job, 132, 161
  letters to FKH, 85, 109
  relationship with FKH, 132, 134, 138
  WGH's letters to, 153, 161
Lee Highway Association, 176
Library of Congress, 234, 239–240, 258
Lincoln, Abraham, 218, 220, 239
Lincoln, Robert Todd, 114
Lincoln Memorial, 114
Lincoln Memorial University, 162
Lindbergh baby kidnapping, 208
Lindsey, Estelle Lawton, 210–211, 214
Livermore, Mrs. Arthur, 127
Lloyd George, David, 247
Lodge, Henry Cabot, 222
Lodge, Mrs. Henry Cabot, 67
Longshore, Frank, 263
Longshore, Hazel, 259, 261, 263, 264, 265
Longworth, Alice Roosevelt
  description of FKH, 3, 25
  Front Porch campaign and, 53
  honeymoon, 25
  relationship with Hardings, 25, 35–36, 110, 141
  at Republican convention, 49
  on WGH, 36, 185
  White House visits, 110, 141
Longworth, Nicholas
  drinking habits, 95
  friendship with Hardings, 35–36, 141
  Front Porch campaign and, 53, 53(photo)
  honeymoon, 25
  at Republican convention (1920), 49
Lorimer, George, 167

Lorimer, Mrs. George H., 127, 130
Lowden, Frank O., 49
Lowell, A. Laurence, 110
Lynchings, 54, 88

Madison, Dolly (journalist), 99, 104, 139
Marcia, Madame. *See* Champrey, Marcia
Marion, Ohio
  centennial observation, 109, 137–138
  concern about FKH during illness, 151
  FKH in as widow, 238, 243–247, 256–258
  friends from, 33, 79–80, 171, 258–259
  Front Porch campaign, 51–57, 53(photo), 55(photo), 242
  Harding friends, 21, 33, 79–80, 171, 258–259
  Harding home as museum, 242, 246, 264, 331n146
  Harding homes, 18, 21–22, 31, 66, 227, 238, 254
  Harding mausoleum, 230, 242, 245–247, 255, 264, 331n146
  Harding memorials, 242–243, 245–247
  Hardings' visit during presidency, 109–110, 137–138
  Jewish residents, 134
  Kling family, 10–11, 12
  opposition to Prohibition, 27
  residents looking for Washington jobs, 132
  train station, 69
  WGH's funeral, 225–230, 228(photo), 321n111
  See also White Oaks Farm sanitarium
Marion Star, 38
  building, 238, 264
  FKH's work, 19, 20, 23, 249, 254
  newsboys, 19–20
  purchase by WGH, 18
  sale by WGH, 179–180, 210
  stories on FKH's last illness, 259, 261
  WGH's income from, 33
  WGH's writings, 27
Marketing, 4–5, 46, 55
Marks, Stella, 122
Marshall, Lois, 64
Marshall, Thomas R., 64
Masons, 177
Mayflower
  cruises, 113, 115, 135, 138, 141–142, 143
  Delaware trip, 177–178
  history, 287n76
  New England voyage, 89
  trips on, 86–87, 90, 91, 114, 195
Mayo, Charles, 145, 147, 148, 148(photo), 152
Mayo, Mrs. Charles, 147, 152
McCandless, James S., 144
McCormick, Ruth Hanna, 128, 129
McGee, R. W., 81
McKinley, Ida, 192, 328n102
McKinley, William, 51, 218, 220, 224
McLean, Edward "Ned," 35, 80
  divorce, 248
  in Florida, 165, 166
  friendship with WGH, 36
  Harding Memorial Administration and, 246
  horse given to FKH, 94
  houseboat, 165, 168
  house used by Daugherty, 89
  inaugural ball, 66, 71
  Mayflower cruises, 138
  newspapers owned, 35, 36, 237
  New Year's ball, 155
  travels with Hardings, 62, 113
  White House visits, 79, 149, 153, 155
McLean, Emily, 108, 237

McLean, Evalyn Walsh, 65(photo)
  book by, 165–166, 167
  Boone on, 87
  in Cincinnati, 237, 258
  clothing sent to FKH, 119
  divorce, 248
  FKH's letters to, 143–144, 160, 179, 236–237, 248
  on FKH's political ambition, 35
  in Florida, 164, 165, 166, 237, 248
  Friendship estate, 36, 139, 231, 233–234, 236–237
  friendship with FKH, 35, 36, 86, 94, 108, 111, 113, 138, 166–167, 233, 253, 260
  health, 174–175, 179
  houseboat, 165, 168
  inaugural ball, 71
  letters to FKH, 160, 166–167, 237
  money extorted by Means, 208
  New Year's ball, 155
  New York shopping trips, 68
  travels with Hardings, 62, 110, 113, 166
  WGH's funerals and, 220, 224–225
  WGH's presidential campaign and, 43
  White House visits, 78, 79, 80, 147, 149, 152, 155
McNary, Charles, 196
Means, Gaston B., 3, 180, 208, 316n33
Media
  newsreels, 46, 91
  radio, 154, 183, 247
  use in presidential campaign, 46, 52, 55
  See also Advertising; Press
Meek, Mary Broadfield, 68
Mellon, Andrew W., 73, 79, 153, 246
Merchant marine, 163, 229
Mezger, Esther
  bequest from FKH, 264
  children, 96, 108–109
  FKH's letters to, 101, 113, 137, 140, 155, 156, 164, 169, 171, 175, 178, 234, 250, 253
  letters to FKH, 247–248
  money sent by FKH, 96, 108–109, 118, 155, 156, 169, 234, 247
  relationship with FKH, 140, 259
  White House visits, 114–115
  See also DeWolfe, Esther Neely
Mezger, Helen Elizabeth, 96, 108–109, 169
Mezger, Roscoe, 96, 175, 247–248
Miller, E. F., 218
Miller, Kristie, 75
Miners, 134–135, 136, 186
Mondell, Frank, 163
Moore, Alexander, 245
Moore, A. P., 68
Moore, Charles, 239, 258
Moore, Robert Walton, 126
Morello, John, 5
Mosby-Coleman, Mrs., 249
Moton, Robert, 114
Movies, 4–5, 48, 168, 173
Movie stars
  Front Porch visits, 54–55, 55(photo)
  at White House, 5, 75, 110
Muskingum College, 137

National American Institute of Homeopaths, 102–103
National American Woman Suffrage Association (NAWSA), 129
National Highway System, 176, 309n63
National Horse Show, 113
National Republican Club, 127–129
National Society Daughters of Founders and Patriots of America, 12
National Society of the Daughters of 1812, 86, 112

National Women's Party (NWP), 127, 129
Navy Department, Denby as secretary, 62, 85, 243, 251
See also Henderson; *Mayflower*
NAWSA. *See* National American Woman Suffrage Association
Neely, George, 22
New, Catherine
   friendship with FKH, 109, 235, 237
   letters from FKH, 67
   travels with Hardings, 68, 86, 89
   White House visits, 78, 79, 86, 155, 160–161
New, Harry
   as pallbearer for FKH, 264
   as postmaster, 226, 301n10
   relationship with FKH, 235, 245, 253
   relationship with WGH, 90
   as senator, 130
   travels with Hardings, 89
   WGH's funerals and, 226
   White House visits, 79, 145, 155, 160–161
Newspapers. *See* Journalists; *Marion Star*; Press
Newsreels, 46, 91
New Year's reception (1922), 97, 99–101, 100(photo)
New York City, trips to, 68, 91, 171–172, 245
Noblett, Elizabeth, 123
Nurses. *See* Powderly, Ruth V.
NWP. *See* National Women's Party

Obama, Barack, 119
Obama, Michelle, 119
Ogburn, William F., 47–48
Ohio
   governors, 27
   Point Pleasant, 112
   presidential primary (1920), 45
   state senate, 21
   WGH as lieutenant governor, 21
Ohio Central College, 17, 137
Ohio Historical Society, 234, 239
O'Malley, Henry, 125

Page, William Tyler, 222
Palace Hotel, San Francisco, 197, 198–202, 203–206
Panama, 62, 63(photo)
Panama Canal, 181–182
Pennsylvania Republican Women's Club, 130
Pepper, George Wharton, 137
Pershing, John J., 121, 217, 222, 228, 243
Pets. *See* Dogs
Philippine Parliamentary Mission, 115, 116(photo)
Phillips, Carrie, 24(photo)
   affair with WGH, 23–26, 27–28, 29, 30, 39
   blackmailing of WGH, 41, 58, 280n138
   death, 272n55
   friendship with Hardings, 23, 25–26, 27
   in Germany, 26, 27–28, 29
   travels with Hardings, 25–26, 27
   visits to Marion, 28, 29, 39, 56
   WGH's letters and poems to, 23, 39, 239
Phillips, David Graham, 48
Phillips, Isabelle, 23, 26
Phillips, Jim, 23, 24(photo), 25–26, 39, 58
Phipps, Lawrence C., 184
Physicians, 145, 147, 148, 148(photo), 152, 198–199, 202, 206
   See also Boone, Joel; Sawyer, Charles
Pickford, Mary, 54–55
Pittsburgh Women's Republican Marching Club, 56

Poindexter, Mrs. Miles, 46, 71
Point Pleasant, Ohio, 112
Politics. *See* Harding, Warren G., political career; Presidential campaign; Republican Party; Women's political involvement
Popular culture, context of Harding administration, 4–5, 55, 75
  See also Movies
Powderly, Ruth V.
  on Alaska trip, 174, 175, 192
  bequest from FKH, 264
  care of FKH, 82, 144, 205, 232, 233, 234
  care of WGH, 204
  on funeral train, 217
Presidential campaign (1920)
  "black blood" issue, 58–60
  Coolidge as running mate, 50
  Cox as opponent, 48–49, 51, 53, 61
  election victory, 60–62
  expenditures, 46
  FKH's role, 45–46, 49, 51, 52, 54, 57, 62, 66
  Front Porch campaign, 51–57, 53(photo), 55(photo), 242
  issues, 54
  movie star supporters, 54–55, 55(photo)
  nomination, 47, 49–51
  platform, 54
  primaries, 45
  Republican convention, 49–51
  scandals, 57–60
  speeches, 51
  trips, 57
  use of media, 46, 52, 55
  WGH's decision to run, 43–45, 50–51
Press
  McLean's newspapers, 35, 36, 237
  wages of pressmen, 238
  WGH's relations with, 53, 120, 149
  See also Journalists; *Marion Star*
Press, FKH's relations with
  coverage of visiting delegations, 5, 86, 110, 115
  cultivation of press, 115–116, 120
  descriptions of clothing, 102, 104, 117, 119, 120, 172, 188, 200
  informal discussions, 4, 68, 115–116
  interviews, 168–169
  interviews refused, 4, 68, 115, 184–185, 201
  photographs, 5, 116
  work at *Marion Star*, 19, 20, 23, 249, 254
  See also Women journalists
Princeton University, 115
Prisons
  FKH's interest in prisoners, 133
  for women, 125–126, 163
Proctor, William H., 59
Prohibition
  effects on White House events, 185
  enforcement, 89, 132, 243, 325n36
  FKH's view of, 95
  WGH's view of, 27, 95, 185, 312n32
  Wilson's veto, 284n18
Psychics. *See* Champrey, Marcia

Race relations
  FKH's views, 6, 50
  WGH's speech in Birmingham, 92, 288–289n105
  WGH's views, 6, 50, 55–56, 58, 92, 288–289n105
  See also African Americans
Rachmaninoff, Sergei, 114
Radicals, 187, 188
Radio broadcasts, 154, 183, 247
Railroads
  in Alaska, 191–192
  cross-country journey to Alaska, 182–190
  funeral train, 209, 212, 213, 213(photo), 215–219
  "Inaugural Special" train, 69
  strikes, 136, 138, 140, 141

Rapp, O. S., 264, 321n111
Reagan, Nancy, 48
Red Cross, 37
Remsberg, Charity M. (Mrs. Elton E.), 17, 201, 214, 217, 238
Republican Glee Club, Columbus, 50, 61, 137, 138, 249–250, 264
Republican National Committee, 129, 130, 133, 136
Republican Party
  conventions, 28, 34, 49–51
  Hughes presidential candidacy (1916), 34, 35
  Taft and Roosevelt supporters, 27, 28
  women's groups, 6, 127–130, 173
Reynolds, Mrs. R., 67
Richards, Edmund, 12
Ring, Blanche, 55, 55(photo)
Ringling, John, 113
Robertson, Alice G., 129, 130
Robinson, Corrine Roosevelt, 73
Rockwell, William, 81
Rolph, James, 198
Roosevelt, Edith, 5, 46, 73, 81, 171, 328n102
Roosevelt, Eleanor, 1, 126, 133
Roosevelt, Theodore
  death, 41
  as president, 198, 287n76
  presidential candidacy (1912), 28
  presidential papers, 239
  Republican Party split and, 27, 28
Roosevelt, Theodore, Jr., 121, 141
Rosing, Vladimir, 106
Rumpf, Louise H., 135
Russell, Francis, 3–4, 20, 22, 23, 28, 29, 39, 59, 234
Russell, J. E., 132
Russell, Lillian, 54–55, 68, 111

Salt Lake City, Utah, 185–186
San Francisco
  Harding Park Golf Club, 246
  Palace Hotel, 197, 198–202, 203–206

Sawyer, Carl
  bequest from FKH, 264, 332n152
  Boone and, 262
  care of FKH, 41, 145, 259, 260, 261
  Harding Memorial Administration and, 255
  as pallbearer for FKH, 264
Sawyer, Charles, 148(photo)
  on Alaska trip, 181, 182, 183, 192, 198
  Boone and, 94, 111, 196, 262
  campaign trips for WGH, 55
  care of FKH, 41, 64–65, 94, 179, 192, 224, 256, 259
  care of FKH as widow, 217, 234
  care of FKH during 1922 crisis, 143, 144–145, 147–148, 149, 151
  care of WGH, 192, 207, 208
  care of WGH during final illness, 196, 198–199, 201–202, 203, 204, 205
  in Coolidge administration, 230, 237, 244, 256, 262
  death, 258, 263
  on election night, 61
  at Federal Bureau of Hospitalization, 123–124
  on FKH, 206, 211
  on funeral train, 217
  Harding administration post, 65, 72
  Harding Memorial Administration and, 246, 255, 256
  as Hardings' personal physician in White House, 72, 82, 172
  at inauguration, 70
  Mayflower cruises, 138, 141
  relationship with FKH, 65, 230, 231, 237, 257, 259, 262
  sanitarium, 23
  travels with Hardings, 89, 113, 165
  WGH's funerals and, 224–225, 227
  White House visits, 78, 79, 152
  See also White Oaks Farm sanitarium
Sawyer, Mandy, 145
  on Alaska trip, 182, 198

Sawyer, Mandy (*continued*)
  Boone and, 250
  on funeral train, 217
  relationship with FKH, 65, 234, 249, 255, 256–257, 261
  White House visits, 152
Scandals
  effects on WGH's reputation, 263
  FKH's silence on, 253
  Forbes thefts, 124, 158–159
  investigations, 252
  in presidential campaign (1920), 57–60
  in veterans hospitals, 123–124, 158–159
  See also Teapot Dome scandal
Schaffner, Charles, 238, 265
Scobey, Evaland, 149
  FKH's letters to, 101
  letters from FKH, 66–67
  letters from WGH, 95
  travels with Hardings, 27
  visits from Hardings, 31, 38
  White House visits, 78
Scobey, Frank
  on blacks, 50
  drinking habits, 95
  encouraging WGH to run for president, 30, 41–42
  friendship with Hardings, 27, 31, 38, 62, 95
  White House visits, 78, 149
Seattle, Washington, 194–196
Secret Service
  agents, 73
  on Alaska trip, 187
  arrival on election night, 61
  on Florida trip, 165
  protection of FKH, 5, 57, 73, 81
  See also Starling, Edmund
Senate
  debate on disarmament treaties, 108
  Teapot Dome investigation, 111, 194, 243
  See also Congress

Senate wives
  Congressional Club, 104–105
  friends of FKH, 32, 33, 46, 64, 71, 104–105, 109, 113
  White House reception for, 91
Seward, Alaska, 190, 192
Sherrill, Clarence O., 83, 103, 231, 322n129
Shriners, 144, 176–177
Silverman, Jacob, 125
Sinclair, Harry, 111, 243
Sitka, Alaska, 192–193, 193(photo)
Small, Robert, 236
Smith, H. W., 182
Smith, Harry C., 92
Smith, Jess
  Daugherty and, 89, 175
  Florida trip, 164, 167
  health problems, 160
  inaugural ball and, 66
  Prohibition enforcement, 89
  relationship with FKH, 89–90
  relationship with WGH, 307n123
  suicide, 175, 180–181
  travels with Hardings, 89, 164
  White House visits, 149, 152
Smith, Laura, 240
Smoot, Reed, 186
Social events at White House
  concerts, 113–114
  Congressional Club reception, 104–105
  covered by women journalists, 5, 93–94, 103–104
  delegations received, 174(photo)
  Easter Egg Rolls, 80, 81(photo), 112, 170
  effects of Prohibition, 185
  Fourth of July reception, 88
  frequency, 102, 108, 110
  New Year's reception (1922), 97, 99–101, 100(photo)
  planning, 80
  receptions, 103, 105, 106, 108, 112, 117, 152, 162–163, 173, 177, 292n26

state dinners, 102
veterans' parties, 121
women's groups, 110, 173
Social life
  bridge games, 71, 87, 91, 141
  charity balls, 104
  during FKH's recovery, 152, 153, 154, 155, 160–161
  poker evenings, 35–36, 71, 96, 141
  as Senate wife, 35–36
  at White House, 68, 71–72, 79, 95–96, 109
  See also Friends of FKH
Social workers, 173
Society for Southern Relief, 104
Sousa, John Philip, 112
Southern Industrial Association, 135
Sparkes, Boyden, 167
Sproul, William Cameron, 125, 139
St. Paul's Episcopal Church (Marion), 238, 264
Stanfield, Robert, 196
Starling, Edmund
  on Alaska trip, 181
  on Britton, 40
  on driving, 137
  on FKH, 106, 180
  on funeral train, 216
  relationship with FKH, 83
  on social events, 94
  travels with Hardings, 89, 112, 166, 195, 197
  view of Hardings, 71–72
  on WGH, 51, 95–96, 157, 166
  WGH's death and, 206
State Department, Hughes as secretary, 62, 73, 79, 155, 220, 293n44
Stewart, Martha, 126
Sullivan, Mark, 3, 52, 71, 72, 154
Sumners, Hatton, 254
Supreme Court justices
  at WGH's funeral, 222
  White House events for, 105, 106, 117, 152
  See also Taft, William Howard

Sutherland, Mrs. George, 46
Swank, Jesse, 21, 229, 263

Tacoma, Washington, 189
Taft, Helen, 74
Taft, Nellie, 28, 73–74, 83–84, 93, 106, 149
Taft, William Howard
  as chief justice, 105, 252
  Lincoln Memorial dedication, 114
  as president, 28, 198, 287n76
  presidential papers, 239
  re-election campaign, 28
  Republican Party split and, 27
  summer White House, 25–26
  WGH and, 28
  WGH's funerals and, 219, 222, 224, 227, 229
Teapot Dome scandal
  damage to WGH's reputation, 2, 111, 241–242, 244
  FKH's view of, 244
  Hardings' awareness of, 183, 243–244, 325n40
  investigations, 111, 194, 243
Terrell, Mary Church, 58
Thomas, Norman, 20
Thomas, Robert Young, 59
Tillinghast, Mrs. James D., 127
Todd, Mrs. David, 130, 153
Trains. *See* Railroads
Travels
  to Atlantic City, 90–91, 195
  beneficial effects, 113
  camping trip, 88–89
  on Chautauqua circuit, 26, 31, 39
  to Cuba, 25
  between election and inauguration, 62, 68–69
  to Europe, 25, 27
  to Florida, 25, 26(photo), 42–43, 68–69, 110, 161, 163–170, 171
  to Hawaii, 31, 159
  "Inaugural Special" train, 69
  to New Hampshire, 37–38

Travels (*continued*)
   to New Jersey, 88, 90–91, 113, 115, 195
   to New York City, 68, 91, 171–172, 245
   to Ohio, 109–110, 112, 137
   to Panama, 62, 63(photo)
   with Phillipses, 25–26, 27
   plane ride, 62, 63(photo)
   during presidential campaign, 57
   to South, 92
   to Texas, 31, 38, 62
   See also Alaska trip; *Mayflower*
Trinity Baptist Church (Marion), 21, 229, 238, 263, 264

Uhl, Eva B., 79
Underwood, Alice, 134–135
United Mine Workers, 134–135, 136
Upham, Fred, 246
Upton, Harriet Taylor, 52, 129

Vancouver, British Columbia, 193–194
Van Fleet, George H., 38, 239, 264
Varady, Rozal, 106
Vern (face artist), 105–106
Veterans
   activists, 124
   bonus bill, 88, 121, 124, 151, 296n106
   bonus march, 124
   of Civil War, 54, 104, 122, 123
   disabled, 121–124
   FKH's aid to, 23, 87, 121–124
   government benefits, 54
   hospital visits, 87, 89, 121, 122(photo), 123
   White House events for, 121
Veterans Bureau
   conditions in hospitals, 123–124
   establishment, 54
   Forbes as head, 62, 123, 124, 158–159
   staff, 121, 122
Veterans hospitals, scandals related to, 123–124, 158–159

Votaw, Carolyn, 31, 40, 126, 141, 147, 238, 243
Voting. *See* Women's suffrage

Waddell, Chauncey Lockhart, 135
Wadsworth, James, 151
Wakefield National Memorial Association, 258
Wallace, Henry, 73, 145, 182, 206, 226, 243, 255
Wallace, May, 182, 205, 255, 258
Walter Reed Army Hospital, 79, 121, 123
Walters, Winfield Scott, 133
Wanamaker, John, 245
Warburton, Mrs. Barclay, 130
Warner, May, 149
War Risk Insurance Bureau, 158
Warwick, Jack, 17, 18
Washington, D.C.
   charity balls, 104
   cherry trees, 73, 111
   decoration of Wyoming Avenue home, 33, 46
   Friendship estate, 36, 139, 231, 233–234, 236–237
   Hardings' homes, 33, 66, 138–139
   Knickerbocker theater, 106
   Lincoln Memorial dedication, 114
   slums, 74
   WGH's funeral, 212, 219–225, 223(photo), 225(photo)
   Zero Mile Marker, 176, 309n163
   See also White House; Willard Hotel
Washington, George, 239, 258
Washington Disarmament Conference, 88, 92–94, 96, 106–108, 120, 169, 247, 293n45
Washington Nationals, 112
Washington Post, 35, 54
Wayne, Frances, 184
Weeks, John
   on Front Porch, 53(photo)

Harding Memorial Administration and, 246
as pallbearer for FKH, 264
as secretary of war, 81–82, 122
summer home, 37–38, 89
travels with Hardings, 91, 110, 113, 164, 165
WGH's funerals and, 226
White House visits, 79, 153
Weeks, Mrs. John, 53(photo), 79, 93, 106, 110, 113, 164, 165
Welliver, Judson C., 53, 182, 216
West, James, 214
West Virginia
  Alderson Federal Prison Camp, 126
  miners, 134–135
  presidential pardon of robbers, 133–134
WGH Memorial Foundation, 59
Wharton, Edith, "Autre Temps," 48
White, Henry, 41
White, William Allen, 19, 58, 88
White House
  expenses, 84
  FKH's departure, 230–235
  floral decorations, 82–83, 103, 173, 221
  gardens, 76, 111, 139, 170–171, 221
  grounds open to public, 76–77, 89, 266
  Harding portrait, 255–256
  housekeeping, 82–84
  maintenance, 83
  meals, 80, 84
  medical facilities, 158
  public visits, 76–77, 88, 89, 99–101, 102, 152, 177, 266
  Rose Garden, 74, 171
  sitting room, 163
  stables, 94
  staff, 80–82, 83–84
  WGH's body resting in state, 220–221
  See also First Lady, FKH as; Social events at White House
White Oaks Farm sanitarium, 65
  FKH's stays, 28, 209, 238, 255, 258–261, 263
  Hardings' visits, 31, 34–35
Wiggin, Mary C., 132
Wilbur, Ray Lyman, 198–199, 202, 206, 315n23
Willard Hotel
  FKH's stay as widow, 248, 249, 250–251, 253, 254–255
  Hardings' stay before inauguration, 69, 70
  vice presidential rooms, 64, 114
Williams, George, 168
Williams, James, 76
Williams, Margaret Lindsay, 255–256
Wilson, Edith Bolling Galt
  clothing, 68
  courtship, 287n76
  as first lady, 52, 64, 72, 74–75, 284n18
  Madame Marcia and, 47
  at WGH's funeral, 222
  at WGH's inauguration, 70, 72(photo)
Wilson, Ellen Axson, 32, 74, 149, 150, 171, 266
Wilson, Woodrow
  election as president, 28
  funeral, 253
  at Harding's inauguration, 70
  isolation in White House, 52, 75, 100
  legacy, 61
  Paris trip, 41
  Prohibition veto, 284n18
  stroke and incapacity, 72, 74, 75, 149, 207
Wilson, Woodrow *(continued)*
  at WGH's funeral, 222
  wives, 32, 47, 74–75, 287n76
  on women's suffrage, 74–75
Women
  employment, 131, 132, 135

Women (*continued*)
   federal prison, 125–126, 163
   roles in marriage, 131
   Southern, 135
Women journalists
   on Alaska trip, 184
   coverage of FKH as First Lady, 93–94, 117, 184–185
   interviews of first ladies, 74
   interviews of FKH, 168–169
   invited to White House events, 5, 93–94, 103–104, 266
   Mayflower cruises, 138
   meeting with FKH in San Francisco, 200–201
   receptions for, 162–163, 171–172
Women's organizations, 86, 110, 112, 126, 173, 293n44
Women's political involvement
   FKH's feminism, 18, 126–127, 130–131
   FKH's support, 6, 86, 120–121, 127, 128, 201
   groups visiting White House, 81, 129
   members of Congress, 129, 130
   in 1920s, 6, 293n44
   in Republican Party, 127–130, 173

Women's suffrage
   activists, 74–75, 127, 129
   FKH's first vote, 6, 60, 61(photo)
   WGH's support, 35, 54, 56, 113
   Wilson's view, 74–75
Wood, Leonard, 44, 49
Woods, John, 143, 161
Woods, Mrs. John, 143, 161
Woodyard, Mrs. Harry C., 46
Work, Hubert, 182, 198–199, 205, 206, 226, 259
Work, Laura, 184–185, 258
World War I
   Boone's service, 111
   effects on daily life, 38
   FKH's activities to support soldiers, 37
   peace treaty with Germany, 88
   WGH's support, 39
   See also Veterans
Wrigley, William, 119, 172, 202
Wynn, Katherine, 82, 156, 175, 178, 264

Yachts. *See Mayflower*
Yellowstone National Park, 187

Zion National Park, 186

www.ingramcontent.com/pod-product-compliance
Lightning Source LLC
Chambersburg PA
CBHW070748230426
43665CB00017B/2292